Society and Development

Society and Development

REGIONAL PERSPECTIVES

EDITED BY

SURJIT SINGH | DHRUV RAINA

Northern Regional Centre
Indian Council of Social Science Research, New Delhi

RAWAT PUBLICATIONS
Jaipur • New Delhi • Bangalore • Guwahati • Kolkata

ISBN 978-81-316-0730-5

The publication of this book was financially supported by the Northern Regional Centre, ICSSR. The opinions expressed and the research finding are those of the contributors. The NRC accepts no responsibility for the same.

Published by
Prem Rawat for **Rawat Publications**
Satyam Apts, Sector 3, Jawahar Nagar, Jaipur 302 004 (India)
Phone: 0141 265 1748 / 7006 Fax: 0141 265 1748
E-mail: info@rawatbooks.com
Website: www.rawatbooks.com

New Delhi Office
4858/24, Ansari Road, Daryaganj, New Delhi 110 002
Phone: 011 2326 3290

Also at *Bangalore, Guwahati* and *Kolkata*

Typeset by Rawat Computers, Jaipur

Printed at Chaman Enterprises, New Delhi

Contents

Contributors

Surjit Singh, Professor and Director, Institute of Development Studies, Jaipur.

Dhruv Raina, Professor, Zakir Husain Centre for Educational Studies, School of Social Sciences, Jawaharlal Nehru University, New Delhi.

Abu Huzaifa, Doctoral Research Fellow, Centre for Study of Regional Development, School of Social Sciences, Jawaharlal Nehru University, New Delhi.

Abdul Matin, Doctoral Research Fellow, Centre for Political Studies, School of Social Sciences, Jawaharlal Nehru University, New Delhi.

Ajit Kumar Singh, Former Director, Giri Institute of Development Studies, Lucknow, ICSSR National Fellow.

Anjali Dash, Research Analyst, Institute of Economic Growth, Delhi.

Aradhana Singh, Doctoral Research Fellow, Department Sociology and Social Work, Hemwati Nandan Bahuguna, Garhwal University (A Central University), Srinagar, Garhwal, Uttarakhand.

Bhaswati Thakurta, Research Associate, Centre for Women's Development Studies, New Delhi.

Bhuwnesh Jain, Deputy Director, Nehru Yuvak Kendra, New Delhi.

Devesh Vijay, Associate Professor, Department of History, Zakir Husain Delhi College, University of Delhi currently Fellow, Nehru Memorial Museum and Library, New Delhi.

Kamal Chaudhary, Doctoral Research Fellow, Centre for the Study of Regional Development (CSRD), School of Social Sciences, Jawaharlal Nehru University, New Delhi.

Kamal Asif, ICSSR Post-Doctoral Fellow, Department of Geography, Aligarh Muslim University, Aligarh.

Kamal Narain Joshi, Former Senior Fellow, Institute of Development Studies , Jaipur, Rajasthan.

Kshipra Sharma, Doctoral Research Fellow, Centre for Political Studies, School of Social Sciences, Jawaharlal Nehru University, New Delhi.

Leon A. Morenas, Associate Professor, School of Planning and Architecture, New Delhi.

Nilabja Ghosh, Associate Professor, Institute of Economic Growth, Delhi.

Nripendra Kishore Mishra, Professor, Department of Economics, Banaras Hindu University, Varanasi.

Ruchika Chaudhary, Research Scholar, CSRD, Jawaharlal Nehru University, New Delhi.

Shailender Kumar Hooda, Assistant Professor, Institute for Studies in Industrial Development, New Delhi.

Udai Bhan Singh, Assistant Professor of Economics, Amity Business School, Amity University Rajasthan, Jaipur.

Varsha Joshi, Associate Professor, Institute of Development Studies, Jaipur.

Yatindra Singh Sisodia, Professor and Director, M.P. Institute of Social Science Research, Ujjain.

Editorial

The idea that the ICSSR should play an active role in organizing 'Social Science Congresses' at the regional level has been in circulation for some time. There are many reasons justifying the organization of such congresses. When the Northern Regional Centre decided to do so in October 2012, at least three goals were foremost on its agenda. The first was to initiate a conversation among the social scientists – both teachers and researchers – in the region on issues and debates that were of pressing concern amongst economists, sociologists, anthropologists, political scientists and scholars in development studies. In order to conceptualize the Congress, a number of leading social scientists were invited to identify the themes for the Congress, and the practice was continued into the Second and the Third Congresses. In doing so, it was felt that while the papers to be presented would draw upon the strengths of the social science disciplines, the engagements with the themes and problems to be discussed should have a strong interdisciplinary thrust, and that the papers should emphasize the interdisciplinary nature of problematic tackled by social science researchers. In other words, the sessions were not organized on disciplinary lines at all, but thematically. Retrospectively, it was found that this was a more comprehensive format for a dialogue across and between disciplines.

Secondly, the Congress was also meant to provide a forum for students from different states in the region to acquaint themselves with some of the leading research trends in the social sciences and to meet social scientists who are at the frontiers of their respective academic fields. In this way, it was hoped that the Congress would help build bridges between the centres of social science research and the colleges and state universities. Panel discussions and the invited lectures were organized in order to inspire conversations of the type mentioned. One panel discussion was devoted exclusively to concerns specific to the state of Rajasthan. Professor K.L. Sharma organized one such panel entitled 'Redefining Rajasthan'. Another panel discussion was on 'Gender and Development'. A third related objective was to provide research scholars in the region with a forum to present and discuss their research findings, as well as acquaint themselves with the researches of their colleagues located at other universities and Research Institutes. Over the coming years, it is hoped that through these Congresses the research scholars would develop a network or association of social scientists in the region, for that surely is an unstated objective of any Congress.

While the proposed themes were broad, they were focused enough to accommodate many sub themes. As a result, a substantial number of papers addressed the themes of regional development; marginalization and representation; changing village economy, issues of governance at the state level etc. Leading social scientists were invited to speak on and discuss relevant themes relating to the changing nature of the village and village economy, to emerging issues in higher education.

While about fifty odd papers were presented at the first of these Congresses organized in collaboration with the Institute of Development Studies, Jaipur, about 18 of the presented papers were short-listed for publication in the first proceedings. In that sense, the papers published have been refereed before publication, keeping in mind the need to encourage publication practices. Again with the passage of time, we hope that the number of papers successfully passing the referee's scrutinizing gaze will increase. Finally, this Congress could not have been organized without the enthusiastic support – both in terms of ideas and organizational facilities – provided by the late Prof. Surjit Singh, the former Director, IDS, Jaipur. His untimely death is deeply lamented, and it is he who is the rightful editor of this volume. I hope the contributors will understand the factors behind the delay in publishing these proceedings. But on behalf of NRC, I do hope that the first proceedings mark the recognition of the serious scholarly engagement in social science research at the regional level.

Dhruv Raina

1

Regional Distribution and Growth of Bank Credit

A Critical View

ABU HUZAIFA

Since the introduction of the Lead Bank Scheme in 1969, several changes have taken place in the country, especially after 1991 with the beginning of financial sector reforms of the Indian economy. Today, the commercial banks are much more focused on their financial management and have improved their competitiveness and efficiency. Although priority sector obligations have continued to be in force for both private sector and public sector banks (PSBs), attention has increasingly been drawn to the fact that large sections of the population remain outside the formal banking structure and the real and financial sectors continue to lag behind in certain regions. While policies are in place to facilitate flow of credit to the more vulnerable sectors/sections of society, there is a need to ensure greater dissemination and implementation of these policies at the grassroot level, besides getting timely information and better assessment of outcomes.

However, the large segment of vulnerable and weaker section of the society lives in the rural areas. Without bringing these rural people into the financial stream of the banking system, the realization of goal of supplying adequate credit to the masses cannot be attained. One of the most intriguing features of India's agrarian economy in the recent years is the persistence of agrarian distress in many regions, even while agriculture credit flow has risen sharply. Rising flow of agriculture credit is normally associated with buoyancy in the farm sectors. In

India, institutional credit for agriculture was viewed from the angle of protecting farmers from the grip of money lenders. Under the 40 per cent priority sector lending, 18 per cent is available to the agricultural sector. Thus the agriculture credit is the availability rather than a supply in the Indian economy. It was hardly considered as an instrument of production enhancement. Traditionally, the role of agriculture credit is of giving push to development process.

Considering the fact of lacking funds in Indian economy, the availability of adequate credit is the lubricant that keeps the wheels of development moving in all the sectors. Although there has been a great expansion of the formal banking sector, the share of informal lending to the rural household increased in the reform period. It is often said that the benefits of the institutional credit, no matter for which sector, have been largely shared by relatively prosperous regions of the country and comparatively richer section in each region. Considering these facts, the main objectives of this study is to examine not only the district and state level variations in the distribution of agriculture and the overall credit supplied by Scheduled Commercial Banks (SCBs), and their growth patterns, but also their policy implications, if any. The specific objectives of the study were following:

Objectives

- To study the relative role of institutional and non-institutional sources of credit across the states and analyse changes there in during 1981, 1992 and 2002.
- To identify the nature and extent of the concentration in the flow of agriculture credit and total credit for all the sectors supplied by SCBs in the year 2008–09.

Materials and Methods

For the purpose of the study, state-wise and source-wise data on cash loans were collected from the reports on 37th, 48th and 59th Rounds of the National Sample Survey (NSS) pertaining to the years of 1971–72, 1981–82, 1991–92 and 2001–2002. The data related to the bank branches of Scheduled Commercial Banks (SCBs) has been collected from the *Branch Statistics*, a publication of the RBI. The data related to outstanding credit of SCBs comes from statistical statement related to banks and the report on currency and finance (various issues), RBI. In order to get per capita availability of credit, district and state-level population from Census 2011 have been used. Rural population for the normalization agriculture credit (per capita credit) and total population for the total credit were taken as the basis of per capita.

The analysis in the study is undertaken for 17 major states, viz. Andhra Pradesh, Assam, Bihar (undivided), Gujarat, Haryana, Karnataka, Kerala, Madhya Pradesh (undivided), Maharashtra, Odisha, Punjab, Rajasthan, Tamil Nadu, Uttar Pradesh (undivided), West Bengal, Jammu & Kashmir and Himachal Pradesh. These states account for more than 95 per cent of the population and 93 per cent of the Net Domestic Product (NDP) in the country (see, Rao, 1999). In addition to this, these states have been contributing, on an average, 90 per cent of the total deposits in the country through Scheduled Commercial Banks (SCBs), including Regional Rural Banks (RRBs) for the last 20 years. Out of the total agriculture credit provided in the country through SCBs and RRBs, on an average, 96 per cent of it goes to these states (RBI, various years). Various techniques like coefficient of variation (CV), ranking methods, and percentage have been used in the study.

The comparative analysis between credit supply to agricultural sector and all the sectors have also been made to examine the regional variation in the location of bank branches and distribution of credit. In order to see the regional concentration, the top seven districts in receiving credit in absolute amount have been ranked across the states. As the number of districts and their areas differ across the states, the classification of the district on the basis of per capita availability of credit has been made to avoid scaling problem. The supply of credit has been normalized on per capita rural and total population. There are 552 districts in the 17 major states[1] which are undertaken in the paper. The availability of credit in top 10 per cent districts (55 districts) has been compared with the bottom 20 per cent districts (110 districts) in both absolute (% of total) and per capita credit for agricultural sector and all the sectors.

Empirical Analysis

Role of Institutional and Non-institutional Sources of Credit

In order to get the changes in share of institutional and non-institutional sources of credit in total outstanding, a comparative analysis of four rounds of the data showing source-wise and class-wise distribution of credit was attempted. It is obvious from Table 1 that there was a remarkable increase in the percentage share of institutional credit to total rural credit in the decades of 1970s in all the regions, except Assam where it witnessed marginal decline. In the next decades, Assam had shown increase from 30.6 per cent to 66 per cent share of institutional credit. But in the reforms period, its share declines around 37 per cent.

Table 1

Percentage Share of Institutional Agencies in Outstanding Cash Debt of Rural Households in 17 Major States

State	Institutional				Non-Institutional			
	1971	1981	1991	2002	1971	1981	1991	2002
AP	13.7	40.9	34	31.4	86.3	59.1	66	68.6
Assam	34.7	30.6	66	37.5	65.3	69.4	34	62.6
Bihar	10.7	47.2	73	41.7	89.3	52.8	27	58.5
Gujarat	46.9	70	75	69.5	53.1	30	25	30.5
Haryana	26.4	75.8	73	67.6	73.6	24.2	27	32.5
Himachal	23.9	74.5	62	65.3	76.1	25.5	38	34.7
Jammu	20.4	43.5	76	67.6	79.6	56.5	24	32.3
Karnataka	29.7	78.2	78	68.9	70.3	21.8	22	31.2
Kerala	44.4	78.6	92	82.3	55.6	21.4	8	17.6
MP	31.6	66.3	73	56.9	68.4	33.7	27	43
Maharashtra	67.4	86.4	82	83.8	32.6	13.6	18	16.2
Odisha	30	81	80	74.8	70	19	20	25.1
Punjab	36	74.2	79	47.9	64	25.8	21	52.1
Rajasthan	9.4	40.9	40	34.2	90.6	59.1	60	65.8
Tamil Nadu	22.1	44.3	58	53.4	77.9	55.7	42	46.5
UP	23.4	55.1	69	60.3	76.6	44.9	31	39.7
West Bengal	30.6	65.5	82	58	69.4	34.5	18	42.1
All India	29.2	61.2	66	57.7	70.8	38.8	34	42.4

Data based on NSSO 26th, 37th, 48th and 59th Round.

Note: The 17 major states include, Bihar, Jharkhand, Uttarakhand in UP and Chhattisgarh in MP.

Considering the country as whole, institutional sources accounted for about 29 per cent of the total cash loans in 1971 which increased to 61 per cent in 1981 and 66 per cent in 1991 and further marginally declines to 57.7 per cent. While the share of non-institutional credit increased to 42.4 per cent in 2002 from 34 per cent in 1991. Thus, the rapid expansion of banking facilities in rural areas through nationalization of banks could not be sustained at the state level in the decade of

1980s and 1990s. In the period of liberalization, the dependency of the rural households on the non-institutional sources of credit increased in all the states, except Himachal Pradesh and Maharashtra where it witnessed marginal decline. The reason behind it shows the decaying structure of institutional credit and the definitional change in the priority sector lending. The marginal increase in the institutional share in Himachal Pradesh shows its extensive efforts of crop diversification and development of flowery-culture in the state. However, the dependency of rural households shows massive increase in Bihar and Punjab. In case of Bihar, there might be low absorption capacity and consumption purpose borrowing which leads to the development of non-institutional lending in the reform period.

Table 2 gives the source-wise distribution of outstanding cash loans in 2001–02 in various regions. It may be seen from the table that bank credit accounted for the highest percentage share (about 35.6%) in the total supply of cash loans in rural India, followed by money lenders (25.7%), cooperatives (19.6%), other sources, including relatives and friends (11.5%), traders (5.2%) and government (2.5%). In the states of Assam, Bihar, Jammu & Kashmir, Rajasthan and Uttar Pradesh, however, the percentage share of cooperatives was found to be comparatively very low i.e. less than 10 per cent of total credit. The banks, including the RRBs and commercial banks (CBs), were found to be major suppliers of the rural credit in Jammu & Kashmir (54.3), Uttar Pradesh (51.2%), Kerala (49.1%), Himachal Pradesh (47.6%), Odisha (43.7), and Haryana (42.6%).

Table 2

Distribution of Debt by Sources Across Major States 2002 in per cent

State	*Institutional*				*Non-institutional*			
	Govt	*Coop*	*Bank*	*All*	*ML*	*Trader*	*Others*	*All*
Andhra Pradesh	1	10.4	20	31.4	53.4	4.8	10.4	68.6
Assam	7	2.7	27.8	37.5	15.5	12	35.1	62.6
Bihar	2.2	2.5	37	41.7	32.8	1.1	24.6	58.5
Gujarat	0.5	41.8	27.2	69.5	6.5	4.4	19.6	30.5
Haryana	1.1	23.9	42.6	67.6	24.1	3.1	5.3	32.5
Himachal Pradesh	6.1	11.6	47.6	65.3	7.2	5.5	22	34.7
J&K	13.1	0.2	54.3	67.6	1.1	15.5	15.7	32.3
Karnataka	1.9	16.9	50.1	68.9	20	1.9	9.3	31.2

Cont'd...

...Cont'd

Kerala	4.9	28.3	49.1	82.3	7.4	1.7	8.5	17.6
MP	1.9	16.9	38.1	56.9	22.6	9	11.4	43
Maharashtra	1.2	48.5	34.1	83.8	6.8	0.8	8.6	16.2
Odisha	13	18.1	43.7	74.8	14.8	0.8	9.5	25.1
Punjab	1.9	17.6	28.4	47.9	36.3	8.2	7.6	52.1
Rajasthan	1.3	5.9	27	34.2	36.5	19.2	10.1	65.8
Tamil Nadu	2	23.3	28.1	53.4	39.7	0.4	6.4	46.5
UP	2.4	6.7	51.2	60.3	19.1	2.9	17.7	39.7
West Bengal	10.3	19.2	28.5	58	13	10.7	18.4	42.1
All India	2.5	19.6	35.6	57.7	25.7	5.2	11.5	42.4

Data based on NSSO 59th Round. ML denotes share of money lenders (professional and traditional money lenders); Coop used for cooperatives.

Table 2 further reveals that the money lenders, the second largest suppliers, contributed significantly (greater than the national average percentage share of 25.7) to the total supply of the credit in many regions including Andhra Pradesh (53.4%), Bihar (32.8%), Punjab (36.3%), Rajasthan (36.5%), Tamil Nadu (39.7%) which indicate how the relatively better-off farmers in these regions tended to invest their surplus resources in the usurious money lending rather than in modern technical inputs. Similarly, the traders contributed significant amount in the State of Jammu & Kashmir, Rajasthan and West Bengal where it is more than 10 per cent of the total supply of the credit.

It is well known that the 1990s were a period of sharp fall in the growth of agriculture credit flow in India. Numerous studies and reports have argued that one of the major factors associated with the agrarian distress in the late 1990s and 2000s was an increase in the rural indebtedness, especially to money lenders. According to All India Debt and Investment Survey (AIDIS), the share of the total debt of cultivator households taken from the formal sources fell from 64 per cent in 1992 to 57 per cent in 2003. In the same period, the share of total debt taken from the money lenders almost doubled from 10.5 per cent to 19.6 per cent. The reversal of agriculture credit flow had taken place in the 2000s. As in the early 2000s, the growth of credit to agriculture began to pick up. Commercial Banks and Regional Rural Banks played an important role in the revival of agriculture credit.

Regional Variation in the Location of Bank Branches and Distribution of Credit: A Comparative Analysis of Agriculture Sector and All the Sectors

The present section deals with the regional variation in the distribution of bank branches and credit. First, we will take total number of Scheduled Commercial Bank branches operating in India. The results depicted in Table 3 show that state-wise classification of districts according to number of branches of commercial bank operating in them shows that out of 582 districts in the country, 26 per cent (151) districts had less than 50 branches each, 33 per cent (188) had branches between 51 to 100, 19 per cent (112) had branches between 151–200

Table 3

State Classification of Districts According to No. of Branches of Commercial Banks As on March 2002

State	*Below 50*	*51–100*	*101–150*	*151–200*	*Above 200*	*Sum*
Andhra Pradesh	0	0	3	9	11	23
Assam	13	9	0	1	0	23
Bihar	15	21	17	4	1	58
Gujarat	3	8	6	4	4	25
Haryana	2	14	3	0	0	19
Himachal	5	5	1	1	0	12
Jammu & Kashmir	8	3	2	1	0	14
Karnataka	0	6	8	8	5	27
Kerala	0	2	1	1	10	14
Madhya Pradesh	16	31	10	3	1	61
Maharashtra	3	11	8	4	8	34
Odisha	10	13	4	3	0	30
Punjab	3	3	4	3	4	17
Rajasthan	3	14	10	4	1	32
Tamil Nadu	2	7	9	6	6	30
Uttar Pradesh	11	36	20	10	6	83
West Bengal	0	2	5	3	8	18
Union Territories and other states	57	3	1	1	0	62
India	151	188	112	66	65	582
% of Total	26	33	19	11	11	100

Source: Branch Statistics, March 2010, RBI.

and 22 per cent districts had more than 151 branches. By seeing at the regional level, it can be observed that there are high concentration of bank branches in the state of Andhra Pradesh and Kerala. In Andhra Pradesh, out of 23 districts, 20 districts had more than 151 branches. In Kerala 11 districts in out of 14 had more than 151 bank branches. Thus the concentration of bank branches is highly biased towards developed states (Table 3).

Figure 1 *Percentage of Total Number of SCBs Branches (in Numbers)*

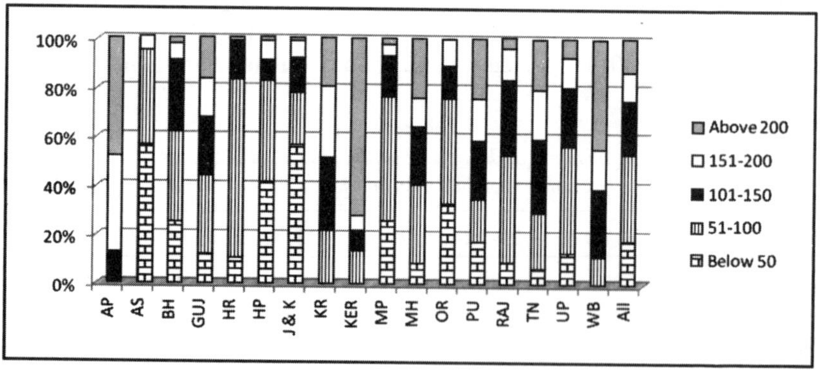

Source: Table 3

As the classification of the district is concerned according to the number of bank branches, the cylinder diagram has been used to show the number of districts in per cent in all the states. On the basis of the five categories made for the number of bank branches, it is clear from Figure 1 that most of the districts in Andhra Pradesh, Kerala and West Bengal have more than 200 branches each, whereas most of the districts in Assam, Jammu and Kashmir and Himachal Pradesh have less than 50 bank branches. The low concentration of branches is justifiable because most of the bank branches in these states may be serving very few people, as these areas have low density of population. If we see the second category from below (51–100 branches), there is a large percentage of districts in Haryana (more than 70%), followed by Madhya Pradesh, Odisha, Rajasthan and Uttar Pradesh.

Now come over to the classification of the rural bank branches of SCBs across the states. State-wise classification of districts (Table 4) according to number of rural branches of Commercial Bank operating in them shows that out of 582 districts in the country, 20.45 per cent (119) districts had less than 25 branches each, 30.07 per cent (175) had branches between 26 and 50, 23.02 per cent (134) had branches between 51and 75, 13.2 per cent (81) between 76 and 100; 12.03 per cent districts had more than 100 branches. By seeing at the state level, it can be observed that there is a high concentration of Rural Bank Branches in the state of Andhra Pradesh, West Bengal and Karnataka. There are more than 100 branches in 15 districts out of 23 in Andhra Pradesh, followed by seven districts in the category 76–100 branches.

Table 4

State Classification of Districts According to Number of Branches of Rural Bank Branches As on March 2002

State	*Below 25*	*26–50*	*51–75*	*76–100*	*Above 100*	*Sum*
AP	1	0	0	7	15	23
Assam	7	13	3	0	0	23
Bihar	8	15	19	8	8	58
Gujarat	3	5	11	4	2	25
Haryana	3	14	2	0	0	19
Himachal	2	6	1	2	1	12
Jammu	3	8	1	2	0	14
Karnataka	0	5	7	7	8	27
Kerala	9	4	0	1	0	14
Madhya	10	33	14	4	0	61
Maharashtra	0	12	7	9	6	34
Odisha	7	6	13	2	2	30
Punjab	3	5	2	5	2	17
Rajasthan	1	13	12	4	2	32
Tamil Nadu	3	5	16	4	2	30
UP	5	27	22	18	11	83
West Bengal	0	1	3	3	11	18
UT and other states	54	3	1	1	0	59
India	119	175	134	81	70	579
Per cent of Total	20.45	30.07	23.02	13.92	12.03	100

Source: Branch Statistics, RBI.

In order to get much clear picture as whole, the total number of districts at the given classification of bank branches has been depicted in percentage in Figure 2. It is obvious from the figure that like the total number of bank branches, the Rural Bank Branches are highly concentrated in West Bengal and Andhra Pradesh. In Kerala, unlike the total number of bank branches, there is a low concentration of Rural Bank

Figure 2 *Percentage of Total Number of SCBs Rural Branches (in Numbers)*

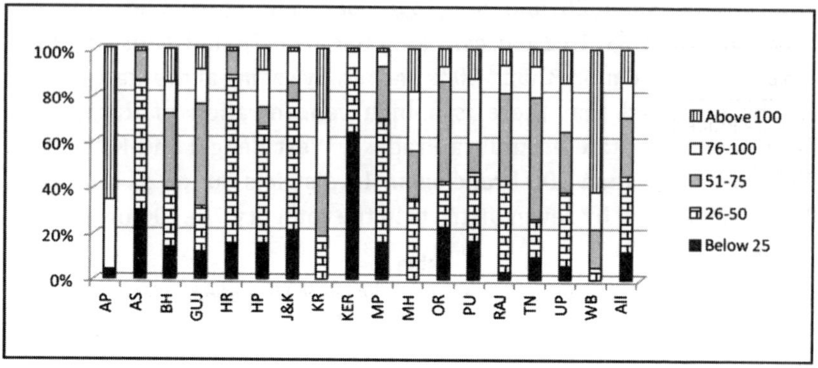

Source: Table 4

Branches, as most of the districts in it have less than 25 Rural Bank Branches. If we combine the last two categories from below of the Rural Bank Branches, we can see that most of the districts in Assam, Himachal Pradesh (HP), Jammu and Kashmir (J&K), Haryana (HR) and Madhya Pradesh (MP) have less than 50 bank branches. The only exception is the state of Haryana, that is because of urban oriented growth rate of the state which led to the modest expansion of bank branches in the rural areas.

The district-level distribution of credit across the states has also been undertaken to get much clear picture between rural and urban-divide. Let us first see the distribution of total credit supplied by the SCBs. The urban orientation of banking system is also evident from the fact that there is a high degree of concentration of bank credit in the developed cities like Mumbai, Kolkata, Hyderabad, Bangalore, etc. which are having more than 40 lakh population each. It is obvious from Table 5 that the share of these cities in deposits is much less than their share of credit. In West Bengal, Kolkata alone accounted for 72 per cent of the credit available for the state as a whole. In Maharashtra, Mumbai city alone accounted 76 per cent of the credit available for the state. In Tamil Nadu, Chennai city accounted 54 per cent of the total credit available to the state. There is also high concentration in the other states like Andhra Pradesh, Himachal Pradesh, Karnataka and Jammu & Kashmir. The city of Hyderabad (AP), Bangalore Urban (KR), Shimla and Solan (HP) accounted for 46 per cent, 68 per cent, 28 per cent and 23 per cent, respectively of the credit supplied to the respective state (Table 5).

Table 5

Concentration of Total Credit in the Top Seven Districts in the 17 Major States on March 2009 (% Share)

State	*Rank 1*	*Rank 2*	*Rank 3*	*Rank 4*	*Rank 5*	*Rank 6*	*Rank 7*	*Total for 7*
Andhra Pradesh	45.96	9.6	5.95	4.29	3.97	3.29	3.05	76.1
Assam	17.6	14.91	7.14	5.75	5.01	4.61	4.31	59.32
Bihar	10.05	9.23	8.98	6.58	5.86	3.73	3.44	47.87
Gujarat	31.87	14.01	10.84	8.73	5.18	3.12	3.03	76.79
Haryana	21.72	11.94	9.15	7.86	7.83	6.06	4.86	69.43
Himachal Pradesh	28.13	23.43	9.64	7.9	6.8	6.61	4.55	87.05
J & K	41.27	26.68	6.08	4.56	3.56	2.53	2.31	86.98
Karnataka	68.08	3.63	2.97	2.93	2.72	2.19	1.47	83.99
Kerala	27.44	15.29	8.97	7.1	6.88	6.08	5.51	77.28
Madhya Pradesh	21.78	11.61	4.26	4.09	3.96	3.49	3.03	52.22
Maharashtra	76.01	6.89	4.05	2.72	1.69	1.32	1.08	93.76
Odisha	26.56	12.91	9.5	5.25	4.66	4.17	3.64	66.69
Punjab	29.11	26.42	10.38	6.52	3.16	3.01	2.75	81.36
Rajasthan	42.11	5.57	5.48	5.4	4.35	4.07	3.43	70.42
Tamil Nadu	54.59	15.14	2.77	2.64	2.06	1.93	1.64	80.77
Uttar Pradesh	16.92	10.78	5.1	4.33	4.27	3.44	3.09	47.92
West Bengal	72.79	4.27	3.77	3.01	2.69	1.96	1.81	90.3

Source: Calculated from Basic Statistical Returns of Scheduled Commercial Banks in India Volume – 38, March 2010, Reserve Bank of India.

Ranking of the districts according to their share in the total credit for the state indicates that more than 65 per cent credit was concentrated in the first seven districts, exception being Assam, Bihar, MP and UP. The cities like Kolkata, Mumbai and Shimla have accounted around 39 per cent each of total agriculture credit supplied to the particular state. The availability of credit does not only depend on the supply but also demand aspects. The demand for credit depends on the absorption capacity and economic activities of any region. As these metro-centric cities are highly developed and having great absorption capacity, there is no reason to criticise the concentration of credit in these regions.

Table 6

Concentration of Agriculture Credit in the Top Seven Districts in the 17 Major States in March 2009

State	Rank 1	Rank 2	Rank 3	Rank 4	Rank 5	Rank 6	Rank 7	Total for 7
Andhra Pradesh	12.93	8.7	8.36	6.3	5.94	5.79	5.28	53.31
Assam	9.35	7.73	7.58	7.17	6.26	5.6	5.05	48.74
Bihar	5.07	4.72	4.16	3.59	3.56	3.52	3.33	27.95
Gujarat	27	8.27	6.94	5.48	5.02	4.7	4.32	61.73
Haryana	10.32	10.01	8.76	6.61	6.01	5.76	5.64	53.11
Himachal Pradesh	39.85	15.69	9.61	7.29	6.49	4.64	4.4	87.97
J&K	22.45	17.34	10.64	7.98	7.2	6.57	4.4	76.58
Karnataka	16.02	7.97	6.45	5.18	4.54	4.16	3.7	48.02
Kerala	14.23	9.78	8.37	7.95	7.52	7.46	7.29	62.59
Madhya Pradesh	5.67	4.41	3.53	3.37	3.22	3.09	2.96	26.24
Maharashtra	39.13	7.44	6.73	3.84	3.53	3.47	3.37	67.51
Odisha	11.75	7.18	6.7	6	5.75	5.01	4.97	47.36
Punjab	29.22	9.87	7.23	7.13	6.46	5.58	5.19	70.66
Rajasthan	17.44	7.4	6.29	6.05	4.82	3.82	3.36	49.19
Tamil Nadu	15.88	9	4.49	4.46	4.32	4.27	4.24	46.66
Uttar Pradesh	5.92	3.78	3.78	3.14	3.13	2.96	2.7	25.4
West Bengal	39.02	12.44	7.64	6.07	5.68	3.55	3.48	77.88

Source: Ibid.

There is also high concentration in the other states like Gujarat, Punjab and Jammu & Kashmir. Coefficient of variation is also being calculated for all districts of the 17 major states. It is obvious that there is high inequality in the distribution of agriculture credit in Punjab where coefficient of variation stood at 3.03. There are also other states like Maharashtra, West Bengal, Himachal Pradesh and Jammu and Kashmir having high inequality in the distribution of agriculture credit.

Per Capita Supply of Total Credit and Agriculture Credit

We cannot compare the availability of credit on the absolute amount, because the areas and population along with the number of districts may differ in across the states. In order to overcome this limitation to some extent, the district-wise population has been taken to get per capita availability of credit across the states. On the basis of district-wise per capita supply of credit across the states, the coefficient of variation shows that the regional inequality in the distribution of credit is much higher in Madhya Pradesh (4.83), West Bengal (3.14), Tamil Nadu (2.02) and Andhra Pradesh (2.06) compared to other regions.

Table 7

State-wise Classification of Districts According to Per Capita Availability SCBs Credit (in ₹) 2009

State	Below 3,000	3,000–5,999	6,000–9,999	10,000–15,000	Above 15,000	Total Districts	Mean	SD	CV
Andhra Pradesh	1	3	11	3	6	23	19,331	39,896	2.06
Assam	11	9	3	1	3	27	5,612	6,676	1.19
Bihar	44	10	5	1	2	62	3,191	3,631	1.14
Gujarat	4	3	2	4	13	26	21,331	22,182	1.04
Haryana	1	1	5	4	9	20	20,958	20,798	0.99
Himachal Pradesh	0	1	6	1	4	12	16,986	16,268	0.96
J & K	10	4	6	0	2	22	7,059	10,168	1.44
Karnataka	0	4	10	7	8	29	7,261	16,614	1.50
Kerala	0	2	1	1	10	14	26,422	26,635	1.01
Madhya Pradesh	9	19	21	9	8	66	53,032	2,56,258	4.83
Maharashtra	7	13	6	2	7	35	8,955	10,940	1.22
Odisha	9	12	4	2	3	30	6,622	7,437	1.12
Punjab	0	2	4	7	7	20	21,559	25,615	1.19
Rajasthan	4	17	5	4	3	33	7,480	8,057	1.08
Tamil Nadu	2	6	9	3	11	31	23,829	48,193	2.02
Uttar Pradesh	40	26	6	6	5	83	5,508	7,307	1.33
West Bengal	9	7	2	0	1	19	14,235	44,683	3.14
All						552	14,265	68,159	4.78

Source: Calculated from Basic Statistical Returns Of Scheduled Commercial Banks in India Volume – 38, March 2010, Reserve Bank of India.

However, the classification of district on the basis of availability of credit has been made. Figure 3, made on the basis Table 7, shows that most of the districts in the developed states like Kerala, Gujarat and Haryana had more than ₹ 15,000 per capita supply of credit in 2009. To some extent, Punjab and Tamil Nadu are on the same trend. The high per capita availability of credit in these states shows their development and greater absorption capacity compare to other states. If we see the poor states like Bihar, Assam, Jammu and Kashmir, and Uttar Pradesh, there is a large percentage of districts in them where per capita supply of credit is very low (below ₹ 3,000). The low per capita supply of credit in Bihar and UP shows high density of population, while in other two states there might be low absorption capacity. The only exception is West Bengal where more than 80 per cent of total districts have less than 3,000 per capita supply of credit.

Figure 3 *Percentage of Total Districts in Obtaining PC Total Credit (in ₹) March 2009*

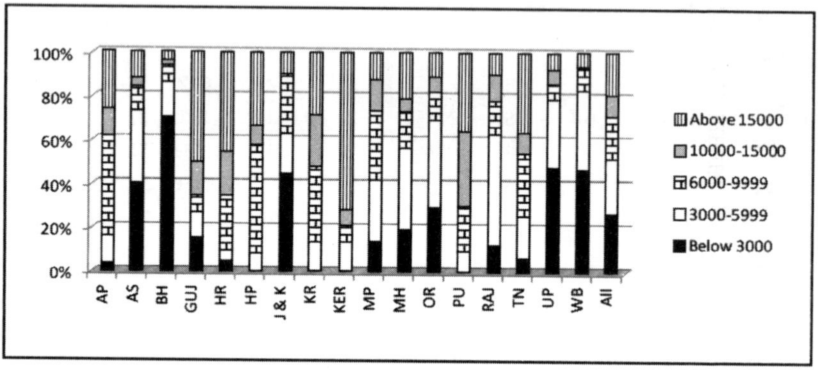

Source: Table 7

Table 8

State Classification of Districts According to Per Capita Agriculture Credit (₹)

State	*Below 1,000*	*1,000–1,999*	*2,000–2,999*	*3,000–4,000*	*Above 4000*	*Total Districts*	*Mean*	*SD*	*CV*
Andhra Pradesh	0	1	6	5	10	22	4,520	2,240	0.50
Assam	22	4	0	0	1	27	764	1,399	1.83
Bihar	54	8	0	0	0	62	670	300	0.45
Gujarat	1	5	1	6	13	26	7,087	9,862	1.39
Haryana	0	1	0	1	18	20	8,518	8,964	1.05
Himachal Pradesh	3	5	2	0	2	12	2,418	2,451	1.01
J & K	14	3	3	1	1	22	2,125	5,698	2.68
Karnataka	0	0	4	3	22	29	2,085	7,265	1.06
Kerala	0	0	1	2	11	14	7,848	4,149	0.53
Madhya Pradesh	8	16	9	8	25	66	2,190	1,501	0.69
Maharashtra	3	17	6	4	3	33	4,435	4,249	0.96
Odisha	7	20	2	0	1	30	1,346	771	0.57
Punjab	0	0	1	1	18	20	8,087	7,694	0.95
Rajasthan	1	9	12	4	7	33	3,008	1,907	0.63
Tamil Nadu	1	0	3	8	18	30	8,269	9,109	1.10
Uttar Pradesh	31	21	13	11	7	83	1,953	1,535	0.79
West Bengal	12	4	2	0	0	18	906	574	0.63
All						547	1,351	5,382	3.98

Figure 4 *Percentage of Total Districts in Obtaining PC Agricultural Credit (in ₹) March 2009*

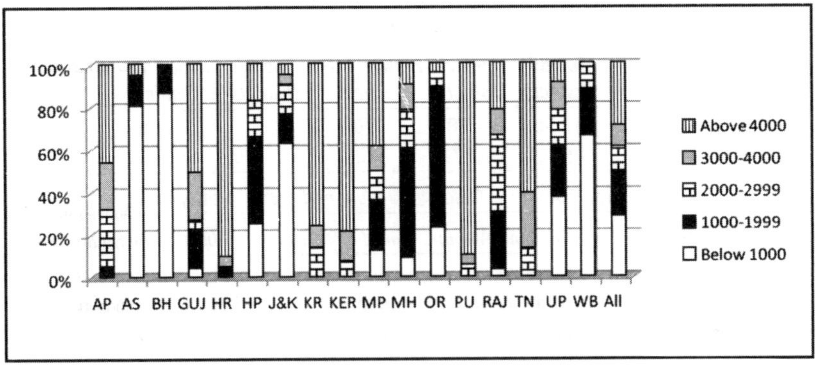

Source: Table 8

Now come to the availability of per capita agriculture credit. Here also, the most developed like southern region (Karnataka, Andhra Pradesh, Tamil Nadu), Punjab and Haryana have been garnering major share of agriculture credit, as most of the districts in these states are receiving more than ₹ 4,000 per capita agriculture credit (Figure 4). The poor states like the per capita total supply of credit are also suffering low per capita availability of agriculture credit. The only exception is Maharashtra where the low per capita availability of agriculture credit might be existing because of high density of population in the rural areas. While inequality in the distribution of per capita credit is high in both the cases, the variation in the distribution of agriculture credit is less severe than all the sectors.

Table 9 shows that the major cities of India like Mumbai, Bangalore, Hyderabad, Ahmedabad, Kolkata, and Chennai are big players in the credit market; they acquire major chunk of supply of agricultural and total credit. If we compare the top 10 per cent with the bottom 20 per cent of the total district of the 17 major states, it is obvious from Table 5 that the former (55 districts) is getting 72 per cent of total supply of credit (in absolute amount), whereas the bottom 20 per cent (110 districts) is just 0.94 per cent. In case of agriculture credit, the top 10 per cent (55 districts) is getting 40 per cent of the total supply of credit, while bottom 20 per cent (110 districts) is just getting 1.7 per cent. Thus, we can say that the level of inequality is much higher in case of supply of credit to all the sectors compared to the agriculture credit.

Table 9

Share of Top 10 per cent of Total Districts and Bottom 20 per cent of Total Districts

	Agricultural Sectors			*All Sectors*		
	Top 55 Districts	*Top Five Districts*	*Bottom 110 Districts*	*Top 55 Districts*	*Top Five Districts*	*Bottom 110 Districts*
Absolute Amount (%)	40.56	11.28	1.70	72.47	43.56	0.94
Per Capita Average	14,611	43,971	322	82,465	4,66,122	1295

Top Five Districts in Absolute Amount and Credit per Capita

Credit per Capita	*Absolute Amount*	*Credit Per Capita*	*Absolute Amount Mumbai*
Ahmedabad	Mumbai	Mumbai	Mumbai
Panchkula	Ahmedabad	Chennai	Bangalore Urban
Bangalore Urban	Patiala	Kolkata	Chennai
Patiala	Chennai	Hyderabad	Kolkata
The Nilgiris	Bangalore Urban	Bangalore Urban	Hyderabad

Source: Ibid.

Sector-wise Share of Bank Credit in 17 Major States

The credit advancement of Scheduled Commercial Banks is biased towards agriculture which is a major employment generating sector in India. Sector-wise analysis indicates that the share of agriculture in total credit available to each state is less than 25 per cent in all the 17 states. Only 5 states like UP, MP, Haryana, Punjab and Rajasthan accounted for more than 20 per cent share of agriculture credit in total credit. In the state of West Bengal (WB) and Maharashtra (MH) where the cities of Kolkata and Mumbai accounted above 70 per cent of the total credit allotted to each state, the share of agriculture credit is less than 10 per cent (MH 4.8%, WB 7.5%). Both in Kerala and UP, the share of agriculture and industry is showing marginal difference but in Kerala, the share of others which includes personal loans, transports operators, trade, finance, etc. accounted more than 70 per cent of bank credit available to it, whereas this share is more than 50 per cent in UP.

Table 10

Sector-wise Share of Bank Credit in 17 Major States (in %) 2009

	Agriculture	*Industry*	*Others*	*Total Credit*
AP	16.8	33.2	50	1,736,793,225
Assam	8.7	21.8	69.5	1,54,698,923
Bihar	17	30.2	52.8	4,79,317,441

Cont'd...

...Cont'd

Gujarat	14.9	48.1	37.1	1,472,815,655
Haryana	22.1	35	42.9	5,00,381,771
HP	14.6	40.8	44.7	98,517,992
J & K	7	21.9	71.1	1,41,428,479
Karnataka	12.4	34.6	53.1	19,76,302,455
Kerala	16.5	15.9	67.6	7,29,446,226
Madhya	24.4	35.2	40.4	6,73,440,037
Maharashtra	4.2	44.2	51.6	6,309,099,143
Odisha	14.2	32.4	53.4	3,36,238,822
Punjab	20.1	38.1	41.8	7,62,015,632
Rajasthan	21.9	34.8	43.3	7,28,185,441
Tamil Nadu	11.4	37.5	51.1	2,258,110,261
UP	24.3	25.2	50.5	1,244,868,312
West Bengal	7.5	42.9	49.6	1,255,114,987
All India	15.2	33.6	51.2	20,856,774,802

Source: Statistical Statement Related to Banks and Report on Currency and Finance, RBI 2010.

Figure 5 *Sector-wise Share of Bank Credit in 17 Major States (in %) on March 2009*

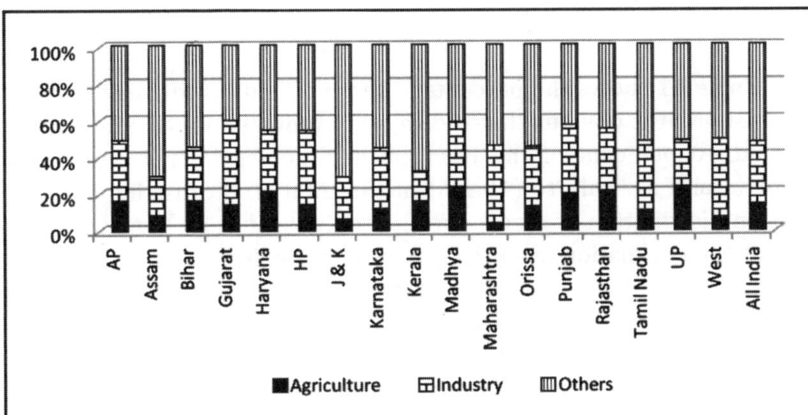

Source: Table 10

The share of industry moves in between 50 and 20 per cent of the total credit, exception being Kerala where industry share is 15.9 per cent. Out of the 17 states, Kerala is the only state where the share of agriculture credit is more than the share of industry. In the wake of the global financial crisis, the focus of recent policy initiatives was maintaining financial stability along with arresting the moderation in the growth momentum. Accordingly, the initiatives taken by the Reserve Bank were mainly aimed at strengthening the banking system and financial markets, while ensuring uninterrupted flow of credit to the different sectors of the economy.

Table 11

Population Group-wise Bank Credit – Percentage Share According to Occupation 2009

Occupation	*Rural*	*Semi-Urban*	*Urban*	*Metropolitan*	*All-India*
Agriculture	38.7	27.7	9.6	3.2	10.9
Industry	24.9	22.1	36.6	46.6	39.8
Transport Operators	1.2	1.2	1.5	2.5	2
Professional and Other services	3.8	4.2	7.4	10.8	8.7
Personal Loans	16.3	29.1	28	15.8	19.4
Trade	10.6	11.5	11.2	8.8	9.7
Finance	1.9	0.8	2.6	9.7	6.6
All Others	2.6	3.5	3.2	2.5	2.7
Total Bank Credit	100	100	100	100	100

Source: Calculated from Basic Statistical Returns of Scheduled Commercial Banks in India Volume – 38, March 2010, Reserve Bank of India.

Table 11 shows the percentage share of bank credit according to occupation. It is obvious that the share of industry at all India level is around 40 per cent of the total credit followed by personal loans (19.4%) and agriculture (10.9%) of the total credit distributed. This uneven distribution of credit does not only exist at all India level but also at the occupation level. The share of agriculture and the industry accounted for 38.7 per cent and 24.9 per cent, respectively, of the total credit distributed in the rural area. These two sectors have received more than 60 per cent of the total rural credit.

Sector-wise Compound Annual Growth Rate (CAGR) of credit has been calculated in Table 12. It is quite clear from Table 12 that the CAGR of total bank credit was 17.2 per cent in the pre-reforms period (1980–81 to 1989–90). It declines by 16 per cent in the first decade of reforms. In the period 2001 to 2009, the total bank credit registered more than 20 per cent annual growth rate. Seeing at the sector level, it is obvious that the personal loans registered 22.7 per cent CAGR in the first decade of reform period followed by trade (17.3%), professional services (16.8%), industry (15.4%), agriculture (10.6%) and transport operators (9.6%). In the period 2001 to 2009, professional services experienced 32.8 per cent growth rate followed by personal loan (26.6%), transport operators (23.50%), agriculture (21.9%), trade (20.33%) and industry (19.04%).

Table 12

Sector-wise Credit of Commercial Banks – Compound Annual Growth Rate (in %)

Period	*Agriculture*	*Industry*	*Transport Operators*	*Professional Services*	*Personal Loans*	*Trade*	*Total Bank Credit*
1980–81 to 1989–90	18.1	17.4	13.6	20.7	25.3	11.8	17.2
1990–91 to 1999–00	10.6	15.4	9.4	16.8	22.7	17.3	16
2000–01 to 2008–09	21.99	19.04	23.5	32.88	26.67	20.33	20.2

Source: Basic Statistical Returns of Scheduled Commercial Banks, Various Issues, Reserve Bank of India.

Thus, it can be said that agriculture sector had been neglected in the initial stage of reform period. In the first decade of reform period, all the sectors have shown decline in the CAGR compared to pre-reform period, exception being trade which registered 17.3 per cent CAGR (more than 11.8%). But the decline in the share of agriculture credit was more than the other sectors.

Conclusion

In the period of liberalization, the dependency of the rural households on the non-institutional sources of credit increased in all the states, except Himachal Pradesh and Maharashtra where it witnessed marginal decline. The money lenders were the major source of borrowing in the informal sector. The compound annual growth of agriculture credit supplied by SCBs, which was 10.75 per cent between 1990 and 2000, increased to 21.99 per cent in the period 2000 to 2009. This revival of agriculture credit in 2000s came from the indirect finance of commercial banks, definitional change in agriculture credit, and increase in the numbers of loans, an urban and metro-centric supply of agriculture credit. The urban and metro-centric orientation of banking system is evident from the fact that there is a high degree of concentration of bank credit in the developed cities like Mumbai, Kolkata, Hyderabad, Bangalore, etc. which are having more than 40 lakh population each.

However, the top 10 per cent (55 districts) of the total districts in 17 major states is getting 72 per cent of total supply of credit (in absolute amount), whereas the bottom 20 per cent (110 districts) is just getting 0.94 per cent. In case of agriculture, the top 10 per cent is garnering 40 per cent of the total supply of credit, while bottom 20 per cent is just getting 1.7 per cent of the total agriculture credit. Thus, we can see that the level of inequality is much higher in case of total supply of credit compared to agriculture credit.

The credit advancement of Scheduled Commercial Banks is biased towards agriculture which is a major employment generating sector in India. Sector-wise analysis indicates that the share of agriculture in total credit available to each is less than 25 per cent in all the 17 states. There is uneven distribution of credit which not only exists at all India level but also at the occupation level. The share of agriculture and the industry accounted for 38.7 per cent and 24.9 per cent, respectively, of the total credit distributed in the rural area.

In the first decade of reform period, all the sectors have shown decline in the CAGR of bank credit compared to pre-reform period, exception being trade which registered 17.3 per cent CAGR (more than 11.8%). But the decline in the share of agriculture credit was more than that in the other sectors. Accordingly, the initiatives taken by the Reserve Bank were mainly aimed at strengthening the banking system and financial markets, while ensuring uninterrupted flow of credit to the different sectors of the economy.

However, the study observed that the distribution of credit, no matter from which source (formal or informal) in both agriculture and total bank credit is highly skewed in favour of the advanced states like Punjab, Haryana, Maharashtra, Andhra Pradesh and Tamil Nadu. There are two types of tendencies which have been observed in the case of credit distribution from the informal sources. First, due to enough income generating activities they have concentrated in the well-developed states. Second, their high share of lending in the hilly regions shows the inability or low penetration of formal sources in providing adequate credit. In the first case, the conventional lending (informal) has been promoted from the formal sources themselves.

Note

1. Some of the districts have been merged due to non-availability of data separately. In case of agriculture credit, there is no rural population in metropolitan cities like Mumbai, Kolkata, Bangalore, etc. That is why there are only 547 districts in per capita agriculture credit.

References

Beck, T., Demirguc-Kunt, A. and Martinez Peria, M.S. (2006). *Reaching Out: Access and Use of Banking Services Across Countries*, World Bank, Washington, D.C., July.

Bell, C. (1990). 'Interactions between Institutional and Informal Credit Agencies in Rural India', *The World Bank Economic Review*, 4 (3): 297–327.

Bhalla, G.S. and Singh, G. (2010). *Growth of Indian Agriculture: A District Level Study*, Final Report of Planning Commission Project.

Chavan, P. (2005). 'How Inclusive are Banks under Financial Liberalisation?', *Economic and Political Weekly*, 40 (43): 4647–49.

Dev, S.M. (2008). *Inclusive Growth in India: Agriculture, Poverty and Human Development*, Oxford University Press, New Delhi.

Gadgil, M.V. (1994). 'Formal Agricultural Credit System in India: Shape of Things to Come', *Indian Journal of Agricultural Economics*, XLIX (3): 476–90.

Gulati, Ashok (2009). 'Emerging Trends in Indian Agriculture: What Can We Learn from These?', 2nd Prof. Dayanath Jha Memorial Lecture, National Centre for Agricultural Economics and Policy Research, New Delhi.

Hoff, K. and Stiglitz, J.E. (1997). 'Moneylenders and Bankers: Price-Increasing Subsidies in a Monopolistically Competitive Market', *Journal of Development Economics*, 52: 429–62.

Honohan, P. (2008). 'Cross-Country Variation in Household Access to Financial Services', *Journal of Banking and Finance*, 32: 2493–500.

Jamir, Limaakum (1996). *Institutional Credit for Agricultural Development: A Regional Analysis* (M.Phil. Dissertation), Jawaharlal Nehru University, New Delhi.

Kar, Jyotimoyee (2010). 'Institutional Credit, Transaction Cost and Informal Sector: A Case Study of Indian Villages', *Indian Journal of Labour Economics*, 53 (2): 397–408.

Kumar, Anjani, Singh, Dhiraj K. and Kumar, Prabhat (2007). 'Performance of Rural Credit and Factors Affecting the Choice of Credit Sources', *Indian Journal of Agricultural Economics*, 62 (3): 297–313.

Kumara, A., Singh, K.M. and Sinha, S. (2010). 'Institutional Credit to Agriculture Sector in India: Status, Performance and Determinants', *Agricultural Economics Research Review*, 23 (2), July–December: 253–64.

Ministry of Finance (2007). *Report of the Expert Group on Agricultural Indebtedness*, Department of Economic Affairs, Government of India, New Delhi.

Mohan, Rakesh (2004). 'Agricultural Credit in India: Status, Issues and Future Agenda', *Reserve Bank of India Bulletin*.

NABARD (1980–81 to 2001–02). *Statistical Statement Relating to Cooperative Movement*, various issues.

Nasir, S. and Singh, R.K.P. (2003). 'Agriculture Credit Flow in Bihar: An Economic Analysis', *Indian Journal of Agricultural Economics*, 58 (1): 137–45.

NSSO (2003). *All-India Debt and Investment Survey, NSS 59th Round, Household Assets Holding, Indebtedness, Current Borrowings and Repayments of Social Groups in India*, Report No. 503 (59/18.2/4).

——. (2005a). *Situation Assessment Survey of Farmers: Indebtedness of Farmer Households, NSS 59th Round*, Report No. 498 (59/33/1), Ministry of Statistics and Programme Implementation, Government of India, New Delhi.

——. (2005b). *Household Indebtedness in India as on 30.06.2002, All India Debt and Investment Survey, NSS 59th Round.*

Rangarajan, C. (2005). 'Agricultural Credit: Reaching the Marginalised Farmers', Lecture delivered at the Bankers conference (BANCON), Kolkata, November 12.

Ray, S.K. (2008). 'Availability of Institutional Credit, Change in Cropping Pattern and Agricultural Growth in West Bengal: A District Level Analysis', *Indian Journal of Regional Science*, 40 (1): 34–42.

——. (2006). 'Institutional Credit, Cropping Pattern, Commercialisation of Agriculture and Agricultural Growth in West Bengal: A District Level Analysis', *Indian Economic Journal*, 53 (1): 58–75.

Reserve Bank of India (2004). *Report of the Advisory Committee on Flow of Credit to Agriculture and Related Activities from Banking System*, Mumbai.

——. *Basic Statistical Returns of Scheduled Commercial Banks in India*, various issues, Mumbai.

Sahu, Gagan Bihari (2007). 'Supply Analysis of Institutional Credit to Agriculture for Major States in India', *Indian Journal of Agricultural Economics*, 62 (4): 664–78.

Singh, Surjit (1998). 'The Informal Sector: Some Linkages and Credit Issues', Working Paper No. 0098, Institute of Development Studies, Jaipur.

——. (2005). 'Agricultural Credit in the Post-Reform Period', Working Paper No. 0145, Institute of Development Studies, Jaipur.

Sriram, M.S. (2007). 'Productivity of Rural Credit: A Review of Issues and Some Recent Literature', *International Journal of Rural Management*, 3 (2): 245–68.

Stiglitz, J.E. and Weiss, A. (1981). 'Credit Rationing in Markets with Imperfect Information', *American Economic Review*, 71: 393–410.

Swaminathan, M.S. (2007). *Agriculture Cannot Wait: New Horizons in Indian Agriculture*, Academic Foundation and National Academy of Agricultural Sciences, New Delhi.

2

In Search of Inclusion

The Role of Muslims in West Bengal's Electoral Politics

ABDUL MATIN

Muslims constitute the second largest religious community and single largest minority community in West Bengal, comprising more than 25.2 per cent (as per 2001 Census) of the total population. The Muslim population is scattered almost all over West Bengal but is mostly concentrated in the districts of Murshidabad, Maldah, Birbhum, Howrah, Kolkata, South 24 Parganas, North 24 Parganas, Coochbehar, Burdwan, East Medinipur, Hooghly, Bankura, Nadia, North Dinajpur, etc. Out of the 19 districts in West Bengal, 12 fall under the list of Minority Concentrated Districts (MCDs) as notified by the Government of India and the socio-economic status of Muslims there is well below the national average.[1]

Right from the Dr Gopal Singh Committee to the recent Sachar Committee (a Prime Minister's High Level Committee) constituted to enquire into the socio-economic and educational status of Muslims in India, Muslims have been found to be the most under-developed and under-represented among all religious communities in India, in terms of social, economic, educational and political development. The condition of the Muslim community in India is more abject than that of the presently notified backward classes.[2]

In the case of West Bengal, the scenario is worse with the Bengali Muslim community falling below the national average for Muslims in the socio-economic, educational and political contexts. In the aftermath of the publication of the Sachar Committee Report in 2006, several Muslim organizations came into existence in West Bengal, which started questioning the Communist Party of India (Marxist)-led Left Front government that had been ruling the state for more than three decades. The representation of Muslims in education, politics, employment, is abysmally low in West Bengal as compared to the national average. Infant mortality rates, poverty, illiteracy, malnutrition, under nutrition, unemployment are very high among the Muslims in West Bengal.[3]

Even though the much-celebrated land reforms programme of the Left Front government directly benefitted large chunks of rural Muslims and SC households in the districts of South 24 Parganas, North 24 Parganas, Nadia, Murshidabad, Hooghly, Burdwan, etc. a huge number of Muslims are still in the vicious cycle of poverty. The result of the last Assembly election of West Bengal which took place in 2011 and put an end to the more than three decades of uninterrupted Left rule in the state made the position of the CPI(M) in the electoral arena clearly visible. The role of the Muslim electorate in sealing the fate of the Left in the election cannot be overemphasized.

Out of a total of 294 Assembly Constituencies, CPI(M) got only 40 seats and the rest of the Left parties (RSP, Forward bloc, CPI) were able to manage only 20 seats. In major districts that have been historically strongholds of the Left like South 24 Parganas, North 24 Parganas, Hooghly, Howrah, Nadia, etc. out of 88 Assembly constituencies in three districts CPM got only nine seats. This happened for the first time after the late 1970s in the history of West Bengal.[4]

The large majority of Muslims in West Bengal have always stood with the Left parties due to various historical and political reasons, one of course being the partition of the state and another important reasons could be the issue of security. But what went wrong in the process that after three decades of unflinching support, Muslims suddenly lost faith in the Left parties and disenchantment with them? My entire paper analyses how and why Muslims play an important role in the electoral politics of West Bengal and how the political parties, mainly Trinamool Congress, started communicating with and responding to the community in the state in a way that immensely helped the Trinamool Congress led by Mamata Banerjee to overthrow the strong Left Front government in the 2011 Assembly Elections.

Socio-economic and Educational Status of Muslims in West Bengal

The socio-economic condition of Muslims in West Bengal is extremely poor even after the 34 years of Left rule in the state. The rate of poverty (both urban and rural), unemployment, malnutrition, child mortality, illiteracy, dropout rates, etc. are extremely high among the Muslims of West Bengal. The representation of Muslims in government employment, education, bureaucracy, judiciary, executive, legislative, etc. is very low compared to the proportion of the community's population in the state.

Education

Education is pivotal to the development of any society. The literacy rate is considered one of the most important indicators of social development and help in the improvement of the quality of life. The wide spread of education in society leads to removal of iniquities in asset ownership, capabilities and opportunities which not only empower individuals to be aware about their rights but also promotes social cohesion and sustainability.[5] The literacy rate among the Muslims in West Bengal is abysmally low and dropout rate is very high. The state of higher education is much more vulnerable, with the representation of Muslims in higher education, either as students or staff, being almost negligible. As far as literacy rate of female is concerned, it is absolutely dismal.

Table 1

Literacy Rates Among Various Religious Communities in West Bengal

Religious Communities	*Persons*	*Male*	*Female*
All Religions	68.64	77.02	51.61
Hindus	72.44	81.12	63.09
Muslims	57.47	64.61	49.75
Christians	69.72	77.20	62.30
Sikhs	87.19	91.37	81.98
Buddhists	74.73	83.09	66.22
Jains	92.81	96.46	88.87
Others	51.53	68.63	34.24
Religion not stated	—	71.52	54.84

Source: Census of India, 2001, Government of India.

Table 2

Educational Level Differentials in West Bengal, 2001 and 2007–08

	Muslim		SCs/STs		Others	
	2007–08	2001	2007–08	2001	2007–08	2001
Matriculation and above	15	12	17	13	39	38
Middle	50	26	52	30	62	58
Primary	85	50	90	54	93	80

Source: (i) Estimated by Dr Abusaleh Shariff from the unit level records of the 64th Round NSSO (ii) Census of India 2001.

Table 3

Representation of Muslims in Higher Education in West Bengal

Name of University	Total No. of Faculty Members	Total No. of Muslim Faculty Members	% of Muslim Faculty Members	Total No. of Administrative Officials	No. of Muslim Administrative Officials	% of Muslim Administrative Officials
University of Calcutta	604	19	3.15	39	3	7.69
Jadavpur University	632	5	0.79	36	0	0
Kalyani University	216	1	0.46	17	0	0
Rabindrabharati University	149	1	0.67	19	0	0
Bengal Engineering and Science University	209	4	1.91	16	0	0
Burdwan University	230	8	3.48	48	2	4.16
Vidyasagar University	112	6	5.36	22	1	4.55
North Bengal University	177	3	1.69	36	1	2.78
Bidhan Chandra Agricultural University	265	9	3.40	Not available	Not available	Not available

Source: Annual Reports and website of concern universities, till 2010.

Table 4

Representation of Muslim in State Government Employment

States	*Muslim Population (%)*	*Total Number of Employees*	*Share of Muslims in State Employment (%)*	*Education Department*	*Health Women and Child Welfare Department*	*Home Department*	*Transport Department*	*Other Department*
West Bengal	25.2	1,34,972	2.1	—	1.0	7.1	—	2.4
Kerala	24.7	2,68,733	10.4	12.3	10.5	10.7	9.2	10.2
Uttar Pradesh	18.5	1,34,053	5.1	—	5.6	9.8	4.2	5.0
Bihar	16.5	78,114	7.6	12.3	2.6	6.9	10.9	7.6
Assam	30.9	81,261	11.2	—	10.8	11.3	11.8	11.7
Jharkhand	13.8	15,374	6.7	—	3.4	7.4	—	7.0
Karnataka	12.2	5,28,401	8.5	11.9	5.0	4.2	7.5	7.0
Delhi	11.7	1,35,877	3.2	7.2	1.7	2.2	1.1	0.9
Maharashtra	10.6	9,15,643	4.4	4.7	2.8	4.2	—	3.8
Andhra Pradesh*	9.2	8,76,291	8.8	7.9	6.4	14.6	10.0	8.9
Gujarat	9.1	7,54,533	5.4	4.5	1.5	5.6	16.3	5.3
Tamil Nadu	5.6	5,29,597	3.2	5.5	3.5	2.5	2.4	2.2
Sum of States	15.4	44,52,851	6.3	6.5	4.4	7.3	6.5	6.0

*Does not provide for group ABCD employees, only total employees and Muslim employees is provided.

Source: Sachar Committee Report, Government of India p. 370.

Economic Status

The economic situation of Muslims in West Bengal is very alarming and abysmally low. The poverty rate as well as unemployment and under-employment rate among Bengali Muslims is quite disturbing. According to the Sachar Committee Report, the rural poverty rate of Muslims in West Bengal is 33 per cent, which is higher than the corresponding rates in Kerala, Assam, Karnataka, Maharashtra, Andhra Pradesh, etc.

The work participation rates among Muslims in West Bengal are lower than the national average. Many people migrate out of the state in search of jobs, especially to Hyderabad, Kerala, Delhi, Mumbai, Gujarat, etc. In terms of sectoral employment, the share of Muslims in wage earning employment in manufacturing and industrial enterprises is relatively higher than Hindus but the long-term trend shows reduction in total employment due to closure and modernization of industry. Most of the labour force in the state is self-employed. A staggering 55 per cent of the state's Muslims fall into this category with almost no links to modern markets.[6]

The situation of Muslims in State government employment is worse, with only 2.1 per cent of Muslims being State government employees.

Political Representation

Muslims in West Bengal are under-represented not only in employment but also in the political arena. Muslims are not represented adequately in local self-government, State Legislative Assembly, Cabinet, Executive and so on. Although political representation not necessarily leads to economic and social empowerment but it certainly helps in political empowerment which gives sense of inclusiveness in the political process.

Table 5

Representation of Muslim in West Bengal State Legislative Assembly

Year	*Total Members of W.B. Legislative Assembly*	*Muslim Members in W.B. Legislative Assembly*	*Percentage of Muslim Members in W.B. Legislative Assembly*	*Expected Presentation as per Proportion of Muslim Population*
1952	238	22	9.66	46
1957	252	25	9.92	49
1962	252	27	10.71	50
1967	280	35	12.5	56
1969	280	36	12.86	56

Cont'd...

...Cont'd

1971	279	29	10.39	57
1972	280	35	12.5	57
1977	294	37	12.59	60
1983	292	36	12.24	63
1987	294	35	11.91	63
1991	294	42	14.29	69
1996	294	40	13.61	69
2001	294	39	13.27	69
2006	294	46	15.64	72
2011	294	59	20.06	75

Source: A. Ansari, Political Representation of Muslims in India and reports of Election Commission of India, New Delhi.

Therefore, from the above mentioned data and reports, the socio-economic, educational and political backwardness of Muslims in West Bengal is crystal clear and so is the pressing need for inclusion and development. Interestingly in the 2011 Assembly Election, the representation of Muslims reached around 20 per cent. This is for the first time in the electoral history of West Bengal in the post-Independence India.

Political Parties and the Issue of the Inclusion of Muslims in West Bengal

West Bengal is a very unique state as far as its Muslim populace is concerned. It is among the few states where, in spite of a huge Muslim population, there is no presence of Muslim political parties after Independence. This is in stark contrast to many other states with considerable Muslim population such as Assam, Andhra Pradesh and Kerala which have the AIUDF, AIMIM and Muslim League, respectively. Muslims in West Bengal have always chosen to vote for the mainstream political parties, whether it was the Congress in the early 1950s and late 1960s or the Communist Party of India from the late 1970s. The 'religion' factor hardly played an important role in the electoral politics of the state. Before the Sachar Committee Report, no political party in West Bengal had taken the issues of 'development deficit' of Muslim seriously. It was only after the publication of the Sachar Committee Report that the question of inclusion, development, welfare of Muslim minority, etc. came into political debates both at the central as well as in the state level.

The Muslim community plays a very significant role in deciding the fate of any political party in West Bengal because of its huge numbers in the state. It is not possible for any political party in West Bengal to form a government without the significant support of the Muslims. Out of 294 Assembly Constituencies, there are around 70 to 75 constituencies where Muslims comprise between 40 to 50 per cent of the total electorate and 60 to 65 constituencies where Muslims comprise between 20 to 30 per cent of the total electorate. As a result, the role of Muslims in the electoral landscape of West Bengal is very vital for any party to come to power in the state.

Inclusive policies for Muslims such as reservation in jobs and education, scholarships and other developmental schemes and policies were never present in the agenda of either political parties or governments in West Bengal for a very long time. Such issues sprang to dominance in the realm of politics due to the findings of the Sachar Committee Report (SCR) and the massive mobilization and assertions of Muslim community-based organizations in the state following this. Before the publication of the Sachar Committee Report, political parties cutting across all ideologies and affiliations never even mentioned the issues of the development of Muslims in the state in their election manifesto. But there has been a drastic change after the SCR Report. Presently, almost all political parties have devoted a separate chapter in their election manifesto for the development of the minority community.

Role of Muslim Community-based Organizations in Electoral Mobilization

Muslim organizations, intelligentsia and religious leaders played a crucial role in creating an anti-Left attitude among the Muslim masses. After the publication of the Sachar Committee Report in 2006, several Muslim organizations, both at the local and state level mobilized and sensitize Muslims of West Bengal about their socio-economic backwardness.

Organizations like Jamiat Ulama-e-Hind (JUH) led by Siddiqullah Chowdhury, Mojaddedia Anath Foundation led by Peerzada Toha Siddique, Furfura Sharif Minority Development Organisation led by Peerzada Toyeb Siddique, All Bengal Minority Youth Federation led by Md.Qamruzzaman, West Bengal Madrasah Students Union, Jamaat-e-Islami, Students Islamic Organisation, Paschim Bongo Ahle Sunnah-wal-Jamat Committee, Popular Front of India, All India Minority Forum led by Idris Ali and many other small organizations played an important role in mobilizing Muslim masses against the incumbent Left government.

Local Muslim newspapers in both Bengali and Urdu such as *Kalom, Mizan, Gati, Janatar Adalat, Bongonoor, Akhbar-e-Mashrikh, Azad Hind,* etc. played distinct role in creating public opinion against the Left Front government and educating the Muslim masses, by highlighting Muslim issues and problems and providing enough space for Muslim organizations to articulate their views and opinions.

Jamiat Ulama-e-Hind

Jamiat Ulama-e-Hind (JUH) is one of the most influential Islamic organizations in India, having a very strong presence among Muslims throughout the country. In West Bengal, under the leadership of Maulana Siddiqullah Chowdhury (General Secretary of State JUH), it played a crucial role in mobilizing Muslim masses against the Left government. JUH organized hundreds of mass meetings and rallies throughout Bengal on various issues related to the Muslim community like reservations in jobs and education, land acquisition, infrastructure development, etc. which appealed to large numbers of common Muslims in the state.

While speaking at a public mass meeting in Kolkata, Maulana Chowdhury said, 'We demand 20 per cent reservation for Muslims because currently only 2.5 per cent Muslims are there in government jobs while they comprise 30 per cent of the total population of the state. We gave an ultimatum to the government to take a decision on the matter at the earliest because we cannot wait anymore. We are fed up of empty promises for the last 30 years, now the government has to step in practically.'[7]

Mojaddedia Anath Foundation

The Mojaddedia Anath Foundation led by Peerzada Toha Siddique[8], one of the chief religious clerics and *peer* of Furfura Sharif (an important Sufi shrine and Muslim pilgrimage site in West Bengal), attracted millions of followers throughout Bengal, especially among the rural peasantry. Peerzada Toha Siddique organized hundreds of religious gatherings (Waz-Mahfil) across Bengal, particularly in the southern regions, where he openly criticized and waged war against the incumbent CPI(M) government for not doing any substantial development for the Muslim community and urged Muslims not to vote for CPI(M).

On 13 April 2010, when Mamata Banerjee visited Furfura Sharif[9] to mark the laying of the foundation stone for construction of new railway lines between Dankuni and Furfura Sharif, in the district of

Hooghly, Peerzada Toha Siddique vehemently criticized Left Front government throughout the meeting in the presence of Mamata Banerjee (then Union Railway Minister) and said:

> When it came to putting up flags and banners, you needed us. When you wanted bombs made and hurled, you needed us. When it came to brandishing pistols and shooting people, our help was required. When you needed to fill up the Shahid Minar or Brigade Parade Ground (popular sites for political rallies in Kolkata), you wooed us. Later, you sat on high pedestals and enjoyed while we suffered. It is time we 'kick' you down. For 33 years, you have played football with us. Now it is time for us to play football .... I can only assure Mamta that of the 30 million Muslims in the state; at least 25 million are on her side. Just because we are not directly involved in politics does not mean that we do not understand politics. We have had enough of '*dekchhi, hochchhe, hobey*' (lit. 'I see, it is happening, it shall be done.' Implies empty or false promises). We don't want any more of that. Jyoti Basu (LF Chief Minister of West Bengal from 1977 to 2000) had finished us off and Buddhadeb Bhattacharjee followed in his footsteps. Don't use us any longer![10]

In front of a crowd of thousands of people at Furfura Sharif, Maulana Noor-ur Rehman Barkati, the Imam of Tipu Sultan Mosque in Kolkata, said, 'The "Red" has destroyed Bengal. The people are with Mamata and it is high time to make her Chief Minister. She is the undisputed Queen of Bengal and she only can save the state from complete ruin.'[11]

Furfura Sharif Minority Development Organization

A Muslim organization led by Peerzada Toyeb Siddique[12] (a great grandson of the famous Sufi saint of Furfura Sharif) and Md. Anisul Haque (former Secretary of West Bengal Madrasah Students Union), Furfura Sharif Minority Development Organization played quite significant role in mobilizing educated Muslim youths and students in West Bengal against the Left government in West Bengal.

They regularly organized mass meetings, public rallies and seminars, especially before the Assembly elections, in various parts of Bengal and gave an ultimatum to the government regarding the implementation of the recommendations of Sachar Committee and Ranganath Mishra Commission. Peerzada Toyeb Siddique has always been vociferous against the Left regime in Bengal.

In April 2010, Furfura Sharif Minority Development Organization held a Minority Convention at Maula Ali Youth Centre in Kolkata, which discussed the issue of reservation for Muslims in government service and education, as recommended by the Sachar Committee and Ranganath Mishra Commission. There, in the presence of Mr Partha Chatterjee, then Opposition Leader of West Bengal Legislative Assembly, Peerzada Toyeb Siddique gave an ultimatum to the Left Front government in West Bengal to act on Sachar Committee recommendations and warned that otherwise the Muslims of West Bengal would teach a lesson to the CPI(M) government.[13]

All Bengal Minority Youth Federation

All Bengal Minority Youth Federation (ABMYF) led by former *madrasah* student leaders Md. Qamruzzaman played an active role in the anti-Left Muslim mobilizations in West Bengal. ABMYF organized various road shows, mass gatherings and seminars to educate and mobilize the Muslim Community in West Bengal, especially in the suburban region of Kolkata.[14]

West Bengal Madrasah Students Union

WBMSU is the most revolutionary *madrasah* students' youth organization in West Bengal. They have a strong network spreading throughout all *madrasahs* in West Bengal. They are the most vocal among the Muslim youth organizations in West Bengal. When the Left Front government removed the word '*madrasah*' from the age-old Calcutta Aliah Madrasah and rechristened it Aliah University, the MSU bursted into protest against the Left Front government's anti-*madrasah* stand. They regularly organized *dharnas*, road blocks, *gherao*, etc. They showed the black flag to the then Chief Minister, Buddhadeb Bhattacharya when he came to attend a programme at Aliah University in Kolkata. Mamata Banerjee and other leaders of Trinamool Congress used to constantly keep in touch with the MSU, who were a great source of strength to them in the fight against the incumbent Left government in West Bengal.[15]

Students Islamic Organization

Students Islamic Organization, the student wing of Jamaat-e-Islami, also played quite an important role among the Muslim youths in West Bengal. The West Bengal Chapter of Students Islamic Organization (SIO) launched a state-wide 10 day-campaign on Muslim reservations and various other issues. The SIO state President said: 'We demand the implementation of Ranganath Mishra Commission Report at the national level. In West Bengal, where Muslims are more than 25 per cent we want 20 per cent reservation to the economically backward sections of the Muslim community cutting across castes'.[16]

Popular Front of India, Paschim Bongo Ahle Sunnah-wal-Jamat, All India Minority Forum, Milli Council, etc. also played an impressing role in the mobilization of the Muslim community in West Bengal against Left Front government by organizing various programmes and activities in the state of West Bengal.

Kenneth Bo Neilson argues that West Bengal minority are in many respects excluded from both the developmental and political process of the state. Muslims score significantly lower on the range of socio-economic indicators compared to other section of the population and their political representation is also poor. However, the Muslim community-based organizations seeks to address and overcome this 'development deficit'. As part of the mobilization, Muslim organizations have used their electoral strength to promote their issues of concern. They put huge pressure on all political parties in the states to pay attention to the welfare and development of the Muslim community that had been hitherto neglected. [17]

Thus, we observe that Muslims played a major active role in the electoral politics of the state and contributed tremendously to the changing landscape of electoral politics in West Bengal.

Conclusion

The gross neglect, exclusion and backwardness suffered by the Muslims of West Bengal under the 33-year-long Left regime reached a point where the genuine grievances could no longer be swept under the carpet, especially with the publication of the Sachar Committee and Ranganath Mishra Commission Reports. This culminated in Muslims of West Bengal coming together onto a common platform for inclusion and development of the community, rising above class, sectarian and partisan divides. The overwhelming anti-Left sentiment, thus, generated among the Muslims, was a key factor in the epoch-making victory of the Trinamool Congress over the Left Front, which had been in power for more than three decades, in the 2011 State Assembly Elections. The defeat of CPI(M)-led Left Front government has changed the political landscape and power equations in West Bengal forever.

Notes

1. Report published by the Ministry of Minority Affairs, Government of India.
2. Sachar Committee Report, a Prime Minister's High Level Committee on the Social, Economic and Educational Status of Muslim Community in India, 2006.

3. Human Development Index Report, Government of West Bengal, 2004, pp. 25–26.
4. Statistics published by the Election Commission of India, 2011.
5. Sanjeer Alam, 'Education and Exclusion of Muslims', in Zoya Hasan and Mushirul Hasan (eds), 'Assessing UPA Government's Response to Muslim Deprivation', *India: Social Development Report 2012: Minorities at the Margins*, Council of Social Development, Oxford University Press, 2012, pp. 242–43.
6. Abusaleh Shariff, *India Today*, 2009.
7. Manzar Bilal, 'India: Demand Grows for Reservation for WB Muslims', *The Muslim News*, 2 February 2010.
8. Peerzada Toha Siddique is the great grandson of *Peer* Abu Bakar Siddique, the founder of the Furfura Sharif order in the district of Hooghly.
9. Furfura Sharif is one of the most important Sufi religious shrines in the Hooghly district of West Bengal. It has a huge influence among rural Bengali Muslims not only in West Bengal but also in Assam, Tripura and Bangladesh.
10. Jayanta Gupta and Falguni Banerjee, 'Muslim Clerics Wow Support to Mamata', *The Times of India*, Kolkata, 14 April 2010.
11. Ibid.
12. Peerzaada Toyeb Siddique is the great grandson of Peer Choto Huzur of Furfura Sharif.
13. *Sangbad Pratidin*, Kolkata, 30 April 2010.
14. Zahidul Haque, 'WB Muslims Likely to Form New Group for Reservation', twocircles.net, 11 April 2010.
15. *Indian Express*, Kolkata, December 2010.
16. Mumtaz Alam Falahi, 'SIO Launches Muslim Reservation Campaign in W.B.', 21 April 2010, twocircles.net, Kolkata.
17. Kenneth Bo Neilson, 'In Search of Development: Muslims and Electoral Politics in Indian State', *Forum for Development Studies*, 38 (3), 2011, pp. 345–70.

References

Ahmed, Rafiuddin (1981). *The Bengali Muslims, 1871–1906: A Quest for Identity*, Oxford University Press, New Delhi.

Alam, Javeed (2006). 'Turning Point', A Special Issue on Sachar Committee Report in *Frontline*, December 15: 9–13.

Alam, Mohd Sanjeer (2009). 'Is Relative Size of Minority Population Linked to Underdevelopment?', *Economic and Political Weekly*, XLVI (24), November 28: 10–13.

Bardhan, Pranab (2011). 'The Avoidable Tragedy of the Left in India-II', *Economic and Political Weekly*, June: 10–13.

Bhattacharya, Dwaipayan (1999). 'Politics of Middleness: The Changing Character of the CPIM in Rural West Bengal (1977–90)', in Ben Royal, Barbara Harris-White and Sugato Bose (eds), *Sonar Bangla? Agricultural Growth and the Agrarian Change in West Bengal and Bangladesh*, Sage Publications, New Delhi.

Chatterjee, Jyotiprasad and Basu, Suprio (2009). 'West Bengal: Mandate for Change', *Economic and Political Weekly*, September 26.

Chatterji, Joya (1994). *Bengal Divided: Hindu Communalism and Partition 1932–1947*, Cambridge University Press, Cambridge.

——. (1998). 'The Bengali Muslims: A Contradiction in Terms? An Overview of the Debate on Bengali Muslim Identity', in Mushirul Hasan (ed.), *Islam: Communities and the Nation: Muslim Identities in South Asia and Beyond*, Manohar Publications, Delhi.

Dasgupta, Avhijit (2009). 'On the Margins: Muslims in West Bengal', *Economic and Political Weekly*, April 18.

Desai, Manali (2001). 'Party Formation, Political Power and the Capacity for Reform: Comparing Left Parties in Kerala and West Bengal', *Social Forces*, 80 (1), September: 37–60.

Eaton, Richard M. (1997). *Rise of Islam and the Bengal Frontier, 1204–1760*, Oxford University Press, Delhi.

Ghosh, Buddahadeb (2008). 'The Subaltern and Politics at the Grassroots', *Economic and Political Weekly*, August 9.

Gupta, Monobina (2010). *Left Politics in Bengal: Time Travels among Bhadralok Marxists*, Orient Blackswan, Hyderabad.

Hasan, Zoya (2009). *Politics of Inclusion: Castes, Minorities and Affirmative Action*, Second Impression, Oxford University Press, New Delhi.

Khalidi, Omar (1995). *Indian Muslims since Independence*, Vikas Publishing House, New Delhi.

Narayan, Badri (2011). *The Making of Dalit Public in North India: Uttar Pradesh, 1950–Present*, Oxford University Press, New Delhi.

Neilson, Kenneth Bo (2011). 'In Search of Development: Muslims and Electoral Politics in Indian State', *Forum for Development Studies*, 38 (3): 345–70.

Rudd, Arild (2003). *Poetics of Village Politics: The Making of West Bengal Rural Communism*, Oxford University Press, New Delhi.

Sikand, Yoginder (2006). 'Behind their Plight', A Special Issue on Sachar Committee Report in *Frontline*, December 15.

Weiner, Myron and Osgood, John (eds) (1974). *Electoral Politics in the Indian States: The Communist Parties of West Bengal*, Manohar Book Service, New Delhi.

Yadav, Yogendra (2011). 'How West Bengal Voted', *The Hindu*, May 16.

Government Documents and Reports

Human Development Index Report (2004). Government of West Bengal, Kolkata.

Ranganath Mishra Commission Report (2007).

Sachar Committee Report, a Prime Minister's High Level Committee on the Social, Economic and Educational Status of the Muslim Community of India (2006). Government of India, New Delhi.

Statistical Report on the General Election of the West Bengal Legislative Assembly (2006 and 2011). Election Commission of India.

Newspapers and Magazines

Mizaan, Gati, Janatar Adalat, Bangonoor.

Saaptahik Qalom, 22 May 2011.

Sangbad Pratidin, Kolkata edition.

The Hindu, Kolkata edition.

The Times of India, Kolkata edition.

Websites

Official Website of Election Commission of India, www.eci.nic

Official Website of Government of West Bengal, www.banglarrmukh.com

Official Website of Ministry of Minority Affairs, Government of India, www.minorityaffairs.com

3

Changing Structure of Rural Economy in India

AJIT KUMAR SINGH

The process of economic development has been historically characterized by a gradual shift from agriculture to industry and later to services as has been highlighted by economic historians and development economists like Clark, Fisher and Kuznets. The development models of Lewis, Jorgenson, etc. also highlight the process of the structural shift. These shifts result in higher income levels in the agricultural sector as well as the whole economy.

It is a well known fact that in India the rate of decline in the share of agriculture in GDP has been much faster than the rate of decline in the share of agriculture in the work force. The slow process of growth of non-agricultural employment has led to overcrowding in agriculture and contributed to the process of marginalization of holdings in India. A positive correlation between high proportion of marginal holdings and rural poverty at the state level has been observed by scholars (Singh, 2011). The pace of reduction of rural poverty in India has been slow because of the slow pace of structural transformation in the rural labour force.

In this paper, we have highlighted some aspects of structural change in rural India in the recent decades. We first discuss the international experience of structural change. This is followed by a discussion of the growth of rural workers by sectors. The shifts in structure of rural workforce have then been examined. The analysis has been done in terms of male and female workers and total workers. The paper also discusses the composition of rural GDP and the share of rural GDP in national GDP by sectors. The final section summarizes the main findings.

The International Experience

The international experience confirms that a rapid shift to non-agricultural development is associated with fast decline in rural poverty. The examples of Japan and Taiwan, both marked by the dominance of small size of holdings, are quite instructive in this context. In Japan, there has been a continuous decline in the number of agricultural workers since 1875 except in immediate post World War II period. Thus, over a 100-year period from 1875 to 1977, more than 2.2 million agricultural workers, i.e. 15 per cent of the agricultural work force, shifted out of agriculture in Japan (Hirashima, 1980). Over this period, cultivated land expanded by about one-third. The result was that cultivated land per agricultural worker increased steadily over the period and led to improved per worker productivity.

In Taiwan also, we observe a sharp shift in employment towards non-agricultural sector. Thus, in a short period of two decades from 1956 to 1976 the number of non-agricultural workers increased by 3.1 million, while agricultural workers increased by only 0.5 million workers (Lee and Chen, 1980). This resulted in a drastic change in the workforce structure as the share of agricultural workers declined from 65.2 per cent to 29.1 per cent, while that of non-agricultural sector increased from 34.8 per cent to 70.9 per cent. Thus, the rapid growth of the non-agricultural sector was able to absorb bulk of the increase in labour force.

The rapidly growing economies of far eastern countries like Indonesia, Japan, Malaysia, Thailand and China, have also witnessed a sharp change in the structure of their employment. Thus, the rural population in China has declined from 82.6 per cent in 1970 to 56 per cent in 2009. Similar transformation in population settlement was also observed in case of countries like Malaysia, Philippines and Japan (*World Development Indicators)*. In contrast, India's rural population declined by only 10 percentage points over the same period – from 80.2 per cent to 70.2 per cent.

Rapid urbanization in these countries has been accompanied by a sharp decrease in the proportion of agricultural workers and a corresponding increase in the proportion of non-agricultural workers. In 1965, majority of workforce in these countries with the exception of Japan was employed in agriculture. But over time, there has been a sharp decline in the agricultural workforce in these countries. Thus, in 2007, the proportion of agricultural workers to total workers was 53.5 per cent in China, 41.8 per cent in Indonesia, 42.1 per cent in Thailand, 36.1 per cent in Philippines and only 4.2 per cent in Japan (Table 1). In contrast, the structural shift in employment has been much slower in India, where still more than half of the workforce is employed in agriculture.

Table 1

Workers Employed in Agriculture as per cent of Total Employment

Year	*China*	*India*	*Indonesia*	*Japan*	*Malaysia*	*Philippines*	*Thailand*
1965	81.0	73.0	71.0	26.0	59.0	56.0	82.0
1980	74.0	70.0	57.0	11.0	42.0	52.0	71.0
1990	53.5	65.6	55.9	7.2	26.0	45.2	63.3
2000	46.3	58.5	45.3	5.1	18.4	37.4	48.5
2007	42.3	52.1	41.2	4.2	14.8	36.1	41.7

Source: World Development Indicators 1965 and 1980 and International Labour Organization, *Key Indicators of Labour Market Data Base*, Geneva.

The shift to non-agricultural employment has resulted in a sharp decline in poverty ratio in the countries studied. Both India and China had around 60 per cent of population living below poverty line of one dollar a day in 1990. Today, poverty ratio stands at 41.6 per cent in India and 16 per cent in China and about 2 per cent in Malaysia and Thailand (UNSD website).

Growth of Rural Workers

Table 2 shows the trends in the work participation rates in rural India. Female WPR has remained distinctly lower than the male WPR and shows higher fluctuation. The male WPR shows a variation in a small range around 54 per cent. It declined between 1993–94 and 1900–2000, but shows a rise thereafter. Female WPR has, however, declined after 1993–94. The decline was quite sharp during the period 2004–05 to 2009–10, during which FWPR declined by 6.6 percentage points.

Table 3 shows the growth of total workers in rural India during the period 1993–94 and 2009–10. The growth of total rural workers shows a fluctuating trend between various NSS Rounds. Employment was almost stagnant between the period 1993–94 and 1900–2000. The growth rate of employment jumped to 3.25 per cent during the period 1900–2000 and 2004–05, but became negative in the next round. The growth rates of male and female rural workers also show a divergent trend. The male rural workers have registered a steady but slow increase in their numbers. Female workers show very marked variations from one NSS round to another.

Table 2

Work Participation Rates in Rural India (UPSS)

NSS Round	*Year*	*Male*	*Female*
50	1993–94	55.3	32.8
55	1900–2000	53.1	29.9
61	2004–05	54.6	32.7
66	2009–10	54.7	26.1

Source: NSS Rounds

Table 3

Growth in Number of Rural Workers in India (UPSS)

NSS Round	*Year*	*No of Workers (in Millions)*			*CAGR (%)*		
		Male	*Female*	*Total*	*Male*	*Female*	*Total*
50	1993–94	187.7	104.7	292.4			
55	1900–2000	198.6	105.7	304.3	0.95	0.16	0.19
61	2004–05	218.9	124	342.9	1.97	3.25	3.25
66	2009–10	232.3	104.8	337.1	1.20	-3.31	-3.31

Source: NSS Rounds

One of the explanations given for the slow growth of women workers is that more and more girls are going to schools, which has led to their lower participation in work. However, as Himanshu (2011) has emphasized economic factors are also behind the observed fluctuations in FWPR. To quote him: '... large poverty and distress also lead to a situation of vulnerability where participation in the labour market is not out of choice but is governed by changes in the income level. This is true for a majority of workers classified as reserve labour and includes women, children and the elderly' (Himanshu, 2011: 57). Therefore, when there is distress situation in the rural economy women are forced to join work force to supplement their household income, but tend to withdraw from workforce when the economic condition of the household improves.

Status of Rural Workers

The status of workers indicates the quality of work. NSS classifies workers into three categories according to their status, namely, self-employed, regular and casual. Self-employed workers are own account workers whether engaged in farming or other activities like artisans and shopkeepers. Regular workers are those who are employed on a regular basis in the public or the private sector. They are assured of employment and get various social security benefits if employed in the organized sector. Casual workers, on the other hand, do not get assured employment and are devoid of any social security benefit.

NSS surveys reveal that over time, the proportion of self-employed workers is going down and that of casual workers has been increasing both in the case of male and female workers (Table 4). The number of casual workers is increasing because the size of holdings is getting reduced and the marginal farmers are joining the ranks of casual workers to supplement their income. Regular workers form a small proportion of workers – 8.5 per cent in case of males and 4.4 per cent in case of females. The proportion of male rural workers has ranged between 8 and 9 per cent in the last four rounds, while that of female rural workers shows a small increase.

Table 4

Status of Rural Workers in India (%)

NSS Round	*Year*	*Male*			*Female*		
		Self-Employed	*Regular*	*Casual*	*Self-Employed*	*Regular*	*Casual*
50	1993–94	57.9	8.3	33.8	58.5	2.8	38.7
55	1900–2000	55.0	8.8	36.2	57.3	3.1	39.6
61	2004–05	58.1	9.0	32.9	63.7	3.7	32.6
66	2009–10	53.5	8.5	38.0	55.7	4.4	39.9

Source: NSS Rounds

Growth of Rural Workers by Sectors

Table 5 shows the number of rural workers by sectors during various NSS rounds since 1977–78. Total rural workers in the primary sector increased from 193.2 million in 1977–78 to 229.4 million in 1993–94 i.e. the green revolution period. The increase in primary sector workers slackened after that but remained positive till 2004–05. However, there was a net decline of nearly 20 million workers in the primary sector in the rural areas, which also resulted in decline in total rural workers during this period. The secondary and tertiary sector workers show a continuous increase throughout the period.

Table 5

Number of Rural Workers by Sectors (in Million)

NSS Round		Rural Males			Rural Females			Total Rural Workers			
No	Period	Primary	Secondary	Tertiary	Primary	Secondary	Tertiary	Primary	Secondary	Tertiary	Total
32	July 1977–June 1978	112.9	12.3	14.7	70.3	5.3	4.1	183.2	17.6	18.8	219.6
38	January– December 1983	119.2	15.4	18.8	79.3	6.7	4.4	198.5	22.1	23.2	243.8
43	July 1987–June 1988	122.8	19.9	22.1	78.8	9.3	4.9	201.6	29.2	27.0	257.8
50	July 1993–June 1994	139.1	21.0	27.6	90.3	8.7	5.8	229.4	29.7	33.4	292.5
55	July 1999–June2000	141.8	25.0	31.8	90.3	9.4	6.0	232.1	34.4	37.8	304.3
61	July 2004–June 2005	145.5	33.9	39.4	103.3	12.6	8.2	248.8	46.5	47.6	342.9
66	July 2009–June 2010	145.9	44.8	41.3	83.1	13.6	8.0	229.0	58.4	49.3	336.7

Source: NSS Rounds. Taken from Himanshu (2011).

Table 6

Compound Annual Growth Rate of Rural Workers by Sectors (%)

Period	Rural Males			Rural Females			Total Rural Workers			
	Primary	Secondary	Tertiary	Primary	Secondary	Tertiary	Primary	Secondary	Tertiary	Total
1983 to 1993–94	1.41	2.86	3.55	1.19	2.40	2.54	1.32	2.72	3.37	1.67
1993–94 to 2004–05	0.41	4.45	3.29	1.23	3.42	3.20	0.74	4.16	3.27	1.46
2004–05 to 2009–10	0.05	5.73	0.95	-4.26	1.54	-0.49	-1.64	4.66	0.70	-0.36

Source: Computed from Table 5.

Looking at the growth of rural employment by sex, we find that rural male workers have continuously increased, the increase being more marked in the secondary and tertiary sectors (Table 5). The increase in the number of female rural workers was slower. The period 2004–05 to 2009–10 witnessed a huge decline in female workers in the primary sector-nearly 20 million. There was a small decline in the number of tertiary sector female workers. However, secondary sector female workers show an increase of one million during this period.

Table 6 shows the CAGR of rural workers by sectors during the various sub-periods. Total rural workers increased at a CAGR of 1.67 per cent during 1983 to 1993–94. The growth rate declined to 1.46 per cent in the period from 1993–94 to 2004–05 and became negative in the last phase due to decline in primary sector workers. The secondary sector workers have grown rapidly throughout the period under study. The tertiary sector workers also increased rapidly till 2005–06 but show a lower growth thereafter. Similar trends are observed in the growth rate of rural male workers. The growth rate of female workers increased during 1993–94 and 2004–05 as compared to the previous decade. But the growth rate of female workers became negative in case of primary and tertiary sectors and slowed own in case of secondary sector. Most of the increase in the secondary sector workers seems to be distress type of diversification in low paid activities due to low incomes in the agricultural sector.

Distribution of Rural Workers by Sex

The share of rural male and female workers in the primary sector remained more or less stable between the period 1977–78 and 1999–2000 with male workers accounting for about 60 per cent and females about 40 per cent of primary workers (Table 7). The share of male workers in primary sector dropped in 2004–05 but sharply increased in 2009–10, due to a sharp decline in female workers. Thus, the general impression that male workers are leaving agriculture and there is greater feminization of agricultural workers does not appear to hold true. The proportion of female workers in the secondary and tertiary sector has been much lower and has declined over time. Thus, female rural workers accounted for over one-third of rural workers in the primary sector, one-fourth in the secondary sector and one-sixth in the tertiary sector.

Table 7

Distribution of Rural Workers by Sectors and Sex (%)

NSS Round		Males			Females		
No.	Period	Primary	Secondary	Tertiary	Primary	Secondary	Tertiary
32	July 1977–June 1978	61.63	69.89	78.19	38.37	30.11	21.81
38	January–December 1983	60.05	69.68	81.03	39.95	30.32	18.97
43	July 1987– June 1988	60.91	68.15	81.85	39.09	31.85	18.15
50	July 1993– June 1994	60.64	70.71	82.63	39.36	29.29	17.37
55	July 1999– June 2000	61.09	72.67	84.13	38.91	27.33	15.87
61	July 2004– June 2005	58.48	72.90	82.77	41.52	27.10	17.23
66	July 2009– June 2010	63.71	76.71	83.77	36.29	23.29	16.23

Source: NSS Rounds

Structural Shifts in Rural Workers

The rural workforce structure has been undergoing a steady but slow process of sectoral shifts in favour of the secondary and tertiary sectors (Table 8). The proportion of workers in the primary sector gradually declined from 83.4 per cent in 1977–78 to 76.3 per cent in 1999–2000. The process of shift accelerated somewhat after that as the absorptive power of the agricultural sector shrunk. The share of the primary sector declined by nearly 8 per cent point during the decade 1999–2000 and 2009–10. The share of secondary sector workers increased in the 1980s but remained stable during the 1990s. The last decade, however, shows a big jump in the share of the secondary sector workers. The tertiary sector shows a steady increase in its share throughout the period. On the whole, the data reveal that the process of shift in the employment structure in India has been rather modest and even now over two-third workers are employed in the primary sector, mostly in agriculture.

The pattern of structural shift has been different for males and females (Table 9). The proportion of male workers in the primary sector declined by about 18 percentage points during the last three decades – from 80.6 per cent in 1977–78 to 62.8 per cent in 2009–10. The pace of decline was faster in the last decade. During this period, the share of secondary sector workers more than doubled – from 8.8 per cent to 19.3 per cent. The share of tertiary sector workers also improved sharply from 10.5 per cent to 17.8 per cent. On the other hand, the process of structural shift in female rural workers was much slower. The share of primary sector in case of female workers declined only by 9 percentage points over the entire period – from 88.1 per cent in 1977–78 to 79.3 per cent in 2009–10. The shift was mainly in favour of the secondary sector and to a lesser extent in case of the tertiary sector.

Table 8

Shifts in Sectoral Structure of Rural Workers in India

NSS Round		Total Rural Workers		
No.	*Period*	*Primary*	*Secondary*	*Tertiary*
32	July 1977–June 1978	83.4	8.0	8.6
38	January–December 1983	81.4	9.1	9.5
43	July 1987–June 1988	78.2	11.3	10.5
50	July 1993–June 1994	78.4	10.2	11.4
55	July 1999–June 2000	76.3	11.3	12.4
61	July 2004–June 2005	72.6	13.6	13.9
66	July 2009–June 2010	68.0	17.3	14.6

Source: NSS Rounds

Table 9

Shifts in Sectoral Structure of Rural Workers in India by Sex (%)

NSS Round		Rural Males			Rural Females		
No.	Period	*Primary*	*Secondary*	*Tertiary*	*Primary*	*Secondary*	*Tertiary*
32	July 1977–June 1978	80.6	8.8	10.5	88.1	6.7	5.1
38	January–December 1983	77.5	10.0	12.2	87.5	7.4	4.8
43	July 1987–June 1988	74.5	12.1	13.4	84.7	10.0	5.3
50	July 1993–June 1994	74.1	11.2	14.7	86.2	8.3	5.5
55	July 1999–June 2000	71.4	12.6	16.0	85.4	8.9	5.7
61	July 2004–June 2005	66.5	15.5	18.0	83.3	10.2	6.6
66	July 2009–June 2010	62.8	19.3	17.8	79.3	13.0	7.6

Source: NSS Rounds

Share of Rural Areas in GDP of India by Sectors

We now discuss the structure of the rural economy in terms of income. Table 10 shows the contribution of the rural sector in the national GDP. Rural areas contributed a little less than half of the country's GDP. About 95 per cent of agricultural GDP, 42.5 per cent of manufacturing GDP, 45 per cent of construction GDP, 41 per cent of trade, hotel and restaurant GDP and 33 per cent of transport, storage and communication GDP originated in the rural areas in 2004–05. But, only one-sixth of national GDP originated in the rural areas in case of modern services like communication, banking and insurance.

Table 10

Contribution of Rural Areas in GDP of India (%)

Sector	*1999–2000*	*2004–2005*
Agriculture and Animal Husbandry	93.83	95.50
Forestry and Logging	94.00	91.67
Fishing	79.24	73.65
Mining and Quarrying	42.39	66.28
Manufacturing	41.54	42.52
Registered	39.90	41.93
Unregistered	44.31	43.42
Construction	43.32	45.46
Electricity, Gas and Water Supply	45.44	33.25
Transport, Storage and Communication	29.30	33.40
Railway	30.98	30.98
Other Means of Transport and Storage	28.48	38.01
Communication	30.76	17.03
Trade, Hotel and Restaurant	27.05	40.90
Banking and Insurance	14.52	14.82
Real Estate, ownership of Dwellings and Business Services	32.07	35.81
Public Administration	19.91	16.11
Other Services	36.25	36.28
Net Domestic Product	48.31	47.98
Population	72.53	71.41

Source: CSO

The rural economy is no longer predominantly agricultural as far as composition of rural income is concerned. In 2004–05, only 38.3 per cent of rural GDP was contributed by the agricultural and allied sectors (Table 11). Manufacturing contributed about 12 per cent of rural GDP and construction about 8 per cent of GDP. Tertiary sector now accounts for 37.5 per cent of rural GDP. Trade, hotel and restaurant contribute about 15 per cent of rural GDP.

Table 12 gives the share of different sectors in rural employment and rural GDP in 2004–05. The table reveals that the share of primary sector GDP is much lower than the share of this sector in employment. The situation is reverse in case of the secondary and tertiary sectors. The secondary sector contributes one and a half times in GDP as compared to its share in employment. The ratio is 2.7 times in case of the tertiary sector. This implies large inter-sectoral variations in the per worker productivity in the three sectors. Thus, per worker productivity in secondary sector is 2.6 times higher and that of tertiary sector productivity 4.7 times higher as compared to the productivity in the primary sector.

Table 11

Structure of the Rural and Urban GDP in India: 2004–05

Sl. No.	*Sector*	*Rural*	*Urban*	*Total*
1	Agriculture, Animal Husbandry forestry and Fishing	38.34	2.24	19.56
2	Mining and Quarrying	3.7	1.74	2.68
	Primary Sector	**42.04**	**3.98**	**22.24**
3	Manufacturing	11.86	14.79	13.38
4	Electricity, Gas and Water Supply	0.66	1.23	0.96
5	Construction	7.91	8.75	8.35
	Secondary Sector	**20.43**	**24.77**	**22.69**
6	Trade, Hotel and Restaurant	14.98	19.97	17.57
7	Transport, Storage and Communication	5.81	10.69	8.35
8	Financing, insurance, real estate and business services	8.41	21.05	14.99
9	Community, Social and Personal Services	8.31	19.54	14.15
	Tertiary Sector	**37.51**	**71.25**	**55.06**
10	Net Domestic Product	100.0	100.0	100

Source: CSO

Table 12

Share of Different Sectors in Rural Employment and Rural GDP, 2004–05

Sector	*Share in Employment*	*Share in GDP*	*Ratio of Share in GDP to Share in Employment*	*Per Worker GDP (in ₹)*
Primary Sector	72.6	42.04	0.58	21,442
Secondary Sector	13.6	20.43	1.50	55,625
Tertiary Sector	13.9	37.51	2.70	99,924

A recent study of farm households of UP by the present author reveals that even in case of farmers, non-agricultural sources of income play an important role (Table 13). According to the study, agricultural income (including income from animal husbandry) contributed about two-thirds of the income of farm households, while the non-agricultural sources contributed about one-third of household income. A marginal farmer earned only 37 per cent of his income from agriculture. This proportion goes up to 56 per cent for small farmers, to 63 per cent for medium farmers and 73 per cent for large farmers. Livestock and fishery contribute 15 per cent of income on marginal and small farms and only 5.3 per cent on large farms. Non-agricultural sources of income contributed about half of the income of marginal farmers. This share is around 28 per cent for small farmers, 26.6 per cent for medium farmers and only 22 per cent for large farmers. As the table shows, services have become an important source of income for farm households.

Table 13

Percentage Distribution of Annual Income of Farmers by Source and Land Size Categories in UP: 2011–12

Sources of Income	*Marginal Farmers*	*Small Farmers*	*Medium Farmers*	*Large Farmers*	*All Farmers*
Agriculture	38.18	57.95	66.39	67.67	53.31
Livestock and Fisheries	16.37	13.61	9.89	7.23	12.87
Total Agriculture and Allied Activities	54.55	71.56	76.28	74.90	66.18
Industry, Artisans and Trade	2.24	0.57	1.77	1.88	2.12
Wage	12.88	2.47	0.31	0.00	5.74
Service	19.16	14.59	11.73	15.10	15.66
Others	11.17	10.81	9.91	8.12	10.21
Total Non-Agriculture	45.45	28.44	23.72	25.10	33.73
Total Household Income (in ₹)	75,166	1,17,002	1,99,763	3,65,042	1,13,815

Source: Singh (2013).

Conclusion

This paper has looked at some aspects of structural change in the rural economy at the national level. The main findings of the paper are summarized below.

1. The process of urbanization as well structural change in the rural economy in India has been quite slow in contrast with the rapidly growing economies of far eastern countries like Indonesia, Japan, Malaysia, Thailand and China, which have witnessed a sharp change in the structure of their employment.
2. The male WPR in rural areas shows a variation in a small range around 54 per cent. The female WPR has remained distinctly lower than the male WPR and shows higher fluctuation. Female WPR has, however, declined after 1993–94. The increase in school enrollment of girls is one of the factors leading to their lower participation in

work. Moreover, women workers constitute a marginal and vulnerable section of rural labour. Whenever there is a distress situation in the rural economy women are forced to join work force to supplement their household income, but tend to withdraw from workforce when the economic condition of the household improves.

3. Rural employment was almost stagnant between the period 1993–94 and 1900–2000. The growth rate of employment jumped to 3.25 per cent during the period 1900–2000 and 2004–05, but became negative in the next round. The growth rates of male and female rural workers also show a divergent trend. The male rural workers have registered a steady but slow increase in their numbers. Female workers show very marked variations from one NSS round to another.

4. Over time, the proportion of self-employed workers is going down and that of casual workers has been increasing both in the case of male and female workers.

5 Total rural workers in the primary sector increased steadily in the green revolution period, but the increase slackened after that but remained positive till 2004–05. However, there was a net decline of nearly 20 million workers in the primary sector in the rural areas, which also resulted in decline in total rural workers during this period.

6. Rural male workers have continuously increased, the increase being more marked in the secondary and tertiary sectors. The increase in the number of female rural workers was slower. The period from 2004–05 to 2009–10 witnessed a huge decline in female workers in the primary sector.

7. The share of rural male and female workers in the primary sector remained more or less stable over time with male workers accounting for about 60 per cent and females about 40 per cent of primary workers. Thus, the general impression that male workers are leaving agriculture and there is greater feminization of agricultural workers does not appear to hold true. Female rural workers accounted for over one-third of rural workers in the primary sector, one-fourth in the secondary sector and one-sixth in the tertiary sector.

8. The rural workforce structure has been undergoing a steady but slow process of sectoral shifts in favour of the secondary and tertiary sectors. The process of structural shift in female rural workers was much slower.

9. Rural areas contributed a little less than half of the country's GDP in 2004–05. About 95 per cent of agricultural GDP, 42.5 per cent of manufacturing GDP, 45 per cent of construction GDP, 41 per cent of trade, hotel and restaurant GDP and 33 per cent of transport, storage and communication GDP originated in the rural areas in 2004–05. But only one-sixth of national GDP originated in the rural areas in case of modern services like communication, banking and insurance.
10. The rural economy is no longer predominantly agricultural as far as composition of rural income is concerned. Only 38.3 per cent of rural GDP was contributed by the agricultural and allied sectors in 2004–05. Secondary sector contributed about 20 per cent and tertiary sector 37.5 per cent of rural GDP.
11. Due to overcrowding in agriculture, labour productivity has been low in this sector. Per worker productivity in secondary sector is 2.6 times higher and that of tertiary sector productivity 4.7 times higher as compared to the productivity in the primary sector.

On the whole, our analysis reveals that the process of shift in the employment structure in India has been rather modest and even now over two-third workers are employed in the primary sector, mostly in agriculture. This has been one of the major factors contributing to low labour productivity in agriculture and high incidence of rural poverty. The countries which have seen sharp reduction in rural poverty has witnessed a very rapid shift towards non-agricultural employment. Development policy in India should, therefore, put especial emphasis on faster expansion of non-agricultural activities both in the rural and the urban areas.

References

Central Statistical Organisation (Undated). *National Account Statistics (Annual)*, Ministry of Statistics and Plan Implementation, Government of India, New Delhi.

Himanshu (2011). 'Employment Trends in India: A Re-examination', *Economic and Political Weekly*, (XLVI) 37, September 10.

Hirashima, Shigemochi (1980). 'Institutional and Macro Aspects of Labour Absorption in Japanese Agriculture', in ILO, *Labour Absorption in Agriculture: The East Asian Experience*, Asian Employment Programme, Asian Regional Team for Employment Promotion (ARTEP), Bangkok.

International Labour Organization (2003). *Key Indicators of Labour Market Data Base*, Geneva.

Lee, Teng-hui, Chen, His-huang and Chen, Yueh-eh (1980). 'Labour Absorption in Taiwan Agriculture', in ILO, *Labour Absorption in Agriculture: The East Asian Experience*, Asian Employment Programme, Asian Regional Team for Employment Promotion (ARTEP), Bangkok.

NSSO (Undated). *Reports on Employment and Unemployment Situation in India*, various rounds, Ministry of Statistics and Plan Implementation, Government of India, New Delhi.

Singh, Ajit Kumar (2011). 'Agrarian Change, Non-Farm Employment and Poverty in India', in Suresh Pal (ed.), *Agriculture for Inclusive Growth*, Indian Agricultural Research Institute, New Delhi.

——. (2013). *Estimation of Farmers Income: Final Report*, Giri Institute of Development Studies, Lucknow (mimeo).

UNSD (Undated). *http:/mdgs.un.org/unsd/mdg/Data.aspx*

World Bank (Undated). *World Development Indicators (Annual)*, Washington, D.C.

4

Urbanization, Poverty and Health

ANJALI DASH

The world's urban population is growing fast. In Asia, 2.2 billion people are expected to live in cities by 2020. Urban settlements are also increasing in size and number. Asia now has 11 megacities, each with more than 10 million people. In addition, hundreds of cities throughout the region have population between 0.5 million and 9 million, whereas smaller towns and cities have people by hundreds of millions (World Bank, 2000; Ali, 2006; DFID, 2001). Cities are important to national economies because they are the focal points for important activities like trade, commerce, industry and government administration. Cities are also centres for education, health care, technological innovation, entrepreneurship and governance. They provide access to large markets for goods and services and communication with backward linkages to the rural hinterland and forward linkages to globalized markets. Cities also create opportunities for jobs, employment and livelihood. Indian cities are no exception to this. On the positive side, economic growth, which is partially driven by urban development, increases the income of poor people. In addition, cities have the resources to improve the conditions within which people live and work, and they create the context within which the poor people can demand and obtain redress from political and bureaucratic systems. Urban population increase are, in part, fuelled by rural-urban migration as people seek new employment and livelihood opportunities in urban centres.

Despite these advantages, most of the cities face significant problems. A large segment of urban population suffers from high birth and death rate resulting in lower economic productivity and lower standard of living. Problems of hunger, under-nutrition and associated disorders are closely linked with poverty. There is also a link between over-crowding and rate of crimes. To improve the quality of life in these habitats, crores of rupees have been spent on implementing many programmes in the country since Independence. In general, the thrust of these programmes has been on improvement of habitats, participation of the local population programmes, public distribution, and skill upgradation, credit support for self-employment and preventive strategy for integrated development of small and medium towns (Reports of National Commission of Urbanisation, 1988). Person living in cities suffer from homelessness, joblessness, personal and social insecurity and other deprival.

Among the Indian states, we are focusing to a Bimaru state Madhya Pradesh, where many people are living below poverty line in both urban and rural areas. As we have already mentioned that people are migrating to the urban cities for the sake of employment and, thus, urban population is increasing and so is the urban poverty rate. The illiterate migrants are converting themselves into slum dwellers.

Ujjain city is situated in M.P. In the early stage of reforms, there is not much variation in urban poverty inside the Ujjain city. But nowadays, population of Ujjain city is increasing and so the population of slum dwellers, which are the major point of urban poverty. Before going to the depth of this study, we should know about the basic concept of poverty and also the current scenario of Indian's urban poverty as well as Madhya Pradesh.

What Do We Mean by Poverty?

Planning Commission of India has measured poverty as income poverty taking the criteria of daily calorie intake, i.e. 2,400 calories per person per day for rural people and 2,100 calories for urban people. Those getting less than this benchmark calorie intake are considered as below poverty line. But we can't confine our efforts only economically but also socially, politically and physically. The person who does not have shelter, food and cloth is called poor. Here, it's clear that due to poverty, health situation is poor on one side and in another way, due to poor health standard, people are unable to work as a skilled labour and their productivity will be reduced. So in that case, he/she cannot improve his/her standard of living and suffering from hunger and consequently will die. Dandekar-Rath and the Tendulkar Committee have defined relative as well absolute poverty on the different dimensions of poverty.

Urban Poverty

Rural and urban poverty are interrelated. Many point to the important connections between the two, as, household livelihood or survival strategies have both rural and urban components (Satterthwaite, 1995). How urban and rural households adopt a range of diversification strategies, by having one foot in rural activities and another in urban (Baker, 1995). Conceptualizing urban poverty as a separate category from rural poverty is also problematic because of different yardsticks for defining urban in different countries. The urban-rural divide is more a continuum rather than a rigid dichotomy. Urban poverty refers to all people who are living below poverty line in urban areas. Urban poverty is a complex, multidimensional problem with origin in both developing and developed domains depending upon its nature and extent (Shing, 2006). The quality of life of people is influenced by the phenomenon of urbanization. Urban poor basically live in slum areas in city/town.

The Slums

Slums are a physical and spatial manifestation of urban poverty. In India, 'slums' have been defined under Section 3 of the Slum Areas Act 1956 as areas where building is a compact area of at least 300 population or about 60–70 households of poorly-built congested tenements in unhygienic environment usually with inadequate infrastructure and lacking in proper sanitary and drinking water facilities. The word 'slum' itself is thought to be derived from 'slumber' meaning 'unknown' as is said to describe the people living in black streets on alleys. The slums are known by different terms in different towns of India. The National Sample Survey Organization (NSSO), 58th Round, define slum as: 'A compact settlement with a collection of poorly built tenements, mostly of temporary nature, crowded together usually with inadequate sanitary and drinking water facilities in unhygienic conditions. Such an area, for the purpose of this survey, was considered as 'non-notified slum' if at least 20 households lived in that area. Areas notified as slums by the respective municipalities, corporations, local bodies or development authorities are treated as 'notified slums'.

According to UNDP, the proportion of slum households is the proportion of urban population who are living in small cluster or *jhuggi*. A slum household is defined as a group of individuals living under the same roof lacking one or more of the following conditions: access to improved water, access to improved sanitation, sufficient-living area, durability of housing and security of tenure. A slum household is defined by

UN-HABITAT as a group of individuals living under the same roof that lack one or more (in some cities, two or more) of the following conditions: security of tenure, structural quality and durability of dwellings; access to safe water, access to sanitation facilities and sufficient living area.

Slum in Madhya Pradesh

Slum is defined as per the clause 3 given in the Madhya Pradesh Gandi Basti Kshetra (Sudhas Thatha Nirmulan) Adhiniyam, 1976 which states that: 'where the competent authority upon report from any of its officers or other information in its possession is satisfied in respect of any area that the building in that area in any respect is unfit for human habitation or areas by reason of dilapidation overcrowding, faulty arrangement and design of such building, hazardous and unwholesome trade carried on therein, narrowness and faulty arrangement of streets, lack of ventilation, light, sanitation facilities or any combination of the factors are detrimental to safety, health, or moral, it may, by notification, declare such area to be slum area'.

An Overview of Slum and Poverty

Are slums really the 'locus' of urban poverty? Is poverty in slums one of the potent forces that maintain the 'vicious circle' from which it is difficult for people to break out? Whether poverty and slums have a direct correlation is a proposition which is required to be analysed on two scores: (i) slums are the centre of poverty and (ii) poverty is the breeding ground of slums.

Types of Slums: Slums/informal housing can also be classified according to the diverse processes of land/housing supply and varying degree of tenure security in the following manner: (a) Freehold land (inner city blighted areas) (b) Urban villages and land owned by village panchayats, (c) *Chawls/Bastis,* (d) Encroachments on public/private land (squatters), (e) Government/private leasehold land (resettlement colonies), (f) Slums on the urban periphery, (g) Illegal land subdivisions/unauthorized colonies/revenue layouts/gramathana layouts (where land ownership may be legal or quasi legal but land subdivision is illegal), (h) Refugee resettlement colonies, and (i) Pavement dwellers, although small in percentage, are found in large mega cities.

Concept of Urbanization, Health and Poverty

The role of health in influencing economic outcomes has been well understood at the micro level. Healthier workers are likely to be able to work longer, generally more productive than their relatively less healthy counterparts, and consequently able to secure higher earnings than the latter, all else being the same; illness and disease shorten the working lives of people, thereby reducing their lifetime earnings. Better health also has a positive effect on the learning abilities of children, and leads to better educational outcomes (school completion rates, higher mean years of schooling, achievements) and increases the efficiency of human capital formation by individuals and households (Strauss and Thomas, 1998; Schultz, 1999). Health has a positive and statistically significant effect on the rate of growth of Gross Domestic Product (GDP) per capita. Higher incomes potentially permit individuals (and societies) to afford better nutrition, better health care and, presumably, achieve better health.

The cost of ill health can drive vulnerable households into poverty and can deepen the poverty gap for households that could have been categorized as poor even before the accrual of illness-related cost (Russel, 2001; Wagstaff and van Doorslaer, 2003). For example, if the head of a household with very young children, which relies on subsistence agriculture, has an episode of service malaria during harvest time, the household may have to incur debts to pay for health care and may also lose most of their harvest and he may become 'medical poverty trap'. Whilst the mutual relationship between poverty and ill health in general, are recognized and a plethora of studies on this issue have been published over the last decade. The specific effect of costs associated with ill health at the household level. Ill health is not only disease specific, but also depends heavily on the particular socio-economic, cultural and geographic environment. Thus, the poverty dynamics (standard of living, nutrition, education, income, economic equality, health status, employment, agriculture, etc.) is associated with illness and vary across households and context. On the basis of this, we have developed a small concept of illness and poverty relation which is shown in Figure 1.

This study is based upon both secondary as well as primary data collection. Secondary sources are based on various governmental reports and also published or unpublished research like CDPU, NSSO, HDR, MUPA, Economic Survey of India and Madhya Pradesh, etc. However, the primary data have been collected from slums/*bastis* of Ujjain city. This data is qualitative in nature. As Madhya Pradesh is a Bimaru state, no doubt here more rural people are living below poverty line, but one thing must be kept in our mind about what is happening with the people who are living in scatter slum/*basti*. So a motto of this paper is to understand the situation of urban poor and how we can improve the quality of life with implementation of a programme called

Figure 1 *Conceptual Framework of Urbanization, Poverty and Health*

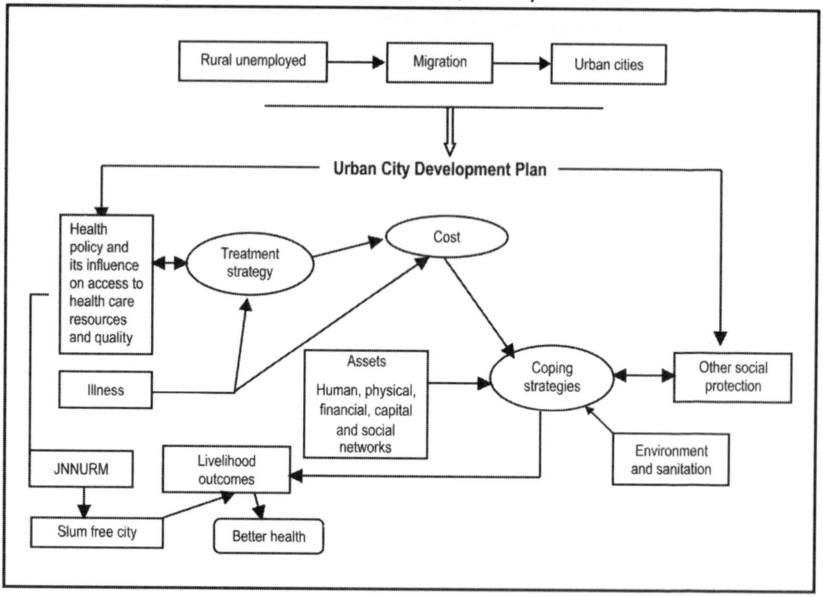

slum free city development plan. We used random sampling to choose Ujjain city and use purposive sampling for slum/*basti*. Data has been collected on 1 January 2013. Statistical tools of the study were Focus Group Discussion (FGD), observation and field base experiences.

Poverty Scenario in India and Madhya Pradesh

In India, rural poverty level was 57.33 per cent in 1971, 35.55 per cent in 1991 and in urban areas it was 45.89 per cent and 32.43 per cent, respectively. After the economic reforms in 1991 the rural poverty rose. Poor are increasing year after year at greater pace during the economic reforms period. The poor are unable to pay for medicine when they are sick and are unable to afford even two meals a day. According to U.R. Rao, if the poor in India start eating one more meal a day, the godown would be empty and India will have to import large quantity of foodgrains. He states emphatically that over 100 million people in the country go to bed each day with hungry stomachs. While foodgrains production has reduced a stagnant plateau, population continues to steadily increase which may result in a specter of millions dying of naked starvation in the coming decades. Figure 2 shows that poverty head count ratio of urban area is high in Odisha followed by M.P. In M.P., poverty head count ratio is more in urban areas as compared to rural among major states of India (Figure 3).

Figure 2 *Poverty Head Count Ratio in Urban India, 2004–05*

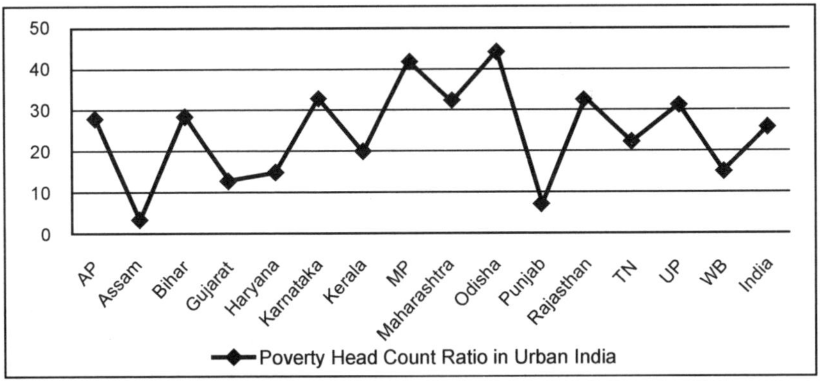

Source: Indian Planning Commission, GoI.

Figure 3 *Sector wise Poverty HCR in 2004–05*

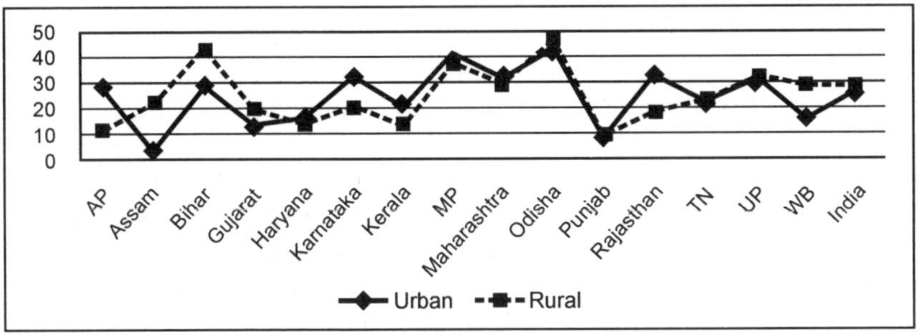

Source: Indian Planning Commission, GoI.

Poverty Measures

Poverty can be measured either in relative or in absolute terms. But the Indian Planning Commission measured as Head Count Ratio (HCR) of the number of poor to the total population. A poor household is defined as a household with an expenditure level below a specific poverty line. Poverty line differs from different rounds. Head Count Ratio (HCR), Poverty Gap (PG) and Squared Poverty Gap (SPG)

$$HCR = \frac{m}{n} \quad PG = \left(\frac{1}{n}\right)\sum_{i=1}^{m}\left(\frac{z-y_i}{z}\right)$$

$$SPG = \left(\frac{1}{n}\right)\sum_{i=1}^{m}\left(\frac{z-y_i}{z}\right)^2$$

Whereas: m = no. of poor population, n = total population, z = poverty line, y_i = income of ith person.

In urban India, a large number of Scheduled Castes (SCs) are located in poverty line as compared to Scheduled Tribes (STs). More than 70 per cent poor Indian resides in six states: Uttar Pradesh, Bihar, Madhya Pradesh, Maharashtra, West Bengal and Odisha. Among the Indian states, Maharashtra emerged on the top with the maximum share of slum population in India i.e. about 26 per cent followed by Andhra Pradesh (13%) and Uttar Pradesh (10%). But nowadays, slum populations are increasing all over the country by enlarging the population. Odisha comes at the first position in this case than Madhya Pradesh. At national level it occupied 39.9 per cent. People move from villages to towns/cities in search of employment. But usually they do not own any shelter and lack money also. Thus, when they find any work, they are forced to find shelter in *jhuggi*/*jhopri*/basti.

Poverty in Madhya Pradesh

Madhya Pradesh is being counted in Bimaru states. It may rank 12th in HDI but it ranks the third poorest, economically, among the low category states in the year 2004–05, unlike Bihar and Odisha. Poverty in Madhya Pradesh is declining at par with India, but the rate of decline of poverty in Madhya Pradesh is less than India. There are several factors contributing to the decline in the poverty ratio. Increase in agricultural production, literacy rate, employment ratio, etc. are the factors influencing poverty. After 1992, new economic reformation gave a boost to Indian economy including the economy of the states. Poverty ratios are substantially higher among the STs (57.16%); it is significantly higher as compared to the SCs (41.21%). The non-backward communities perform better head count ratio (12.78%) in Madhya Pradesh as compared to India (14.98%). This proves the inequality among social groups.

Figure 4 *Urban Population live Below Poverty Line*

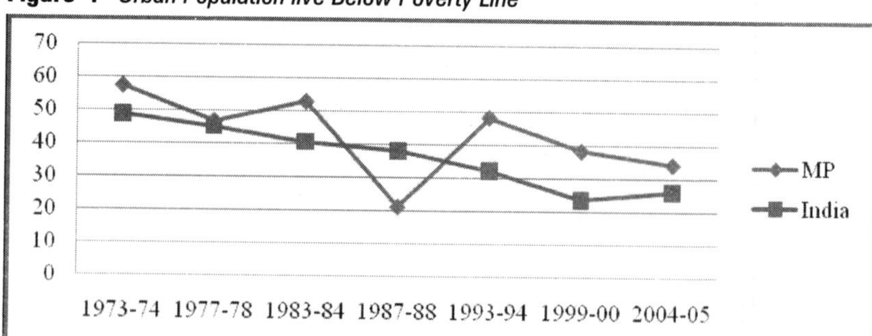

Profile of Ujjain City

Ujjain city is an ancient city of central India, in the Malwa region of Madhya Pradesh. The religious importance of Ujjain town has been attributed to the presence of the deity Mahakaleshwar on the banks of the holy river Kshipra. Presently, Ujjain is a Commissionaire and district headquarter in the state of Madhya Pradesh. It is also a major city among the seven towns of Ujjain district. Ujjain is the 'Greenwich Mean Time' of India for Panchang. The tilting of earth at an angle 23.182778°N 75.777222°E latitude on its axis and geographical line of Tropic of Cancer has a special cosmic influence making it fit for an absolute time location. This historic city is situated at a height of 1,678 ft. from the mean sea level.

As of 2001 India Census, Ujjain had a population of 429,933. Males constitute 52 per cent of the population and females 48 per cent. Ujjain has an average literacy rate of 72 per cent, higher than the national average of 59.5 per cent: male literacy is 79 per cent, and female literacy is 66 per cent. In Ujjain, 13 per cent of the population is under 7 years. The current Census (2011) population of Ujjain Municipal Corporation

Figure 5 *Ujjain City Map*

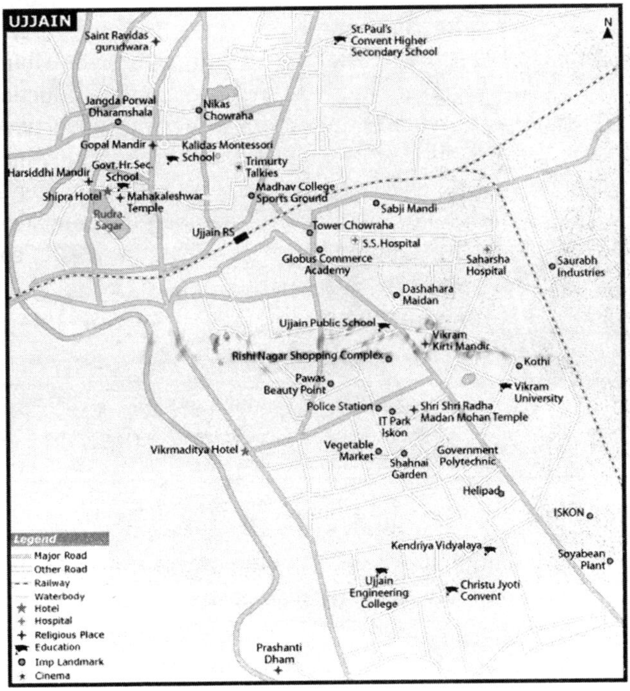

(UMC) is 5.15 lakhs and the total number of wards is 54. The city has experienced relatively moderate growth rates in population during the last three decades from 1981 to 2011. Growth rate of population in Ujjain city is growing rapidly from the last few decades.

The city has been divided into two parts. The old city which lies north of the broad gauge railway line is more densely populated as compared to the newer areas. This is an overcrowded area. There is no drainage system in this area and pollution is more due to waste materials. This is a congested type of area. The UMC should ensure safe and pollution free city, but in reality what is happening in the city is evident in Figure 6.

Figure 6 *Inside the Ujjain City*

Poverty and Slum

Ujjain today is the most poorly interpreted city of India. Its antiquity is not apparent immediately. The city was destroyed completely at some point in history. There is no system in place that would address this issue in future either. The 129 slums in the city present a picture of poverty in the city of Ujjain. The authorities are not willing to help them find the 'dream' they aspire for, or simply ignore them.

It is indispensable to analyse the status of poverty for any city development exercise. Besides, it becomes more important in the state like Madhya Pradesh where level of poverty is relatively higher. Slums in Ujjain are spread all over the city, with the maximum number located in wards 53 (having 11 slums), 54 (having 11 slums), 11 and 27 (7 and 9 slums each). A total of 1, 89, 387 persons in Ujjain have been identified as those living below poverty line (Table 1 and 2). This would mean that more than 40 per cent of the total population in the city is living below poverty line.

Table 1

Number of Poor in Ujjain

Year	*Number of Poor*
1993-94	25,280
1999-00	1,44,705
2004-05	1,89,387

Source: CDPU.

Although the figures available suggest that a majority of slum dwellers in Ujjain are living below poverty line, it can be analysed from Table 3 that nearly half of the population in Ujjain city is below poverty line. A major poor population lives in the old city areas where they do have the ancestral shelter to live in, but are unemployed.

Table 2

Ward-wise Information of Slums in Ujjain City

Ward No.	*No. of HHs*	*Slums Households*	*No. of Slums*	*Slum Population*	*Total Population*	*% Slum Population*
1	1,364	741	8	3,600	9477	38
2	2,123	1275	7	6,710	11,242	60
3	2,449	675	3	3,965	13,171	30
4	1,127	260	2	1,600	6,610	24
5	2,288	565	4	3,550	13,146	27
6	914	215	1	1,302	5,715	23
7	1,008	233	1	1,547	5,969	26
9	1,298	605	4	4,200	9,643	44

Cont'd...

...Cont'd

11	1,859	1022	7	6,209	10,929	57
24	1,559	450	1	250	9,061	3
25	1,652	490	4	3,150	8,955	35
26	1,228	300	1	2,000	6,386	31
27	3,526	1760	9	9,618	18,427	32
28	1,934	322	3	1,865	9,991	19
32	1,067	44	1	259	7,013	4
33	1,303	235	1	1,409	8,694	16
35	1,590	397	7	2,006	8,847	23
36	2,010	526	3	2,833	11,672	24
37	2,208	657	6	4,264	11,857	36
38	1,804	595	5	3,675	9,425	39
39	2,570	151	2	875	13,707	6
41	1,524	140	1	1,064	7,307	15
42	2,143	55	1	275	9,729	3
43	3,341	180	1	1,060	15,558	7
46	1,808	136	3	570	9,536	6
48	978	140	1	600	5,398	11
49	1,629	438	2	1,656	9,121	18
50	1,650	189	1	766	8,740	9
52	1,474	427	3	1,364	7,665	18
53	2,095	1665	11	9,785	10,925	90
54	2,673	1801	11	10,362	14,350	72

Source: City Development Plan Ujjain, 2006.

Slums and squatter settlements are essentially the products of urban poverty. In the context of urban basic service delivery, almost by definition, the population living in slums lacks access to the basic infrastructure services like safe water, sanitation, solid waste collection and disposal, drainage, roads, street lights, neighbourhood amenities like safe play areas for children, community facilities, and electricity connections.

Table 3

BPL Card Holders in Ujjain City

Ward No.	*2004*	*2012*	*Ward No.*	*2004*	*2012*
1	1067	1638	28	858	1438
2	1232	1879	29	123	181
3	737	1255	30	405	428
4	671	1210	31	619	893

Cont'd...

...Cont'd

5	1514	2421	32	987	1409
6	1514	1843	33	901	1433
7	305	809	34	649	909
8	219	265	35	698	801
9	741	1196	36	1549	2118
10	589	888	37	1773	1847
11	1227	1633	38	1289	1594
12	180	533	39	879	896
13	153	161	40	413	460
14	111	199	41	244	279
15	125	182	42	43	59
16	261	267	43	644	715
17	219	425	44	303	305
18	117	128	45	0	0
19	175	200	46	355	438
20	223	373	47	405	4252
21	309	823	48	384	547
22	357	588	49	1483	1984
23	549	1009	50	428	569
24	608	900	51	70	100
25	402	808	52	800	965
26	1234	1912	53	1404	1870
27	1724	2585	54	2965	3867

Source: UMC.

Urban Poverty Reduction Programmes

The anti-poverty strategies, government policies and alleviation programmes have approached the poverty eradication problem in the three different ways such as (i) enhancing productive employment and income for the poor; (ii) focus on the basic needs, services and health; and (iii) community and infrastructural development. There have been two broad traditions in policy approaches to urban poverty (Amis, 1995; Moser, 1995). The first sets of approaches have focused on the physical infrastructure problems of housing, sanitation, water, land use and transportation.

Recently initiated programme is: Basic Services to the Urban Poor (BSUP) under Jawaharlal Lal Nehru Urban Renewal Mission (JNNURM) beginning from the year 2005/2006. JNNURM is a seven year mission. The major objectives for the BSUP programme are: focused attention to integrated development of basic services to the poor; the basic services include security of tenure at affordable prices, improving housing, water supply, and sanitation. The projects on further augmentation, construction and maintenance of basic infrastructure projects shall come under the financial provisions of the JNNURM project fund.

Table 4

Various Programmes Held in Ujjain City

Schemes	Sub Category	Duration	Aims	Governing Body	Status Till Date
JNNURM	BSUP	2005–2012	Provide basic services to the urban poor	UMC	Running process
	IHSDP	NA	NA	NA	NA
	RAY	Up to 2017	Provide basic needs to the urban poor	UMC	Pilot survey finished
EAS+ LIG		2012	Housing facility to the urban poor	MPHB	On process
SJSRY		1997– till now	Loan provider to the urban poor	DUDA	On process
ISHUP		2007	Affordable housing for all	MHUPA	Running process

Source: Author's estimation.

Slum Rehabilitation Scheme (BSUP)

Dwelling Units: 1,320, total slums: 10, dwelling unit size: 29.7sq.m, proposed site: Gond Basti (312 units): Pawasa (1,008 units), total cost per dwelling unit: ₹ 1,31,887.00. This project contains 10 slums of the city. It builds for slum dwellers in three *bastis* called Gond Basti, Narsingh Ghat basti and Pawasa Phase (Rajeev Ratan Colony and Gourd Samaj Basti). Almost whole work has been completed in Pawasa Phase whereas in Gond Basti, it's over up to 70 per cent. Poor slums have already shifted in these two dwelling houses but in case of Narsingh Ghat basti, they are still struggling for the sake of a house. BSUP work has stopped from the last one year. This project should have been finished in 2012 but still, it is an ongoing process. According to Nodal Agency, this project has been extended for one more year.

Rajeev Aawas Yojana (RAY)

Rajeev Aawas Yojana aimed at ushering in slum-free urban India. Bringing existing slums within the formal system and enabling them to avail the same level of basic amenities as the rest of the town; redressing the failures of the formal system that lie behind the creation of slums; and tackling the shortages of urban land and housing that keep shelter, out of reach of the urban poor and force them to resort to extra-legal solutions in a bid to retain their sources of livelihood and employment.

RAY was started in Ujjain in 2010. But it concentrated on four slums of Ujjain city. Till date it's about to complete baseline survey of this project. These four slum *bastis* contain Akta Nagar, Santi Nagar, Agar Rajim and Moti Nagar. Now it is in process to work properly.

Swarna Jayanti Shahari Rozgar Yojana (SJSRY)

SJSRY was launched by the Government of India on 01.12.1997. This scheme subsumed the earlier three urban poverty alleviation programmes, namely Urban Basic Services for the Poor (UBSP), Nehru Rozgar Yojana (NRY) and Prime Minister's Integrated Urban Poverty Eradication Programme (PMIUPEP). An independent evaluation of SJSRY was carried out by the Ministry of Housing & Urban Poverty Alleviation in 2006 to assess the impact of the scheme in improving the conditions of the urban poor. It provides financial support up to ₹ 2 lakhs to the urban poor for their housing. For Ujjain in financial year 2012–13, ₹ 60 lakh was sanctioned to benefit 200 poor households but in actual, as per DUDA information, 476 households are getting benefit at a cost of ₹ 32.25 lakhs. SJSRY will have five major components, namely: (i) Urban Self Employment Programme (USEP) (ii) Urban Women Self-help Programme (UWSP) (iii) Skill Training for Employment Promotion amongst Urban Poor (STEP-UP) (iv) Urban Wage Employment Programme (UWEP) (v) Urban Community Development Network (UCDN).

Figure 7 *Framework for Slum Free City Plan*

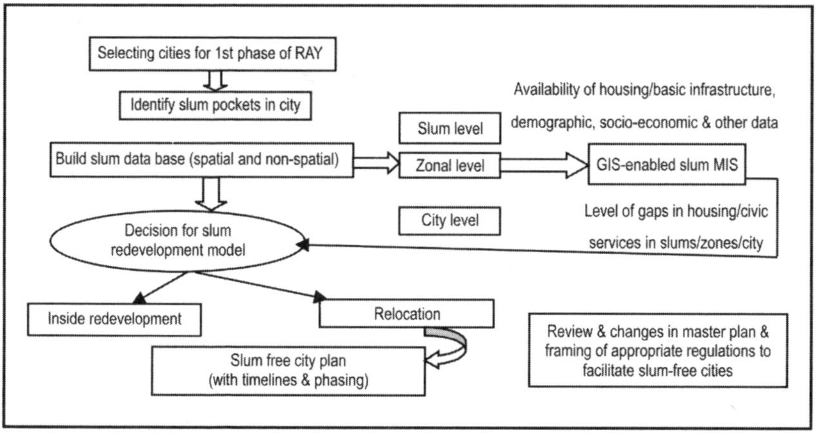

Perception of Service Levels in Ujjain

For the urban poor dweller, all the civic services listed in the Act are essential because high priced private services – whether it is transport or health – are beyond their means. The views of poor households in Ujjain must influence the strategy for improvement of service levels in slums. In terms of satisfaction of the urban poor with the levels of basic services, electricity is the only service that they have few complaints about. Sanitation is the least satisfactory of all public services. Women, in particular, articulated the need for functional public toilets close to their slum. Some also desired individual low cost toilets. The perception of these services, therefore, differs for the Urban Local Body (ULB) and urban poor as shown for example in Figure 8. Provision, pricing and scope of the urban services are seen to be differing widely in several instances leading to depriving them of an access to some of the services for the urban poor.

Figure 8 *Perception of Urban Services by ULB and Urban Poor*

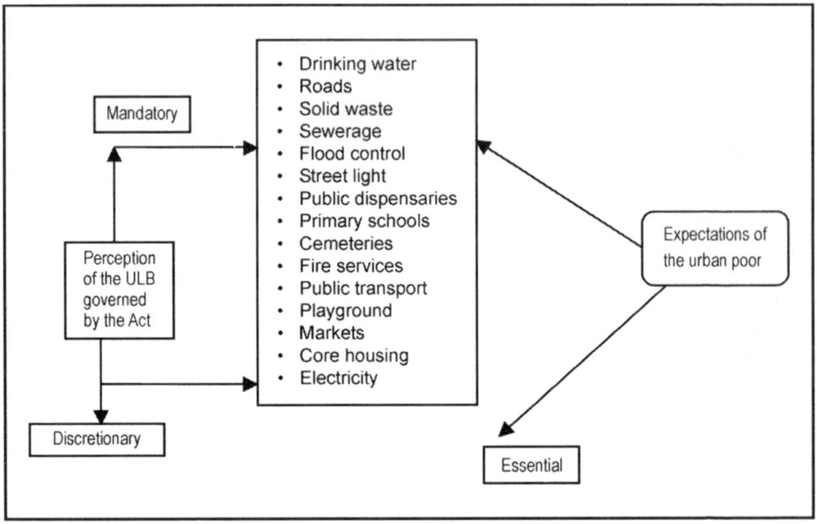

Actual Scenario of Urban Poverty and Slum in Ujjain City

We have described the earlier mentioned information by the help of various governmental documentation. So here, we would like to focus on grass-roots level, the reality of the slum living conditions and how they are surviving their lives. We visited three slum *bastis* to know the grass-roots level reality and analyse this section. Gond Basti, Narsingh Ghat Basti and Jabran Colony are three slum areas of Ujjain city (Figure 9).

Figure 9 *Living Conditions of the Poor Households*

Living Conditions and Access to Services: In urban centres, people are dependent on the provision of public and private services to mitigate the environmental effects of the overcrowded conditions in which they live – accumulations of solid waste, human excrement, and stagnant water in polluted open drains. They cannot dispose of their rubbish on open wastelands, or relieve themselves in forests, and they cannot rely on common property resources as alternative sources of income, water and fuel. Unfortunately, many poor people do not have access to those services – water, drain clearance, solid waste disposal systems – which could improve the environmental conditions within which they live. This means that urban poverty is invariably associated with poor quality housing, often in overcrowded unsanitary slum settlements, and with ill health which is related to the spread of infectious diseases like Tuberculosis (TB), and the constant threat of exposure to environmental hazards such as mosquito infested drains, and fires and floods, which could destroy their homes altogether. Poverty is also associated with a lack of access to a wider range of services, including health, education and law and order, on the grounds of cost, discriminatory practices, and the failure of urban managers to keep pace with the demands of growing settlements on the peri-urban fringe. They live on the most precarious sites and in untenable conditions along polluted canal banks, on pavements, and along railway lines, in constant fear of eviction or relocation. They represent a sizeable proportion of the urban poor.

The social composition of a majority of slums comprises Scheduled Castes, Scheduled Tribes and other backward castes. Most of the slums or *mohallas* have predominantly one caste staying in it, for example, Patels or Chamars/Harijans or Bain Samaj, or people from one place of origin. However, in some of the slums, the original settlement housed a single caste or social group, but later, other social groups also started moving in, creating a wider social mix. Life in urban areas can be costly. People need access to cash to cover the higher cost of living in urban areas than rural areas, where essential items, including food and many non-food items (such as rent, energy, transport, water from private vendors, and sanitation from pay-as-you-use facilities) have to be purchased. Poor people's capacity to meet these needs is dependent on having somewhere secured to live, preferably close to their work, their capacity to sell their labour for money, and their ability to draw on and use social support systems. As income streams become more insecure, poor people can be pushed increasingly into debt, forced to take loans from private money lenders who charge exorbitantly high rates of interest.

Housing Condition

Housing is also an important productive asset since access to credit to secure a livelihood may depend on property ownership. The price and availability of land for housing remains an important influence on housing prices and conditions leading to the development of illegal or informal land markets, where the poor have limited capacity to pay. Quantity, accessibility and tenure of housing are all important and have *gender-specific* dimensions. The housing conditions are divided into

Kutcha and *Pucca* types. The analysis shows that most of the houses are entirely made of makeshift materials – wood, bamboo and plastic/ tarpaulin sheets.

Due to Basic Services for Urban Poor (BSUP), some families are getting houses in multi-storey apartment i.e. around 140 family shifted to this building in Gond Basti. Basically, BSUP have been first started in Gond Basti and Narsingh Ghat Basti which are mostly slum populated areas. Housing and living condition of these families are so simple. Only 140 HHs are staying in multi-storey apartment and remaining are in *jhuggi/jhopri*. Size of the room is 5/7 made of bamboo and tile. In multi-storey apartment, there are two rooms 10/10 including kitchen and toilet. For a large family it is very difficult to manage in this small size of room.

Figure 10 *Housing Condition of the Basti*

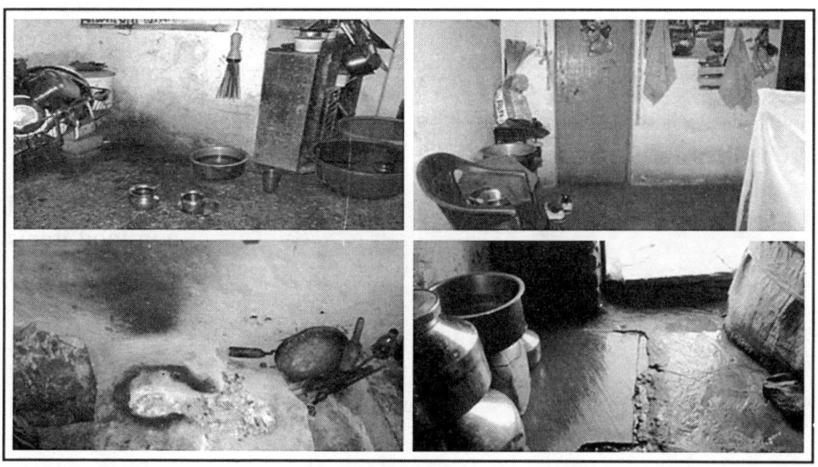

Drainage and Electric Facility in the Slum

More than half of the slum population in Ujjain city does not have any toilet and drainage facilities. They are living illegally and in unauthorized colonies. This deplorable situation in the provision of sanitation services to the poor has been a result of urbanization and consequent increase in demand as well as the incapability of executing agencies to provide a reliable and efficient level of services to its people. The Ujjain Municipal Corporation (UMC) is responsible for providing basic amenities like water, electricity and sanitation to all citizens in both the plan and non-plan areas of the city. Within the UMC, direct responsibilities for services provision in the slums and *jhuggi/jhopri* cluster rests with the JNNURM and RAY. But in multi-storey apartment, electricity is available but there is no drainage facility. Electricity also, is used only for household purpose. There is no street light in these slum *bastis*. One big problem they are facing in using electricity is the high cost of electric bill. Sometimes in a month, they have to pay ₹ 500 and sometimes ₹ 5,000. Just imagine here that when people are unable to give a proper meal for a day to their family, in that case how they can afford this. Families those are unable to pay the electric bills are barred from using these services. Even though there is access to electricity but people are unable to afford that service and the family are excluded from use of that service. In that case, how can we reduce poverty by providing basic services to the poor? Not only are they suffering from lack of use of electricity but also health hygiene situation due to no drainage facility. Figure 11 shows how dirty water discarded from toilet is disposed on the road.

Figure 11 *Drainage System of the Slum City Ujjain*

Drinking Water Facility in the Slum Basti

Access to individual water connections (which is ideal) in Ujjain slums is low and most slum households do not have easy access to public sources of supply (public stand post hand pumps/wells) within 100 metres of their dwellings (UNCHS Habitat's norm of 200 metres). The accessibility comes out to be one source of water per 150 persons, which is very low. In summer season, the situation becomes more critical. In this locality, there is one (or two) tubewells which also do not work properly (see Figure 12).

Figure 12 *Drinking Water Facility of the Basti*

Poverty, Employment and Livelihoods

There is gender-differentiated access to employment and income-earning opportunities in urban areas. Unemployment and underemployment have been major concerns for many urban economies. Recent studies suggest that the urban poor have suffered significantly from structural adjustment through reduction in employment creation and downward pressure on real wages. New categories of the poor have been identified, for example, former state employees who have been retrenched. There is evidence that in many countries, gender segmentation in the labour market remains widespread (Gilbert, 1997) and that woman's work remains characterized by insecurity and low returns. Furthermore, many different facets of women's work, both unpaid and paid, are not recognized by urban planners. The deregulation and casualization of the labour market has led to an increase in home working, particularly among women, which sometimes leads to greater exposure to environmental risk, both in terms of human pathogens and industrial toxic compounds at home or in the workplace (Home Net, 1996; Gilbert, 1997). People of the slum areas depend on unsecure daily wage labour. Male of the family stay in the house and smoking, drinking is common for them due to lack of employment. Women of these families are working on different grounds. They wash utensils and get ₹ 300 to ₹ 500 per month. With this money they are helping in the survival of their families.

Urban Environment, Health and Poverty

The determinants of health in urban areas are complex, but social and cultural factors, including composition of the family and cultural restrictions are important (Fustukian, 1996). Poor health can reduce capacity to earn an income, and health treatment can use up scarce savings or lead to debt. Women play a crucial role in informal health care in low-income households and communities, in their role as wives and mothers, and continue to be used as conduits to children in promotional and preventative health campaigns. This raises questions as to who in a household gets access to health care when user charges are imposed. Poverty and health are inter-related to each other. Due to unhygienic situations, people are suffering from various communicable and non-communicable diseases due to the lack of health care facilities. The people living in slum areas of Ujjain city are far away from health care services. About 80 per cent of the families are living below the poverty line in slum *basti*. So they do not have a willingness to pay for health care services. They are unable to afford for private health care services and depend on governmental hospital. As Ujjain has a district hospital, poor people are using these services. But when we raise the question on health camp in the *basti* then the condition is not better. In rainy season, they suffer from various types of diseases due to lack of sanitation. Level of mortality and morbidity is high in this place. When they require any health practitioner in that time, they do not find one.

The first picture in Figure 13 shows the community toilet provided by government, the second one is the playground of the children which is covered by waste water and the last one is another community toilet where the discarded waste water is openly released on the road.

Figure 13 *Community Toilet Facility and Playground*

Education Facility

The education system of the slum *basti* is very poor. More than half of the people are illiterate in this society. Children up to six years of age in these *bastis* go to ICDS Aanganwadi centres to learn something but children very rarely continue school after this. Those families, who are sending their children to the government primary school, because of the

Figure 14 *Hygienic Situations of the Slum Households*

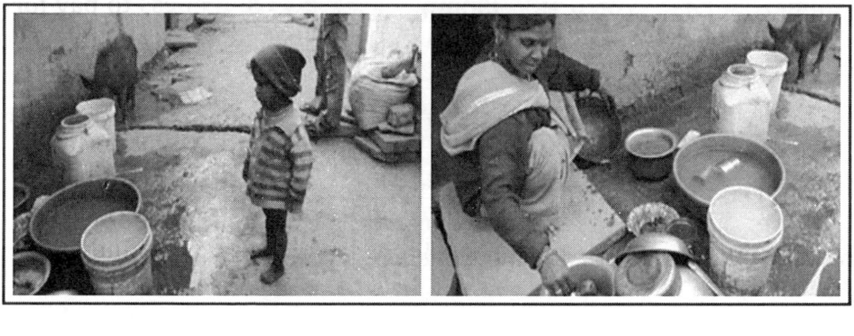

low cost of services, are not aware about the quality of service provided by the teachers. When we interact with school children, they say that they want to read English and Mathematics but teaching quality is very poor. School children are not only suffering from poor quality of services but also poor sanitation facility in the school. The school having a toilet is also in a very bad condition; as can be seen in Figure 15.

Figure 15 *Toilet Facility in the Primary School and Our Future*

Basic Services for Urban Poor in Narsingh Ghat Basti

Access to basic services is now deemed a criterion for identification of the poor and poor areas in a city (essentially slums). The responsibility for service provision in an equitable manner lies with municipal government, which finds it difficult to meet growing gaps in service levels of a burgeoning urban poor population. This scheme provides house to the urban poor as multi-storey apartment. This multi-storey apartment is their dream. At least they can stay in a good house. Progress work of the multi-storey apartment has stopped from last one and half years. Now the condition of this incomplete multi-storey apartment has worsened (see Figure 16). Nobody is taking care of the building and day by day, the condition is deteriorating.

View of BPL Cardholders

On a BPL card, a household gets 10 kg wheat per month at ₹ 3 and 5 litres kerosene at ₹ 16 per litre which is not sufficient for a family. We have seen in our previous section that every year more BPL cards are issued to poor families. But the question is that what is the quality of wheat, which is provided by the government? It can be seen in Figure 17

Figure 16 *Incomplete BSUP Work*

Figure 17 *Quality of Wheat Provided by Government to the BPL Holders*

as to how the poor people are living their daily lives. Some families do not even have a BPL card.

For slum people, it is very difficult to meet out their daily needs. Daily market is far away from these *bastis*. There is no playground for the kids.

Overview on Access to Basic Services

Table 5 gives an overall picture of accessibility of slum dwellers to the basic services:

Table 5

Access to Basic Services

Year	*No. of Slums*	*Percentage of Slum Dwellers Having Access to*		
		Water Supply (%)	*Drainage System (%)*	*Waste Service Collection (%)*
1991	108	20	20	35
2001	113	30	30	40
2005	129	40	50	50

Source: UMC

It can be analysed that nearly half of the slum population in Ujjain does not have accessibility to the basic services. There is an increase in the coverage of basic services to the slum dwellers but lack of interest among dwellers to take legal connections is a major problem.

Conclusion

This whole paper is based on the secondary sources as well as observations and discussions with government officials, community-based organizations and slum dwellers. Urbanization is a rising problem, as people are migrating from rural to urban cities in great numbers. The growing number of slums and squatters in metropolitan cities in India coupled with sub-standard living conditions of urban-poor has become a major concern in urban and regional planning (Dhul, 1996). There are a number of reasons responsible for this situation such as availability and accessibility to basic needs, inadequate housing and income-generating opportunities, access to services, urban land pressure, etc. Due to migration, urban poverty is increasing, which has major implications on the basic services and infrastructure. There is wide disparity in the poverty ratio between urban and rural poverty. Urban poverty still remains one of the major issues in Indian planning.

Health and poverty are interrelated to each other. It is also a community phenomenon. It is related to everything which affects human beings. Crowdedness and poor environmental sanitation are associated with morbidity and mortality from TB, malnutrition, maternal child disorders and untreated psychoses. In the northern city, in the down part of the town where the local administration has long been concerned about the high cost city services and the need for urban renewal, the immigrant tends to congregate. There is already unemployment in the cities. So when new residents come to the city, they do not find any job and have no access to the minimum requirements of the life.

Urban poor do not have basic services. They struggle for health, education and livelihood. There is, thus, an urgent need to address the issue of urban poverty. In this context, it may be stated that the Central government has an important role to play in the formulation of realistic policies, plans, programmes as well as in programme/scheme implementation and monitoring. Since poor are deprived of the benefits of the schemes, it is necessary for the implementing agencies to ensure that the benefits of the schemes should reach them. It is clear that due to urbanization, India became developed but in reality, it's raising urban poverty through migration which is breaking down the whole development model. If they are healthy then their capability, power of earning would be more and they can do better for improving their living condition with high income. They can provide better health check-up and education to their children. So the government should not only focus more on the rural poor but also on the urban one. The government should supervise the service delivery system which is implemented to provide the basic services to the slums.

References

Ali, S. (ed.) (2006). *Dimensions of Urban Poverty*, Rawat Publications, Jaipur.

Amis, P. (1995). 'Making Sense of Poverty', in IIED, 'Urban Poverty: Characteristics, Causes and Consequences', *Environment and Urbanization*, 7 (1).

Baker, J. (1995). 'Survival and Accumulation Strategies at the Rural-urban Interface in North-west Tanzania', in IIED, 'Urban Poverty: Characteristics, Causes and Consequences', *Environment and Urbanization*, 7 (1).

Basta, S.S. (1977). 'Malnutrition and Health in Low-income Urban Areas of the Third World', *Ecology of Food and Nutrition*, 6: 113–24.

Beall, J. (1997). 'Assessing and Responding to Urban Poverty: Lessons from Pakistan', *IDS Bulletin*, 28 (2).

Berlinguer, G. (1993). 'The Interchange of Disease and Health between the Old and New Worlds', *International Journal of Health Services*, 23 (4): 703–15.

Census of India (2011).

City Development Plan Ujjain (2006–07).

Dash, A. (2009). *Access to Health Care in Rural Odisha* (M.Phil. Dissertation), Sambalpur University, Odisha.

De Haan, Arjan (1997). 'Rural-urban Migration and Poverty: The Case of India', *IDS Bulletin*, 28 (2).

Duhl, L.J. (1966). 'Urbanisation, Poverty and Health', *Journal of Urban Health*, 42 (5), May: 369–79.

Fustukian, S. (1996). 'Strategies to Strengthen Urban Health and Social Development', in N. Hall, R. Hart and D. Mitlin (eds), *The Urban Opportunity: The Work of NGOs in Cities of the South*, ITDG, London.

Gaur, K.D. and Jawa, R. (2000). 'Urban Poverty Alleviation Strategies', *Social Change*, 30 (1&2), March–June: 74–91.

Gilbert, A. (1997). 'Work and Poverty during Economic Restructuring: The Experience of Bogota, Colombia', *IDS Bulletin*, 28 (2).

Gilbert, A. and Gugler, J. (1992). *Cities, Poverty and Development: Urbanization in the Third World*, Oxford University Press, Oxford.

GoI. *Annual Report 2011–12*.

——. (2011). *Slum Census*.

Home Net (1996). 'Rights for Home Workers', *Home Net Newsletter*, 5.

ILO (1996). 'Social Exclusion and Anti-poverty Strategies', Research Findings on the Patterns and Causes of Social Exclusion and the Design of Policies to Promote Integration, Geneva.

Kundu, Amitabh and Moitra, S. (1999). 'Access of Urban Poor to Basic Services: An Analysis in the Context of Changing Prospective of Urban Governance in India', in O.P. Mathur (ed.), *The Challenges of Urban Governance*, NIPF, New Delhi.

Moser, C. (1995). 'Women, Gender and Urban Development Policy: Challenges for Current and Future Research', *Third World Planning Review*, 17 (2).

——. (1996). 'Confronting Crisis: A Comparative Study of Household Responses to Poverty and Vulnerability in Four Poor Urban Communities', Environmentally Sustainable Development Studies and Monographs Series No. 8, World Bank, Washington, D.C.

Moser, C. and Chant, S. (1985). 'The Role of Women in the Execution of Low-income Housing Projects Training Module', DPU Gender and Planning Working Paper No. 6, University College London, London.

Moser, C. and Holland, J. (1995). *A Participatory Study of Urban Poverty and Violence in Jamaica: Summary Finding*, Urban Development Division, World Bank, Washington, D.C.

NSS Report No. 534: Some Characteristics of Urban Slums, 2008–09.

Russell, S. (2001). 'The Economic Burden of Illness for Household in Developing Countries: A Review of Studies Focusing on Malaria, TB and HIV/AIDS', *American Journal of Tropical Medicine and Hygiene*, 71 (Supp 2): 147–55.

Satterthwaite, D. (1995a). 'The Under-estimation and Misrepresentation of Urban Poverty', in IIED, 'Urban Poverty: Characteristics, Causes and Consequences', *Environment and Urbanization*, 7 (1).

——. (1995b). 'Viewpoint: The Underestimation of Urban Poverty and of its Health Consequences', *Third World Planning Review*, 17 (4).

Schultz, T. (1999). 'Health and Schooling Investment in Africa', Paper 549, Yale-Economic Growth Centre.

Statistical Handbook Ujjain (2011).

Strauss, J. and Thomas, D. (1998). 'Health, Nutrition, and Economic Development', *Journal of Economic Literature*, 36 (2), January: 766–817.

Ujjain Gazetteer (1991).

Wagstaff, A. and van Doorslaer, E. (2003). 'Catastrophe and Impoverishment in Paying for Health Care with Applications to Vietnam 1993–98', *Health Economics*, 12: 921–34.

Wratten, E. (1995). 'Conceptualising Urban Poverty', in IIED, 'Urban Poverty: Characteristics, Causes and Consequences', *Environment and Urbanization*, 7 (1).

5

Land Matters

Addressing the Importance of Land Rights in the Development and Empowerment of Women in the Hill State of Uttarakhand

ARADHANA SINGH

Land is one of the most fundamental resources to women's living conditions in Uttarakhand. Here, women are the main workers in fields; they work for more than 15–18 hours per day collecting fuel, fodder, water in addition to looking after animals, children and the elderly at home. According to Vir Singh's (1987) assessment in the Indian Himalaya, a pair of bullocks works for 1064 hours, a man for 1212 hours and a woman for 3485 hours a year on one hectare farm: a woman works longer than men and farm animals combined. Historically, also women of Uttarakhand have played a major role in social and environmental movements: the well documented *'chipko'* (hug the trees) movement led by women of Reni village in Garhwal region of Uttarakhand, agitations against mining in Khirakot, Shama, Chaurasthal in Kumaon region, direct confrontations with the liquor mafia to ban selling of liquor in villages and women's contribution in the recent movement for creating a separate state of Uttarakhand. Despite their central role in social movements and agricultural production, their land rights are still largely discriminated against. In Uttarakhand, close to 57 per cent of cultivators and nearly 84 per cent of agricultural workers are women (Mehta, 2008). This significantly makes the land issues more important for the Uttarakhand women. Land is a source of economic empowerment and represents a key factor in the struggle for equity and equality. Rights to use and control land are, therefore, central to Uttarakhand women's livelihoods.

The traditional exclusion of women from land ownership on gender grounds is the most damaging human rights violation. Women continue to face discrimination in accessing and owning land. Most women in the region have access to farmland only through their husbands or fathers as they are only granted usufructuary rights as land title passes through the male line. Without rights to land, women's economic and physical security is compromised. Land ownership and control over land also plays a critical role in determining social status and political power. Large landowners often play dominant roles in their communities, including holding political office and controlling employment of agricultural labourers. Conversely, landless people are often the poorest and least powerful members of their communities.

Construction of Gender in Uttarakhand

The socio-political and economic conditions of the region have given rise to different constructions of gender, particularly, in relation to the role of women. For the women of this region, engagement in both productive and reproductive activities became a necessary adjunct of everyday existence. The rugged terrain, the lack of irrigational resources, and the migration of the male members of the household for service-based occupations in the army, police and other services made the women de-facto cultivators. Moreover, the use of family labour as the chief source of labour supply in a subsistence economy ensured women's participation in agricultural activities in large numbers. This active participatory role of women became a part of the peasant culture and ethos in due course of time. This cultural ethos can be seen to exist in a fairly homogenous form among all castes and classes of the region and among the high and low with small variations.

There is also effect of familial ideology which naturalizes and universalizes the construction of women as mothers and wives, as economically dependent, passive, dutiful and self-sacrificing within all personal laws. This homogenizing discourse within the cultural ideology of the family obscures all the different experiences of women in individual or group situations (Kapur and Cossman, 1996).

The Significance of Land as Property

In agrarian economies, arable land is the most valued form of property, for its economic as well as its political and symbolic importance. It is a productive, wealth-creating, and livelihood-sustaining asset. Traditionally it has been the basis of political power and social status. For many, it provides a sense of identity and rootedness within the village; and often in people's minds land has a durability and permanence which no other asset possesses (Agarwal, 1994: 17).

Status of Women's Land Rights in Uttarakhand

According to Agricultural census, (Government of India, 2005–06), of the total individual operational holdings in Uttarakhand, about 8.9 per cent were operated by women covering 8.4 per cent of the total land. The same data in the 2000–01 was 7.8 per cent operated by women covering 7.9 per cent of the total land. There is an increase of one per cent in the land being operated by women, which is a desirable trend albeit very low and too slow. The same GOI report reveals that the total individual operational holdings in India, about 12.4 per cent were operated by women covering 9.9 per cent of the total land. In the lowest size class (below 0.5 hectare), the percentage of individual landholdings operated by women was relatively higher 13.8, covering 12.5 per cent of the area operated by them. It is also observed from the data that there is a kind of inverse relationship between size class of holding and women's access to operational land. Although the data doesn't clearly say whether the land operated by women is also owned by them, it more or less indicates the same. The FAO report (2010–11) states that rural women in most of the developing countries are less likely to own land and control its produce. Wherever they have access to land, it is often of poorer quality and in smaller plots. It is further seen in the GOI report that in the states like Andhra Pradesh, Goa, Karnataka, Kerala, and Tamil Nadu, the percentage share of women in total number and area of operational holdings was comparatively higher than other states. In some Eastern states, namely Assam, West Bengal and Odisha and Northern state of Punjab, the percentage share of women in the total number of operational holdings as well as area was relatively low. Personal interviews with several people with *patwaris* and *kanungos* revealed that only widows, unmarried daughters or daughter without brothers had inherited land in the state. Earlier ideas about inheritance excluded women completely from its ambit, and even now women continue to be deprived of their inheritance rights and are simply assumed to be economically dependent (Kapur and Cossman, 1996). The ownership of land by purchase is generally rare and depends on the initiatives of a man. Where such ownership exists; women are merely instruments as the effective ownership lies in the hands of a man.

Importance of Land Rights for Women

Land is not just a productive asset and a source of material wealth, but equally a source of security, status and recognition. Women's access to and control over land can potentially lead to gender equality alongside addressing material deprivation (Quimsumbing and Maluccio, 2003).

Agarwal (1995 b) observes in the context of South Asia that arable land is the most valued form of property, for its economic, political and symbolic significance. It provides security to married women and widows. Women, more than men, consider land as key to livelihood security. It is a wealth-creating and livelihood-sustaining asset. It has also been termed as a metaphor for power, wealth and status. Land ownership provides opportunities for women to enter decision-making processes and gain confidence to face heavy odds (Sud, 2007).

Studies on land and agriculture encompassing Asia and Africa by Agarwal, 2003; Lastarria-Cornhiel, 2002; Kelkar, Nathan and Walters, 2003; FAO, 2006; Song and Chen, 2006 noticed that gender inequalities affect rural and agricultural development. Their study also reveals that ensuring equal rights to land and assets for women and men increases economic opportunities, encourages investment in land and crop production, improves household food security, enhances women's agency, and leads to better agricultural management.

In regions where agriculture dominates livelihoods, land is also important for women for reducing the risk of poverty and enhancing food security. Land also increases aggregate wage rates and access to credit. Besides, studies show that property and asset ownership by mothers leads to better outcomes for the survival, education and health of children, than assets owned only by fathers. Even in societies such as in Bangladesh where husbands control most household resources, expenditures on children's clothing and education were higher and the rate of illness among girls was lower in households where women owned assets (Quimsumbing and de la Briere, 2000; Hallman, 2000). In Bangladesh and South Africa, for instance, a study found that the assets that women bring into a marriage, though fewer than those that men bring, play a significant role in household decision-making (Quimsumbing and Maluccio, 2003). Higher female earnings and bargaining power translate into greater investment in children's education, health and nutrition, which leads to economic growth in the long-term (DFID, 2010).

Research in Kerala found that 49 per cent of women with no property reported physical violence, whereas 7 per cent of women with property did, controlling for a wide range of other factors such as household economic status, education, employment, and other variables (Panda, 2002).

In addition to welfare gains, gender equality in land rights can enhance productive efficiency. Property ownership may confer incentives to work harder or take greater economic risk. Studies carried out in countries as diverse as China, Ghana, Pakistan, Thailand, and Vietnam have found a clear association between secure land tenure and increased outputs or improvements to quality of land (Mason and Carlsson, 2004). Land ownership (Giovarelli and Lastarria, 2004) can serve as collateral, improving women's access to credit, which in turn can increase output. This can be especially crucial where women are the principal farmers.

Agarwal, in her pioneering work on land rights for women in South Asia emphasizes that supporting women's legitimate share in landed property can prove to be the single most critical entry point for women's empowerment in South Asia. Independent land access could create an enabling environment for women's agency, thereby setting in motion a process for social and political empowerment (Agarwal, 1994).

Researchers and women respondents alike have recognized multiple benefits to be gained from women's ownership of land. First, holding land in her own name or jointly with her husband, gives a woman a secure right to land if she separates from her husband, is deserted or is widowed. Second, ownership of land gives a woman control over, and a continuing right to, a major source of income whereby she is able to directly benefit her children. Third, land ownership enhances a woman's ability to access credit as it gives her an asset that can be used as collateral. Fourth, land ownership increases a woman's respect and leverage within her family. Fifth, land ownership can qualify women for benefits under programmes that require beneficiaries to own land.

Women's access to and control over land has also gained sharp focus due to the contemporary issues of climate change and displacement due to large scale developmental projects. Women need to be assisted in devising coping mechanisms to confront these new challenges. Women with property rights are more likely to be active members of their communities, and as a result, community institutions themselves are more likely to be responsive to the needs of women.

There is considerable evidence to show that the lack of assets enhances vulnerability and also poverty. Asset-less women are subject to threats of violence and inequalities within the household. Thus, effective land rights for women, coupled with equal access to credit, technical information, and other inputs, are important for improving women's welfare, their bargaining power within the household, broader economic efficiency and increase in their social status as members of the community.

Constitutional Provisions and Initiative by Government of India

The Constitution of India provides for equal rights and opportunities to all its citizens irrespective of gender.

Article 14 of the Constitution of India confers equal rights and opportunities on men and women. Article 15 prohibits discrimination on several grounds including sex, and Article 15(3) empowers the State to make affirmative discrimination in favour of women. Article 39 provides for the state to direct its policy towards providing to men and women equally the right to means of livelihood and equal pay for equal work. Constitutional protection is provided to ensure humane work and maternity relief (Article 42) and provisions against practices derogatory to the dignity of women [Article 51(A) (e)].

Although the legal and constitutional edifice of the country effectively affirms and upholds the principles of equity in gender relations, women by and large have been denied access and control of land and other productive resources.

At the start of developmental planning, especially from the first to the Fifth Plan (1951–1979), the emphasis of GOI was on 'welfare' together with the welfare of other disadvantaged groups. Then there was a shift in the Sixth Plan (1980–85) from 'welfare' to 'development' by placing more emphasis on health, education and employment. The Seventh and Eighth Plan (1985–97) continued this 'women in development' strategy with focus on employment, including self-employment, and human development. The Ninth Plan (1997–2002) made a significant shift from development to 'empowerment of women' with a focus on creating an enabling environment.

Furthermore, in the Tenth Five Year Plan (2002–07), the Ministry of Finance, Government of India, introduced a scheme of giving concession on stamp duty to women property buyers. This move can be seen as a hope that it would empower women and improve their economic status preventing them from exploitation. The Eleventh Five Year Plan (2007–2012) also encouraged more ownership rights for women by offering incentives for ownership of property in women's name so that more property is registered in the name of women.

Prospects of Gender Equality: Constraints and Challenges

Women's land rights are put forth as a way to realize human rights, increase economic efficiency, productivity, empower women, and promote general welfare and well-being. Women's land rights are addressed because they are seen as a tool to promote development. Despite the increasing prevalence of these claims, little effort has gone into realizing them. There is a pressing need to establish a comprehensive understanding of the challenges and barriers in legal, social, administrative measures and customary practices to women's right entitlement to land in order to make the process of land entitlement easier for women. There are three avenues via a female can own land – Family, Market and State (Agarwal, 2003). The access of land to women is mainly through inheritance i.e. family and limited through the market and state.

Legal Constraints

The inheritance laws of both Hindus and Muslims treat agricultural land differently from other property. For instance, the Hindu Succession Act (HSA) of 1956 exempted tenancy rights in agricultural land from its purview. Women's inheritance rights in tenancy land, thus, depend on state-level tenurial laws. In most north-western states, tenurial laws specify an order of devolution. This order strongly favours inheritance by male agnatic heirs, women coming very low in the order of heirs, as was the case under archaic customs. Surprisingly, these inequalities cannot be challenged on constitutional grounds because land reform laws come under the Ninth Schedule of the Constitution.

A second source of inequality in Hindu law lies in the continued recognition in the HSA of *Mitakshara* joint family property in which sons have rights by birth but not daughters.

Social and Administrative Constraints

Dowry continues to be one of the major reasons that daughters do not receive or ask for their share of the birth, families' land, dowry is considered as their share of the family property. Despite this line of thinking, dowry is not actually an asset for most women as it goes directly to and is controlled by their husbands or in-laws.

Sometimes these high dowry and weddings expenses are met by selling families' land; this also keeps daughters from inheriting any of her birth families' land.

Many women give up their shares in parental land in favour of their brothers. In the absence of an effective state social security system, brothers are seen as an important source of social security, especially in case of marital breakup. Cultural constructions of gender, including how a 'good sister' would behave, also discourage women from asserting their rights, as does the emphasis on female seclusion in many areas (Agarwal, 1998).

Where women do not voluntarily relinquish their claims, male relatives file court cases, forge wills, use threats and even resort to physical violence. In eastern India, most of the witch murders among tribal groups in recent decades are found to be of widows who typically have customary claims (mostly usufruct rights) to land (Kelkar and Nathan, 1993; Chaudhuri, 1987).

To top it all, unhelpful approach of government officials who have deep rooted social biases obstruct the implementation of laws in women's favour. This is especially seen in the recording of daughter's inheritance shares by the village *patwari* in northern India.

There is a notion among families that if a daughter asks for her share in property it will destroy the family ties especially that of the brother-sister.

Post–marital residence of the women offer operational difficulties. This is compounded by high illiteracy, high fertility, and social restrictions on women's mobility and public interaction.

There is a taboo against female ploughing the land. This increases women's dependence on male help; reduce yields if ploughing is not done in time. It is believed that land belongs to the one who tills which disqualifies women as claimants where the policy is applicable.

Biases in Land Distribution Schemes

In the view of the government under any schemes of land reform, poverty-alleviation, or resettlement, land is typically allotted to male household heads. This happens because of myriad reasons – the social perception of men as breadwinners and women as dependents, land transfers made to men are assumed to benefit all family members, the social perception regarding women's lesser capabilities and appropriate roles, the household is viewed as a space of harmony which is eroded by the property considerations. Typically a family unit is defined as constituted of the cultivator, spouse, and minor children. An adult son is usually counted as a separate unit and, therefore, entitled to additional land, but an adult daughter is not (Agarwal, 1998).

Conclusion

Women constitute nearly half of the total society. Hence, women's development is considered necessary from the point of view of the developmental policy of the state. Women's empowerment, including their economic empowerment, is an issue of true human and humane development. But the issue of equality of the rights of male and female involves the transformation of the structure of beliefs, rites, practices, etc. being strongly biased in favour of men. This transformation is possible only when its desirability is widely realized. If the legitimacy of women's right to own land is recognized and realized by the people at large, it may become easy for the government to create appropriate legal instruments for the acquisition of land rights by women and, further, such recognition of the legitimacy of women's right may also help women in retaining their control over their lands. In Uttarakhand, an ideological movement is, therefore, required for mobilizing people to consider the desirability of equality of the rights of men and that of women.

Acknowledgements

I would like especially to thank Prof. Dipankar Gupta for giving detailed and thought-provoking comments that led to substantial improvements. I would also like to thank the editor of this volume.

References

Agarwal, B. (1994). 'Gender and Command Over Property: A Critical Gap in Economic Analysis and Policy in South Asia', *World Development*, 22 (10): 1455–78.

——. (1995a). *A Field of One's Own*, Cambridge University Press, Cambridge.

——. (1995b). 'Women's Legal Rights in Agricultural Land in India', *Economic and Political Weekly*, 30 (12): A39–56.

——. (1998). 'Gender and Legal Rights in Agricultural Land in India', *Economic and Political Weekly*, XXX (12).

——. (2002). 'Are We Not Peasants Too? Land Rights and Women's Claims in India', Seeds No. 21, Population Council, New York.

——. (2003). 'Women's Land Rights and the Trap of Neo-Conservatism: A Response to Jackson', *Journal of Agrarian Change*, 3 (4): 571–85.

Chaudhuri, A.B. (1987). *The Santals: Religion and Rituals*, Ashish Publishing House, New Delhi.

Chowdhry, P. (2009). *Gender Discrimination in Land Ownership*, Sage Publications, New Delhi.

Department for International Development (DFID) (2002). *Better Livelihoods for Poor People: The Role of Land Policy*, London.

FAO (2006). *The State of Food Insecurity in the World*, Food and Agriculture Organization of the United Nations, Rome.

——. (2011). *The State of Food and Agriculture, 2010–2011: Women in Agriculture, Closing the Gender Gap for Development*, Food and Agriculture Organization of the United Nations, Rome.

Giovarelli, R. and Lastarria, S. (2004). 'Gender Issues in Land Administration and Land Reform', paper presented at the Gender and Rural Development and the Land Thematic group jointly sponsored brown bag lunch, April 29, World Bank, Washington, D.C.

Government of India (2005–06). Ministry of Agriculture, Agricultural Census, All India, New Delhi.

——. (2000). Ninth Five Year Plan: 1997–2002, Planning Commission, New Delhi.

——. (2008). Eleventh Five Year Plan: 2007–2012, Planning Commission, New Delhi.

Guivant, S. Julia (2003). UNRISD Programme Papers on Social Policy and Development, PP SPD 14: Agrarian Change Gender and Land Rights, July.

Gupta, Jayoti (1997). 'Women Second in Land Agenda', *Economic and Political Weekly*, May 4.

Hallman, K. (2000). 'Mother-Father Resource Control, Marriage Payments, and Girl-Boy Health in Rural Bangladesh', Food Consumption and Nutrition Division Discussion Paper 93, International Food Policy Research Institute, Washington, D.C.

Kapur, Ratna and Cossman, Brenda (1996). *Feminist Engagements with Law in India*, Sage Publications, Thousand Oaks, London, in association with The Book Review Literary Trust, New Delhi.

Kelkar, G. and Nathan, D. (1993). *Gender and Tribe: Women, Land and Forests in Jharkhand*, Zed Books, London and Kali for Women, New Delhi.

Kelkar, G., Dev, N. and Walters, P. (eds) (2003). *Gender Relations in Forest Societies: Patriarchy at Odds*, Sage Publications, Delhi.

Lastarria-Cornhiel, Susana (2002). 'The Impact of Changing Patterns of Land Rights on Rural Women', Land Tenure Center, University of Wisconsin-Madison, paper presented at the expert group meeting on the situation of rural women within the context of globalization, Ulaanbaatar, June.

Mason, K. and Carlsson, H. (2004). 'The Impact of Gender Equality in Land Rights on Development', paper presented at the Human Rights and Development: Towards Mutual Reinforcement conference hosted by the New York University School of Law, New York, March 1.

Mehta, G.S. (2008). *Towards Improving Livelihoods in Mountains: Options and Strategies*, Zenith Books International, Delhi.

Panda, P. (2002). 'Rights-Based Strategies in the Prevention of Domestic Violence', ICRW Working Paper 344, International Center for Research on Women, Washington, D.C.

Quimsumbing, A. and de la Briere, B. (2000). 'Women's Assets and Intrahousehold Allocation in Bangladesh: Testing Measures of Bargaining Power', Food Consumption and Nutrition Division Discussion Paper 86, International Food Policy Research Institute, Washington, D.C.

Quisumbing, A. and Maluccio, J.A. (2003). 'Resources at Marriage and Intrahousehold Allocation: Evidence from Bangladesh, Ethiopia, Indonesia, and South Africa', *Oxford Bulletin of Economics and Statistics*, 65 (3): 283–327.

Singh, Vir (1987). 'Hills of Hardship', *The Hindustan Times Weekly*, January 18.

Song, Shunfeng and Chen, Aimin (2006). *China's Rural Economy After WTO: Problems and Strategies*, Ashgate Publishing, Farnham, UK.

Sud, Nikita (2007). 'From Land to the Tiller to Land Liberalization', *Modern Asian Studies*, 41 (3): 603–37.

World Bank (2001). *Engendering Development through Gender Equality in Rights, Resources, and Voice*, World Bank and Oxford University Press, Washington, D.C., January.

6

Decentralization for Good Governance and Development

Empirical Evidence from India

SHAILENDER KUMAR HOODA

Decentralization has been emerged as a highly popular strategy for improving public sector efficiency, responsiveness, and accountability in the developing world. Both theoretical and empirical literatures argued that decentralization brings services closer to the people and increase local citizen participation, democratic elections and financial and political equity (for detail see Hooda, 2012). Their close relation with the local people enables them to know the local problems and needs and, therefore, enables them better to enforce and coordinate policies and programmes. Decentralization has administrative problem-solving capacities and leads to effective service delivery in policy-fields like education, water quality, health, sanitation, food safety, environmental protections and regional development.

While presenting the relationship between decentralization and good governance, the studies have argued that decentralization often serves as an instrument to strengthen the transparency, voice and accountability of policy-making, these dimensions in one sense are important components of good governance. According to Ronald and Henry (2000), decentralization offers a key element of the enabling environment for good governance through which responsibilities are transferred from the central government to the local level, where citizens can more readily participate in decisions that affect them.

Decentralization offers partnerships between local government institutions, civil society organizations and the private sector for attainment of good governance.

The concept of good governance, however, is highly complex and is surrounded by intense controversy (Mundle et al., 2012). The Mundle study has reported that the term 'governance' is defined as the use of political authority and exercise of control over a society and the management of resources for social and economic development (Landell-Mills and Serageldin, 1991). Governance has been applied to the processes through which public decisions are made (Ronald and Henry, 2000). These definitions emphasize the political nature and the management aspect of governance. However, it does not define the nature of the relationship between the authorities (the governors) and the public (the governed). Charlick (1992) looked at governance as the effective management of public affairs through the generation of a regime (set of rules) accepted as legitimate, for the purpose of promoting and enhancing societal values sought by individuals and groups. The fundamental principles of good governance include respect for the rule of law and human rights, political openness, participation and inclusiveness, equality and non-discrimination, effective and efficient processes and institutions, transparency, and accountability.

Some literatures have highlighted that decentralization and (good) governance, in many ways, is reciprocal. Ebimaro (2006) asserts that decentralization is synonymous with good government. Decentralization is a process of transferring power, resources and responsibilities from the central to the sub-national levels of government, while governance is a new mode of government characterized by heterarchy rather than by hierarchy, creating a horizontal relationship among a multitude of actors both public and private. Decentralization aims to promote good governance by enabling citizen participation and democratic elections. In other words, the outcome of decentralization should result in a more participatory government for citizens and improved delivery of public services because of the local participation and accountability (Green, 2005).

Given this complex phenomena, over the last 50 years or so, decentralization is assumed a prerequisite for good governance (Oyugi, 2000). One of the benefits that can be expected from decentralization is the realization of good governance (Litvack, Ahmad and Bird, 1998).

Good governance in turn is crucial for successful development by providing principles and indicators for a successful decentralization, such as per capita income (Grindle, 2007). The mutual relationship between decentralization or regional autonomy and good governance has been easily accepted. Nharnet Team (2005) supports the idea on such mutual relationship by stating that decentralization is the logical application of the core characteristics of good governance at the sub-national and local levels. These characteristics include accountability, transparency, rule of law and responsiveness. This statement infers that without decentralization, good governance seems to be unsuccessfully implemented. Similarly, the Centre for Democracy and Governance (2000) confidently says that when effective decentralization and democratic local governance advance in tandem, local governments – and the communities they govern – gain the authority, resources, and skills to make responsive choices and to act on them effectively and accountably.

Some studies have highlighted that decentralization constitutes a strategy to achieve good governance; the failure of good governance (if any) might be caused by unsuccessful decentralization framework. The failure of decentralization is caused mostly by the low capacity of local government. From the beginning of decentralization policy, there was wide anxiety on the capacity of local government to run the new wave of government management. Such concern implies that government capacity constitutes condition *sine qua non* for rewarding decentralization.

The above discussion reveals that one major challenge is how to segregate and measure the extent of decentralization and good governance and how to associate them. We believe that the empirical results are highly sensitive to type(s) and way the decentralization and good governance variable(s) are measured. This study, therefore, first works out an appropriate measure of decentralization and good governance in Indian context (across 16 major states of India) and then their association. This further highlights some issues and strategies to renew the spirit of decentralization in order to achieve more meaningful good governance in India. The specific research questions that the study asks are: does decentralization lead to good governance in rural area of India at state level; does decentralization lead to high level of development in Indian states; is there any nexus between decentralization, governance and development?

Data and Methods

Measuring Decentralization: Considering the fact that empirical results of the impact of decentralization are highly sensitive to type(s) and way the decentralization variable(s) are measured, this section measures an appropriate and multidimensional comprehensive measure of the extent of decentralization, in a well defined methodological framework, in India at major states level.

Choice of Indicators and Methodology: There is considerable debate in identifying the dimensions and methodology adopted for measuring the level of decentralization. This methodological debate is influenced by the experience of decentralization in specific contexts, including its strengths, weakness and challenges before the decentralization. For measuring the status of decentralization in (Kerala) India, John and Chathukulam (2003) study includes scope, intensity, commitment, and demand for decentralization, effect in society and the theory and practice. Kearney (1999) constructed an index of decentralization for 49 countries (including India) using dimensions on government structure, regional and local executive, revenue raising authority and revenue sharing criteria, etc. World Bank (2000), in its overview of India's rural decentralization, has used three political, administrative and fiscal parameters. The Eleventh Finance Commission (EFC) 2000–2005 of India introduced the index of decentralization, based on funds, functions and functionaries (3Fs) and used 10 indicators in totality (GOI, 2000, EFC Report). Alok and Bhandari (2004) study, expanding the scopes of the EFC exercise, provide a fairly comprehensive measure of index of devolution and comprise three broad dimensions of devolution of 3Fs and construct the index on the scoring scale basis. Further, NCAER (March 2007) used the same methodology for constructing the 'working index of devolution for assessing environment for PRIs in the states' with some modification in the indicators as proposed by Alok and Bhandari (2004).

These measures have some limitations and lack in including broader and multidimensional indicators. That is, these studies have ignored the political dimensions of decentralization. This is, however, an important dimensions which provides a fairly better understanding of citizens' participation as well as the level of democracy in a particular country/state. Further, the information on some of the important indicators like administrative, fiscal and functional decentralization have not been included. We present a distinct and comprehensive measure of decentralization. That is, we have captured the fiscal, functional, political and administrative dimensions of decentralization. On the importance of these dimensions, it is presumed that decentralizing the budget (fiscal dimension) is the most important step in decentralization, which enables the local governments to meet the needs of the people and better provisioning of local services, such as the health services. The fiscal decentralization, however, provides more revenue raising, expenditure allocations and other finance responsibilities to local bodies but we believe that its effectiveness requires calibration with other dimensions (like political and administrative) of decentralization. The political participation brings the decision-making closer to the people and, thereby, increase democratization. The active participation of the people, especially the women, in politics is expected to persuade the decision of local authorities in their interests and priorities. Thus, political participation, in a way, improves the effectiveness of fiscal decentralization. The administrative decentralization is necessary to implement political decisions. This is also an important precondition for fiscal decentralization to be effective because the efficiency in the delivery of public services particularly depends on administrative efficiency and accountability.

All these dimensions (presented in Table 1) of decentralization are captured by including the parameters on devolution of funds, functions, functionaries (administrative) and political powers and authorities that are devolved to local government (the Panchayat Raj Institutions-PRIs) under the 73rd Constitutional Amendment Act (CAA) of India and some other indicators that capture the extent of decentralization. This index of decentralization not only captures the extent of fiscal decentralization (funds) but also gives adequate or appropriate weight to the structure and content of devolution, as manifested in to whom the power is transferred (functionary) and for what the power is transferred (function) and what is the extent of community/political participation at the local level. Such identification of the level of decentralization is not only helpful in identifying the nature and extent of implementation of 73rd Amendment at the state level but also tells the extent of local participation in politics. In short, this index shows whether the decentralized institutions are functionally, financially, politically and administratively viable institutions at the local level and if they can help to achieve good governance and high level of development in the country.

Table 1

Measuring the Extent of Decentralization in Indian States

Indicators	*Methodology for measurement*
Calculating the political participation index	
Constitution of State Election Commission (SEC)	If, Yes = 5, No = 0
Holding elections to PRIs every five years	If Yes = 5; No = 0
Share of women and reserved class panchayats representatives	If <=25=1; if >25&<=29=2; if >29&<=33=3; if >33& <=37= 4; if >37=5
% of total voters' turnout in assembly election	If < 45%=1; 45 – 65% = 3; > 65% = 5
Women voted as % of men voted in assembly election	If < 75%=1; 75–85% = 3; > 85% = 5
% of women contested in assembly election	< 2%=1; 2 – 3% = 3; > 3% = 5
% of women elected in assembly election	< 4%=1; 4 – 6% = 3; > 6% = 5
a. Political participation sub-indices	*Arithmetic mean of all the above indicators*
Calculating the sub-index of functions devolution	
De facto transfer of 29 functions to Panchayats	[(Number transferred/29)*5]
Activity mapping has been conducted for the 29 functions?	[(Number of functions for which activity mapping is done/29)*5]
b. Functions devolution sub-indices	*Arithmetic mean of all functions items*
Calculating the sub-index of finances devolution	
Authorization to the village panchayats as per the PRIs Act to collect appropriate taxes, duties, tolls and non-taxes fees.	[(Number of taxes items assigned/38)*5] [(Number of non-taxes items assigned/29)*5]
PRIs own revenue as % of Expenditure of PRIs	Less than 5% =1; 5 – 10% = 2; 11 – 15% = 3; 16 – 20% = 4; More than or equal to 21% = 5
PRIs own revenue as % of state own revenue	Less than 1% = 1; 1–2% = 2; 2–3% =3; 3–4% = 4; more than 4% = 5
Per capita (as per rural population) real (at 1993–94 prices) expenditure on core services (like, health, education, water supply, street light, roads, etc.) by PRIs	Less than ₹ 50 = 1; 51–100 = 2; 101–150 =3; 151–200 = 4; more than 200 = 5
Constitution of State Finance Commission (SFC)	If No SFC has been constituted = 0; Only 1st SFC report received = 2; 2nd SFC report received = 3; 3rd SFC report received = 5; (used highest score)
Timely actions on the latest SFC's major recommendations	> Two years = 1; <2 years>one year = 2; < 1 year > six months = 3; < Six months = 5

Cont'd...

...Cont'd

% of funds devolved to PRIs that are 'untied' to any scheme	<5% are untied=1; 5–25% untied=2; 25–50% untied=3; 50–75% untied=4; >75% untied=5
Release of Funds to PRIs: Compliance of the State Government in sending the TFC grant without delay (data from NCAER)	>60 Days=1, 45–60=2, 30–45=3, 15–30=4, <15 Days=5
Is the allocation of SFC funds to the PRIs based on an apportionment formula?	If allocation is based on development or equitable criteria and include more than three items = 5, if three items= 4; if two items =3; if one item= 2; if ad-hoc grant = 1
c. Finances devolution sub-indices	*Arithmetic mean of all finance items*
Calculating the sub-index of functionaries devolution	
whether staff transferred, for instance, whether (i) only general staff transferred; (ii) functionaries of departments transferred but without any control over them by elected representatives; (iii) functionaries of departments transferred with some degree of control invested in the elected representatives (such as sanction of leave); (iv) functionaries transferred and under substantial control of the elected representatives	If item (iv)= 5; if item (iii)=4; if item (ii)=3; if item (i)=1; if no information average of below three items
How many functionaries has been transferred	[(Number of functionaries transferred/29)*5]
General support to panchayats at present: Government has specified expert institutions and entities to support PRIs for preparation of Annual Plans and for capacity building (data taken from NCAER)	Yes = 5 No = 1
What is the amount of money provided for the training of PRI's elected functionaries in the state budget? (₹ per year per elected functionary) (data taken from NCAER)	Less than or equal to ₹ 1000= 1; More than ₹ 1000 =5
Has the state's department of Panchayati Raj brought out its Annual Report for the last fiscal year?	Yes=5, No=0
d. Functionaries devolution sub-indices	*Arithmetic mean of all functionaries items*
The Rural Decentralization Index (RDI)	Arithmetic mean of the above sub-indices (a to d) The value of RDI further is normalized to be between 0 and 100 by take the formula: RDI = (DIi*100)/5

Source: Hooda, S.K. (2012), unpublished Thesis.

The Political Participation Index is constructed by assigning more weight to women participation. This idea comes from the literature that highlights that more participation of women in politics lead to good governance. The data information is collected from State Election Report (various years) and State of Panchayat Raj Report (2006). The sub-index of functions includes whether 29 functions have been assigned to PR's and whether activity mapping carried out on these functions. As the assignment of duties across PRIs is based on detailed activity mapping. The activity mapping is a way of unbundling subjects into component activities and mapping them against functions which empower the Panchayat by law and with subsidiarity principle (GOI, 2006). Therefore, the inclusion of these items of activity mapping in indices analysis is the first step towards high 'quality' of devolution and strengthens decentralization. The information on functions devolution sub-index indicators are collected from MoPRI (2006), the State of Panchayats – A Mid-Term Review and Appraisal Report, Ministry of Panchayati Raj, Vol. I, II & III; and the State of Panchayat Raj Report (2007 & 2008).

For measuring the finances devolution sub-index, 67 items of taxes and duties (Rao and Rao, 2007) are included. The previous measure (NCAER, 2007), however, has included six type of taxes and duties namely, property/house tax; profession tax; land tax/cess; taxes/tolls on vehicles; entertainment tax/fees; and licence fees which village panchayats generally impose. The inclusion of 67 tax and non-tax items makes finance devolution index more robust and comprehensive. Further, the indicator – share of PRIs own revenue in state's own revenue – provide the information about the degree of autonomy of PRIs to collect funds. Its high share leads to greater autonomy of PRIs to spend on various services as per the local resident requirements. Next, a higher share of PRIs' expenditure on core services (like, health, education, water supply, street light, roads, etc.) in per capita real terms shows the actual spending by PRIs on these services and shows the priority of PRIs towards core services.

The indicator whether the allocation of SFCs funds to the PRIs is based on any apportionment (development or equitable) criteria or not is more important from the standpoint of equal distribution of financial resources across the districts in a particular state. This further leads to equal (low variation) availability of different type of social and economic services across the districts in a particular state. Capturing such variation helps us to design an appropriate policy for devolving the finance across the districts. Data information is collected from the 11th to 13th Union Finance Commission Reports and various State Finance Commission Reports, and Rao and Rao (2007), 'Expanding the Resource Envelop of Panchayats: Augmenting Own Revenues', paper presented at NIPFP, New Delhi.

As a result of data limitations, the functionaries sub-index is measured by using indicators of NCAER (2007) study. However, these variables to some extent are modified and restructured. For instance, whether (i) only general staff is transferred; (ii) functionaries of departments transferred but without any control over them by elected representatives; (iii) functionaries of departments transferred with some degree of control invested in the elected representatives (such as sanction of leave); (iv) functionaries transferred and under substantial control of the elected representatives. The information is collected from NCAER (2007) and State of Panchayat Report (2007 & 2008).

The index of decentralization is constructed by using scaling score method for the year of 2006–07. The scaling score value varies between 0 (a lower score value) and 5 (a high score value). For calculating the aggregate index of the extent of (rural) decentralization, the arithmetic mean of all the sub-indices (i.e. sub-indices of political, fiscal, functional and functionaries/administrative) is worked out. Further, the value of DIH is normalized between 0 to 100 score (Table 1).

Measuring Good Governance: Measuring the extent of governance is very complex and involves multidimensional phenomenon. The dimensions of good governance that have been discussed in the literature are voice and accountability, political stability, government effectiveness in implementation of health and education policy; rule of law/regulatory authority, control of corruption. Each dimension could have several additional sub-dimensions, each represented by one or more different variables. Moreover, there are some dimensions that are not directly observable. Particularly challenging is the task of combining all the indicators and sub-indicators into a single aggregate index of good governance that can capture the multidimensional features of a government in all its complexity. In analysing the determinants of good governance, some of the studies cited earlier have identified indicators of individual dimensions of governance, which they have then sought to relate to other independent variables or other indicators of governance (La Porta et al., 1999). However, these studies have not attempted to aggregate the individual indicators into a single index of good governance (Mundle et al., 2012).

Some studies, however, map their set of selected indicators onto a few major dimensions of governance and combine them into a single index using some aggregation rule (Mundle et al., 2012). However, two opposite approaches have been adopted in the selection of indicators. In one approach, which seeks to use all available information, hundreds of indicators are mapped onto the major dimensions. In the other parsimonious approach, only some indicators are adopted to represent the major dimensions of governance. The Mundle (2012) study has provided a measure of quality of governance for Indian states. They specifically included three branches of a developmental state i.e. the executive, the judiciary, and the legislature. Given the focus on a developmental state, the executive pillar is expanded into four key dimensions: delivery of infrastructure services, delivery of social services, fiscal performance and maintenance of law and order. The deliveries of legal services are included under judicial pillar and quality of legislature under the legislative pillar.

The Mundle (2012) study, however, provides fairly a good idea of the quality of governance in the Indian states by including some important output as well input variables but at the same time has ignored some other significant outcome variables of our interest. For instance, the purpose of this study is just not to capture the extent of good governance (that includes Mundle study indicators) but to show its association with decentralization. Under the decentralization, discussed above, the judiciary and legislature powers/authorities to local government have not been provided to Indian states. Therefore, providing the association of good governance (that include judiciary and legislative powers) with decentralization will be unrealistic. The most dominant literatures, discussed above, reveal that decentralization can lead to effective delivery of services (that is, the executive pillar) at the ground level. The measure of good governance, therefore, includes the indicators on executive pillar that are synonymies of effective delivery in the present study. That is, the dimensions relating to execution of infrastructure and social services delivery are included. Under infrastructure, service delivery indicators of the availability of potable water, sanitation, irrigation, roads and power/energy and under social services, the standard indicators on the outcome of health and education (presented in Table 2) are included.

Table 2

Indicators to Measure the Extent of Good Governance for Effective Service Delivery

Infrastructure service delivery in rural area	Rural Road Density Per 1000 km, 2007
	Rural Road Density Per 1000 Population, 2007
	Percentage of Households Having Electricity in India 2007–08
	% of Net Irrigated Area (NIA) to Net Sown Area (NSA), 2001
	Percentage Distribution of Households by Improved Source of Drinking Water, 2008–09
	Household with access to sanitation facility (%), 2005–06
Health services delivery in rural area	Institutional Birth, 2005–06
	Child Full Immunization 2005–06
	MMR 2005–06
	IMR - 2008–09
	Sex Ratio (0–6 years)
Education services delivery in rural area	% Children (Age 3–4) in anganwadi or pre-school)
	Gross enrolment ratio 2007–08
	Literacy rate 2007–08

Source: Ministry of Health and Family Welfare, Family Welfare Statistics in India - 2009, New Delhi; Ministry of Health and Family Welfare, National Family Health Survey (NFHS-3), Government of India, MoHFW, New Delhi; Government of India (2011), 'India Human Development Report 2011', Planning Commission, GoI, New Delhi; ASER (2008), 'Annual Status of Education Report (Rural) 2008', 13 January 2009, www.asercentre.org; Government of India, Department of Drinking Water Supply, Ministry of Rural Development, 2004–05, New Delhi; Government of India (2008), 'Statistics of School Education, 2007–08', Ministry of Human Resource Development, GoI, New Delhi; GoI, Directorate of Economics & Statistics of respective State Governments, and for All-India - Central Statistical Organization; Government of India, 'Census of India 2001', Registrar General of India, GoI, New Delhi; Government of India, 'Central Electricity Authority, Ministry of Power, GoI; GoI, Statistical Abstract India 2005–06, Ministry of Statistics and Programme Implementation; Government of India, 'Basic Road Statistics of India', Ministry of Road Transport and Highways, Transport Research Wing, New Delhi, August 2012.

The index of good governance is constructed by using actual indicators as well as their transformed values (Table 2). Considering the sensitivity, advantages as well as disadvantages, of different methods of aggregation, this study has computed the index of effective service delivery or good governance by applying the average of the Sum of Ranks (i.e. Modified Borda Scores/ranking) methodology. The average of the Sum of Ranks is a variant of the Borda count method that derives its name from the 18th century French mathematician and political scientist Jean Charles de Borda. The Borda count is a form of preferential voting where voters rank candidates in order of preference and the rankings are converted into points. Candidates score one point for being ranked last, two for being next to last and so on. The candidate who receives the most number of points is declared the winner. Thus, this method tends to elect the most broadly acceptable candidate, rather than the one supported by the majority (Sandler, 2001; Gill et al., 2002, Mundle et al., 2012). In our adaptation of this technique for the present exercise, we have given 16 points to the state ranked first for a particular indicator, 16 being our sample size. The second rank holder receives 15 points and so on until the worst performing state receives just 1 point. This procedure is repeated for all the indicators. The points received by the states under each dimension are then added up to give us the sub-index of good governance for that dimension. The final index of good governance is obtained by averaging of different sub-indices. An obvious limitation of this approach is that those dimensions that have more underlying indicators will get a proportionately higher weight in the final index, though this may have no intrinsic justification.

To show the association between decentralization and development, the level of development in the present study is measured in terms of per capita gross state domestic product (GSDP) of a particular state. The good governance in the study is measured using indicators on delivery of social and economic services in the rural area. To identify the gain from decentralization for a specific service delivery, the association between decentralization and good governance is provided for each (economic, infrastructure, health and equation) services superlatively.

Result and Discussions

Extent of Decentralization in India

Considering the high rationality of scaling score criteria, presented in Table 1, the state should have achieved score value 100 to have high level of rural decentralization in the state – an indicator to promote the effective service delivery. The findings indicate that none of the state has achieved 100 point score with considerable variation across states. The score value of overall rural decentralization index indicates that the states like Kerala, West Bengal, Karnataka and Tamil Nadu have scored high point out of 100. Some low (Bihar) and high income (Gujarat and Punjab) states have scored very low score value compared to the others (Table 3).

Table 3
Extent of Rural Decentralization in India

State	*Functions sub-indices*	*Finances sub-indices*	*Functionaries sub-indices*	*Political participation indices (PPI)*	*Overall Score: Rural Decentralization Index (RDI)*
Bihar	75	37	30	69	53
Punjab	22	59	37	97	54
Gujarat	48	40	32	97	54
Himachal Pradesh	41	51	50	86	57
Odisha	74	44	40	91	62
Uttar Pradesh	71	54	41	83	62
Andhra Pradesh	64	64	37	89	64
Maharashtra	88	52	32	83	64
Madhya Pradesh	47	58	61	91	64
Haryana	86	64	33	80	66
Rajasthan	59	59	75	80	68
Assam	100	49	35	97	70
Tamil Nadu	63	58	89	86	74
Karnataka	93	50	69	89	75
West Bengal	100	53	86	89	82
Kerala	85	80	80	91	84

Source: Author's estimation using information provided in Table 1.

The political participation is reported to be high in most of the Indian states. It can be argued that implementation of political participation, in a democratic country like India, is easier to do in many ways. Such types of level of participation are similar to international experiences (World Bank, 2000). That is, the experiences across the world show that electing local governments or political participation seems to be much easier than vesting them with administrative control over significant functions or fiscal autonomy.

The score of devolution of fiscal, functional and functionaries' powers is much lower than the score of political decentralization. The extent of different sub-indices varies considerably across and within a state in India. During the time of implementation of 73rd CAA, however, it was expected that there will be uniformity across all states in political, functional, finances and administrative decentralization. But, the results show that the feature of rural decentralization in India is unbalanced in nature (Figure 1). However, in order for decentralization to be

Figure 1 *Nature of Rural Decentralization in India*

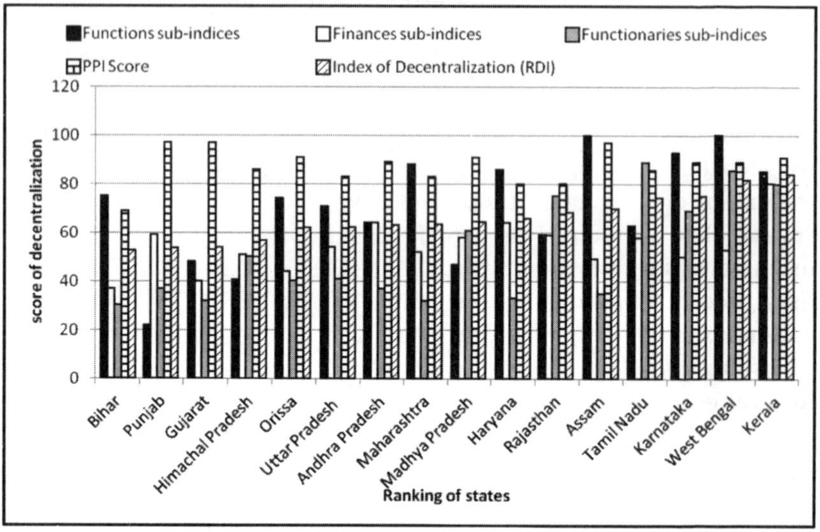

Source: Table 3.

effective, it needs to be balanced along the key dimensions – political, administrative, functional and fiscal.

The unbalancing nature of the different dimensions/sub-indices has resulted in high variation in the level of overall rural decentralization in India. For instance, the functions have not been fully transferred in some of the states. The activity mapping was to be carried out to clarify the role of PRIs at different levels. This also has not been carried out in some states. Even with just these two indicators, there is still a large gap in achieving the level of devolution in the sphere of functions and results in low level of functional devolution and consequently in overall decentralization.

The devolution of finance shows the degree of autonomy to the PRIs in determining their spending priorities. This provides the fiscal power to local government and involves the devolution of taxing and spending powers along with the arrangements for rectifying the mismatches in resources and responsibilities. Empowering the local governments with finances is relevant not only because of its instrumental significance in providing an efficient delivery of public services and local goods, but also because of the failure of national and state government in providing basic services of comparable quality to the citizens (Oommen, 2006). It is realized that any talk of the effectiveness of the local bodies in the absence of a strong finances base is of no use. The fiscal empowerment of local tiers is the key variable in this new dispensation of governance. The fiscal power of any level of government (centre, state or local) generally depends on collection of revenue from different sources by levy of tax and imposition of duties on different items as well as on their rates, so as to collect more revenue to meet their expenditure requirements. The data analysis shows that the extent of fiscal decentralization is very low in Indian states. This reveals that even after the constitutional amendment in 1993, India ostensibly transfers very little funds to PRIs and results in low level of fiscal decentralization. The estimates of the devolution of finances sub-index or fiscal decentralization reflect wide variation across states. The states like West Bengal, Assam, Karnataka and Bihar have scored low value of finance devolution. This reflects that these states have accorded low priorities in this respect.

Further, the performance of functionaries' sub-indicators also varies widely across states. The reason of such variation is reflected from its indicators. For instance, in many states, the Annual Reports of the states have not been published. The classification of transfers of functionaries from lower to higher degree shows that Kerala has implemented this reform concept widely.

The sub-indices of devolution of all 3Fs powers show considerable variation across the states as well as within a state in different sub-indices. That is, the uniformity in different sub-indices dimensions is lacking in many states. Most of the states, however, have managed high rank in functions and functionaries but not in the finances, except Kerala. Kerala is able to manage high score for all sub-indices. The richer states like Haryana and Maharashtra have devolved functions as well as finances, but score of devolution of functionaries remained low. Some states have high rank in devolution of function but not in the finances as well as functionaries and it results in high variation in overall decentralization index across states. Such unbalancing nature of different dimensions undermines the functioning of the inter-governmental transfer system. It can be argued that unless the imbalance is corrected through greater fiscal and administrative decentralization, Indian states are unlikely to evolve effective PRIs. In short, in order for decentralization to be effective for good governance, these dimensions need to be balanced.

It is expected that when the functions are transferred, there would be pressure to devolve more finances as well. With the transfer of functions, there is also a need for providing trained functionaries who can then be accountable for their responsibilities. The analysis across the state do not meet our expectation and shows considerable variation across sub-indices which is a challenge in empowering the Panchayat with different equipment to perform better at the local level, particularly in delivering of local services. To sum up, these variations in overall index and indices highlight the gaps in implementation of decentralization concept at the local level that need to be bridged by the states to strengthen the functioning of the PRIs. How the extent of decentralization has impacted the level of good governance or effective delivery of services is described in the next section.

Extent of Good Governance

The extent of good governance is measured by taking into account the indicators on social and economic services delivery. This specifically includes the indicators on the delivery of basic infrastructure facilities, health and education services in the rural area of India. The score of good governance – synonym of effective services delivery – reveals that the states of Tamil Nadu, Kerala, Himachal Pradesh, Karnataka and Punjab turn into five best performing states. These states have scored high rank value amongst the others. The states of Rajasthan, Bihar, Uttar Pradesh, Madhya Pradesh and Assam turned in bottom five ranking states. Odisha, Gujarat, Maharashtra, Haryana, Andhra Pradesh and West Bengal came in middle performing states (Table 4).

Table 4

Governance Ranking of States: Borda Count Score

	Infrastructure score	*Social score*	*Health score*	*Education score*	*Overall score of Good Governance (col. 2 to 5)*
1	*2*	*3*	*4*	*5*	*6*
Rajasthan	4.17	4.4	3.80	6.13	4.3
Bihar	6.33	4.0	5.60	2.33	5.2
Uttar Pradesh	8.17	3.6	2.80	5.21	5.9
Madhya Pradesh	6.00	7.0	4.00	9.67	6.5
Assam	7.00	7.4	6.20	10.46	7.2
Odisha	7.33	7.8	7.20	9.25	7.5

Cont'd...

...Cont'd

Gujarat	8.50	8.1	7.00	10.04	8.3
Maharashtra	5.83	11.1	10.60	10.38	8.5
Haryana	10.33	7.1	7.20	6.38	8.7
Andhra Pradesh	10.00	9.1	11.20	5.38	9.6
West Bengal	9.00	10.3	12.20	8.75	9.6
Punjab	11.83	7.5	8.40	6.17	9.7
Karnataka	10.00	10.0	10.20	8.67	10.0
Himachal Pradesh	9.67	11.9	10.20	13.63	10.8
Kerala	10.17	13.6	15.20	11.88	11.9
Tamil Nadu	11.67	13.1	14.20	11.71	12.4

Source: Author's estimation using information from Table 2.

Decentralization and Governance: An Association

The study finds that there is a strong correlation between decentralization and measures of good governance. In other words, the extent of good governance which is considered as a synonym of effective services delivery in the study is positively co-related (with coefficient value around 0.38) with the measure/extent of decentralization in India (Table 5). The correlation coefficient value shows that the extent of decentralization is highly correlated with health service delivery followed by social, education and infrastructure services. To provide a more robust result, the study has also examined the association between the extent of decentralization and the value of human development sub-indices of health and education score. These scores are estimated by Planning Commission (2011) to estimate the human development index (HDI) at the Indian state level. The study finds that our estimate of decentralization is highly and positively correlated with the HDI sub-indices of health and education. This shows that decentralization plays a crucial role in improving the delivery of social services in India.

Interestingly, the extent of decentralization has strong correlation with the score value of social services as compared to the infrastructure services (Figure 2). This may mean that states with high level of decentralization can deliver social services more effectively as compared to the others. Within the social services, which comprises health and education services, the extent of decentralization is highly correlated with health services score as compared to the score value of education services (Figure 3).

Table 5

Correlation Coefficient: Decentralization, Good Governance and Development

	RDI	*BSI*	*BSS*	*BSH*	*BSE*	*BSGG*	*HDIH*	*HDIE*	*NSDP*
1	*2*	*3*	*4*	*5*	*6*	*7*	*8*	*9*	*10*
RDI	1								
BSI	0.1369	1							
BSS	0.4926	0.5282*	1						
BSH	0.5207*	0.6217*	0.9243*	1					
BSE	0.3607	0.1894	0.7828*	0.5104*	1				
BSGG	0.3862	0.8291*	0.9125*	0.9084*	0.6039*	1			
HDIH	0.4025	0.5540*	0.7768*	0.8596*	0.3897	0.7811*	1		
HDIE	0.361	0.423	0.7420*	0.6198*	0.7524*	0.6923*	0.7115*	1	
NSDP	0.185	0.5989*	0.6628*	0.6188*	0.4587	0.7249*	0.6834*	-0.1551	1

Note: RDI-Rural Decentralization Index; BSI-Borda count score for infrastructure service delivery; BSS-Borda count score for social service delivery; BSH-Borda count score for health service delivery; BSE-Borda count score for education service delivery; BSGG-Borda count score for overall good governance; HDIH is the health sub-indices of overall Human Development Index (HDI) of Indian states; HDIE is the education sub-indices of overall Human Development Index (HDI) of Indian states; NSDP-per capita net state domestic product – a measure of the level of development in the state* 5 per cent level of significance.

Source: Table 4.

Figure 2 *Extent of Decentralization and Score of Good Governance for Effective Services Delivery*

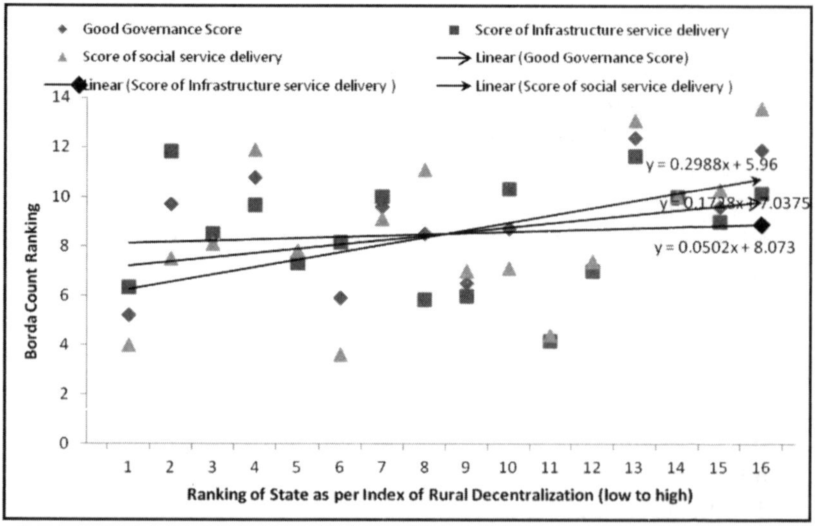

Source: Table 3 and 4.

Figure 3 *Extent of Decentralization and Score of Health and Education Services Delivery*

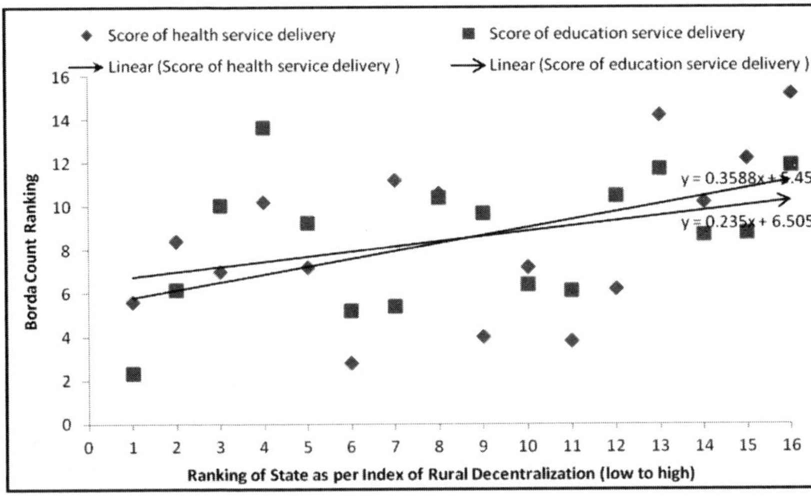

Source: Table 3 and 4.

The high association of the extent of decentralization in the delivery of health services motivates us to examine whether decentralization really improves the access to health care services, particularly amongst the low socio-economic stratum. That is, we would like to see whether extent of decentralization matter more for better access to health care in India. Examining the association between the decentralization and access to health care by socio-economic stratum, however, is not so easy to arrive. For the purpose, household level data on access to health care is required. To show such type of relationship this study uses the NSS 60th Round unit level data on health care utilization. The utilization (an indicator of access to health care) status then is examined by identifying the states with low and high decentralized states. The utilization of health care services for outpatient visit, Ante-natal (ANC), child delivery and child immunization received are examined in the study. The results show that the status of utilization for all type of care is recorded high in high decentralized (high than the average value of decentralization index) states as compared to low decentralized states. The percentage of child delivery in public facilities out of total delivery recorded nearly three times (about 30.1%) more in high decentralized states as compared to the low (only 10.8%) decentralized states (Table 6). The percentage of ANC received from public facility was found nearly double in high decentralized states (about

51.0%) as compared to low decentralized states (about 26.4%). Similar type of trends emerge in case of outpatient visit. The immunization services received by child (age 0–4 years) are also recorded high in high decentralized states (about 926 per 1000 child) as compared to low decentralized (about 894 per 1000 child) states. This shows that level of decentralization not only ensures effective delivery of health services but also ensures high access to health care utilization from public facility (which are more cost effective) in rural India.

The results also show that the status of utilization of different type of care from public facility is comparatively high amongst the low socio-economic stratum group (like the poorest quintiles and the SC/STs and OBC category) in rural area. Specifically, the status of utilization, like for child delivery, from public facility decreases with the level of income and the social status in high decentralized states. This means that states with high level of decentralization ensure high utilization of public services for child delivery amongst the poorest and the SC/STs as compared to their other counterparts. These trends, however, are not reflected in low decentralized states (Table 6). The rate of child immunization was also recorded high amongst the SC/STs and the poorest in high decentralized states as compared to low decentralized states. The lower quintiles and SC/STs women generally receive higher proportion of ANC services from government sources in high decentralized states as compared to the low decentralized states (Table 6).

It is also revealed from the data analysis that trends of outpatient visits in total visit increases with level of income and by social status. That is, it is the general population which tends to derive the maximum benefit of outpatient services. But, in high decentralized states, these outpatient visits, particularly in government facilities, are distributed in favour of the lower quintiles (Monthly Per Capita Expenditure-MPCE class) and SC/STs. That is, the SC/STs accounted for 33.9 per cent of outpatient treatment from government facilities and the general population about 20.5 per cent in high decentralization states. Across economic stratum it has been noticed that the poorest quintiles accounted about 29.4 per cent of outpatient treatment from government facilities whereas the richest quintiles about 27.7 per cent in high decentralized states. This may mean that the SCs/STs and the poorest quintiles (i.e. the population with low socio-economic status) have more reliance on the public provider. This reflects presumably the fact that outpatient services in public facilities are more readily accessible to priority population in area where the extent of decentralization is high.

Table 6

Decentralization and Access to Health Care Utilization by Socio-Economic Stratum (in %)

		Outpatient Visit (OPV)		ANC Services		Child Delivery		Child Immunization	
Socio-Economic Status		Low DIH	High DIH	Low DIH	High DIH	Low DIH	High DIH	Low DIH	High DIH
Social Status	SC/STs	22.7	33.9	33.9	53.9	9.3	32.1	882	933
	OBCs	14.1	27.7	22.6	54.2	11.0	35.6	885	914
	Others	18.8	20.5	21.2	45.6	13.3	22.5	916	933
Economic Status	Poorest	20.0	29.4	33.3	55.6	15.9	34.4	878	909
	II	17.9	28.9	23.9	54.5	7.4	34.7	895	927
	Middle	15.0	25.6	17.4	57.2	9.2	32.1	910	941
	IV	17.3	21.5	35.8	31.9	13.3	22.8	891	941
	Richest	18.5	27.7	25.5	54.0	8.9	24.3	906	930
Total		17.8	26.5	26.4	51.0	10.8	30.1	894	926

Note: Outpatient visit shows percentage of ailing members received treatment from government facility out of total who took treatment on medical advice during last 15 days; ANC is anti-natal care services which shows percentage of ANC received from government facility out of total pregnant women (who received ANC from public + private + not received) during last 365 days; child delivery is percentage of child delivery in public facility out of total (public + private + home) delivery during last 365 days; and child immunization includes number of children (age 0–4 years) per 1,000 children received basic immunization services during last 365 days. DIH is devolution index to health, estimated using health related funds, functions and functionaries powers to PRIs (for details see Hooda, SK, 2012).

Source: Utilization data is taken from NSS 60th Round Unit Level records

The status of utilization is recorded high amongst the poor and the SC/STs than their other counterparts in high decentralized states in comparison. The states with low level of decentralization, however, were unable to ensure the same pattern of utilization. This reflects that the high level of decentralization does not only ensures high level of utilization from public facilities but also addresses the issue of equity in utilizing the health care services in the rural area.

The study goes further to show the relationship between decentralization and health outcomes at the individual state level. For the purpose, the association between the extent of decentralization and infant mortality rate of rural area is presented in Figure 4. The results show that the extent of decentralization (on funds, functions and functionaries powers) is negatively associated with the rural IMR (Figure 4). This indicates that high level of decentralization leads to low infant mortality rate in the rural areas. The correlation between these two variables turns highly significant (significant at 5% level) with

Figure 4 *Decentralization and Rural IMR: An Association*

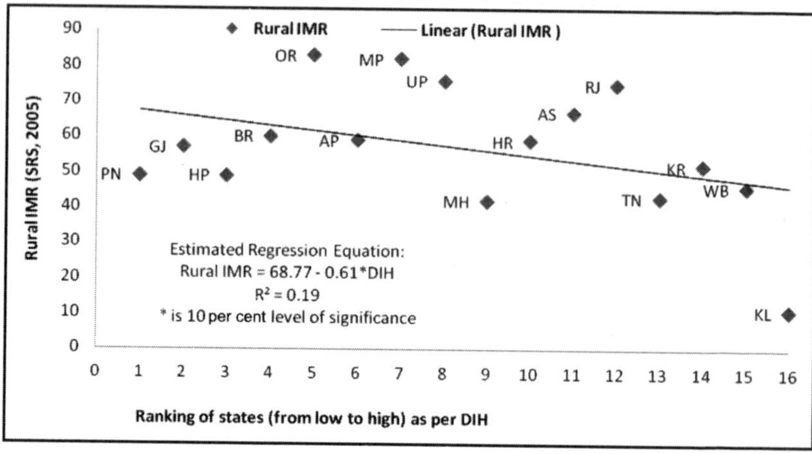

Note: The DIH is devolution index to health, estimated using devolution of health related funds, functions and functionaries powers to PRIs (for details see Hooda, SK, 2012)

coefficient value about –0.43. The regression coefficient between these variables show basis point increment in the value of decentralization reduces the infant mortality rate in the rural area by –0.61 with 10 per cent level of significance. Thus, decentralization leads to lower infant mortality rate in the rural area.

This analysis shows that decentralization does not only help in improving the effective delivery of health services but also addresses the issue of equity and further helps in reducing the infant mortality rates in the rural area of India. These findings meet the expectation of different policy dialogue, particularly the objective of Primary Health Care Approach, National Health Policy and National Rural Health Mission and MDGs. That is, decentralization particularly ensures high status of service utilization amongst the priority population and effective service delivery with greater equity as per the population needs. These findings have some profound implications for policy initiatives. That is, government needs to promote decentralized structure of health service delivery in the rural India. This will ensure the financial protection to the needy population in the rural India.

Association between Decentralization, Good Governance and Development

The extent of decentralization associated positively with the level of development, measured in terms of per capita NSDP, of a state (Figure

5). The correlation coefficient value between these two turned around 0.185 (Table 5) and regression coefficient around 0.02 (Figure 5). This indicates that decentralization, however, associated positively with the level of development but its coefficient value shows that this association is not significant. Interestingly, the score value of good governance even shows high positive correlated with level of development (Table 5 and Figure 6). The correlation coefficient value turned around 0.72 with 5 per cent level of significance (Table 5).

Figure 5 *Decentralization and Development*

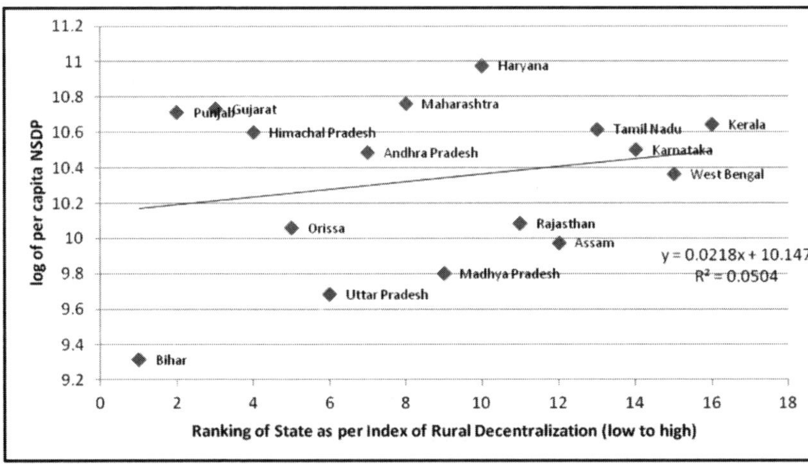

Source: Authors' estimation

Figure 6 *Governance and Development*

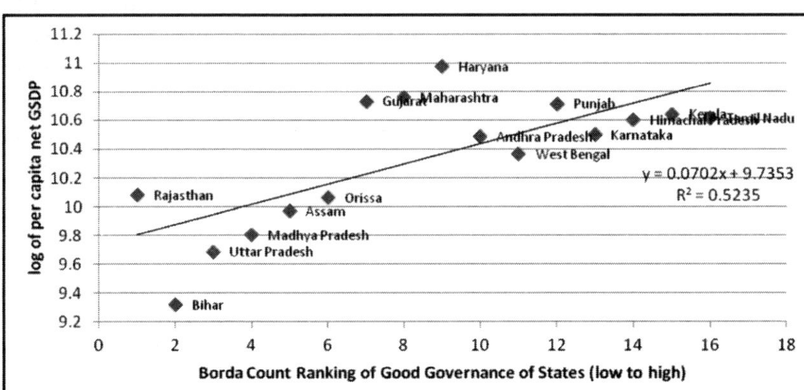

Source: Authors' estimation

It emerges from our analysis that decentralization first leads to good governance (or better service delivery), this then leads to high level of development in Indian states. That is, there exists a nexus between decentralization, governance and development in Indian states. This can be understood from the following nexuses.

Decentralization ⇒ Good Governance ⇒ Development

The high inter-correlation between governance and development may be partly because of their mutual interaction through feedback effects and partly because of development and governance having the same underlying drivers. For instance, higher income may facilitate better governance through larger pools of public resources in economic and social services. Equally, more efficient allocation of public resources in cases of good governance can also eventually lead to higher incomes. Such co-movement and interdependence of development and governance has led to the Besley and Persson (2011), and Mundle (2012), concept of development clusters. This correlation between governance and development is also confirmed in our analysis of the effective delivery (governance) in Indian states.

Conclusions

The analysis of the association between extent of decentralization, development and governance shows that a well-designed and proper implemented decentralized policy leads to good governance and high level of development in a particular state. Specifically, the high level of decentralization leads to better delivery of services at the local level in terms of better infrastructure delivery, education attainment and health standard, high human development, etc. The extent (high) of decentralization even turns effective in providing the financial protection to a needy (poor) person by ensuring high access to publically provided health facilities (which are more cost-effective).

Further, the level of good governance (measured through effective service delivery) is highly correlated with high level of development. That is, governance leads to high level of development in the country. Thus, it can be argued that a well-designed and proper implemented decentralized policy ensures effective delivery of services, good governance and high level of development across the Indian states. Therefore, decentralized delivery structure is highly advocated for effective delivery system. However, inadequate devolution of funds, functions and functionaries powers to local bodies at the same time can limit the local panchayat to perform better, which has also emerged from our analysis, therefore needs to be strengthened in every Indian state.

References

Alok, V.N. and Bhandari, L. (2004). 'Rating the Policy and Functional Environment of PRIs in Different States of India: A Concept Paper', paper presented at the Fifth Roundtable of Ministers in Charge of Panchayati Raj, Srinagar, India, October 28–29, retrieved from http://www.panchayat.gov.in.

Besley, T. and Persson, T. (2011). *Pillars of Prosperity*, Princeton University Press, Princeton.

Center for Democracy and Governance (2000). *Decentralization and Democratic Local Governance Programming Handbook*, Technical Publication Series, US. Agency for International Development.

Charlick, Robert (1992). *The Concept of Governance and its Implications for AID Development Assistance Program in Africa*, Associates in Rural Development, Washington, D.C., p. 16.

Ebimaro, Sampson (2006). 'Why Performance-Oriented Political Decentralization Matters in Good Governance and Sustainable Development: Comparison between Japan and Nigeria', retrieved from net.

Gill, J. and Gainous, J. (2002). 'Why Does Voting Get So Complicated? A Review of Theories for Analysing Democratic Participation', *Statistical Science*, 17 (4): 383–404.

Government of India (2000). *Report of 11th Finance Commission*, Ministry of Finance, GoI 2000–2005, New Delhi.

——. (2004). *National Sample Survey Organization (NSSO): Sixtieth Round on Morbidity and Health Care (Schedule 25.0)*, January–June, New Delhi.

——. (2009). *The State of Panchayats: An Independent Assessment 2007–08*, Ministry of Panchayati Raj, New Delhi.

——. (various years). *State Election Report of Various States*, Election Commission of India, New Delhi.

Green, Keith (2005). 'Decentralization and Good Governance: The Case of Indonesia', MPRA Paper No. 18097, Munich Personal RePEc Archive.

Grindle, Merilee S. (2007). 'Good Enough Governance Revisited', *Development Policy Review*, 25 (5).

Hooda, S.K. (2012). 'Decentralization and Financing of Public Health Care Services in Rural India: A State Level Analysis', Unpublished Thesis, Jawaharlal Nehru University, New Delhi.

John, M.S. and Chathukulam, J. (2003). 'Measuring Decentralisation: The Case of Kerala (India)', *Public Administration and Development*, 23 (4), October: 347–60.

Johnson, Ronald W. and Minis, Henry P. (2000). *Toward Democratic Decentralization: Approaches to Promoting Good Governance*, World Bank, Washington, D.C.

Kearney, Christine (1999). 'Decentralization Index', December 30, retrieved from http://www.econ.brown.edu/faculty/henderson/decentralization.pdf

Kundu, A. (1984). *Measurement of Urban Processes: A Study in Regionalisation*, Popular Prakashan, Bombay.

La Porta, R., Lopez-de-Silanes, F., Shleifer, A. and Vishny, R. (1999). 'The Quality of Government', *Journal of Law, Economics and Organisation*, 15 (1).

Landell-Mills, P. and Serageldin, I. (1991). *Governance and the External Factor*, World Bank Annual Conference, Washington, D.C.

Litvack, Jennie, Ahmad, Junaid and Bird, Richard (1998). *Rethinking Decentralization in Developing Countries*, World Bank, Washington, D.C.

MoPRI (2006). *The State of Panchayats: A Mid Term Review and Appraisal Report*, Ministry of Panchayati Raj, Vols I, II & III.

Mundle, S., Chakraborty, Pinaki, Chowdhury, Samik and Sikdar, Satadru (2012). 'The Quality of Governance: How Have Indian States Performed?', *Economic and Political Weekly*, XLVII (49), December 8.

NCAER (2007). *An Index of Devolution for Assessing Environment for Panchayati Raj Institutions in the States*, National Council of Applied Economic Research, New Delhi.

Nharnet Team (2005). *Decentralized Governance, a Global Sampling of Experiences*, UNDP Monograph on Decentralization.

Oommen, M.A. (2006). 'Fiscal Decentralisation to the Sub-State Level Government', *Economic and Political Weekly*, March 11.

Oyugi, W.O. (2000). *Decentralization for Good Governance and Development: The Unending Debate*, United Nations Centre for Regional Development, Geneva.

Rao, G.M. and Rao, UA. (2007). 'Expanding the Resource Envelop of Panchayats: Augmenting Own Revenues', paper presented at NIPFP, New Delhi.

Sandler, T. (2001). *Economic Concepts for the Social Sciences*, Cambridge University Press, Cambridge.

World Bank (2000). *Overview of Rural Decentralization in India*, Vol. 1.

7

From Development-Induced Displacement to the Verge of Migration

A Case Study of Displaced Santali Women in Bankura District of West Bengal

BHASWATI THAKURTA

The concept of development-induced displacement historically is associated with the construction of dams for hydroelectric power and irrigation purpose. Other factors are mining, construction of industrial plants, and conservation projects, etc. Development-induced displacement is a social problem affecting multiple levels of human organization, from tribal and village communities to well developed urban areas. According to Michael M. Cernea, the main causes of development-induced displacement include water supply (construction of dams, artificial reservoirs, irrigation projects), urban infrastructure, transportation (roads, highways, canals); energy (mining, power plants, oil exploration and extraction, pipelines), agriculture expansion, parks and forest reserves and population redistribution schemes (Cernea, 1999).

The climate change is the result of exploitation of nature. Sea-level rise and loss of coastal wetlands and mangroves have increased the damage due to coastal flooding which is a result of unsustainable human developments. Millions of people are projected to be flooded annually due to sea-level rise. Densely-populated and low-lying areas are especially at risk. Their adaptive capacity is relatively low and they have other challenges as well, such as tropical storms. Due to deforestation, annual rainfall decreased and agriculture suffered, it also gave rise to the problem of water scarcity.

If we ponder on the factors of displacement and migration, development and climate change, these two factors, are interrelated and human species are acting as a facilitator in the process of climate change by the name of development which is unsustainable in the mask of sustainability. In this regard, we have to put a little bit emphasis of the term 'Hu-man', who is acting as a facilitator in the process of policy-making. The designers of the project are men. Their conventional method is not only due to insensitive planning but also the result of inequality in the society. The structure that we call society or the institution has given a very particular and unequal stand for women and all the marginals (including both men and women).

Generally, the flow of the wave is towards development to climate change. Displacement also undergoes a drastic alteration in the form of migration caused by climate change directly and indirectly by some unsustainable plans.

Figure 1 *The Interconnected Incidents which Lead to Displacement and Migration*

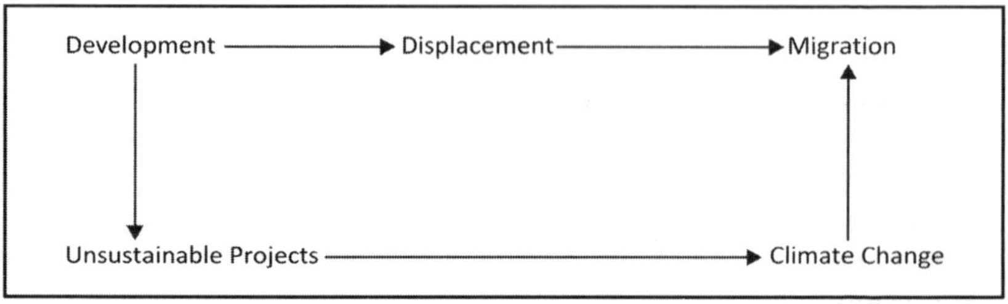

Since displacement is the sub set of migration, this study focuses on development as a displacement factor and climate change as a migration factor.

Research Methodology

The field research has been done in two villages; in one of them the whole community has been displaced and in the other, some families. The villages are *Dharashole* in *Beliatore Forest Range* and *Malibonya* in *Pirrorgarhi Forest Range* of Bankura North and South division, respectively. The one-to-one interviews of the community women and informal chat are the main source of the collection of their story. The old women of the village as well as new women members in the community that arrived from other tribal villages through matrimonial relations are the focus group. The Old women focus on the hardship of displacement and the initial struggle of settling in the new place and the young women are concerned about the climate change factors like poor agriculture due to less rainfall, water scarcity, increased deforestation, and elephant attack which at times compel them to ponder on migration.

Gender Issue in Development and Displacement and the Context of Re-settlement

Gender is a powerful social and cultural construct determining the ways in which social relations are structured between men and women. Gender is central to how societies assign roles, responsibilities, resources and rights between men and women (Mehta and Srinivasan, 2000). Gender is not merely about bodies; it also includes the institutionalization of masculine and feminine values in the practices of organizations, institutions and the state. Gendered values and practices, thus, have the potential of marginalizing certain groups of people, including peasants of developing countries, tribals, women and poor. In the context of development projects, gender becomes especially significant for several reasons. Gender and class (class/race) based division of labour, distribution of property and power, structure people's interactions with nature and in the process structure effects of environmental change on people and their responses to it (Agarwal, 1996). The differences in the divisions of power, labour and property, based upon perceived and ritualized gender differences, result in women and men of the same class-experiencing environment in different ways; hence, having a different knowledge of the environment. For example, peasants and rural women, especially poor, play a crucial role as providers, producers and managers. As such, these women experience displacement in a specifically gendered way as it affects their everyday lives.

Gender is also an indicator of the so-called development. If we look at the true positive side of development, which includes the equality of genders, class, caste, which is hard to achieve by nature but still we can easily make out that gender is one of the indicators or controlling factors. If development does not change women's lives then it is not a true development. State institutions often end up marginalizing women because of their ignorance as to what constitutes gender sensitive programmes that are suitable to local needs of the people. The standpoint to look at the context of the displaced community of santals and the women is based on the parameters of both caste and gender discrimination.

Gender in Local Context of *Santal* Community in Bankura

The *Santal* (also spelled as *Santhal*) are the largest tribal community in India and live mainly in the states of Jharkhand, West Bengal, Bihar, Orrisa. Santali women are central to the economy of their society. They take part in agricultural production, gather forest produce, do wage labour where available (from government or forest department works, *Tendu*[1], *Shal*[2] leaf and road contractors, etc.) and almost singly handled bear the whole burden of domestic work, child-rearing, rearing of cattle/livestock, going to markets to sell their produce, do the marketing for their families, etc. In one word, except those tasks which are a taboo for them, they do all the work.

There seems to be fairly firmly defined and gender-based division of house maintenance tasks. Men repair the roof, but women are in charge of wall maintenance. Close female relatives often work together. Walls are plastered with mud and rice or wheat straw twice a year. Every five to eight years, women demolish part of the house and rebuild it with new walls. Women are also in charge of making tiles. This type of work is usually done in June, before the onset of the monsoon and prior to peak times in agriculture.

Importantly, however, in most of the regions, in most of the tribes Santali women have no property rights over land. While Santal families survive predominantly on account of women's work, it is primarily men who have full usufructory and other rights over land and other resources. But customary law has allowed women usufructory rights to some extent.

According to a report prepared by the British ruler, Gautzer on the *Santhal Paraganas* during 1922 to 1935, called the *Gautzer's Settlement Report*, in *Santhali Adivasi Law* only males can inherit land, where sons jointly succeed their father. An unmarried daughter has no right in the immovable property. A widow has no claim on her deceased husband's property if there are male relatives. If a widow does not remarry, then her rights to maintenance will continue. There is no uniform customary law for Santal and it often varies across villages and could be significantly different between areas.

The Report on the Committee on the Status of Women in India (CSWI) – Towards Equality (1974), on the one hand, made a review a prevailing unequal status of women in the country with the help of empirical evidences and, on the other hand, made feasible recommendations for removal of the same to achieve the goals enshrined in the Constitution (Banerjee, 1995).

The Report dwelt at length on the situation of poverty in the country and on the large concentration of women in unorganized sectors, and emphasized that women in poverty should receive priority in all measures to promote and sustain women's equality. A project was initiated by the International Labour Organization in the *Ranibandh* block of Bankura district in collaboration with the Centre for Women's Development Studies, New Delhi, in 1981. They did initial study on tribal communities especially on the Santals of the region. The *Ranibandh* is the part of the most underdeveloped part of Bankura, which is not far from the *Kangshabati Dam*; it is situated in the same block. The area has a large concentration of tribal populations. Originally a part of the vast area known as *Junglemahal* (forest area), it used to be inhabited mainly by Santals, a forest-dwelling tribe.

During the last three centuries, other people also came in as settlers, forests disappeared even more rapidly in the 20th century, and soil erosion was faster on the hilly slopes. Even cultivable land became increasingly less productive and droughts were frequent.

Over the last few decades, thousands of men and women and children had taken to seasonal migration to the green revolution districts of Hooghly and Burdwan for employment in agriculture. The local bureaucracy believed that such migration gave them a taste of higher standards of living in the developed regions, hence its popularity among women and children. The tribals had main grievance was against the forest policy of the government. For the tribal women, forests provided the basic means of livelihood. They used to collect free of cost fruits, flowers or leaves of *Mahua,*[3] *Peasal,*[4] *Kendu*[5] and others. They used to gather leaves and brushwood and other minor forest produce without paying any charges. But during the last three decades, gradually their customary rights had been abrogated. They were harassed, prosecuted, insulted and above all were deprived of their supplemental income from forest (Bandyopadhyay, 1980).

Deforestation had left them no option other than *namal* (in *Santali* language seasonal migration). The wages were of ₹ 8.00 per day, paid partly in cash and partly in food grains, fuel, salt and oil. The recruited labour occasionally found temporary shelters in the work place, provided by the employers. The pace of work was set by the regular attached labour, and any woman or adolescent who fell behind would be sacked on the spot but would have to wait till the end of the season to be paid along with the rest. Infant mortality, abortions and a gradual loss of health were common. Sexual molestation by the employer or his recruiting agent was a fact of life and a price that often had to be paid when one needed work desperately (Mazumdar, 1998).

Alienated from their traditional habitat and deprived of local brews made of *Mahua* with cash in hand, the men spent much of their wages on other more harmful and costly liquors. The net savings that a woman could bring home after a trek ranged between ₹ 30–70, much of which generally went to repay their debts (Mazumdar, 1998).

During their absence, because the old people left behind could not take adequate care, their few livestock disappeared, or their uninhabited houses collapsed during heavy rain. So they had to borrow again to repair homes, or replace their lost goods. The surviving children, trekking with their mothers three or four times a year, could never get to school.

Nor did they ever acquire the forest lore and skills which had helped their grandparents and parents to survive in earlier days. The disorganization of their lives also precipitated the destruction of other social norms. Eviction and desertion of wives and children by husbands had become widespread, wife-beating had increased and women could not get justice from the traditional caste/tribal councils. In any case, the councils had lost their influence over the younger generation.

Development, Displacement, Climate Change and Migration

In 1956, a giant water dam reservoir was planned at *Mukutmonipur*, (about 12 km from *Khatra* town in the district of Bankura, WB), under a big vision mooted by the then Chief Minister of Bengal, Dr Bidhan Chandra Roy. The *Mukutmonipur Dam* was planned to provide major irrigation facilities to 8,000 sq km of agricultural land, stretched across Bankura, Purulia, Paschim Medinipur and parts of upper Hoogly. Approximately 2 km from the lake is the *Bangopalpur Reserve Forest*, a home of many species of flora and fauna. Kangshabati Reservoir Project has an irrigation potential of 3, 48,477 ha, covers the districts of Bankura, Midnapore and Hooghly. The project was taken 25 years back when the CWDS did the study of the dwellers of the *Ranibandh* block.

My recent visits are in those villages where they were resettled. The picture of the rest of the Bankura is different as far as standard of living has been concerned but the climate change factor is affecting them adversely.

Dharashole

The village of Dharashole was formed in 1957 when they had to leave their village in Mukutmanipur named *Kusumkumandihi*. They were forced to displace and they came to the Barmashiya forest of *Beliatore* Forest Range. By nature they are forest dwellers, so they select that place that was under the *mouza* of the *Baromashiya* forest. The place was full with *Shal* tree but illegal felling was going on. They had to buy the land from the government to settle down amidst the forest. The scope of work was limited so they cut some portion of the land they had acquired for the cultivation, which depends on the seasonal rain. The Kangshabati project does not help them directly for agricultural irrigation. Though the project promises many villages the irrigation facility, one can find the dry canals in the villages throughout the year.

The illegal felling was out of control and government declared a new plan called Joint Forest Management where both the community and the forest department would protect the forest. They got a piece of forest land for protection. Other villages are not Santal infested. The felling under the protection of FPC is not uncommon.

Patumani Hansda told us, 'in the place where we are living, rainfall is less; forest is decreasing highly; elephants are coming frequently and damaging our harvest. We are not afraid of the animals but since they do not have forest to dwell they will come and destroy our property because we destroyed their house, the forest.

My parents chose this place to live but the place was not arid from the beginning and now since the forest land decreased drastically so the rainfall reduced, the agriculture that we are dependent on depends on seasonal rain, which is also making our living very tough. The seasonal elephant attack is also a part of major discomfort. Majority of the villagers is still landless; they depend on forest products for daily livelihood. Even village men went to the small town as a contractual labour. The source of drinking water in the village is unimaginable. The dark muddy water is used for cleaning and washing, the well in the village is the only source of drinking water, which is in the process of drying. The situation in summer is unbearable for us'.

According to *Phulmani Hansda, Patumani's* daughter-in-law, she was extremely disturbed about the elephant attack in the area when the agricultural land is ready to harvest. Her husband works as contractual labour in the town and she is also highly active in FPC and the minor forest-based business.

According to her, if the system of the protection of the forest with the Forest Department can be done properly then it will be effective for the climate as well. Majority of the family in this village are landless. After the intervention of the Forest Rights Act, they got some vested land. But since the weather is changing rapidly due to disappearing forest then the cultivation in the vested land, which is solely dependent on the seasonal rainfall, is impossible. So they are not benefitted by this act also. The regular felling of the forest according to the working plan of the FPC they benefitted highly. The women's role in the forest protection is very important for the income from the Minor Forest Products and the Felling. The Minor Forest Product-based income is very important for the regular household expenses.

Malibonya

The *Malibonya* village is a tribal village from the beginning and some displaced *Santal* family came to live here. They were easily accepted by the village community. According to them they did not have land yet and the changing weather and scarcity of the work and drinking water insist them to migrate. In the existing Forest Management System, during felling they earn but apart from that the rate of employment is very low. They even do not have the *patta* yet according to the Forest Rights Act.

According to *Lakshmi Hembram* the life was not easy on those days when we are displaced. 'We roam here and there. We are tribals and forest is everything for us. We cannot live without forest. At last we landed in this village'. In JFM, the villagers have to protect a piece of forest land. The FPC here is run by tribal women whereas in *Dharashole* it was run by men but women are more active. The Santal women's contribution in JFM changes the state of their livelihood, the forest where protected (the area they got) is dense and according to the working plan of the JFM the annual felling give them good amount of money.

But how much they try to conserve their area, the rest of neighbouring villages due to different attitude towards forest are not protecting it properly. The community perspective regarding conservation of neighbouring village is less so they are cutting the forest and not protecting them, so automatically the slow process of climate change is set on and elephant problem has increased. The Santali women's initiative is very minuscule if we compare to the rest of male Forest Protection Committees'. Women's function in male Forest Protection Committee is restricted due to certain patriarchal norms, which is not allowing women to work efficiently in joint forestry, so the whole system is suffering as an inevitable result of these consequences and people are willing to migrate.

Lakshmi Hembram was crying while sharing her feelings of having to migrate to the city. The fear of city life and sorrow of leaving the village which was chosen by her husband is, indeed, very painful at this age.

Patumani's eyes also filled with tears while caressing her grandson: 'This place was arid but chosen by our parents, but my grandson's family will not be able to stay here for long. We will not be able to connect ourselves with the nature, with the forest anymore, and we have to be like city dwellers and live the life in city forgetting our ethnic identity and cultural life. We are heading towards a future where we will not be able to maintain our language, custom, everything we are going to lose.'

Conclusion

The *Kangshabati* Reservoir project case study applied a culture-based understanding of *Mukutmonipur* Dam displacement processes in Bankura district of West Bengal through the lens of women. The study asked the question: How do women experience displacement and relocation in the dam project? In a region where women and children make up the majority of displaced population, insensitivity to the needs of women has shaped post-rehabilitation programmes in a way where women face impoverishment, income decline, and leads to destitution. The eight interlinked potential risks intrinsic to displacement identified in Cernea's model as landlessness, joblessness, homelessness, marginalization, food insecurity, increased morbidity and mortality, loss of access to common property and social integration manifest themselves in the daily lives of these displaced women.

They suffer from joblessness and homelessness as many of them live in faraway places; they have lost their own traditional houses and they build new ones with such a hardship because initially they had to stay under the thatched roof. They suffer from a loss of access to commons, which creates fodder and fuel wood shortage and decline in income and food diversity. Women face even further hardship when community support structures disintegrate and family and kinship networks break down. Systems of care, protection, compensation, resettlement and rehabilitation remain largely insensitive to women's needs leading to a fundamentally disenfranchising experience.

In this patriarchal society, women have been denied compensation for land that they cultivate for years but did not have a registration in their name. Cases of ineligibility have been identified in many women headed households and widows, specially these categories of women had faced major hardship in resettlement. Men are the recognized heads of household; therefore, support from the local authority and the village heads for permission to stay in the village was easy if the family is men headed. But in *Santal* community there are many women headed families, they just disappeared. Since the incident is long back they even not able to sustain and nobody know about them. Even *Patumani* or *Lakshmi*, they were unknown about the fate of the women headed households and widows.

The resettlement process is fraught with impoverishment risks (Cernea, 1999). Women are forced into adopting a culture they have never known, and limitations in their social space have prevented them from rebuilding their daily practices in a new environment. Thus, women remain marginalized at the community level as well as at the national level policy-framework because of their disadvantageous position ascribed by patriarchal gender relations, traditionally excluding women from political participation, even at the community level. The narratives of women clearly brought out the insensitivity of state discourses to the needs of women. All policies are conceptualized with male biases in mind, although the national rehabilitation and resettlement policy acknowledges gender as a category. The processes of displacement transform the everyday lives of women from a community owned network to individual private property ownership that undermines the socio-economic status of women. State policies should take into consideration these problems to enable participation of women and move towards gender justice. Ensuing narrative-based approach highlights the concerns of women affected by displacement processes for consideration by policy planners while making decisions that make far reaching transformations in the lives of women in the name of development and public purpose.

Apart from the development and displacement part, the Forest Policy that was adapted were not even women friendly even if they are more connected than their fellow partner to the forest. In the tribal community, both men and women are concerned about the conservation but women are more connected to it than men, but other Forest Protection Committee members are not dedicated like them so illegal felling carries on that results into climate change. Insufficient rainfall adversely affects the seasonal agriculture of the tribal community. Since they are not benefited by *Kangshabati* Canal but *Kangshabati* project displaced them and now the recent situation insists them to migrate again. Even in family the men went to the city for better earning opportunity. The displaced women in both *Dharashole* and *Malibonya* came with their parents or husbands, namely 'Male Guardian' of the village. They were not heads of the family. They cannot even remember the fate of the women-headed households in the time of displacement.

Women never got the importance from the policy makers even in Joint Forest Management in India. It is not unknown to them that women spent the majority of their time in forest and the daily expenses of their families were earned from selling Minor Forest Product, but still they are not a part of Forest Management System. Despite the fact that after many protests against the government policy, women were included in the system but still a gap remained between the policy and its implementation. It has been observed that women controlled FPC works more efficiently than men-run FPC in Bankura. Women do not control all the FPCs, therefore it is quite inevitable that deforestation will go on which will adversely influence the climate, agriculture, and animal attack in the region. Some tribal pockets are green thick patch of forest. Displaced women's role in forest protection and their efforts to make the environment favourable for the living is, indeed, an unequal struggle against the factors forcing them to migrate. No one can tell that how long they will resist.

Notes

1. Tendu – Botanical name *Diospyros Melanoxylon.*
2. Shal – Botanical name *Shorea Robusta.*
3. Mahua – Botanical name *Madhuca Longifolia.*
4. Piasal – Botanical name *Pterocarpus Marsupium.*
5. Kendu – Another name of Tendu.

   All the botanical names are taken from H. Mukherji, *Plant Groups,* New Central Book Agency Private Limited, Kolkata, 1982.

References

Agarwal, B. (1996). *A Field of One's Own: Gender and Land Rights in South Asia,* Cambridge University Press, Cambridge.

Bandyopadhyay, D. (1980). *Travails of Tribal Women,* CWDS, New Delhi.

Banerjee, K.N. (1995). 'Grassroot Empowerment (1975–1990)', A Discussion Paper, CWDS, New Delhi.

Cernea, Michael (1999). 'Why Economic Analysis is Essential to Resettlement: A Sociologist's View', in Michael Cernea (ed.), *The Economics of Involuntary Resettlement: Questions and Challenges,* Chapter 1, World Bank, Washington, D.C., pp. 5–38.

Government of India (1974). *Towards Equality: Report of the Committee on the Status of Women in India,* New Delhi.

Mazumdar, Vina (1998). *Peasant Women Organise for Empowerment: The Bankura Experiment,* CWDS, New Delhi.

Mehta, L. and Srinivasan, B. (2000). 'The Double Bind: A Gender Analysis of Forced Displacement and Resettlement', in Lyla Mehta (ed.), *Displaced by Development: Confronting Marginalisation and Gender Justice,* Chapter 1, Manohar Publications, New Delhi, pp. 3–33.

8

From Colonial Rule to Panchayati Raj

A Study of the Changing Economy in a North Indian Village, Circa 1930–2010

DEVESH VIJAY

The 20th century witnessed momentous transformation in India which had an impact on our villages too. Changes in colonial land settlements, unprecedented peasant mobilization for the freedom struggle and other mass movements, growth of modern transportation and, above all, the abolition of zamindari along with the introduction of a modern Constitution as well as adult franchise and the recent media and communication boom have had a major impact on the way age-old patterns of economic and social relations operate in the countryside now. The economic transformation brought by the 'green' and 'white' revolutions, the growing integration of the rural and urban population and the slow but historic growth of rural roads, electricity, irrigation, vehicles, agricultural machinery and literacy in the past century are hallmarks of this historic churning. No doubt, poverty, stark inequality and dearth of basic facilities persist in most Indian villages. While rural India contributes less than a fourth of India's gross domestic product, it still engages nearly two third of our population. The resultant maze of change and continuity in village, India thus cries out for a close look from social scientists and policy makers at the turn of the new millennium.

Existing Research

While village studies have had a rich tradition in India since colonial times, long term restudies of villages and their economic structure across generations have been scarce in the country.[1] Early 20th century works such as those of the Wisers in Uttar Pradesh and Slater in Tamil Nadu, which have been followed up by some recent scholars have been useful in this context. Their numbers, however, are extremely small.[2] On the other hand, recent sociological works which have analysed class, caste and power relations in villages in detail have often lacked historical depth.[3] Thirdly, attempts at comparing short span village reports also lead us to conflicting viewpoints in our extremely diverse continent.[4] Did the abolition of zamindari and the introduction of agricultural land ceilings after Independence bring about significant changes in local hierarchies as well as agricultural productivity? Has recent liberalization of the Indian economy led to further 'immiserization' of rural labour or created fresh opportunities for many? To what extent has legislation for women's empowerment actually eroded traditional patriarchal relations among different communities? Questions such as these call for extensive restudies of several villages when the Indian countryside is going through accelerating change now.

The Context

As a small contribution in this field, the present work attempts a sketch of change in one village of western Uttar Pradesh during the past 80 years based on a multi method approach with special focus on its changing economy. The name of the studied village is Dhantala. It is situated in the Meerut district of Uttar Pradesh at a distance of about 90 kms from central Delhi. Lying midway between the townships of Mohiddinpur and Kharkoda, this village has been traditionally dominated by Gurjar and Jat landowners. Helped by a family of sweepers that had moved from Dhantala to a slum called Aradhaknagar (in my neighbourhood in Delhi), I managed some boarding and lodging support in the said village when I visited it first, in 1989, while completing my M.Phil. dissertation on migrant labourers in my city.[5]

Dhantala's dwellings are concentrated in a central core of about 200 acres of which roughly sixty acres are residential while the rest consist of common spaces including four schools, a panchayat hall, three temples, three cremation grounds and one graveyard and two ponds. This core is surrounded by agricultural fields spread over 1300 acres approximately, especially towards the east and the south of the built up area.[6]

The residential quarters are further subdivided between *varna* or broader caste groups. While middle castes, including Gurjars and Kumhars live together along major lanes of the village, Muslims and dalits have more excluded clusters. Among Gurjars also, two competing factions (of ex pradhans—Bhagmal and Tekram) are concentrated along separate sides of the hamlet. Similarly, among dalits, Jatavs and Valmikis have adjacent but different clusters. There are a few shops in Dhantala of grocers, artisans, etc. but almost all operate from small rooms facing village lanes from within houses.

Demography

Of the total population of 2,650 in the village, in 2011, about 40 per cent were below 12 years and 13 per cent were above 60 years old. Females made up 45 per cent of the community. The principal castes and communities were upper middle castes or Gurjars and Jats (56%) and lower middle castes or Kumhars and Khatiks (11%).[7] Among others, the dalits or scheduled castes made up 25 per cent including Jatavs (20%) and Valmikis (5%), while Muslims constitute approximately 10 per cent of the population. There is only one upper caste (Bania) family living in Dhantala now, though in early decades there was another Bania and a Brahmin family too.

In 1989, at the time of my first visit to Dhantala, the village had roughly the same communities in similar proportions. However, the population at that time was 2080. The rise in Dhantala's population in preceding 20 years was thus 30 per cent which could have been more but for the emigration of about 100 families to cities such as Delhi and Noida, where population has more than doubled in last two decades.

Precise estimates of numbers living in Dhantala in the early decades of the 20th century could not be tracked by me. Yet, a rough estimate based on district collectorate's land records (available since 1936 in Urdu Language) and the recollections of nonagenarians like Suraj Bhan and Parmanand in Dhantala suggest that the total population of the village at the beginning of our study period was about 800 which had risen to just 1200 by the time of Independence. This indicates approximately four fold rise in Dhantala's population between 1930 and 2011.

Methods

As my aim was to chart the nature of economic changes in one village over the past century along with an account of its changing demography, a multi-method approach incorporating both historical and sociological tools was found relevant. But any effort to combine several methods in research throws up many challenges. In this light, it would be apt to specify the methodological tools applied in the present study along with their respective strengths and limitations.

Written documents – official or personal – constitute a major source of information about the human past specially on events like wars, rulers, revolts, etc. which often attract widespread comment. On subjects like everyday life and slow changes in the economic structure of rural communities, however, archival materials rarely shed enough light. Similarly, local documents like family letters, receipts and diaries also remain inadequate bases for reconstructing the past of semi-literate communities. In the present study, some documents available with old families of Dhantala, as also the land records available from 1936 at the collectorate office in Meerut city, provided significant information on the changing economy at the local level. Yet, a comprehensive account of such history required use of oral history and field surveys too.

Among field methods, quantitative surveys, structured interviews and participant observation have been specially used by sociologists and anthropologists to understand present day social patterns. We have also applied these tools to assess the current shape of demographic and economic shifts as shown in the following sections. But in addition to personal interviews and conversations, we found the technique of group discussions and attending villagers *baithaks* or group sittings very useful since such conversations were not only informative but also more convincing and self-corrective as villagers often shared a lot of information in these and often highlighted incorrect claims of others too.

It may also be noted here that in our attempt to combine quantitative and qualitative research methods during fieldwork, the problem of numeric estimates based on shifting oral evidence was faced. As calculating yields, price ranges wage differentials and rentals, etc. over decades in precise figures based on subjects' recall is open to lapses and constant variation, it is common amongst anthropologists to bypass numerical estimates altogether. I have tried to resist this retreat and have offered as much quantitative evidence on Dhantala's demography and economy as possible but with the strong rejoinder that these estimates can be seen only as broad indicators and not as precise reflections on matters concerned.

Besides quantitative surveys, another ethnographic tool which has been used in the present report as a mirror of changing economic structures is that of life sketches or multiple but short accounts of substantial stretches of individual lives as narrated by subjects themselves and covering a broad spectrum of class, gender and age locations in the community. The full text of these sketches is not being presented here for want of space but when viewed in a comparative frame across generations, these life sketches become a useful lens on changing economic patterns across three generations or about eight decades. Lastly, to get a glimpse into economic changes in the previous century, the tools of oral history, including group discussion as well as individual memoirs and semi structured interviews, were found extremely useful.

Early History and Economy

Before we examine mutations in economic relations in Dhantala over the previous century, it would be useful to note the major turns in the history and material landscape of this village. Many of these are preserved in community lore while some find mention in local histories and family lore and official records also.[8] The family histories transmitted orally or noted in genealogies (called *vanshavalees*), which have been preserved across centuries by 'Bhats' (coming to Dhantala from Baghpat), give us an idea of the village's growth over time. Some elders in Dhantala also kept a record of such information and helped in reconstructing an outline of their past. Besides this, local histories of castes as well as the region around Meerut have been noted by chroniclers like N.T. Parker and Yateendra Verma too. On the basis of these sources, a sketch of Dhantala's early past can be offered.[9]

Dhantala lies in the middle of the Ganga-Yamuna doab which happens to be one of the richest agricultural belts of South Asia. However, being close to Delhi, it was frequently drawn into the turmoil of invasions and violent regime changes from the days of the Mahabharata to the coming of the British in the region in early 19th century. As a result, the site was resettled several times in pre-modern times. From late 18th century, however, a village called Rasoolpur had existed here and the same got the present name as Dhantala from early 20th century.

Much before that, in the 16th century, when Rasoolpur was still to be settled, three Tyagi brothers by the name of Tarak Singh, Kharak Singh and Bijai Singh are said to have founded the villages of Tori, Kharkoda and Bijora, respectively, around the present site of Rasoolpur/Dhantala. Local chronicles also claim that the three Tyagi brothers were recognized as the zamindars of their respective villages by the rulers at Agra and Delhi also. Similarly, Jamshed Ali and Mohammad Ali (who are descendants of the Chaudhris of Tori), also affirmed that their lineage derives from Tarak Singh whose grandsons – Kishan Shah and Ram Shah – embraced Islam in the 17th century adopting the names of Karim Baksh and Rahim Baksh, respectively. They were recognized as the zamindars of Tori and four other villages by the Mughals.[10]

The *haveli* or abode of the principal zamindar or Chaudhri of the area was located in Tori which lie close to the northern boundary of Dhantala. The Chaudhris were keen to extend cultivation in their estates. However, due to disturbed political conditions and the repeated revolts of the Jats and Satnamis in the region, especially in the 17th and early 18th centuries, this did not materialize and it was only in late 18th century that one of the scions of Chaudhry Karim Baksh called Rasool Baksh built his abode on the site of Dhantala and attracted Gurjar shepherds by developing a water channel that exists as a dry bed to the south of Dhantala till today.

Rasool Baksh lived and died on this very site and his grave near the said channel is revered by the villagers till today. It was after this 'pir' or holy man that Dhantala got its first name of Rasoolpur. According to family genealogies available with residents of Dhantala like Khem Singh, Devraj Singh and Mahender Singh, their forefathers (going back roughly ten generations from now) started settling in Rasoolpur/Dhantala in the late 18th century. Thus, a family of Bhadanas (a Gurjar sub caste) living in Dhantala claim to be the eleventh generation of Parasram Bhadana who is said to have settled in Rasoolpur in Vikram Samvat 1835 or 1779 AD.[11] Their scion Mahender Singh is a prosperous farmer and owner of the ration shop in Dhantala now.

However, the founding of Rasoolpur in the late 18th century did not bring about regular settlement initially. Right until the beginning of the 19th century, the region around Meerut was a bone of contention among warring Marathas, Mughals, Pathans and Jats because of which initial settlers were forced to flee Rasoolpur again and again. The rise of the British in the region after the treaty of Surji Arjan Gaon (1803) with the Sindhias marked a turning point in this context. Meerut soon came up as a cantonment and grew into a major market while cessation of wars in the region also encouraged more settlers to migrate to Rasoolpur. Around the same time, the zamindari of Tori and Rasoolpur was inherited by Yahya Khan (1780–1900) who was to play a crucial role in the growth of the village by encouraging new settlers to shift from cattle rearing to cultivation. Yahya Khan died in 1900 at the ripe age of 120 after expanding his estate via marriage (begetting the zamindari of Kakod from his in-laws) and by encouraging cultivation to such an extent that Rasoolpur soon became famous as Rasoolpur–Dhantala because of its remarkable productivity and prosperity. Indeed, the prefix in its name also gradually disappeared and, by 1947, the village was increasingly being referred as just Dhantala or 'the abode of wealth'.

The long period of Yahya Khan's zamindari coincided with the consolidation of British rule in north India. His descendants in Tori – Jamshed Ali and Shahzada – informed me that Khan's power was such that even Queen Victoria had called upon him in 1857 (along with other landed notables) to resist the mutineers. Yahya Khan is said to have remained neutral in this war and extended his estate to about 12,000 acres spread across seven villages in the second half of the 19th century. Dhantala was one such village whose population, as recorded in the collectorate records at Meerut, grew to about 500 by the turn of 20th century from a few dozen when Yahya had taken over from his father Ahlad Khan in early 19th century.[12]

An important measure that helped in expanding cultivation in the estate of Yahya Khan was the fact that he encouraged some dalit families also to become sharecroppers or *kashtkars* of huge tracts instead of just labouring for Gurjar or Jat peasants as customary then. With this encouragement, Dhantala came to be inhabited soon by Jat and Gurjar as well as Kumhar, Muslim, Jatav and Valmiki settlers and the village's population had crossed about 1200 by 1947. Despite this increase, Dhantala had, till 1984, about 400 acres of uncultivated common land whose distribution led to a major tussle, as we shall note later.

Tardy Growth of Infrastructure

The establishment of the British administration in the region in early 19th century was accompanied by the introduction of the Mahalwari land settlement with its rigid tax burden and forced commercialization of agriculture. Although the growth of Meerut city and the spread of the railways was a spur to the village economy, other colonial institutions like the district hospital, canal and tubewell irrigation, electricity, modern education and legal procedures and modern mills in Modinagar and Meerut were out of reach for ordinary villagers till recent times. Even in 1947, Dhantala had no qualified doctor or nurse, middle or primary school, electric poles or a *pucca* road or any motorized vehicle or even a radio set.

In this context, the country's Independence proved to be a major turning point as it not only brought adult franchise, abolition of zamindari, land ceilings and elected panchayats to the village but also the first primary school, a Panchayat *Ghar* and brick lanes within a decade. In the 1960s, the most significant innovation for villagers was the sprouting of the green revolution with the help of high yielding varieties of wheat and rice, specially 'Sunehra Chausanth' or the 'Golden 64' type of wheat which raised farmers' incomes as yields doubled or tripled (depending on the quantity of water and fertilizer used by a cultivator) rapidly. The road skirting the village was also metalled for the first time in the late 1960s and the election of the village head through secret ballot began from 1967.

Land consolidation or 'Chakbandi' of agricultural fields was attempted in the region between 1970 and 1973 but led to considerable litigation. The decade also saw the introduction of power supply in some village homes, the arrival of first tractors in Dhantala and the propagation of Prime Minister Indira Gandhi's Twenty Point Programme for development as also coercive sterilization during the 'National Emergency' declared between 1975–77. In the 1980s the growth of competitive politics in the Panchayat body brought some improvements in Dhantala. The most significant of these was the allotment of three acres of land each among nearly 100 men from village commons after a major agitation organized by the landless in 1983–84. The same decade saw the launch of a milk cooperative, the final completion of the slow work on bricked lanes, the construction of *pucca* houses (each furnished with a hand pump also) for 16 poor families by the state (under the Indira Aawas Yojna) and finally, the arrival of television for rural viewers too. Meanwhile, the construction of a separate temple was also launched near the dalit quarters of Dhantala in 1988.

The 1990s brought a major change in the economic policy of the state and the effects of consequent 'liberalization' were felt in Dhantala too. A number of factories in the local industrial hubs of Modinagar and Meerut were closed while the recruitment for state jobs, especially in grade IV, came to a near halt. On the other hand, a number of new welfare schemes were announced whose implementation on the ground has been highly unsatisfactory. Among the more useful new measures were those launching subsidized rations for 'below poverty line' (BPL) cardholders, mid-day meals for primary school students under state or local administration, pensions for the physically challenged, widows and poor above 65 years in age and the strengthening of the Panchayati Raj through regularization of the five yearly elections and better and direct funding from central government for local bodies.

The last decade also saw improvements in Dhantala's connectivity with the outside world as public and private buses started touching the village directly, personal vehicles increased in the village by leaps, mobile connections arrived in 2003 and satellite television channels could be seen (by better off residents) with the help of newly launched dish TV. *Pucca* buildings have also come up for Dhantala's primary as well as middle school and a new panchayat *Bhavan* and the rundown road connecting the village to nearby towns has been relayed and ambitious schemes like the employment guarantee scheme, universal education and right to food schemes have also been proclaimed with a lot of fanfare. Their implementation on the ground, however, remains a far cry from their claims and proclamations as we shall see below.

The foregoing account of the slow augmentation of facilities and infrastructure in Dhantala may suggest that cumulative improvement, specially over the past 50 years, has taken place in the village which started as a cattle raisers' abode, about 200 years ago. But, given the long stretch of this history and the poor implementation of schemes as well as unequal distribution of their benefits, these improvements seem paltry on the ground specially, when we compare the story of Dhantala with that of villages in the more advanced states of Punjab, Haryana, western Maharashtra, etc. (not to speak of advanced Asian Countries such as Japan and South Korea). Just to recount one instance, electricity reached Dhantala in 1935 when a state tube well was installed for irrigation. Most homes today have electricity connections. Yet, power lines are of little value as not only is there no supply for 12 or more hours daily but even when power is there, voltage is so low that dim bulbs, slow fans, cellphone batteries and a television is all that it supports; the farmers' dire need for adequate storage and irrigation remains unfulfilled even after 60 years of Independence.

Occupational Structure

Having charted the origins of Dhantala and some of the turning points in its broader history, it would be useful to examine the changes witnessed in various sectors of the village's economy over the last century. By 'economy' we are referring here to the production and distribution of goods and services in a community, its occupational structure, consumption patterns as also living standards across classes. For want of space, we shall focus mainly on the production side of the economy and also not dwell on the changing relations between various agrarian and non-agrarian classes in the village here.

A comprehensive profile of the occupational structure of Dhantala in the early 20th century is difficult to obtain today. But the structural records and elders' recollections clearly reveal that cultivation and animal husbandry were the principal occupation of most residents while a number of crafts were catered by one or two families each. Pottery and brick making was handled by a more substantial group of Kumhars from the early decades. In 2011, a detailed survey of household and occupation shows that out of a total work force of 855 (excluding unpaid women workers in peasant households), 502 were dependent on agriculture primarily, while among 353 non-farm workers also many had shares in family fields. Of the 502 agriculturists, 390 were small or marginal peasants (holding less than 10 acres of land); 8 were rich farmers (with more than 15 acres) and 18 were artisans cum cultivators. Among others, 50 were farm workers and 71 non-farm labourers, while 8 were tenant cultivators. Cattle rearing and milk selling to local diaries was common in most homes including that of cultivators. With this overview of the current material setting in Dhantala, we shall now turn to sectoral accounts of changes in the village economy over past eight decades.

Agriculture

With a threefold rise of population between 1936 and 2011 and the distribution of village's vacant land to the landless in 1984, almost the entire agricultural land around Dhantala (of about 1300 acres) has been brought under cultivation. As a result, little vacant land is visible even at village's boundaries where the fields of surrounding hamlets touch those of Dhantala except for a road or a school acting as a dividing point.

Besides rabi crops like wheat and mustard and kharif types like rice and pulses, sugarcane and vegetables including potatoes are also grown in Dhantala. While canal and tank irrigation is absent, tube wells and submersible pumps have now replaced the labour demanding Persian wheels that were in use till the middle of the previous century. As a result, while two crops a year have become a norm (except in the longer cycle sugarcane), groundwater has fallen drastically since the adoption of high yielding seeds in the seventies. According to villagers, till 1970, water was easily struck at about 20 ft depth while pipes have to be dug minimum fifty feet now before water is found.

Dhantala falls in the first 'green revolution' zone of the country and *kisans* and *kashtkars* of the region deserve credit for being the pioneers of High Yielding Variety crops. Many old *kisans* of Dhantala clearly remember how exciting it was to adopt the new varieties of wheat like the Golden 64 (Sunehra Chausanth) and Narma Roja and of rice like Lal Moonji and sugarcane called CO1148. In the 1970s, modern machinery was also adopted by the bigger landowners of Dhantala such as Khem Singh and Devraj Singh. From a time when Persian wheels were the main source of irrigation in early 20th century to the present when electric pumps numbered 150 in the village (including 50 submersibles), Dhantala's better off *kisans* have come a long way. The first tractor was bought in Dhantala by Khem Singh and Bhagmal Gurjars in 1970 and in 1989 their number was 10, while by 2011 it was 50. On the other hand, organic farming being promoted by the administration has not found many takers. In December 2011, I was informed by a prosperous landowner, Pushpender, that for two preceding crops, he and two other farmers had experimented with organic manure in half of their fields. The manure was supplied by state's agents at a lower price than that charged for chemical fertilizers. Yet, not many have followed up on this since yields have been reportedly lower than with fertilizers and organic compost is difficult to develop in required quantity as dung is used for making fuel cakes on a major scale as the region.

Still tube well irrigation and High Yielding Varieties of wheat and rice resulted in dramatic improvements in output after 1970. Elders in Dhantala recall that in the early decades of the 20th century, when neither the high yielding seeds nor electric tube wells and modern pesticides had arrived, crop yields were not even one-fifth of what they are today and four quintals in an acre was considered a good harvest of wheat while un-irrigated patches yielded two quintals maximum. Today, even a poor farmer with low capital expects about 10 quintals of wheat in an acre while better inputs bring upto 20 quintals per acre. Ninety-four-year-old Suraj Bhan recalls that even before the green revolution, crop yields had grown from about four quintals per acre per harvest to about six quintals by 1960 because of better irrigation and electric tube wells. But the jump was faster and much more in the 1970s soon after the introduction of High Yielding Varieties of wheat and rice. Overall, a fivefold rise in wheat yields can be noted between 1920 and 2010 from two to four to ten to twenty quintals per acre now. But water required for the new varieties is also twice less and fertilizers and pesticides are essential. General inflation has grown one hundred and fifty times between 1930 and 2011. On the other hand, the price of wheat rose more than 200 times from ₹ 5 per quintal in 1920s to ₹ 1,100 in 2011.

Due to lack of space, I am not dwelling on the structure of landownership in Dhantala here. Yet, the cultivated area of the village, in 2011, was 1300 acres divided among 572 main cultivators with an average of about three acres per cultivator. However, the wealthiest farming family of Khem Singh, in the village, had about 40 acres while the poorest among landowners were four brothers with puny shares in the half-acre family plot in the same period.

Animal Husbandry

Agriculture is commonly seen as the primary occupation of most villagers. However, the example of Dhantala shows that non-farm incomes and animal husbandry are equally significant in the region's rural economy now. Indeed, besides the introduction of land ceilings in the 1950s and the green revolution in the 1970s, the next major change which deeply affected the economy of Dhantala was the 'white revolution' or growth of milk production and sale through the cooperative movement growing from the 1980s. This revived the importance of animal husbandry which had declined in the middle decades of the 20th century but had once been the sole occupation of settlers in Dhantala. The revival was doubly beneficial since the growing demand for milk and milk products in cities in the last decades of the century put the natural resources of the village to good use while bringing some more cash to small farms which were failing to absorb the labour power of most families.

Cattle rearing are, of course, highly symbiotic with agriculture as fields provide cheap supply of cattle feed while the animals yield dung for both manure and fuel. Ample space around rural homes also provides room for the livestock which is unimaginable in cities. Further, the spare time of village children can also be used in grazing and washing animals easily. The sale of hides, calves and meat also adds to the profitability of this adjunct of agriculture and many of our poor subjects stated that they earn more through dairy than farming now.

Till recent decades, however, what was lacking in this potential chain was transportation and processing link between increasing urban demand and rural dairymen. This came to the region in the form of milk cooperatives that started following the highly successful model presented by the Mother Dairy Cooperative especially after the 1970s. The most important cooperatives buying milk from cattle rears and dairies of Dhantala are Parag, Amul and Paras. In 1990, the price of milk noted by me was ₹ 4 per litre, while in 2011 it was ₹ 40 for a litre of full cream milk.

A rough estimate of income and expenditure accruing from cattle rearing in Dhantala, in 2010, showed that while each buffalo of about 10 litres milk yield per day required upto ₹ 75 of cattle feed, the sale price of its yield could go up to ₹ 300 daily in the eight odd months that it yields milk.[13] Even if we add interest on account of purchase of the animal (a good buffalo was purchased, in 2011, by Bhopal Singh in Dhantala for ₹ 70,000) and some losses due to illness and also barren months (when the buffalo is to recover its fertility after the *gabhin* or delivery and feeding phase), the sale of milk is a more beneficial occupation in the countryside than small scale agriculture of the marginal peasant with limited inputs. What adds to the profitability of cattle rearing is the sale of hides and beef as well as bones for additional income especially among the lower castes and Muslims who have benefitted more from this expanded trade in the last two decades. In fact, the main road linking Hapur with Garhmukteshwar passes close to Dhantala and is dotted by many slaughterhouses exporting meat. Some men from surrounding villages also supply carcasses and livestock to these meat factories.

Unlike cattle, other animals have not been successfully raised for business in Dhantala. Although numerous attempts were made for fishing, pig rearing, poultry, etc. by villagers, frequent outbreaks of disease and death among animals, forced most such ventures to wind up quickly.

Rural Manufacturing

While agriculture and allied activities have shown some development over the previous century, the same cannot be said for manufacturing. Traditionally, Dhantala was home to a variety of craftsmen including carpenters, potters, oil pressers, blacksmiths, cobblers, etc. But as transportation and other links with the urban economy grew and greater mechanization made factory-made tools, implements, cloth and oil, etc. more attractive because of their lower cost and greater durability, the rural clientele of the former began to decline from mid-20th century. Some modern tools and machinery were, no doubt, adopted by village craftsmen too. But the shortage of electricity and other infrastructure in the village has kept modern manufacturing for both rural and the urban market restricted in Dhantala. Among the few processes that have appeared within the secondary economy of Dhantala are: motor winding and mobile, cycle and tyre repair. It is worth highlighting here that the examples of rapid growth of rural industry in South Korea, Indonesia, Taiwan, etc. (besides Meiji Japan and 19th century Germany) indicates that the overwhelming dependence of the residents of Dhantala on low yield farm economy is not inevitable or necessary.

While traditional crafts have declined and few new manufacturers have appeared within Dhantala, in recent decades large scale manufacturing has not picked up in a big way even in towns and cities around the region. Although Meerut became a major hub for wholesale and retail trading and some towns such as Hapur, Moradabad, Khurja, etc. have been famous for crafts like printed cloth, pottery and brassware, large scale modern industry capable of employing surplus labour from villages has not grown much. The limited food processing and sports goods industry of Meerut and nearly Hapur is too meagre to offer non-agricultural employment to 10 million residents of the district as a whole. The story of the Modi family (descended from the early 20th century industrialists Gujjur Mal Modi) who were running several factories and mills in Modinagar (including those of tyres, thread, and sugar and cloth mills) till the 1980s is instructive. After a heroic strike carried by workers under the left banner in the early 1980s, they shifted many of their businesses to Gujarat while their cloth mill was burnt and compensation was claimed from insurance by the industrialist's family allegedly after the removal of most of the machinery, according to the octogenarian Prahlad Singh, who worked in one such mill before the incident.

While manufacturing has been slack in and around Dhantala, construction has picked up both within the village and in surrounding towns in recent decades and demand for both skilled and unskilled workers in masonry, woodwork, etc. has grown significantly while property prices have also risen remarkably including those of agricultural land. Thus, in 1900, the sale price of one acre agricultural plot in Dhantala was about ₹ 100 (though Yahya Khan had reportedly transferred 500 acres of his land in Dhantala to Gopal Singh in lieu of ₹ 10, 000 only, while another village was given away in the 1920s by a landlord in adjoining Muzaffarnagar to a money lender again, for ₹ 10,000 only, according to the septuagenarian Khem Singh). But by 1947, land prices had firmed up in the region as population had begun to rise more consistently and one acre of agricultural land could fetch up to ₹ 1,000 now.[14] The steepest rise in prices has come in recent decades. In 1998, Wahid Khan sold his 1.2 acre field for ₹ 1.25 lakh. By 2007, the rate of similar land in Dhantala had gone up to ₹ 10 lakh per acre while, in 2011, I was witness to the sale of a field in Dhantala at a price of ₹ 25 lakh per acre. The major factor for the steep rise in land prices of late has been the arrival of buyers from near expanding cities in the National Capital Region who have encashed lands there and purchased in villages like Dhantala that are again not too far from cities. Property dealing has, hence, emerged has a major occupation even for villagers like Pushpender and Pawan in Dhantala now.

The Tertiary Economy

While manufacturing remains underdeveloped both in small and large scale ventures in and around Dhantala, the same cannot be said of the service sector in the traditional rural economy. In the traditional rural economy, a host of services including those of the barber, the mid-wife, cobbler, priest, washer man, traditional healers, sweeper, etc. were available for ages. Almost all of these were low tech, family based occupation and restricted in the *varna* idea to specific castes. Gradually, in the 20th century, caste restrictions on the choice of occupations have also loosened in Dhantala, greater mechanization, modern training and better returns appeared in services offered by teachers, health workers, repair shops, flour mills, etc. Besides this, about villagers who have acquired training from vocational institutes in Meerut and Noida also commute to cities to work as accountants, lawyers, compounders, etc. while a smaller number has permanently shifted from the village to towns. A notable fraction of these professionals are from Dalit castes too and have struggled hard on the sole available rope for upward mobility namely, cheap education in government run schools and colleges which also offer some reserved seats to them as per the Constitution. We shall compare the proportion of different castes among these mobile men of Dhantala in the next section.

Besides state employees and educated professionals, another wing of the tertiary sector that has provided employment to village youth in recent decades is the transport sector where repair shops and jobs for drivers, cleaners and suppliers, etc. has absorbed those with little education also. Similarly, the booming property market offers some options both for construction workers as well as landowners wishing to sell part or whole of their fields at much higher prices than before. Other services where both labourers and petty businessmen have found some jobs cutting across rural urban divide are hawking and roadside vends, food industry and cleaners' and sweepers' jobs.

New services available within Dhantala today include mobile repairing and recharging, electric grinding, motor winding and tool repair, etc. For others like banking, postal service, police, hospital, high school and college education, major vehicle or tool repairs, etc. the village is still dependent on towns around. On the whole, services have not been hurt as much as traditional crafts in recent times. Yet, many service providers like Dinesh the tailor and Saifi the blacksmith have to fall back on agricultural income for making ends meet and get small fields cultivated by family or hired labour or tenants.

The most lucrative profession in Dhantala today, however, is the production and sale of cheap liquor. In 2009, it was estimated, in a group discussion attended by me that, on an average, liquor worth ₹ 5,000 is being sold daily in Dhantala. There are three main agents who get illicit liquor costing ₹ 17 per pouch and sell it for ₹ 30. Some villagers are allegedly in the business of making illicit liquor occasionally within Dhantala also. The opening of thousands of authorized liquor shops by the Mayawati government in 2009, however, made bottled alcohol easily available within the village and hurt the local bootleggers pretty hard.

From Jajmani to Cash and Contract

Besides the decline of traditional crafts and services in Dhantala, the erosion of traditional exchange between agriculturists, craftsmen and service providers has been extremely significant recently. Till about 1970, Dhantala's crafts as well as services were centred on the 'jajmani' system also called *lagbandi* locally. Under this, each craftsman or service provider was hereditarily attached to specific peasant families or *jajmans* that were served on a continuous basis by the *kamin* or service provider and supported in turn by the former with payment in grain at harvest ranging between half to two quintal of wheat annually (given to village barber, carpenter, etc.) or half kilo or more of grain daily (to construction worker) or just a few *chapattis* (given to sweepers daily) or, one meal after and some grain given at harvest (to some field labourers).

The majority craftsmen and service providers like barber, carpenter, etc. were paid through harvest payment. In addition, however, the *kamin* or worker could hope for support from his *jajman(s)* in times of crisis as also during festivals and weddings, etc. Some skilled workers like the barber could be, thus, attached to half or the whole village, at times, while each carpenter, blacksmith, etc. was attached to a group of about 20 odd *jajman* families.[15]

The relation between the peasant and the *jajman(s)* was, of course, more exploitative than reciprocal since the former were expected to show full commitment while the protection and wages expected from the latter were not only meagre but also less certain. The labouring *kamins* were mostly outcastes or from lower middle castes, the *jajmans* were typically upper middle caste farmers or zamindars. For example, Rajkali, an 86-year-old ex-sweepress of Dhantala, recollected that she used to clean drains and lift refuse daily from the houses of a dozen *kisan* households, in the middle decades of the century and was in return given two *chapattis* (with stale vegetables occasionally) each in her second round, in the afternoon. In addition, she received up to a third or half of a quintal of wheat or millets at harvest from each patron, but was called as mid-wife during child birth, while her husband carried fire to the cremation ground after each death in the *jajmans*' family.

Another feature of *jajmani* was that each craft or service in Dhantala was associated with a specific sub caste only and the families concerned were not supposed to take up vocations of other sub castes. Such a strong linkage between occupations and sub castes has declined sharply in Dhantala since Independence even as the need for service providers like tailors, barbers and cobblers, etc. remains. Thus, Momin, whose father was a carpenter, now runs a barber's shop in the village while Dinesh, whose family had traditionally been in farming, now owns a tailor's shop. Not only have individuals departed from occupations within their *varna* but also moved into jobs across varnas of late. For example, Manoj is a Jatav who has completed his PhD and is now teaching in a college in Meerut while Ved Prakash is a middle caste Gadariya who has violated all caste norms by, accepting the sweeper's job in Dhantala when it came under Mayawati's government as regular government employment with a salary of ₹ 10,000 per month. Similarly, there are number of Jatavs in Dhantala who have become lawyers, traders, etc. in the last 20 years. On the other extreme, a Brahmin from the village died in 2005 labouring and eating in the temple at Kharkoda during his last days.

Another significant feature of the traditional 'rural' economy which has changed dramatically in Dhantala is the system based on barter exchange. Over the 20th century and especially from the 1970s, cash started replacing goods and services as the medium of exchange in Dhantala. Agricultural workers are, however, still paid in grain often and specially at harvests. But on most fields rented out by owners, dues are still repaid through simple division of the harvested crop.

It is not possible to attribute the decline of the traditional features of Dhantala's economy to a single cause. From the middle of the last century, increased mobility of both goods and men between village and city, an increase in bicycles as means of transporting small commodities, including milk, tools and grocery, etc. and some rise in the purchasing power of villagers due to the steady decline of tax and rent and, with the consolidation of the green revolution from the 1970s, together helped in eroding age old structures such as *jajmani*, barter and the rigid association between specified castes and occupations. But sharp erosion appeared in *jajmani* relations from the 1980s when surplus land was distributed among 110 landless men after an agitation and increased output generated by the green revolution encouraged cash and contractual transactions and better transportation and communication also gave a boost to emigration among the village's Dalits.

The fact that the same services fetch a better price in cities than in the village adds to this trend and help in sustaining poor workers in city slums despite the increased cost of living there. For example, in 2009, I noted that Momin, the barber, was charging ₹ 5 for a hair cut in Dhantala. On the other hand, in a Delhi slum called Aradhaknagar, in the same year, Bishen was charging ₹ 10 for the same job offered on a footpath on a wooden chair while in a saloon, in a lower middle class colony, the price of a hair cut was ₹ 25 then. Similar price ratios can also be seen in village and town economies in other services such as tailoring, driving, etc. Besides the sharp difference in the price fetched by a service in village and city, even the lower price is not available in villages to workers easily. Thus, in Dhantala, Momin's clients often insisted on partial or delayed payment or part cash and part goods payment often.

Thus, while jajmani has disappeared as an occupational structure in Dhantala, some of the ethos regarding clients' claims for payment according to convenience and after considerable delay still remains in the village. Growing Migration to towns is eroding this traditional craft and service economy nevertheless. In my last meeting with Momin, the village barber, in 2011, he talked at length about his plan about shifting to Meerut to work in a saloon on wages first and then to open his own saloon in the city. This, he insisted, would save him from poor delayed payments for his work, common in Dhantala now.

Permanent and Periodic Migration

As the non-agricultural sector offers little income in Dhantala, many villagers seek employment like Momin in surrounding cities now. Between 1989 and 2011, about 98 families are, thus, said to have left Dhantala, restricting its demographic growth to a mere 35 per cent (from 2080 to 2650 over the same period). This is in sharp contrast to the population explosion visible in our cities and particularly in city slums.[16] It was further reported by Dhantala's Pradhan, in 2011, that in preceding four years, 13 families migrated from the village while four came to Dhantala from outside. Of those who left the village on a permanent basis, however many visit for important family functions and festivals still.

Apart from those who have emigrated from Dhantala and return for occasional functions, about 120 residents of Dhantala were commuting in 2011 to surrounding cities for work and returning daily. Going to Meerut, Hapur, Delhi or Ghaziabad by train or bus, in the morning, about 40 of these were lower caste labourers, masons, while another 40 were sweepers and peons, etc. employed in private or public sector units in cities. Amongst commuters a few happen to be clerks, lawyers and small scale entrepreneurs. The latter usually belong to the richer landowning families which employ wage labour on their lands and continue to educate their children for clerical jobs in banks and offices in cities, on salaries ranging, in 2010, between ₹ 20,000 and ₹ 50,000 per month (having risen from about ₹ 2,000 – ₹ 4,000 noted by me in 1989). Many of these have taken up abodes in towns gradually. But the number of commuting Dalit lawyers, clerks and teachers commuting daily is also on the rise and stood at 11 in 2011.

Caste, Education and Consumption

About 100 years ago, the village's caste structure was very different as Dalits were not even allowed to sit close to upper and middle castes then. Today, the Pradhan of Dhantala is a dalit woman. Yet, caste and gender hierarchies are still strong. The first primary school opened in Dhantala in 1948. Now the village has two primary and two middle schools of which one is private in both categories. A third private residential middle school has been opened just outside Dhantala recently by trust run by Jat landowners who also have secure jobs in banks in Delhi. The said school has much better infrastructure and teaching discipline but charges minimum ₹ 300 as monthly tuition fees and is accessible only to prosperous families, many of whom belong to surrounding small towns like Kharkoda and Hapur rather than villages in the district. The government schools and those run by trusts inside Dhantala also have *pucca* buildings now. But a major contrast exists in the salaries paid to teachers there. While the former get about ₹ 2,000 per month, the latter start in the primary wing also at ₹ 30,000 approximately. Correspondingly, the private schools charge ₹ 100 to ₹ 300 as monthly fees from students while the government schools teach for free and also provide meals and some finance for dress and books too. Still many parents who can afford to send their children to the former and even those who cannot appear very keen to do the same. The main reason seems to be more regular teaching and greater attention given to English in the private schools.

Literacy has shot up from a single lettered person in Dhantala, in 1947, to about one-third of the populace in 2011 and approximately two-third in 2011. In absolute terms, of the total population of 2704 in 2011, 1724 were found to be literate. On the other hand, in 1989, out of 961 adults in Dhantala, only 372 were literate. Further, of 1724 literates in Dhantala, in 2011, 105 were graduates or professionally qualified and 32 were independent professionals like doctors, lawyers, technical staff, etc. in nearby towns. Almost all of them, however, went out of the village for work (along with 46 other clerks, accountants, etc. and 35 lower grade workers employed in public or private sector units). Qualified professionals such as doctors, lawyers, etc. living within Dhantala remain small as only one 'registered medical practitioners', one veterinary doctor and three school teachers and two health workers do so, while five others come from adjoining cities to work in Dhantala in day time.

While education has improved slowly over the past half century in Dhantala, ownership of consumer durables has shown a more dramatic shift in preceding three decades. In my first visit, in 1989, I had counted 10 televisions sets, 15 two wheelers, one refrigerator and one car besides 20 tractors and 50 tube wells in the village. By 2011, the corresponding figures had risen to 400, 197, 95, 31, 40 and 204, respectively. Among gadgets that have nearly disappeared over the same period are radios and video cassette players while those that have grown in a big way in the village are mobiles (about 1200), satellite television (64 dishes), washing machines (58) and inverters (50).[17] In the 85 Dalit households too, in 2011, there were 74 televisions, 168 mobiles, 30 two wheelers, 10 inverters, two cars, 15 satellite dishes and eight washing machines. It is pertinent to repeat here that a large number of these gadgets have been purchased second hand from marts in neighbouring towns while a few have come as dowry.

The conspicuous jump in certain gadgets and consumer durables in Dhantala (and the steep rise in the price of agricultural land, as noted before) doesn't imply that poverty had gone down dramatically in the village. While starvation and deaths due to epidemics have come down since the 1970s, undernourishment and poverty still persists in about 50 families which have little land or secure income and are simultaneously caring for physically or mentally challenged members too. While 25 of these families were receiving minimal state aid in the form of subsidised ration or a paltry pension in 2011 and some owned a second hand mobile charged with a ₹ 10 monthly account or even a black and white television set their minimum need for food, shelter and medical care still remain largely unfulfilled as per capita income in the 50 of family of Dhantala was clearly below the rural poverty line of ₹ 21 per day in 2011.

Conclusion

Villages have been considered the mainstay of Indian society on several counts. While three-fourth of India's population still lives in villages, our primary institutions such as family, religion and caste are also more firm in the countryside than in cities. However, village India is also changing rapidly now as electoral politics, increased connectivity, television and mobile phones among others transform its culture and economy increasingly. On the other hand, though much has changed in rural life, in recent decades, Indian villages have retained many old rhythms too. The pace and direction of change, of course, varies from region to region and a number of long term studies of rural relations would be required for a comprehensive understanding of this complex reality.

The paper shows that the economy of Dhantala exhibits profound changes along with significant continuities across eight decades as recalled by three generations living in the community presently. Similar lineages, fields, shrines, dung cakes and livestock that existed a century before can be traced in Dhantala till today. Similarly, marriage customs, purda, open defecation, eating and sleeping routines and, of course, caste remains prominent in the village. On the other hand, schools, roads, tube wells and tractors and, above all, a fourfold increase in population; quickening migration and a tenfold rise in agricultural productivity since early 20th century signify slow but continuous change also in the economy of Dhantala. The tardy pace of this transition, however, does not satisfy growing aspirations of younger villagers in the region. Resultant social tensions could provide a fertile ground to divisive politics with time, it is feared.

Notes

1. For exceptional long term studies of Indian villages refer Kessinger (1974), Wadley (1994) and Dreze et al. (1994).
2. Refer Wiser and Wiser (1971/1998) with a postscript by Susan Wadley. Also see Slater (1921) revisited recently by Guhan and Bharathan (1984).
3. Srinivas (1961), Beteille (1965/1971), Gupta (2005), Breman (2007) on one hand and Mendelsohn (1993) on the other.

4. For contrasting views refer Breman (1993), Leiten and Srivastava (1993) on the one hand and Jaffrelot (2003), Jeffery (1996) on the other.
5. I would like to specially thank Shri Devraj Singh, Shri Khem Singh, Shri Gautamrishi (advocate), Satyaprakash Gautam and Bhopal Singh of Dhantala for their consistent help and patience with my queries.
6. The Gram Pradhan Smt Prakashi's husband Chandrabhan informed me that in native terms, the 'rakba' or total measurement of the village is estimated at 13,500 kucha bigha or about 2600 acres in all.
7. The term 'middle castes' has been used here to refer to so called 'other backward castes' or shudras including upper middle peasant castes such as Jats and Gurjars and lower middle peasant castes like kumhars, dhimars, etc.
8. The land records maintained since early 19th century at Meerut Kachahri and the vanshavalees kept by Bhats at Baghpat and Hardwar are particularly useful in this regard.
9. Parker (1904), Verma (2003) and Kumar (1996).
10. See Verma (2003). Unfortunately, neither this book nor our villagers themselves provide exact years for the founding of these villages.
11. The modern Gregorian calendar starts 56 years after the Vikrami Samvat's year one.
12. I wish to thank here the record keepers at Meerut collectorate especially Mehboob Khan in helping me translate a few land records from Urdu for above information.
13. Poorer farmers spent no more than ₹ 20 on cattle feed generally also obtained no more than four kg milk per day while better cattle rearers spent around ₹ 100 per buffalo on feed to obtain 10 to 12 kg of milk from one buffalo.
14. Gold is reported to have been selling in 1947 at ₹ 50 per tola (ten gram).
15. Here it may be added that to some extent, the element of reciprocal loyalty and patronage between a dependent and a master in the Jajmani arrangement was similar to that seen in feudal ties of medieval Europe. However, clear differences between the two universes were also apparent as the stress on military service and land assignments was obviously absent in the latter. The concerned Jajmans in the Indian version were of course zamindar as well as kisan families and not just state appointed lords.
16. In a Delhi slum called Aradhaknagar, studied by me since 1988, for example, population grew from 490 to 1760 between 1989 and 2009 or by about 250 per cent. Delhi's population as a whole grew from about 50 to 140 lakh over the period.
17. The count of various gadgets per home was made in 2011 by two men from Dhantala separately before being compared again in my presence. I thank Pradeep Kumar and Satyaprakash for their patient work on this tedious job.

References

Beteille, Andre (1965/1971). *Caste, Class and Power*, Oxford University Press, New Delhi.

Breman, Jan (1993). *Beyond Patronage and Exploitation*, Oxford University Press, New Delhi.

——. (2007). *The Poverty Regime in Village India*, Oxford University Press, New Delhi.

Dreze, Jean and Nicholas Stern (1998). *Palanpur: 1957–1993*, Delhi: Institute of Economic Growth.

Guhan, S. and Bharathan, K. (1984). *Dusi: A Resurvey*, Madras Institute of Development Studies, Madras.

Gupta, Dipankar (2005). 'Whither the Indian Village: Culture and Agriculture in 'Rural' India', *Economic and Political Weekly*, February 19.

Jaffrelot, Christophe (2003). *India's Silent Revolution: The Rise of the Low Castes in North Indian Politics*, Permanent Black, Delhi.

Jeffery, Patricia (1996). *Don't Marry Me to a Ploughman*, Westview Press, Boulder, CO.

Kessinger, T.G. (1974). *Vilayatpur: 1848–1968: Social and Economic Change in a North Indian Village*, University of California Press, Berkeley.

Kumar, Vipnesh (1996). *Meerut ke Paanch Hazaar Varsh*, University of Allahabad, Allahabad.

Leiten, G.K. and Srivastava, Ravi (1993). *Unequal Partners: Power Relations, Devolution and Development in Uttar Pradesh*, Sage Publications, New Delhi.

Mendelsohn, Oliver (1993). *The Transformation of Authority in Rural India*, Cambridge University Press, Cambridge.

Parker, N.T. (1904). *Memoirs of a District Magistrate*, National Archives of India, New Delhi.

Slater, G. (1921). *Some South Indian Villages*, Madras University Press, Madras.

Srinivas, M.N. (1961). *The Remembered Village*, Oxford University Press, New Delhi.

Verma, Yateendra (2003). *Gurjaron ka Itihas*, Rastogi Prakashan, Meerut.

Wadley, Susan (1994). *Struggling with Destiny in Karimpur: 1925–1984*, University of California Press, Berkeley.

Wiser, W.H. and Wiser, C.V. (1971/1998). *Behind Mud Walls: 1930–1960*, University of California Press, Berkeley.

9

Development of Urban-Rural Fringe Area Around Aligarh City

An Allusive Review to Frame Out the Challenges

KAMAL ASIF

The speed, direction and depth of an urban centre exhibit wide spatial variations in the developing and the developed world. In the forthcoming decades, rapid urbanization will be one of the greatest challenges in the developing world to ensure human welfare and a viable global environment. According to the current estimates, cities occupy 4 per cent of the world's terrestrial surface, which is a home for almost half the global population, consume three-quarters of natural resources, and generate three-quarters of pollution and wastes. According to the United Nations (2009), this phenomenon is most common in countries of Asia and it has been estimated that the fastest rate of urban growth over the next 25 years will be in medium-sized cities with 1 to 5 million population and that most people will live in smaller cities having less than 1 million people.

The outward movement of city population and immigrated rural people, to develop suburban, industrial, residential, commercial and recreational activity in the urban fringe areas results in a massive socio-economic change of cities. This phenomenon is common in all the developing countries of the world but in the continent of Asia, it is a teething problem resulting in an unplanned development. At the urban scale, development of a fringe area can be seen as the restructuring of urban space in the form of suburbanization. However, from the perspective of the urban centre, suburbanization is a process of decentralization in which many socioeconomic forces are involved, but the pivotal point in the entire process is the availability of cheap land on the periphery of urban centres (Smith, 2013).

The infringement of agricultural land into urban areas is a continuous phenomenon which began with the expansion of cities and accelerated more rapidly since the mid of the 20th century. The loss of agricultural land to human settlements is of serious nature in India. As per the estimates, about 1.5 million hectares of land (mostly agricultural) supported urban growth between 1955 and 1985, and another estimate shows 0.8 million hectares were transformed between 1985 and 2000. With the beginning of the 21st century, it has been estimated that half of the Indian population lives in suburban areas around previously existed cities. The features of urban sprawl, low density land use, heavy reliance on fossil fuels, diverse character of land use, impact on surrounding environment and lack of opportunities are widespread. For a multi-level development of city, it should be stressed that sustainable urban development should include socio-economic and environmental sustainability, i.e. a desire for a general state of urban well-being and a good quality of life for all urban residents. Inoculating a future oriented approach for planning sustainable development of cities and their fringe area is the very urgent need of the time.

Urban-Rural Fringe Area

The conceptual definition of urban fringe was propounded by R.J. Pryor in 1968. It is a zone of transition between the continuously built-up and suburban areas of the central city and rural hinterland. Therefore, it can be assimilated as Urban-Rural Fringe Area which has been defined as 'the area of transition between well recognized urban land use and the area devoted to agriculture'. Therefore, urban-rural fringe is a continuous area that starts beyond the urban limits of cities. A more comprehensive definition of urban fringe, given by Herington (1984), describes the distinctive characteristics that it is 'an area which is partly assimilated in the growing urban complex, which is still partly rural and where many of the residents live in the countryside, but are not socially and economically forming part of it'. The paper is based on Aligarh city and its urban-fringe area.[1]

Urban purposes for which land is brought for basic use are the construction of buildings, housing, parks, roads, railways, etc. Development of Aligarh city has been done in a very helter-skelter way that, the basic urban services did not increase with the increase in population and area of the city. During the last four decades, the

Figure 1 *Study Area and Its Location*

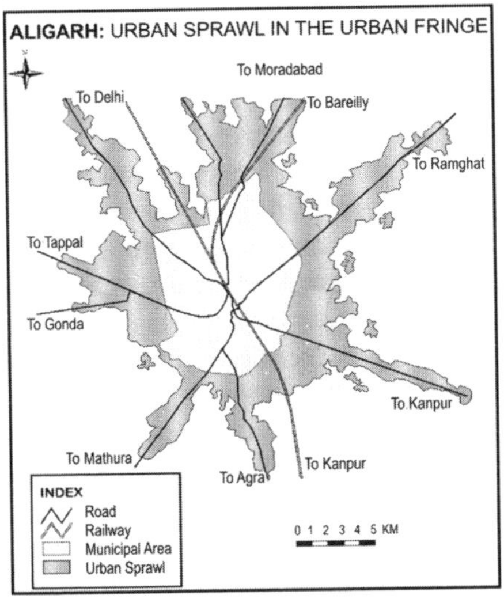

population of Aligarh has increased four times and spread out over much larger area (Figure 1). With reference to environment, the situation seems to be much problematic and directly related to degradation and losses. In Aligarh, due to hasty pace of urbanization, land is needed (for space and material) for day-to-day construction and filling of depressions. In the urban fringe of Aligarh, land degradation occurs due to strip mining, brick kilning, dumping of urban waste and coal ash dumping which is a dilatory matter of great concern.

The paper is mainly based on secondary statistical data obtained from records of various government departments, organizations, national and international research agencies. The discussion has involved an in-depth study for which case study approach was applied to analyse the process and parameters of urban growth and encroachment of agricultural lands in the urban fringe areas. Use of remote sensing was made possible by the affability of Google Earth software programme through which satellite images of Aligarh city was obtained. The imageries of years 2009 and 2011, and municipal maps of 1976, 1991 and 2001 were obtained to prepare urban sprawl map of Aligarh Urban Agglomeration by overlaying techniques with the help of GIS technique Arc view 3.1. For cartographic presentation, the required maps were obtained from different sources and processed. Ability to assess, measure, and monitor urban sprawl depends upon the availability of relevant, accurate and reliable data.[2]

Urban Growth of Aligarh City

A realistic picture of urban growth trends in Aligarh city is revealed if we examine them by urban area and size of population. The total geographical area of Aligarh district is 3,648.31 sq km. It is 32nd largest district of the state of Uttar Pradesh and 38th largest in India in terms of total area. Aligarh is one of the 13 metro cities of the state and is the administrative headquarters of Aligarh district, Aligarh Police Range and Aligarh Division, and has a population of about one million (estimate). Aligarh city grew up as an economic and political centre, but, later growth was very haphazard, which has resulted in a high degree of urban congestion. The core of the city has a marked degree of compactness and a very high density of population. In the course of time, the streets in the city have become narrow and more irregular.

The rapid rate of urbanization in Aligarh is highlighted by the fact that the population has consistently stepped up in each succeeded decade during the past century. In the first census, which was conducted in 1847, the population of Aligarh city recorded 36,181 persons and by 1853 the total population rose to 55,001 persons, though in 1865 it had fallen down to 48,403 persons. Since then, there has been a considerable increase which started even before 1881 and continued to 1901. Afterwards, the population of Aligarh continued to decline for two consecutive decades of 1901–11 and 1911–21 (Table 1). Since 1921, the growth has been steady and it continued upto 1971 with a slight fluctuation in 1951. During the post-Independence period, Aligarh experienced a marked growth of industries in residential areas. The 1961 Census categorized Aligarh as a service-cum-industrial centre but, the 1971 Census reclassified it as industrial-cum-service centre. As the city entered in 1990s, the census reports gave new records of the population growth i.e. 49.75 per cent. In the subsequent Census of 2001, there has been a downfall in the growth rate by 10 per cent, i.e. 39.23 per cent, at that time, the actual population was 6,69,087 persons. During the period of 1901–2011, the population of Aligarh city has been increased by 8,00,491 persons, which shows a growth of 1,110.50 per cent.

According to the provisional reports of the 2011 Census, population of Aligarh is 8,72,575 persons; in which males and females constituted 4,63,123 persons and 4,09,452 persons, respectively, with a growth rate of 30.41 per cent (Table 1 and 3). The sex ratio in Aligarh city is 884 females per 1,000 males. Aligarh city is governed by Municipal Corporation which comes under Aligarh Urban Agglomeration. Although Aligarh city has population of 8,72,575 persons, its urban/metropolitan population is 909,559 persons of which 4,82,828 constitute males and 426,731 as females. Aligarh Metropolitan Area (AMA) includes Aligarh City and three suburbs namely: Ashrafpur Jalal, Kwarasi and Sarsaul (Table 3). According to an estimate made with the help of geospatial method by Farooq and Ahmed (2008), the area of Aligarh city has increased to more than 50.54 sq km and the density automatically increased to 17,265 persons per sq km.

Table 1

Population Growth in Aligarh City (1901–2011)

Census Year	*Total Population*	*Decennial Actual Increase*	*Decennial Growth (%)*
1901	72,084	—	—
1911	66,344	-5,740	-7.96
1921	66,963	+ 619	+ 0.93
1931	83,878	+16,915	+25.26
1941	1,12,655	+98,777	+34.31
1951	1,41,618	+28,963	+25.71
1961	1,85,020	+43,402	+30.65
1971	2,52,314	+67,294	+36.37
1981	3,20,861	+68,547	+27.17
1991	4,80,520	+1,59,659	+49.75
2001	6,69,087	+1,88,567	+39.24
2006	7,89,529	+1,20,442	+18.00
2011*	8,72,575	+2,03,488	+30.41
2021**	12,49,352	+3,76,777	+43.18
1901–2011	8,72,575	+8,00,491	+1,110.50

Source: (a) Aligarh District Census Handbooks: Village and Town Directory, 1971, 1981, 1991 and 2001; (b) *Census of India 2011 (provisional); (c) **Extrapolations made by Aligarh Development Authority (ADA).

Aligarh District: Urban and Rural Population

During 2011 Census, 33.11 per cent people live in urban areas of the district. In total 12,16,581 people live in urban areas of which males are 6,46,035 and females are 5,70,546. The sex ratio in urban region of Aligarh district is 883 as per 2011 Census data. Similarly, child sex ratio in Aligarh district was 873 in 2011 Census. Child population (0–6) in urban region was 1,63,478, of which males and females were 87,264 and 76,214, respectively. This child population figure of Aligarh district is 13.51 per cent of total urban population. Average literacy rate in Aligarh district as per census 2011 is 69.85 per cent of which males and females are 75.84 per cent and 63.08 per cent literates, respectively. In actual number 7,35,584 people are literate in urban region of which males and females are 4,23,781 and 3,11,803, respectively.

According to the 2011 Census, 66.89 per cent population of Aligarh district lives in rural areas of villages. The total Aligarh district population living in rural areas is 2,457,268 of which males and females are 13,12,501 and 11,44,767, respectively (Table 2). In rural areas of Aligarh district, sex ratio is 872 females per 1,000 males. If child sex ratio data of Aligarh district is considered, the figure is 870 girls per 1,000 boys. Child population in the age 0–6 is 3,91,951 in rural areas of which males were 2,09,630 and females were 1,82,321. The child population comprises 15.97 per cent of total rural population of Aligarh district. Literacy rate in rural areas of Aligarh district is 69.48 per cent as per census data 2011. Gender wise, male and female literacy stood at 82.47 and 54.60 per cent, respectively. In total, 14,35,050 people were literate of which males and females were 9,09,529 and 5,25,521, respectively.

Table 2

Aligarh District Information at a Glance

Description	*2001*	*2011*
Actual Population	2,992,286	3,673,849
Male	1,607,402	1,958,536
Female	1,384,884	1,715,313
Population Growth (in %)	22.15	22.78
Area (in sq km)	3,649	3,649
Density (persons/sq km)	820	1,007
Per cent share to UP Population	1.80	1.84
Description	*Rural*	*Urban*
Population (% share)	66.89	33.11
Total Population	2,457,268	1,216,581
Male Population	1,312,501	646,035
Female Population	1,144,767	570,546

Source: Census of India 2001 and 2011 (Provisional).

Table 3

Aligarh City Information at a Glance

Description	*2001*	*2011*
City Population	6,69,087	8,72,575
Male	354,616	463,123
Female	314,471	409,452
Population Growth (in %)	39.24	30.41
Area (in sq km)	40.43	>50.54*

Cont'd...

...Cont'd

Density (persons/sq km)	16,549	17,265
Per cent share to UP urban population	1.93	1.96

Aligarh Metropolitan Region
(Aligarh City, Ashrafpur Jalal, Kwarasi and Sarsaul)
Population: 909,559 (482,828 M and 426,731 F)
Aligarh city is governed by Municipal Corporation which comes under Aligarh Urban Agglomeration.

Source: Census of India 2001 and 2011 (Provisional)

Table 4
Area Under Urban Land Use in Aligarh (1901–2011)

Year	*Area (sq km)*	*Actual Growth (sq km)*	*Growth (%)*
1901–1951	11.06	—	—
1961	31.86	20.80	188.06
1971	34.45	2.59	8.12
1981	34.45	0.00	0.00
1991	40.43	5.98	17.35
2001	44.86	4.43	10.95
2006	50.54	5.68	12.66
2011	56.72	6.18	12.22
2021	113.79	57.07	100.61

Source: (a) Aligarh District Census Handbooks: Village and Town Directory, 1971, 1981, 1991 and 2001.
(b) * Census of India 2011 (provisional)
(c) ** Extrapolations by Aligarh Development Authority (ADA)

The process of outward expansion and consequent encroachment on rural land remained imperceptible over a period of roughly 50 years (1951 to 2001), during which the municipal boundary of the city was increased three times (in 1976, 1991 and 2001, Figure 2). In the first decade of post-Independence, there was a significant engulfment of land (2078.4 ha. in 1961, Table 4), showing 188 per cent growth in the municipal area. This land was primarily acquired for educational, commercial, health and other public uses. Specifically, the outskirts of the city were the preferred locations for these establishments, which are purely agricultural based. The educational institutions served not merely as growth points that opened up new areas, thus forcing farmers to relocate further into the hinterland, but also facilitated a rapid expansion towards their locations and beyond. In continuation, during 1971, the municipal area of the city was increased by engulfing 259 ha. land of the fringe area. After a span of 20 years, the municipal area was

Figure 2 *Expansion of Municipal Area of Aligarh City (1976–2001)*

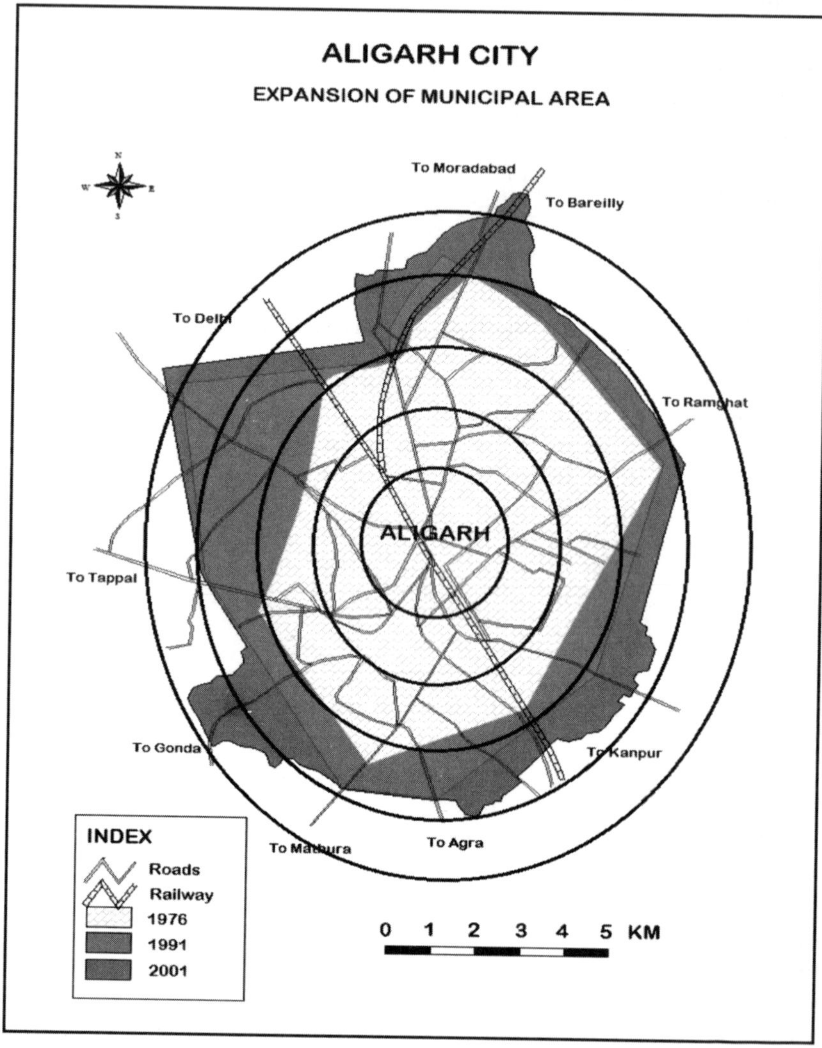

Source: Asif and Rahman, 2012

increased by 598 ha. in 1991, and in the subsequent decade, the municipal area again increased to the extent of 443 ha. (Census, 2001).

Framing Sustainable Governance

Concentration of urban population in medium sized cities like Aligarh, though reflects an imbalance in the pattern of urban development, and is nonetheless suggestive of stable and dynamic urbanizing tendencies. In the case of land resource concerns, the most effective way of allocating the land for agricultural and non-agricultural uses is the proper and wise governance. There are basically only two ways of planning land use: the market process; and central planning involving local, state, or federally administered land-use controls. Despite the widely acknowledged merit of the market in facilitating efficient resource use and material output, various measures are being proposed and implemented to change the pattern of land use. Use of financial incentives to induce owners of agricultural land to retain more land in agriculture could also be an important key in the thrust areas.

Since the clear-cut difference in the value of land converted from agricultural to non-agricultural uses is often quite high, a significant reduction in the conversion of agricultural land has a high opportunity cost (Crosson, 1984). There are two important questions concerning any land-use measure intended to protect agricultural land, whether based on economic incentives or regulations. First, will the measure achieve its stated goal? A land-use control that effectively retains land in agriculture will be costly in terms of tax revenue, or it must be involuntary. Second, will measures to protect agricultural land increase the efficiency of land use? Land shifts out of agriculture because it is economically more productive in other uses. Moreover, the current legislation addressing the environmental problems resulting from urbanization does not address the problem of loss of agricultural land; this factor should be reflected in regional planning (Morello, et al., 2000).

Therefore, socio-economic progress of an area is a continuous phenomenon which forms a basis for the future planning, so that equilibrium is maintained. For Aligarh city, at present, there is a need to do so for sustainable future development. Due to incompetence, poor governance or a lack of resources, the city of Aligarh is badly run and administered. The developmental plans for the city are formulated and somehow implemented through a single governing body, the Aligarh Development Authority (ADA), Aligarh. The agency is further governed by the State Housing and Development Authority, Lucknow. The ADA has formulated and proposed the Master Plan for the next 20 years (2001–2021) in which the area for development has been proposed from 44.86 sq km (2001) to 113.79 sq km (2021) to achieve a growth of 153.65 per cent. Because of vast extrapolated urban area, in the forth-coming decades, there is a need for proper governance of the city and its peripheral areas. Thus, the study proposes that, a separate urban governing body as the 'Urban Fringe Development Authority' (UFDA) should be created by the government to formulate plans exclusively for the development of urban-rural fringe areas.

Framing Sustainable Sector-wise Zones

Sustainable development is the development that meets the needs of the present generation without compromising the ability of future generations to meet their own needs. It has emerged that in the current built-up area of Aligarh city which is intensively occupied, has much pressure of traffic on all roads because most of the community services are present in the main built-up area. To fulfil the basic needs, people of newly developed areas in the fringe depend on the old built-up area; as a result, human pressure increases on roads in old parts of the city. Consequently, a number of environmental and socio-economic problems have emerged during the last decade. Therefore, in order to minimize the pressure of traffic, and for proper and balanced development of city, Aligarh Development Authority (ADA) has prepared a Master Plan 2021. In this plan, the city and its peripheral areas have been divided into five development zones through which proper access of all community services in respective zonal areas will be provided to the residents. Sector-wise zoning and their land utilization has been formulated for sustainable development.

Table 5

Zonal Divisions of Aligarh Metropolitan Area

Areas Included in Different Zones	*Sector Number*
High density residential area	SECTOR – I
Area between Kanpur G.T. Road and Mathura Road.	SECTOR – II
Area between Mathura Road and Delhi G.T. Road.	SECTOR – III
Area between Delhi G.T. Road and Bareilly rail route.	SECTOR – IV
Area between Bareilly rail route and Kanpur G.T. Road (including Harduaganj town)	SECTOR – V

Source: Master Plan 2001–21, ADA.

The main land use activities considering zoning regulations included in the Master Plan are residential, commercial, industrial; offices, public services, parks and farmlands have been taken into consideration. There is also a need to include new ancillary/incidental activities for sustainable development, ensuring the regulatory steps related with the construction of new houses, commercial buildings and

Figure 3 *Map Showing Sector-wise Planning Zones as Recommended by Aligarh Development Authority, Aligarh*

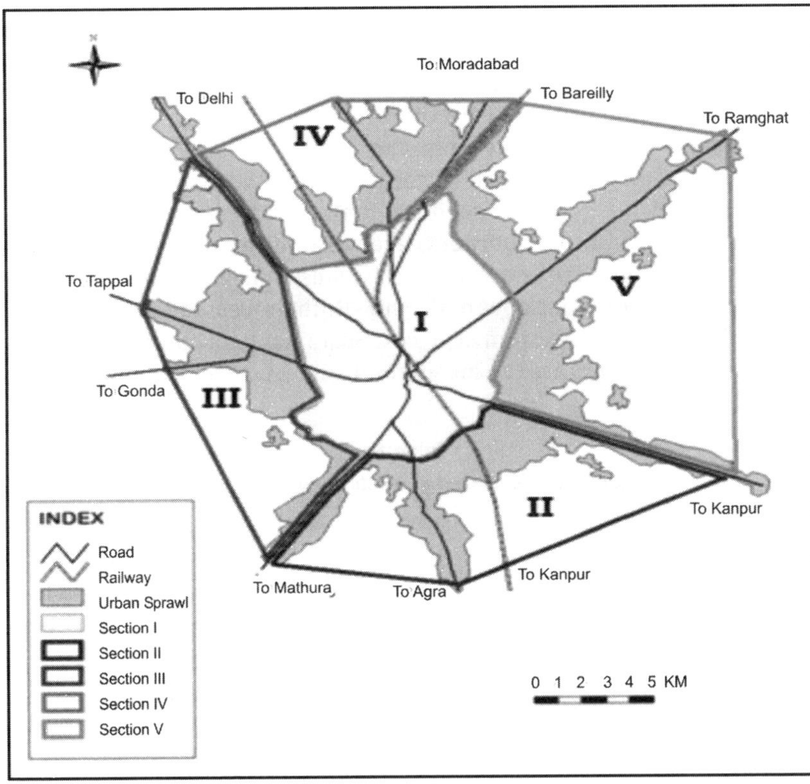

Source: Asif and Rahman, 2012.

others so as to simplify the complexities in traditional zoning regulations and to make zoning user friendly. The operational and economic workout is also necessary so that the basic plan of land use in respective zone should not be deteriorated. New residential colonies where land use is practiced as uncontrolled and illegal will have an option of regulating with the regulations of zonal plan/sector plan/layout plan. The land uses must be examined through transparent process and by a board or a committee constituted by the ADA under special task forces.

Framing Sustainable Waste Management

Increasing urbanization in cities of the developing world is one of the defining features of the 21st century. Infrastructural development on agricultural lands in fringe areas of Aligarh city does not seem to be economically viable and environmentally sustainable. The development should take place without deterioration of productive agricultural lands and destruction of fragile natural environment. Industrial and domestic waste water has contaminated the ground and surface water resources which has become hazardous to the health of the people mainly in the urban fringe areas. Also the dumping of urban waste in agricultural fields has led to the pollution of soil and water. Urban areas 'import' huge amounts of goods – such as fuels, foods and water – from ecosystems beyond their borders, like rural farms, forests, and water catchments. Cities then 'export' their wastes – such as garbage, waste water, air pollution – back out of the city. Both processes have an impact on the delivery of ecosystem services. Sustainable urban and environmental developments are the most important concerns for city planners and policy makers.

Table 6

Category-wise Generation of Waste in Aligarh City (2010)

Waste Generation Category	*Waste Generated Per Month (in MT) (% to total)*
Household or Domestic	7,125 (59.4)
Street Sweeping	2,275 (18.9)
Hotels and Restaurants	200 (1.7)
Markets (e.g. Fruit-vegetable markets, Mandis, etc.)	1,500 (12.5)
Commercial establishments (including offices, institutions, etc.)	900 (7.5)
Total	12,000 (100.0)

Source: Municipal Corporation, Aligarh, 2010.

Being an important industrial and commercial centre, Aligarh is facing the problem of urban waste generation and its disposal, resulting in environmental degradation through air, water and soil pollution. According to the Aligarh Municipal Corporation, during the year 2010, the total quantity of urban waste generated from the municipal area of the city was about 12,000 metric tonnes. The major problem is the generation waste from residential areas (7,125 mt. i.e. 59.4%), Streets (2,275 mt. i.e. 18.9%) and markets (1,500 mt. i.e. 12.5%). Other categories like hotels and restaurants (200 mt.) and institutions (900 mt.) which share 1.7 and 7.5 per cent, respectively (Table 6). According to an estimate, about 60 per cent of this waste is disposed off and dumped in peripheral areas of the city, along the roads and railway lines, while remaining 40 per cent remain dumped in the city in the respective localities and vacant places. All of urban wastes should be dumped in non-agricultural lands and should be processed in treatment units and recycled for making bio-fertilizers and other byproducts. There should be at least four recycling units in all directions around the city to ease the collection of waste and for processing operations.

Framing Sustainable Agro-Processing Clusters

Urbanization affects all sectors of the food system. As the urban population increases, more and more food needs be transported and distributed to the cities. Therefore, easy accessibility of fringe areas is also another advantage of developing agro-industries in the fringe areas. The developments in the post-harvest sector over the past decades and modifications made in marketing, processing and distribution systems ensures the availability of food in urban areas. Thus, the agriculture of urban fringe areas becomes more market-oriented that fills the food delivery gap and generates employment opportunities for the fringe dwellers (Figure 4).

Figure 4 *Diagram Showing Synergy between Urban and Rural Environs for Sustainable Agro-Processing Clusters in Rural-Urban Fringes*

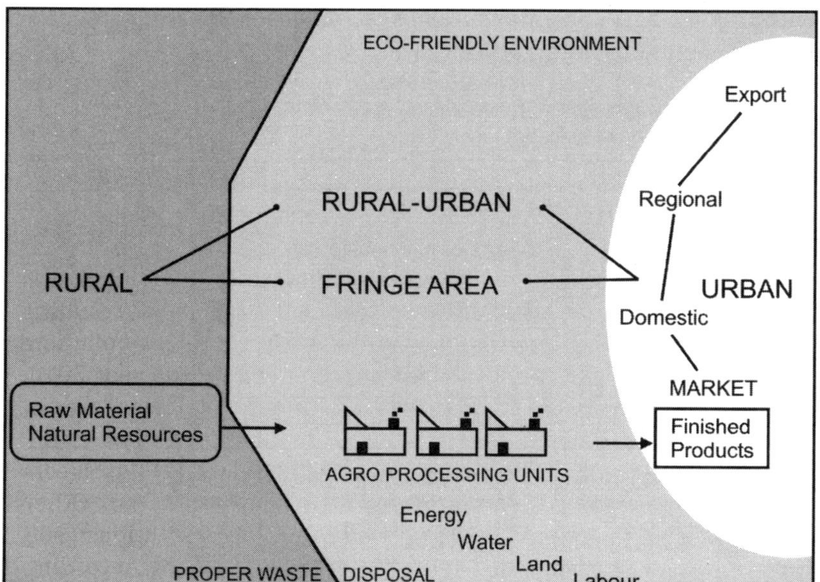

Source: Asif and Rahman, 2012.

Agro-processing clusters can and do contribute for preserving the local agricultural and economic development, and also the sustainable environment of the urban fringe areas. This will help in planning for farming which is ecologically and economically sustainable for a particular fringe area. Moreover, APCs are beneficial for planning at micro level concerning location: land and land development, financial credits, infrastructure, market (domestic and export), and increasing awareness. The scheme is also helpful in developing plans for easy and quick transportation, and storage facilities in fringe areas for sustainable development.

Hence, agro-processing is an employment intensive sector, which is gainful to people living in urban catchment areas rather than the areas, marked with low level of entrepreneurial urge, which hinders the activities due to the constraints of finance, assured market and proper training on technology. On the ground of sustainability, there is wide diversity in agricultural practices in urban fringe areas of Aligarh which permits the production of a wide range of agro-produce, thus catalysing a fast growth of agro-processing activities (Figure 5). Sustainable urban-rural fringe could be accredited with APCs (Agro Processing Clusters) which will be helpful in empowering the rural masses by encouraging agri-entrepreneurships at village level for agricultural development and habitat utilization.

Figure 5 *Sustainable Agro-Processing Activities for Urban-Rural Fringe Areas of Aligarh City*

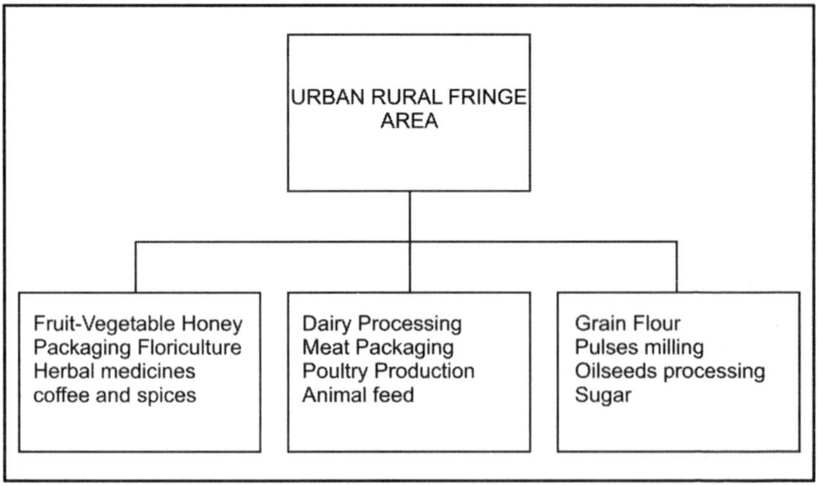

Conclusion

The general agreement about Aligarh is that the urbanization and suburban development in the fringe areas of the city are at a turning point. The question emerged is: which way will it turn? The present study sets out clearly the diversity in the patterns of urban growth in Aligarh City and its surrounding region. In the fringe areas of Aligarh city, there is a wide range of agricultural practices, which permits the production of a wide range of agro-products, thus catalysing a fast growth of agro-based processing activities. The conversion of raw agricultural produce into edible and or marketable products takes place often in urban-rural fringe areas which has equal access to the raw material, labour and the markets. The study began with the question: Can Agro-Processing Clusters (APCs) located in urban-rural fringe areas unleash the synergy among the environmental, agricultural and economic development? The internal working and external environment of clusters and availability of all necessary assets in the fringe areas of Aligarh city suggests an answer in affirmation. Therefore, development of APCs will be helpful in empowering the rural masses by encouraging agri-entrepreneurships at village level, preserving the local agriculture, and providing sustainable livelihood through local resource utilization.

Socio-economic growth is a continuous phenomena in the urban fringe of Aligarh city, therefore, there is a need to maintain equilibrium in planning for achieving a sustainable development. Adoption of sector-wise zonation of the city and its metropolitan area is the present need, and important for future planning. The study also suggests creating a separate governing body as Urban Fringe Development Authority (UFDA) for all cities facing the problems similar to that of Aligarh. To overcome the risks of associated rapid urbanization, there is also a need of rational policies of the government which should be adaptive, participatory, and effective. Planning should be done to frame out sustainable governance, sector-wise zones, urban waste management and development of agro-processing clusters in the urban-rural fringe area around Aligarh city. Moreover, the sustainable management of natural resources should be frame out that can contribute to socio-economic viability of urban and rural areas, for ensuring livelihood, generating employment and for ensuring food security. This study must draw the attention of policy makers to urban planners and land developers, as to how to grow city on a front which is environmentally and socio-economically sustainable.

Notes

1. Aligarh is one of the important major cities of Uttar Pradesh. Aligarh district lies in the alluvial tract formed by the rivers of the Ganga and the Yamuna. This tract is commonly known as *Doab* (a land between the two rivers) which is one of the most important agricultural tracts in the Ganga plain of India.
2. The following publications/records of various government departments were collated and consulted: *Aligarh District Census Handbook: Village and Town Directory* (1971, 1981, 1991 and 2001), Census of India; *Census of India 2011*, http://www.census2011.co.in/census/metropolitan/89–aligarh.html; *District Statistical Diary*, Aligarh 2001 and 2011, Economics and Statistical Division, Lucknow, Uttar Pradesh; *Statistical Abstract of Uttar Pradesh 2010*, Economics and Statistics Division, State Planning Institute, Government of Uttar Pradesh, Lucknow; *Master Plan Reports of Aligarh* 1991–01 and 2001–21, Aligarh Development Authority (ADA), Aligarh; District National Informatics Centre (NIC), Aligarh; *Annual Report 2001*, District Urban Development Authority (DUDA), Aligarh and *Annual Report* (2001, 2006 and 2011), Municipal Corporation, Aligarh.

References

Adeboyejo, A.T. and Abolade, O. (2009). 'Household Responses to Urban Encroachment on the Rural Hinterland in the Ogbomoso Urban Fringe, Nigeria', in A. de Sherbiniin et al. (eds), *Urban Population Development-Environment Dynamics in the Developing World: Case Studies and Lessons Learned*, CICNRD, Paris, pp. 41–75.

Anbumozhi, V. (2007). 'Eco-industrial Clusters in Urban-rural Fringe Areas: A Strategic Approach for Integrated Environmental and Economic Planning', Business and the Environment Research Project, Kansai Research Center, Hyogo, Japan.

Asif, K. (2010). 'Developing Agro-processing Enterprises in the Rural-urban Fringe Areas: A View Point on Sustainable Development and Propelling Rural Prosperity', Emerging Technologies for Sustainable Environment, Proceedings of the International Conference, Department of Civil Engineering, AMU, Aligarh, October 29–30, pp. 592–95.

Asif, K. and Rahman H. (2012). 'A Quest for Developing Agro-processing Centers in Rural-urban Fringe Areas: A Key for Sustainable Development and Propelling Rural Prosperity', in S.S.A. Jafri et al. (eds), *Problems and Management of Rural-urban Fringe*, GIRI Institute of Development Studies, Lucknow, pp. 242–52.

Best, R.H. and Champion, A.G. (1970). 'Regional Conversions of Agricultural Land to Urban Use in England and Wales', reprinted from *Transactions and Papers*, Institute of British Geographers, Publication No. 49, pp. 15–22.

Best, R.H. and Coppock, J.T. (1962). *The Changing Use of Land in Britain*, Chapters 6 & 7, Faber and Faber, London.

Census of India (1971, 1981, 1991 and 2001). *Aligarh District Census Handbooks: Village and Town Directory*.

——. (2011). http://www.census2011.co.in/census/metropolitan/89–aligarh.html

——. (2001). *Uttar Pradesh Administrative Atlas*, Vol. I, Directorate of Census Operations, Uttar Pradesh.

Crosson, P. (1984). 'Agricultural Land: Will there be Enough?', *Environment*, 26 (9): 16–20.

District Statistical Diary, Aligarh (2001 and 2011). Economics and Statistical Division, Lucknow, Uttar Pradesh.

Farooq, S. and Ahmad, S. (2008). 'Urban Sprawl Development around Aligarh City: A Study Aided by Satellite Remote Sensing and GIS', *Journal of Indian Society of Remote Sensing*, 36: 77–88.

Fazal, S. (2009). 'Modelling for Sustainable Urban Expansion: A Case Study using GIS Technique', paper presented at the National Seminar on Problems and Management of Rural-urban Fringe, GIRI Institute of Development Studies, Lucknow, November 17–18.

Harris, C.D. (1968). 'The Pressure of Residential-industrial Land Use', *Man's Role in Changing the Face of the Earth*, 58: 881–95.

Hart, J.F. (1976). 'Urban Encroachment on Rural Areas', *The Geographical Review*, 66 (1): 3–17.

Jones, R.H. (1970). 'Migration to and from the Scotland since 1961', *Transactions of the Institute of British Geographers*, 49: 145–59.

Master Plan Reports of Aligarh (1991–01 and 2001–21). Aligarh Development Authority (ADA), Aligarh.

Morello, J. et al. (2000). 'Urbanization and the Consumption of Fertile Lands and Other Ecological Changes: The Case of Buenos Aires', *Environment and Urbanization*, 12 (2): 119–31.

Oguz, H. (2004). *Modeling Urban Growth and Land Use/Land Cover Change in the Houston Metropolitan Area from 2002–2030*, Ph.D. Dissertation in Forestry, A & M University, Texas.

Pryor, R.J. (1968). 'Defining the Rural-urban Fringe', *Social Forces*, 47 (2): 202–15.

Shafi, M. (1990). 'Agriculture and Rural Transformation in India', *The Geographer*, 37 (1): 1–8.

Siddique, M. (1975). 'Town Planning of Aligarh', *The Geographer*, 22: 55–65.

Smith, N. (2013). 'Gentrification, the Frontier, and the Restructuring of Urban Space', in N.R. Fyfe and J.T. Kenny (eds), *The Urban Geography Reader*, Routledge, New York, pp. 128–37.

State Planning Institute (2010). *Statistical Abstract, Uttar Pradesh*, Economics and Statistics Division, Government of Uttar Pradesh, Lucknow.

United Nations (2012). *World Urbanization Prospects: The 2011 Revision*, Department of Economic and Social Affairs, Population Division, New York.

10

Nowhere Youth in India

Post-Reform Analysis: 1993–94 to 2009–10

KAMAL CHAUDHARY

Increasing number of young people due to falling fertility rates in some parts of the world particularly in developing countries are a major human resource for development as they are the key driving forces in the development process and also capable of making efforts not only in terms of economic aspects but also in terms of bringing social change. According to the United Nations statistics, approximately 18 per cent of the world's population are youth out of which 84 per cent is living in developing countries (United Nations 2007). Gloabally, 73 million young people in 15–24 age cohort are estimated to be unemployed in 2013 which accounts for 12.6 per cent of the total youth population (ILO, 2013). The high rates of unemployment, underemployment and availability of poor quality jobs are some of the major problems of youth labour market and thus, undermine economies' growth potential. Youth unemployment and underemployment are prevalent around the world because young people lack skills, work experience, job search abilities and the financial resources to find employment (United Nations, 2003; ILO, 2006 and Matsumoto, et al., 2012). Existence of weak labour market institutions, educational institutions and informal sector employment further contribute to the challenges faced by young people in the labour market. Two-third of the total youth population is underutilized – either engaged in informal sector, unemployed or underemployed (ILO, 2013).

These challenges are evident in India, which has the largest youth population in the world with around 66 per cent of the total population under the age of 35. But harnessing these resources is a major challenge. Young Indians face major barriers because of poverty and low levels of human capital. Youth while entering the labour market for the first time encounter difficulties in finding a job because they are considered as 'freshers' with no real time experience and often under-employed. They are not provided with social security benefits, health benefits and safety measures and have to work for long hours with meagre or no overtime wage. Also, any disturbance in the economy affects the young people with greater intensity as compared to their adult counterparts. It is also indicated that young people are the first to lose their jobs and the last to gain employment.

The situation is worst when we look at the separate category of young people who are not in employment, education and training. The future outcomes for these young people are even worst as compared to the youth who are underemployed or unemployed but in education or training process, because, by acquiring higher education they can reap better future outcomes. The current paper has been divided into several parts. Section 1 deals with the characteristics of the youth labour market. Section 2 describes the brief review of the related studies. Section 3 comprises of definitions and concepts used in the present study. Section 4 explains about the methodology and data source. Section 5 analyses the trends of youth labour market in the post reform period. Finally, the paper concludes with section 6.

Review of Literature

A review of past related studies are in many ways meaningful and provide basis for current research and help in designing the study. The poor quality of education and rising levels of unemployment has not received adequate attention even though youth have been recognized as the most vital section of the society. It has been argued that the rising levels of unemployment discourage those who are available for work but not actively seeking, from participating in the labour market and thus further complicate the problem. Mitra and Verick (2013) described the situation of employment and unemployment in India. They stated that participation at an early age and low productivity are the two characteristics of youth labour market because early age participation implies forgone skilled training that is essential for gaining formal sector employment. Dev and Venkatanarayana (2011) accentuate that failure to integrate young people in the labour market despite rising levels of educational attainment needs to be paid heed if the benefits of demographic dividend are to be realized. Changes in the age structure due to demographic dividend also creates supply side potential but whether this potential could be realized depends on the policy formulation of the country. The impact of increased percentage of working age population on economic growth using 78 Asian and non-Asian countries has been analysed by Bloom and Williamson in 1998. They found that nearly one-third of the East Asian countries miracle is attributed to the demographic dividend. Their findings have also been supported by Behrman, et al. (1999), Anderson (2001), Bloom, et al. (2003) and Bloom, et al. (2006). Strictly analysed in the case of India, demographic dividend is not the only solution to provide an upward shift in the economic growth as enough jobs are not being created to absorb the rising population of youth entering in the labour market. Another noted phenomenon in the developing countries is the rising unemployment among educated youth. In case of India, 34 per cent of the youth with tertiary level education are unemployed. This is primarily due to rising skill gap and deficient jobs creation in the formal sector of the economy.

Concepts and Definitions

Although the definition of youth may vary from country to country, the Government of India officially defines youth as persons between the ages of 16 and 30 years. The UN, however defined the youth as persons between 15 and 24 years of age because it is argued that 15–24 age cohorts heavily influence the future outcome. As per the New National Youth Policy 2012, youth is defined in India as persons between the ages of 16 and 30. Further youth has been sub-divided into 3 categories according to their different needs and concerns i.e. from 16 to 20, 21 to 25 and 26 to 30.

Youth NEET Rate: Youth Not in Employment, Education or Training

In the context of changing labour markets, a general problem with usual labour-market indicators is that simple comparisons between young people who are employed, unemployed, or not in the labour force are not sufficient to understand the complexity of youth labour market. For this reason, there is a considerable need of a useful complementary indicator which can present the more viable picture. An attempt has been made by calculating 'the Youth NEET Rate' to represent the more appropriate picture of the youth labour market. The Youth NEET Rate is an alternative indicator of the youth unemployment rate, measuring the sum of young people not in employment as well as not in the education or training as a proportion of the total youth population. The NEET rate of youth is commonly used to measure non-utilized youth potential and young people who are at the risk of becoming marginalized in the future as it takes into account the impact of education and training levels.

Data Source and Methodology

For the present study, youth definition of the National Youth Policy 2012 has been used. The Unit Level data of four Employment-Unemployment Surveys carried out by National Sample Survey Office (NSSO) has been used for various indicators of labour market; covering the period from 1993–94 to 2009–10. The data is used for UPSS (Usual principal and subsidiary status) only. Further the youth NEET rate has been calculated to analyse the non-utilized youth in the labour market.

Trend Analysis

Before establishing the facts about non-utilized youth or their inactivity status, an analysis using labour force participation rate, workforce participation rate and unemployment rate has been done to shed light on the nature and structure of youth labour market in India.

Educational Levels of Young People in India

Education plays an important role in the overall development of an individual and also helps in creating better human capital for the country. In 2011, approximately 82.5 per cent of the total youth aged 16–30 are literate. The percentage of youth with middle education or below has fallen down in the last two decades whereas percentage of those with secondary and above has increased. Around 8 per cent of the total youth in 2011–12 completed more than 15 years of schooling compared to just 4 per cent in 1993–94. The same trend has been observed in case of youth studied up to secondary and higher secondary level. This clearly signifies the increased level of educational attainment among youth in India with increased mean years of schooling.

Labour Force Participation Rate (LFPRs)

This section reviews the Labour Force Participation Rate (LFPR's), which captures the number of young people who are either employed or unemployed and searching for a job as a percentage of the youth population. The LFPRs varied between 83–86 per cent for rural males during 1993–94 to 2004–05 periods. Despite the increase in total population, the LFPRs declined sharply by 7 per cent to 76 per cent between 2004–05 and 2009–10. This might be because of the increase in the numbers of years of schooling. The rates for urban males have tended to fluctuate between 73–75 per cent. This shows that the LFPRs are higher for rural males compared to urban males. This might be because of low levels of income in rural areas where males cannot afford to remain unemployed for longer time periods in the patriarchal system; they are the main bread earners of the family.

Figure 1 *Labour Force Participation Rates by Gender and Sector: 1993–94 to 2009–10*

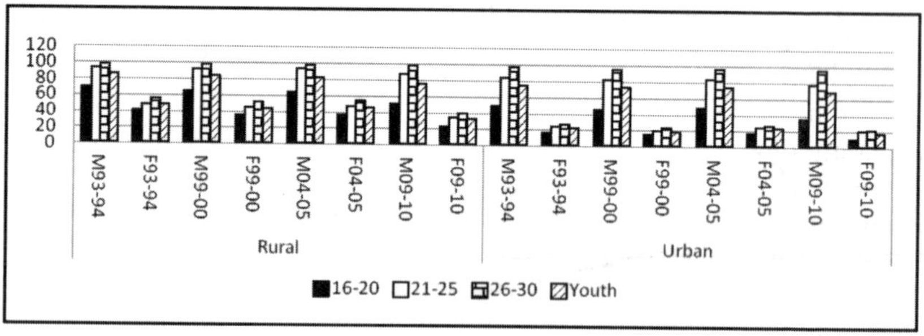

Also the Labour Force participation rates for females fluctuate between 43.5 per cent to 48 per cent in rural areas and between 18.5 per cent to 23 per cent in urban areas. This reflects the fact that the LFPRs are higher for rural females compared to urban females but the overall female participation rate is lower compared to males. If we look at the age specific rates, then for 26–30 age groups, the LFPRs in rural and urban areas have been found to be higher than LFPRs for the working age population (15–59 years). Also LFPRs have been lower for the youth aged 16–20 because of their high enrolment in schools rather than actively seeking jobs in the labour market. A steep decline has been observed in LFPRs of both males and females in rural and urban areas respectively during 2004–05 and 2009–10. The possible reason may be the recent global economic crisis and increasing levels of educational attainments. LFPRs are highest among the youth aged 26–30; followed by 21–25 and 16–20 age cohorts in both the sectors.

Workforce Participation Rate (WPRs)

The trends in WPRs are more or less same as that observed for LFPRs. The WPRs in rural and urban areas have been found to be higher for the

Figure 2 *Workforce Participation Rate by Sector: 1993–94 to 2009–10*

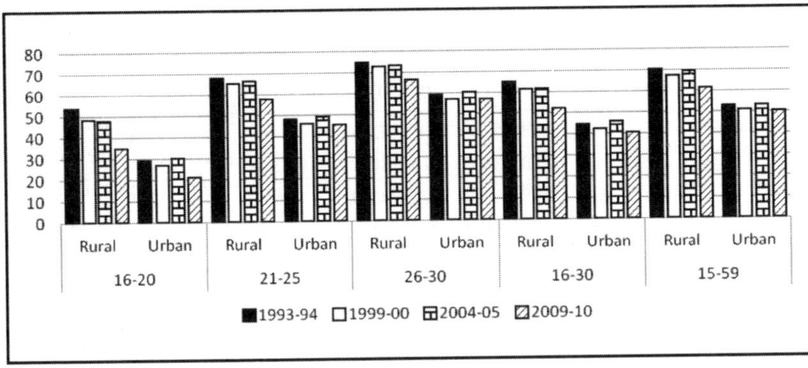

working age population as compared to the youth population. The WPRs have fallen from 1993–94 to 2009–10 with an upward trend shown in the 61st Round (2004–05). The possible reason could be, as economy develops, the workforce participation rates fall because the enrollment rates increase. The WPRs among youth aged 26–30 have been reported even higher than those in the working age group as they have already attained higher education and start looking for the job. Even when productive employment opportunities are not available, males or even females cannot afford to withdraw from the labour market. Rather they start looking for jobs in the informal sector where they largely indulge in a wide range of low productivity activities.

Status of Employment

Table 1 explains a significant increase in the regular salaried workers from 1993–94 to 2009–10 for youth in rural areas. The percentage is significantly high in urban areas. In the developed nations, there is a close relation between self-employment and level of educational attainment as it is argued that it requires more advanced skills and information. But this is not the case with developing countries. Self-employment is found to be higher in rural areas compared to urban areas despite more educated people with advanced skills dwell in urban areas. The overall percentage of self-employed people has gone down with an upward trend shown in 2004–05, in both rural and urban areas. The same is true for casual workers in urban areas but reverse trend has been followed in rural areas with an increase from 39 per cent to 42 per cent. This signifies the casualization of labour in the labour market in the post-reform period.

Table 1

Status of Employment Among Youth (16–30 Years): 1993–94 to 2009–10

	Sector	*1993–94*			*1999–00*			*2004–05*			*2009–10*		
		SE	*RS*	*CL*	*SE*	*RS*	*CL*	*SE*	*RS*	*CL*	*SE*	*RS*	*CL*
16–20	Rural	56.6	4.1	39.3	52.6	4.8	42.6	55.1	5.9	39.1	48.6	6.2	45.2
	Urban	43.3	26.7	30.0	39.0	30.5	30.5	40.9	34.6	24.5	36.4	33.2	30.5
21–25	Rural	55.4	6.2	38.5	53.0	6.2	40.8	56.1	8.0	35.8	49.9	9.0	41.1
	Urban	43.8	34.3	21.9	40.3	38.3	21.4	40.5	41.6	17.8	31.8	48.1	20.0
26–30	Rural	53.3	7.2	39.5	51.7	7.5	40.8	57.1	7.5	35.4	50.3	8.5	41.2
	Urban	40.8	40.4	18.9	42.0	39.8	18.2	43.2	41.6	15.1	37.7	45.4	16.9
16–30	Rural	55.0	**5.9**	39.1	52.4	**6.3**	41.3	56.2	**7.2**	36.6	**49.7**	**8.1**	**42.2**
	Urban	42.4	34.9	22.6	40.7	37.1	22.2	41.7	40.0	18.3	**35.3**	**44.1**	**20.5**
15–59	Rural	56.2	6.9	36.8	54.1	7.4	38.5	58.5	7.6	33.9	52.4	7.8	39.8
	Urban	40.8	41.0	18.3	40.8	41.5	17.7	44.1	40.8	15.2	39.7	42.7	17.5

Source: Various Rounds, National Sample Survey Office (NSSO).

Notes: SE: Self-Employed, CL: Casual Labour, RS: Regular Salaried.

Youth and Unemployment Rates in India

Figure 3 explains that incidence of unemployment is higher in urban areas as compared to rural areas because people in urban areas can choose to remain unemployed as they are enough well off and spend more time in searching better jobs. Despite the fact that there is a wide gap between rural and urban unemployment rates, the unemployment rates in urban areas are showing a declining trend but reverse trend is being followed by rural areas. As shown in the Appendix Table 3, the unemployment rates tended to fluctuate between 3 per cent to 4 per cent in rural areas and between 6.5 per cent to 10 per cent in urban

Figure 3 *Incidence of Unemployment by Sector: 1993–94 to 2009–10*

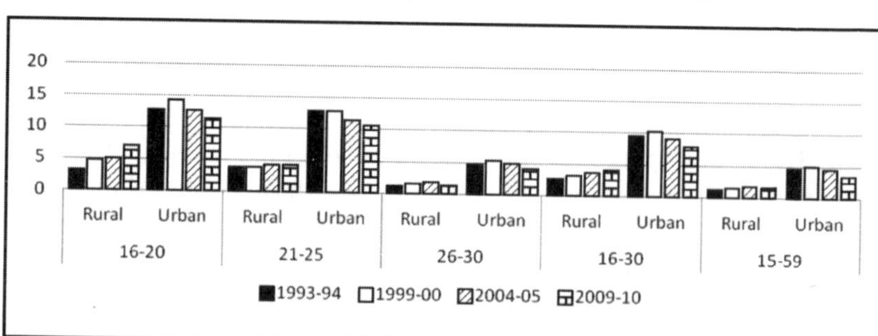

areas. Such high unemployment rates partly reflect the mismatches between skills demand and supply. Further, the incidence of unemployment is highest in the age group of 16–20 years. The possible reason might be those who are early school dropouts find it difficult to get a job in the market. It is lowest in the age group of 26–30.

Transition from School to Work

Although Unemployment rate does not clearly specify the condition of youth labour market, an increasing number of young people neither in employment nor in education or training (NEET Rate) is an alternative indicator of a weak or poor transition between school and work. In other words, it is an indicator of the size of population at risk. Although an increasing proportion of young people are staying in higher education, some leave the school system at secondary and higher secondary levels and are particularly vulnerable. They are less likely to be reintegrated in the labour market because they lack skills and thus have a long term impact on their employment and earning outcomes. Demographic factors, socio-economic factors, cultural boundations and gender role expectations affect the transition process. Many developed countries in order to smooth out school-work transition have implemented study-work programme for young people and thus reduced the NEET rate significantly. In order to analyse the inactivity status of young people in India, Youth NEET Rate has been calculated to represent the more nuanced picture of youth labour market.

Youth Neither in Employment nor in Education or Training

Figure 4 represents the Youth NEET rate for male by location for the period 2004–05 and 2009–10 for the three age categories as well as the youth aged 16–30. The analysis shows that Youth NEET Rate is higher in urban areas compared to rural areas and the gap is visibly large for the age category of 21–25 years. The Youth NEET Rate is lowest in the age

Figure 4 *Youth NEET Rate by Sector for Male: 2004–05 and 2009–10*

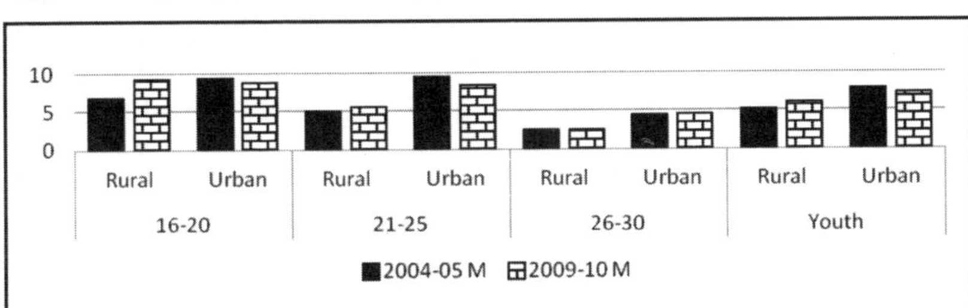

group of 26–30 years. Further it has shown a declining trend in urban areas but the reverse trend is found in the case of rural areas. This indicates the weak transition between school and work in rural areas compared to urban areas and relates to the fact that combined effect of increased economic activities and increasing levels of education in urban areas is helping young people in getting employment than that in rural areas. The same trend has been observed for females in both rural and urban areas and shown Figure 5.

Figure 5 *Youth NEET Rate by Sector for Female: 2004–05 and 2009–10*

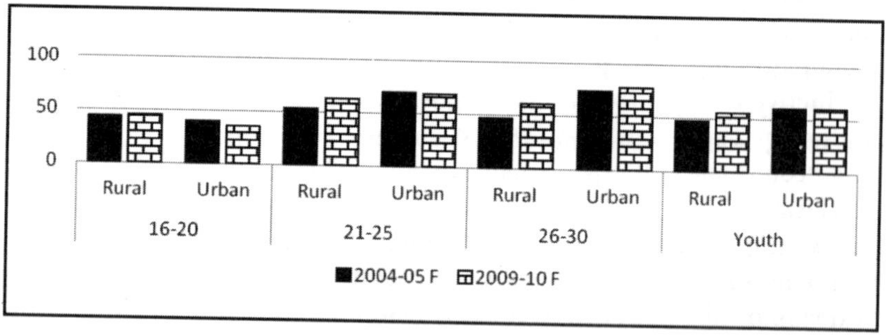

The youth NEET rate has been showing an upward trend in rural areas and downward trend in urban areas for all the youth age cohorts. It is significantly higher among females as compared to males. Further, it is the highest for females aged 21–25 as compared to the overall youth in the country. The Youth NEET Rate has increased from 2004–05 to 2009–10 for both males and females. Rural urban comparison reveals that it has been found higher in urban areas but it has shown a declining trend in urban areas and rising trend in rural areas from 2004–05 to 2009–10. In 2009–10, it has been found the highest for rural youth aged 16–20 years. The same trend is followed in case of females by rural-urban distribution. In comparison to males, the Youth NEET Rate is much higher among females. This may be due to customs and other cultural expectations that they have to look after family rather than participating in the labour force. For 16–20 age groups, it has been showing a declining trend in both rural and urban areas among females. This may be due to rising levels of educational attainment.

Conclusion

The aim of this paper is to provide a profile of youth in India. Despite increase in the levels of educational attainments, participation in the labour market at an early age is prevalent. This leads to forgone skills essential for better earning outcomes later in the life. A significant gender gap exists in LFPRs, WPRs and Unemployment rates for youth in India. Huge differences are observed in indicators of labour market in rural as well as in urban India. A significant proportion of the youth is found out of employment, education or training. The Youth NEET Rate is significantly higher among females as compared to males. This is due to the lack of study-work programmes which could in fact smooth the transition between school and work. In order to tackle the challenges of participation and employability of youth in India, policy interventions should promote a better quality education, on the job training and productive job creation. There is a need to invest in education and skills so that the benefits of the youth could be harnessed in the future and they could be provided with better future opportunities. Also significant gap exists in data of NEET youths, what is needed to have captured of detailed data of NEET for better understanding of youth problems and further policy implications. Overall, the challenge is both in terms of job creation and the preparation of youth for the labour market to make efficient use of India's demographic dividend.

References

Anderson, B. (2001). 'Scandinavian Evidence on Growth and Age Structure', *Regional Studies*, 35 (5).

Behrman, J.R., Duryea, S. and Szekely, M. (1999). 'Aging and Economic Opportunities: Major World Regions Around the Turn of the Century', Working Paper No. 405, Inter-American Development Bank.

Bloom, David E. and Williamson, J.G. (1998). 'Demographic Transitions and Economic Miracles in Emerging Asia', *World Bank Economic Review*, 12 (3): 419–56.

Bloom, David E., Canning, David and Sevilla, Jaypee (2003). 'The Demographic Dividend: A New Perspective on the Economic Consequences of Population Change', Population Matters Monograph MR-1274, RAND, Santa Monica.

Bloom, David E., Canning, David, Wu, Linlin, Liu, Yuanli, Mahal, Ajay and Yip, Winnie (2006). *Demographic Change and Economic Growth: Comparing China and India*, Harvard School of Public Health, Harvard University, Boston, MA.

Dev, M.S. and Venkatanarayana, M. (2011). *Youth Employment and Unemployment in India*, Indira Gandhi Institute of Development Research (IGIDR), Mumbai.

International Labour Organisation (2006). *Global Employment Trends for Youth*, Geneva.

——. (2013). 'Global Employment Trends for Youth', Special Issue on the Impact of the Global Economic Crisis on Youth, Geneva.

Matsumoto, M., Hengge, M. and Islam, I. (2012). 'Tackling the Youth Employment Crisis: A Macroeconomic Perspective', ILO Employment Working Paper No. 124, Geneva.

Mitra, A. and Verick, S. (2013). 'Youth Employment and Unemployment: An Indian Perspective', ILO Asia-Pacific Working Paper Series, International Labour Organisation, New Delhi.

United Nations (2003). *World Youth Report: The Global Situation of Young People*, Economic and Social Affairs Division, New York.

——. (2006). *World Population Prospects*, New York.

——. (2007). *Understanding Youth Issues in Selected Countries in the Asian and Pacific Region*, Economic and Social Commission for Asia and the Pacific, New York.

APPENDIX

Appendix Table 1

Labour Force Participation Rates (LFPRs) by Gender and Rural-Urban Residence, 1993–94 to 2009–10

		1993–94			*1999–00*			*2004–05*			*2009–10*		
		M	*F*	*P*	*M*	*F*	*P*	*M*	*F*	*P*	*M*	*F*	*P*
16–20	Rural	69.9	40.7	55.9	65.0	35.7	50.8	64.4	36.8	51.1	50.9	23.6	38.4
	Urban	49.4	16.0	33.8	46.3	14.5	31.6	48.3	17.2	34.2	35.1	10.7	24.0
	Total	64.3	34.2	50.0	59.7	30.0	45.4	59.9	31.8	46.5	46.5	20.0	34.3
21–25	Rural	93.9	48.8	71.1	92.9	44.4	68.5	93.7	46.7	69.9	88.3	34.6	60.7
	Urban	83.9	24.3	55.8	83.0	19.7	52.9	83.7	25.1	56.0	78.7	21.0	50.8
	Total	91.1	42.5	67.0	90.0	37.8	64.1	90.6	40.6	65.8	85.1	30.5	57.6
26–30	Rural	98.6	55.2	76.1	98.3	51.7	74.2	98.5	54.6	75.5	98.3	40.2	68.0
	Urban	97.2	26.6	62.1	96.6	23.0	60.3	97.2	27.1	63.8	96.6	22.2	59.7
	Total	98.2	47.9	72.5	97.9	44.1	70.4	98.1	47.4	72.2	97.8	34.9	65.5
Youth (16–30)	Rural	86.2	48.0	67.1	83.7	43.6	63.6	83.3	45.6	64.4	75.9	32.5	54.4
	Urban	74.8	22.0	49.6	73.0	18.8	47.2	74.6	22.9	50.5	68.2	17.9	44.2
	Total	83.0	41.3	62.4	80.7	37.0	59.1	80.8	39.6	60.5	73.6	28.3	51.4
15–59	Rural	89.8	52.1	71.2	88.3	48.7	68.7	88.6	52.5	70.6	84.8	39.9	62.6
	Urban	83.3	25.1	55.8	82.3	22.2	53.8	83.4	26.1	56.2	80.9	21.0	52.3
	Total	88.0	45.2	67.1	86.6	41.7	64.6	87.1	45.4	66.6	83.6	34.5	59.6

Source: Various Rounds, National Sample Survey Office (NSSO).

Notes: M: Males, F: Females, P: Persons

Appendix Table 2

Work Force Participation Rate (WPRs) by Gender and Rural-Urban Residence, 1993–94 to 2009–10

		1993–94			1999–00			2004–05			2009–10		
		M	F	P	M	F	P	M	F	P	M	F	P
16–20	Rural	67.3	39.9	54.1	61.4	34.5	48.4	60.7	35.3	48.5	47.0	22.4	35.7
	Urban	43.4	13.7	29.5	39.8	12.3	27.0	42.3	14.8	29.8	31.2	9.4	21.2
	Total	60.7	32.9	47.5	55.3	28.5	42.5	55.5	30.0	43.5	42.5	18.8	31.6
21–25	Rural	89.7	47.5	68.5	88.7	43.1	65.7	90.2	44.2	66.9	84.7	32.6	57.9
	Urban	74.6	19.3	48.5	73.1	16.3	46.1	75.7	20.4	49.5	72.1	17.0	45.5
	Total	85.5	40.3	63.1	84.1	35.9	60.2	85.7	37.5	61.8	80.6	27.9	54.0
26–30	Rural	97.0	54.8	75.2	96.7	51.1	73.1	97.1	53.2	74.1	97.1	39.2	66.9
	Urban	93.2	24.7	59.2	91.8	21.4	57.1	93.5	24.4	60.6	93.5	20.4	57.3
	Total	96.0	47.2	71.0	95.3	43.2	68.7	96.0	45.6	70.3	96.0	33.7	64.0
Youth (16–30)	Rural	83.4	47.2	65.3	80.6	42.6	61.5	80.4	43.8	62.0	72.9	31.2	52.2
	Urban	68.3	19.0	44.8	66.0	16.5	42.4	68.6	19.7	45.8	63.7	15.6	40.7
	Total	79.3	39.9	59.8	76.4	35.6	56.2	76.9	37.4	57.4	70.1	26.6	48.8
15–59	Rural	88.4	51.6	70.2	86.7	48.2	67.6	87.1	51.5	69.4	83.4	39.2	61.5
	Urban	79.8	23.4	53.2	78.4	20.9	51.1	80.2	24.2	53.6	78.5	19.8	50.5
	Total	86.0	44.4	65.7	84.3	40.9	63.0	85.1	44.2	65.0	81.9	33.6	58.3

Source: Various Rounds, National Sample Survey Office (NSSO).

Notes: M: Males, F: Females, P: Persons

Appendix Table 3

Incidence of Unemployment by Gender and Rural-Urban Residence, 1993–94 to 2009–10

		UPSS											
		1993–94			1999–00			2004–05			2009–10		
		M	F	P	M	F	P	M	F	P	M	F	P
16–20	Rural	3.8	2.1	3.2	5.4	3.3	4.7	5.7	4.0	5.1	7.8	5.0	7.0
	Urban	12.3	14.7	12.8	14.1	15.3	14.3	12.4	14.0	12.7	11.2	12.5	11.4
	Total	5.6	3.7	4.9	7.3	4.8	6.6	7.2	5.4	6.6	8.5	6.1	7.9
21–25	Rural	4.4	2.5	3.7	4.5	3.0	4.0	3.8	5.4	4.3	4.1	5.7	4.5
	Urban	11.0	20.3	12.9	11.9	17.0	12.8	9.6	18.6	11.5	8.4	18.8	10.5
	Total	6.1	5.1	5.8	6.5	5.0	6.1	5.4	7.7	6.1	5.4	8.4	6.2

Cont'd...

...Cont'd

26–30	Rural	1.5	0.8	1.2	1.7	1.1	1.5	1.4	2.7	1.9	1.3	2.4	1.6
	Urban	4.1	7.0	4.7	5.0	7.1	5.4	3.8	10.0	5.0	3.2	8.0	4.1
	Total	2.2	1.6	2.0	2.6	1.9	2.4	2.1	3.8	2.7	1.9	3.4	2.3
Youth (16–30)	Rural	3.2	1.7	2.7	3.8	2.4	3.3	3.6	4.0	3.7	4.0	4.2	4.1
	Urban	8.7	13.7	9.7	9.7	12.7	10.3	8.0	14.2	9.3	6.6	13.1	7.9
	Total	4.6	3.4	4.2	5.3	3.8	4.8	4.8	5.5	5.0	4.8	5.8	5.0
15–59	Rural	1.6	0.9	1.3	1.9	1.1	1.6	1.7	1.9	1.8	1.7	1.7	1.7
	Urban	4.2	6.7	4.8	4.7	6.1	5.0	3.9	7.3	4.6	2.9	6.0	3.5
	Total	2.3	1.7	2.1	2.6	1.8	2.4	2.3	2.7	2.4	2.1	2.4	2.2

Source: Various Rounds, National Sample Survey Office (NSSO).

Notes: M: Males, F: Females, P: Persons

Appendix Table 4

Youth NEET Rate by Gender and Rural-Urban Residence, 2004–05 and 2009–10

		2004–05			*2009–10*		
		M	*F*	*P*	*M*	*F*	*P*
16–20	Rural	6.9	43.7	24.6	9.4	44.6	25.5
	Urban	9.3	39.9	23.2	8.8	33.8	20.2
	Total	7.6	42.7	24.2	9.2	41.6	24.0
21–25	Rural	4.9	53.4	29.5	5.5	62.9	35.0
	Urban	9.5	69.3	37.8	8.3	67.1	36.7
	Total	6.3	57.9	31.9	6.4	64.1	35.5
26–30	Rural	2.5	46.4	25.5	2.5	60.1	32.5
	Urban	4.4	74.3	37.8	4.6	77.8	40.9
	Total	3.1	53.7	29.0	3.1	65.3	35.1
Youth (16–30)	Rural	5.0	47.6	26.4	6.2	55.4	30.6
	Urban	7.9	60.5	32.5	7.3	59.4	32.2
	Total	5.9	51.1	28.1	6.5	56.6	31.1

Source: Various Rounds, National Sample Survey Office (NSSO).

Notes: M: Males, F: Females, P: Persons

Appendix Table 5

Educational levels of Youth Population: 1993–94 to 2009–10

	Not Literate	Below Primary	Primary	Middle	Secondary and Higher	Diploma	Graduate and Above
				1993–94			
16–30	38.68	9.77	12.24	16.14	18.86	-	4.3
31–59	53.6	11.86	10.71	9.46	9.71	-	4.66
15–59	45.24	10.79	11.84	13.73	14.11	-	4.3
7+	42.89	17.27	14.28	11.9	10.48	-	3.18
				1999–00			
16–30	31.86	8.89	11.92	19.48	22.56	-	5.28
31–59	49.92	10.87	10.54	10.82	11.83	-	6.02
15–59	40.26	9.86	11.59	16.02	16.84	-	5.44
7+	38.19	16.99	14.52	13.87	12.41	-	4.02
				2004–05			
16–30	25.18	9.12	13.78	20.87	23.44	1.47	6.15
31–59	45.35	10.61	12.19	12.24	11.98	1.28	6.35
15–59	34.93	9.87	13.32	17.32	17.2	1.33	6.03
7+	32.96	16.78	16.65	15.11	12.94	1.01	4.56
				2009–10			
16–30	17.45	7.19	13.12	20.55	31.96	1.43	8.29
31–59	38.71	10.19	12.79	13.68	15.88	0.97	7.79
15–59	27.98	8.68	13.19	18.12	23.16	1.14	7.73
7+	26.93	15.25	16.97	16.3	17.65	0.9	5.99

Source: Various Rounds, National Sample Survey Office (NSSO).

11

Impact of Urbanization on Water Resources

Case of Jaipur Using Remote Sensing Technique

KAMAL NARAIN JOSHI

Urbanization and industrialization has threatened the surface and groundwater resources in and around the urban areas. The unplanned growth of urban settlements and infrastructure development act as an obstacle in the path of water flow which ultimately hampers the recharge process of ground as well as surface water bodies in the area. This process has resulted in the conversion of water potential and agricultural lands into non-agricultural uses. Apart from the diversion of lands for non-agricultural uses, the extensive damage to ecology and environment due to industrial waste, pollution, and misuse of land can also be seen in the urban areas and its periphery. One other important impact is noticed on the natural hydrological system of the city. As the urban areas spread, the natural hydrological features like rivers, nallah and water bodies come in the heart of the city and people start encroaching upon them. It results in either completely or partly blocking of the system. Another important issue that many of the cities have experienced its expansion at the cost of flood risk because they are settled in low-lying areas or along the river/nallah. These lands are often parts of some watersheds or catchments of the water bodies or rivers/nallahs flowing in urban environs. Hence, this process on one hand breaks the hydrological system and, on other hand, creates a permanent recurrent flood damage zone in the city area. The paper tries to understand the anthropogenic activities that have negative or positive impact on water resources of Jaipur city. It aims to assess the impact on water resources due to changes in urban morphology encroachments, unscientific land use, haphazard growth of colonies and emergence of slum, etc. and also suggests strategy which would help to solve the problem.

The paper is based on remote sensing as well as secondary data. The satellite data has been used to prepare thematic maps mainly land use and water resource, a village-wise data from revenue and census department have also been collected and used in the study. The maps have been prepared in GIS environment using Arc Info, MapInfo, ERDAS and Auto-CAD software. For preparing base maps, I have used Survey of India Topographical Sheet on 1:50,000 scale. A GPS survey has been carried out to collect ground truth for interpretation of satellite data. Information from revenue department was also collated. The remote sensing data has been analysed using statistical as well as computer mapping technique supported by field surveys.

The field survey was conducted in two parts phases i.e. reconnaissance survey and detailed survey for ground truth collection and preparation of image interpretation key. A few sites have been re-visited after interpretation of satellite data for final verification.

Three types of data have been used viz. (i) conventional data (ii) remote sensing data and (iii) secondary data from on line department and revenue data.

Conventional Data

1. Topographical Sheets (Survey of India): Nine Topographical Sheets i.e. 45/N/9, 45/N/10, 45/N/13, 45/N/14, 45M/12, 45/M/16, 54/A/4, 54/B/1, 54/B/2 on 1:50,000 scale have been used for all purpose of basic geographical information.
2. Census Data: Census data of series 1971,1981,1991 and 2001 have been used for collecting detailed information at village level. Some information from cadastral map and *zinswari* has also been used.

Remote Sensing Data

The satellite data of the year 1975 (Landsat MSS), 1986 (IRS – LISS II FCC) 1991 (IRS – LISS III FCC) have been used to draw information on land use, geomorphology and hydrological features. IRS-LISS –III and IV data in the form of False Color Composite have been used.

Expansion of the Jaipur City

In 1728, when the wall city of Jaipur was founded, its total area was about 4.81 sq. km. By 1930–31, the limits of the municipal area further extended to the wall of city, and the total area reached to 9.6 sq. km. In 1951 due to rapid increase in population the city area has been further expanded to 40 sq. km. During 1964, with the increasing demand of population problems associated with urbanization like living accommodation, traffic congestion, lack of sanitation and other amenities, etc. there was a felt need of preparing a Master Plan of keeping the needs of the Jaipur city up to 1991. In 1965, a Master Plan of Jaipur city was prepared and 125 revenue villages of surrounding areas of Jaipur city were brought in the urban boundary. The total area reached to 115 sq. km. In 1972, an additional 132 revenue villages were inducted in the urban area and the total area reached up to 385 sq. km, out of which 153 sq. km was the urbanizable area and rest was to develop green belt around Jaipur. In recent past, in 1995, the Master Plan was revised targeting the need of the year 2011. The Master Plan earmarked the notified urban area of Jaipur city to be 96,300 acres (385 sq. km) out of which 38,400 acres (153.6 sq. km) was the urbanizable area (40%) and 57,900 acres (231.4 sq. km) as the green belt (60%).

Physical Environment of Jaipur

The city is surrounded by the Nahargarh hills in the north and Jhalana in the east, which is a part of Aravalli hill-ranges. To the south and the west of the city are also prevailing hillocks but they are isolated and discontinuous in formation. The southern end of the city is open to plain and stretches far and wide towards Sanganer and beyond. The walled city was originally located on the rocky street to provide an easy drainage system on either side of the city but the future exertion of the city took place on the south and west on the alluvial plains formed in the confluence's zone of the Amani Shah nallah in the west and Jawahar Nagar nallah in the east and beyond.

The general slope of the Jaipur city and its surroundings is from north to south and then to south-east. Nearly all the ephemeral streams flow in this direction. Higher elevations in the north exist in the form of low, flat-topped hills of Nahargarh (587 metres), Jaigarh, Amber and Amargarh, which are deeply dissected and eroded. An isolated hillock called 'Moti Dungari' upon which an old royal castle exists is near the Rajasthan University. Further in the south, topographical levels of the plain areas varies between 280 metres along Bandi and Dhund rivers in the south to about 530 metres in the north east of Chomu near Samod hills. The overall trend is a decline of level from the areas bordering the hills in the north to plain in the south, slopes of the plain areas are in general gentle.

The natural drainage of the Jaipur city is largely technically affected. It shows intense gully erosion particularly in the northern hilly region. Dhund River and Amani Shah nallah form a fork like drainage pattern in the confluence zone of which the major part of Jaipur city is situated. The Amani Shah nallah, which originates from the western slopes of Jaigarh hills, flows northwards in the upper reaches, turns south and south-west in its middle course and flows towards east with a broad semi-circle. Finally, it joins river Dhund further downstream. There is another small drainage system in the north foothills which nowadays discharges the city's waste effluents into an artificially impounded lake called the Jal Mahal (Man Sagar). Jal Mahal Lake is a large cesspool now of effluent waste water changing its profile from muddy water mixed with effluents and sludge during rainy season to a dried large puddle surrounded by parched earthen floor during summer seasons.

Climatically, Jaipur is located in the semi-Arid Zone of India. It is characterized by high temperature, low rainfall and mild winter. The mean temperature of Jaipur is 36° varying from 18°C in winter (January) to 40°C in summer (June). Thus, January and June are the coldest and hottest months. The normal rainfall of Jaipur is 600 mm; nearly 90 per cent of which takes place in the summer monsoon period i.e. from June to September, the rest comes from the winter cyclones.

Hydrometeorology

The mean annual rainfall recorded at Sanganer, Amer and Jaipur rain gauge stations was 584.0, 676.5 and 6391.mm respectively, (period 1969–2007). The average mean annual rainfall for these three stations works out to 633 mm for the same period.

The monsoon rainfall which contributes about 96 per cent of total annual rainfall extends from June-end till September, July and August being the wettest months. Based on chegodev's empirical relation, probability of exceeding of average annual rainfall is about 25 per cent and normal drought 19.7 per cent where as probability of reverse and most severe drought is almost negligible. Perusal of rainfall periodicity shows good rainfall spell between 1981 and 1983 (with a flash flood in 1981) whereas the time span 1984–89 witnessed a low precipitation/drought period. This low rainfall spell was broken in 1990. The rainfall during the period of 1990 to 1998 was generally good with the exception of 1991 and 1993 when the rainfall was slightly below mean annual rainfall. Again, between 1998 and 2001, the precipitation was below 40 per cent of mean and the city is witnessing yet another drought.

History of Water Resource Development of Jaipur City

In the beginning of 18th century the area surrounding Jaipur had a good surface drainage network. A perennial river called Dhanvantri river (presently Amanishah Nallah) was flowing in the west of Jaipur city. It originates from the highest point of Nahargarh hills in the north of Jaipur. First it flows northwards in the upper reaches, turns south and south-west in its middle course and finally flows from north to south till it meets river Dhund. The Dund River in the east follows a straight course from the north to south for a considerable distance. Dhund River and Dravywati River (Amanishah Nallah) form a fork like drainage pattern in the confluence zone of which the major part of Jaipur city is situated. There were four natural drainages. Two of these flow to the south west to meet the Amanishah Nala and the other two flow to the north east to meet the Jal Mahal Talao. There is another small drainage system in the north foothills which impounded lake called the Jal Mahal (Man Sagar). The western part of Jaipur is a vast expansion of gently undulating surface and is drained by westerly flowing streams. They are the Bandi River in the northwest and Sadriya Nadi in the west, with their smaller and ephemeral lower order streamlets.

In the beginning of the 18th century, the population of the city was about a lakh and needs were very limited. Water was required for drinking, cooking and washing purposes. These limited needs could very well be met by the local wells. The citizens used to draw water from open wells and *baories* (step wells) in the city.

A moat wall was constructed along the foot hills of Nahargarh keeping in view the dual purpose of keeping the wild animals away from the city as also diverting the rain water to Man Sagar (popularly known as Jai Mahal). This moat wall allowed the water from the hills to percolate into the wells in the areas nearby and, thus, serve as a source of recharge to water supply for the town. Another tank was constructed within the four walls of the city popularly known as Raj Jaimal's Tank which provided recharge to the wells in the northern part of the city. A channel for supply of drinking water to those who could not afford to have their own wells was constructed right from Suraj Pole Gate to Chand Pole Gate and three reservoirs called the *kunds* were constructed which are buried now and are known as Chhoti Chauper, Bari Chauper and the Ramganj Chauper. The water was lifted through traditional means at both the ends and was collected in the *kunds* from where the poorer sections of the community would fetch water.

The first water supply scheme was started for city palace where water from open well was drawn with oxen and was supplied though a small canal. In the mid of 18th century, the walled city was supplied water from Amanishah Nalla though canals upto Chhoti Chauper and Bari Chauper from where people used to take water. Piped water supply to Jaipur for public began in 1874 with the construction of a reservoir of 4.5 MLD capacities across Amanishah Nallah. Open wells were constructed in the Nallah to meet the drinking water demand.

This system could meet the demand of the city till the first quarter of this century. With the population exceeding a lakh and the dependence on the water supply scheme increasing, it was felt that the existing system would not be sustainable. The Amanishah nallah was considered insufficient for further tapping. A new source had to be located which could provide sufficient supply. The source was located at Ramgarh Bundh. This tank was constructed in the year 1903 near village Jamwa Ramgarh at a distance of about 30km from Jaipur. River Banganga originating from the Bairath was tamed and the tank was constructed with a capacity of 2080 meft. The catchment area of the tank was 475 sq. km and with an annual average rainfall of 558 mm the F.T.L being 1260.00 R.L. the live storage capacity was 2030.30 meft. Thus, in the early 1930s the city had two sources viz. The Amanishah Nallah system and the Ramgarh Bund/Laxman Doongri system were considered sufficient to meet the demand of around 150 lakh population.

In the early 1940s, the city witnessed a process of development whereby efforts were made to make it an important centre of industry and trade. Colonies outside the four walls of the city were carved out necessitating extension of the water supply. In the late 1940s, when the process of integration of State resulted in formation of Greater Rajasthan, Jaipur was chosen to be the capital of Rajasthan precisely on account of the fact that it had assured means of water supply. However, this decision resulted in a fast growth and increase in urban population. In 1953, capacity of Pumpage from Ramgarh Lake was increased from 9 MLD to 27 MLD by installation of necessary pumping stations, carrier main filtration plants, distribution mains, etc.

In 1961, the population of Jaipur city had increased to about 4.50 lakh and a demand for water had increased due to increase in the population. Hence, in the year 1963, capacity of lake was further increased from 27 MLD to 54 MLD and filter plant was installed at Laxman Dungari. A pumping station was created at Bundh gate from where the water was to be lifted to the filter plant at Laxman Doongri. Three additional filters were installed at Laxman Doongri and a reservoir with a capacity of 10 lakh gallon was constructed. An additional distribution line diameter was laid from Laxman Doongri to connect the city supply lines. The capacity of this re-organized scheme was 16 lakh gallons per day. Thus, the total supply of water through the schemes went up to 100 lakh per day.

To meet the growing demand of drinking water due to population pressure, the augmentation scheme was sanctioned during 1971–72 taking groundwater as source. The existing capacity of the scheme was 63 MLD.

In the year 1970–71, for the first time it was envisaged that the groundwater should be tapped and supplied in the areas nearby. The city was divided into 14 zones and for each zone, a tube well was bored and commissioned. The capacity of groundwater withdrawal was in from 63 MLD to 99 MLD in 1973–74 by constructing additional tube wells in the outskirt areas. During 1976–77, the supplies from the groundwater was enhanced to the tune of 126 MLD. During 1980–85, to further increase the water supply capacity by 72 MLD, about 18 MLD of water was increased from Ramgarh Lake whereas 54 MLD groundwater from 120 wells. Thus, the total capacity of Jaipur water supply scheme was raised to 234 MLD.

The only sources were the Ramgarh Tank and the groundwater. Amanishah Nallah was being tapped to is fullest capacity and it was found that by more tube wells in the nallah, it would result in reduction in the yield of the existing wells. Jamwa Ramgarh Bundh, the main source of water supply to Jaipur city, had overflown only three times during the total period after its construction. During the past two decades, the storage of water till 1983–84, was maximum at 2250.00 meft and a minimum of 1216–46 meft. However, after 1983–84, the water level never went beyond 54 ft. and in some years it was as low as 29 ft and 36ft. the tank has been silted up to 14ft and reducing the storage capacity. Further aggravating the problem was construction of 25 Anicuts in the catchment area of Ramgarhbundh. This caused interception of water coming to Ramgarh Bundh. Any lean year could result in the Ramgarh Bundh remaining dry. Ramgarh Bundh, therefore, has been no more a source for tapping additional water supply to Jaipur.

Till a regular solution of the problem of feeding Jaipur was not available, the increasing population of Jaipur city and the increasing demand for water could be met only through contingency plans. All the steps taken by the State Government were in the nature of emergency management. Bisalpur dam on river Banas was envisaged that the waters of this dam would be utilized partially for irrigation and partially for supplying drinking water to the cities of Ajmer, Beawar, Kishangarh and villages en route to the district of Ajmer and also for Jaipur city as also towns and villages falling enroot. Bisalpur dam is to have the capacity of 1271.55 mcm at maximum water level and that of 1095.84 mcm at full reservoir level. A scheme has been prepared to supply 340.00 million gallon of water per day from Bisalpur dam to Jaipur city. This will meet the requirements of around 34 lakh of population in the city.

The Bisalpur-Jaipur Water Supply Project (BWSP) has been designed to deliver water from the existing Bisalpur Dam headworks up to Balawala on the south edge of Jaipur City to reduce the city's dependence on its groundwater resources, and includes complementary provisions for supplying water to other areas. The conceptual planning for the BWSP is to utilize the Bisalpur Dam water in a phased manner in order to meet the ever increasing water demands of Jaipur City and reduce the groundwater abstraction to sustainable limits. Phase I of the BWSP with water treatment plant (WTP) designed to supply a total of 400 MLD with a provision of 360 MLD for Jaipur city and 40 MLD for rural area.

The works have been planned and designed for 600 MLD in such a manner so as to facilitate a Phase II expansion programme which is to be taken up in the future to provide a total of 540 MLD of treated water to Jaipur City plus 60 MLD to the rural areas and also to facilitate construction of the Stage II of the Project to achieve a total capacity of 1020 MLD clear water production.

Present Drinking Water Supply for Jaipur

Presently, city water supply is about 400 MLD from about 1067 tube wells and 1800 hand pumps catering about 25 lakhs (2.5 million) of population in Jaipur city with the service level (supply per capita per day) of 160 litres. Public Health and Engineering Department (PHED), Government of Rajasthan, is primarily responsible for planning operation and maintenance of water supply scheme in Jaipur city. In addition to PHED water supply scheme, a number of private tube wells also supply drinking water in Jaipur urban agglomerate area. A recent survey by PHED indicate that there are about 1340 tube wells scattered over various parts of the city and are responsible for the bulk of the total production (347 MLD). In addition, there are about 1845 hand pumps installed at various locations, which help in meeting the demand of the weaker sections of the society tube wells in Jaipur city only.

It is clear that requirement of drinking/domestic water supplies are wholly dependent on groundwater only. With increasing urbanization and industrialization (hence greater dependability on groundwater resources), the water levels are declining and groundwater resources depleting. Since the present level of replenishment of dynamic water resources is not sufficient to meet the demand of Jaipur Urban and its agglomerate area. The Static groundwater resource is undergoing depletion/mining at faster rate.

Impact of Urban Growth on Hydrology

The hydrology of Jaipur is governed by physical characteristics of landscape and geology. The city is surrounded by hills intermountain valleys, pediments and sandy plains. In northern and eastern parts, the Aravalli hill ranges, trending north, east-south, west alternating with intermountain valleys, constitutes significant signatures of physiography. There are as many as 518 rivulets that originate from these hill ranges out of which 398 are of 1st order, 92 of 2nd order and 25 are of 3rd order and three are of 4th order streams. In early stage, the city expansion was restricted to foothills only and no drainage system was disturbed. But as the expansion took place, people started filling, diverting and blocking the stream. At many places the natural streams were used to dump the garbage. As a result, 150 streams out of which 113 of 1st order, 37 of 2nd second order and 10 of 3rd third order stream are blocked or filled for the construction purpose due to expansion of Jaipur city. It has a direct bearing on the availability of surface as well as groundwater. Now the water of these streams goes waste as flood water in the street of urban areas or flows in the urban sewerage system. It creates local flood situation in low lying areas.

Destruction of Groundwater Recharge System

Groundwater is part of the Earth's water or hydrological cycle. When rain falls, a part infiltrates the soil and the remainder evaporates or runs off into rivers. The roots of plants will take up a proportion of this moisture and then lose it through transpiration to the atmosphere, but some will infiltrate more deeply, eventually accumulating above an impermeable bed, saturating available pore space and forming an underground reservoir.

Direct human interventions have led to reduction in groundwater recharge. These include: deforestation, destruction of local water systems and stoppage of river flows. Deforestation also leads to change in river flow regime in the affected area that also affects the recharge in the given area. There are larger and indirect human interventions that have also affected the groundwater recharge systems, including urbanization and concretization of more and more land.

As the built up area increases, more area comes under concretization like houses roads, and other amenities. These areas are not suitable for groundwater recharge as the concretized land does not allow water to penetrate. Hence, the water of that local stream flow on the surface as a surface flow. The local streams of that area also get affected. It does not allow water to penetrate and hence the groundwater recharge area is reduced. The table reveals that the built area in 1986 was only 143.40 sq. km which was increased to 189.70 sq. km in year 2003. It means the potentiality of recharging the groundwater area has been reduced by 46.30 sq. km during last 17 years.

Second important impact of the expansion of built up area is seen in relation to hydro-geo-morphology. Most of the area, about 65 per cent, is covered by alluvial plain which is good for groundwater probability and groundwater recharge. Second largest area is under pediment and intermountain valleys which moderate from groundwater point of view. Now it is clear from Table 1 that the total 65 per cent alluvial area, which was under agricultural land, has reduced by 32 sq. kms. This reduction has a negative impact on groundwater. It is observed that the groundwater of these areas have also gone down by 5.97m in HCM Training Institute, 1.69m in Jhotwara area, 1.81 m at Army Cantonment (Study conducted by Rajasthan Ground Water Board).

The other important observation linking to this phenomenon is that wells of this area which was getting recharge through various streams which it was not concretized also got negatively affected. Table 1 reveals that the distribution of wells and tube wells in the built up area was 789, 1014 and 1116 in the year 1986, 1991, and 2003, respectively. Due to expansion in the built up area, all these wells and tube wells have been in the grip of water deficiency. Again the rate and speed of water recharge depend on the type of surface area being concretized. If the area is fully packed with the cement like in the wall city where no single feet area is left *kutcha,* all is packed wall to wall, then there is no chance of recharging the groundwater. Otherwise the speed and volume of recharge slows down as per the per cent of area concretized.

Table 1

Distribution of Wells and Tube Well in Different Land Use Categories

Major Land Use Category	*Area (sq km)*			*Tube wells*			*Wells*			*Total (wells and tube wells)*		
	1986	*1991*	*2003*	*1986*	*1991*	*2003*	*1986*	*1991*	*2003*	*1986*	*1991*	*2003*
Built up area	143.40	163.32	189.70	545	725	791	244	289	325	789	1014	1116
Forest area	57.45	53.52	59.01	13	33	20	27	34	32	40	67	52
Crop land	217.03	205.80	185.05	1349	1083	1050	449	404	382	1798	1487	1432
Waste land	18.30	13.63	2.24	54	20	—	19	12	—	73	32	—
Total	436.00	436.00	436.00	1861	1861	1861	739	739	739	2600	2600	2600

Source: Based on Interpretation of Satellite Data and GIS.

Other groundwater recharge potential zones are the agricultural land. These lands are often plain and with loose sand which keep the velocity of water low and are helpful in percolating water. The agriculture area in the year 1986 was 217 sq. km which was about 50 per cent of the total geographical area. In year 2003, it has been reduced to 185.05 sq. km. The distribution of wells and tube wells in the same area was 1798 and 1432, respectively, in the year 1986 and 2003.

Depletion of Groundwater

The above table show that within 17 years of urbanization, building of roads, houses and commercial complexes and encroachment of forest lands, agricultural fields, pasturelands and open wasteland has taken place at an unprecedented rate. This has reduced the open areas to a great extent. The open areas were formerly the useful places to soak the rainwater and percolate it down to recharge the aquifers. Hence, the city sprawl has shrunk the vacant surfaces thereby affecting the rainwater supply to water-bearing rocks. The diminished aquifers have now lowered the water table. During the past five years, the water table has sunk by more than one metre per year into the tube wells and this is alarming to the ecology of the city. Thus, the city is in the 'dark zone' of water potentials.

More promising aquifers have been sighted in the southern parts of the city in the vicinity of Sanganer a satellite town, Durgapura Township and further south of Shivdaspura from which large quantities of water are now being exploited and supplied to the city. Here, there are more vacant spaces to absorb more rainwater and replenishments can be expected to be reasonably good. The slope of the lands is also to the south and so the rainwaters of the north flow down to the south and recharge the aquifers of this area. Moreover, the Amanishah Nallah, the Ganda Nallah, the Jawahar Nagar Nallah and the Dhund River, all of them being the natural drains of the city and its environs, bring a heavy discharge of water in the rainy season to add to the richness of the aquifers. It can be asserted, therefore, that these areas of potentially rich aquifers be left unscathed of human activity like residential localities, industrial sites and transportation networks so that they get the constant recharge of rain water.

Encroachment upon forest lands and pasture lands by building residential and industrial areas in Jawahar Nagar, Tilak Nagar, Vishwakarma industrial area, Vidyadhar Nagar and Amba Bari has proved to be suicidal in the total ecological scenario of the city and the damage caused is irreversible. Not only the water table has sunk down in these areas, but also the natural abodes of wilderness have been lost forever. Today, all these areas are the most potent sources of groundwater but the loss of rainwater replenishments to the subsoil layers is having a constant telling-effect to the extent that the vegetation and water resources will soon vanish.

In addition to above, advances in technology have resulted in enormous increase in abstraction of groundwater world-wide thereby disturbing natural groundwater resource balance. Large-scale groundwater development due to urbanization and industrialization has rendered most of the Jaipur Urban area groundwater system as over-exploited. The ever-increasing pace of development of groundwater has also resulted in declining trends in water levels, thereby causing decrease in the yield of the wells.

Degradation of Hills and Water Bodies

There are hillocks even within the towns. These hills provided a natural scenic view to the town and forts were built over them. The population pressure has adversely affected these hillocks and at present these are almost barren. The hill terraces are dotted with encroachments and unauthorized constructions. Extensive removal of vegetation particularly due to deforestation on the slopes of hills and from stable dunes flanking the hills has played a major role in degrading the environment. Due to stone quarrying from the hill slopes of Jhalana and Amagarh and also due to encroachments by way of urban construction activities, the problem of soil erosion has accelerated today. The quarrying has increased the degree of slope of hills causing deterioration in aesthetic view of hills.

In some of these towns mining activities are being carried out. All these activities have affected aesthetic beauty and environment.

For taking care of water needs of the residents of Jaipur, a number of wells and baories (step wells) were dug apart from large ponds. In Amer, 'Maotha Sagar' Bandh Talab, etc. were constructed in order to maintain the water level in other wells and baories. Main baories of Amer are 'Panna Meena', 'Chhela baories', 'Thttar baories', 'Naku bawari', Sarai baories,. 'Vijay bagh baories', and 'Teli baories' On the pattern of baories of Amer, the king of Jaipur Sawai Jai Singh got constructed many baories in various colonies of Jaipur. These baories were constructed in the low-lying areas and basins of hills in order to collect the water and form a large catchment area. The famous baories constructed in that area were 'Kala Hanuman Ki baories', two baories of Gurjar Ghati namely 'Kalyan ji temple baories' and near 'Atreya School', in Jai Singhpura Khore, near Chullgiri, seven baories of Galta, 'Khon Nagoriyas', 'Jagga ki baories', Yagnashala ki baories', 'Parsashramdwara ki baories', etc. The main purpose of these baories was to enable continuous water supply for residents of these areas and also to maintain water level. These water bodies were not only a source of drinking water but also served as recreational places. They had well connected inlet drainage system spread over protected catchment areas. However, the haphazard growth of towns has adversely affected these systems. In absence of sewerage system, these water bodies have been converted into cess pools for collection of domestic sewage.

Suggestions to Augment and Restore the Urban Water Resources

Conservation of Surface Water: The Amanishah Nallah, the Jawahar Nagar Nallah and the Dhund River form the major drainage of the Jaipur urban area. All of them, being the natural drains of the city, bring a heavy discharge of water in the rainy season to add to the richness of the aquifers. It can be asserted, therefore, that these areas of potentially rich aquifers are left unscathed of human activity like residential localities, industrial sites and transportation networks, etc. More promising aquifers have been sighted in the southern parts of the city in the vicinity of Sanganer, Durgapura and further south of Shivdaspura from which large quantities of water are now being exploited and supplied to the city.

Here, there are more vacant spaces to absorb more rainwater and replenishments can be expected to be reasonable good. The slope of the lands is also towards the south so the rain waters of the north that flow down to the south can recharge the aquifers of this area. Hence, these open spaces be used for parks and recreation spots creating water ponds, etc. so that their openness be used for the recharge of groundwater;

There were six dams constructed on the main water course of Amanishah Nallah, namely Athuni Kund, Babu-Ka-Bandh, Majar Dam, Amanishah Water Works and Dam, Rawalji-Ka-Buandh, Khawasji-ka-Bundh, Gular Dam, and Ramchandrapura Dam. Out of these, two dams are in operation, others were breached during the flood periods of 1960 and 1981. Unfortunately, the water spread area of four dams, namely Athuni Kund, Majar Dam, Amanishah Water work and Rawalji–ka-Bundh have been much encroached upon by the people though they are located in the centre of city. Therefore, these should be repaired and kept free from the pollution.

Many major water ponds of the villages and their drainage which have not come under the influence of urbanization should be protected and their water course be kept intact so that when they come in the periphery of urban area they can be used as a source of surface water.

There are as many as 17 anicuts in the urban territory. There maintenance is very poor. The irrigation department does have sufficient funds to repair these structures. They are very important as the urban area is facing acute water shortage. Hence, their maintenance should be ensured.

There are a number of traditional water harvesting structures like step wells, baories, wells and *taals*. Their condition is also poor. Recently, the Government of Rajasthan has shown some interest in reviving them in the name of conservation of cultural heritage. All these structures which are not in use due to lack of maintenance should be revived.

Conservation of Groundwater: Advances in technology have resulted in enormous increase in abstraction of groundwater world-wide, thereby disturbing natural groundwater resource balance. Large-scale groundwater development due to urbanization and industrialization has rendered most of the Jaipur Urban area groundwater system as over-exploited. Recharge to groundwater is also diminishing because of the shrinkage in the open areas. The ever-increasing pace of development of groundwater has also resulted in declining trends in water levels, thereby causing decrease in the yield of the wells.

Construction of Sub-Surface Barriers/Check Dams: In order to arrest and recharge monsoon run-off rain water, construct subsurface barriers/check dams across the ephemeral Amanishah Nallah and associated streamlets also. Filter dykes/inverted wells within the impoundment area so as to allow speedy percolation of the water. Construction of such structures is likely to result in additional recharge of groundwater.

Artificial Recharge from Paved Areas: Artificial recharge from paved area run off, i.e. from roads, footpath, etc. can be recharged by constructing recharge shafts/trenches, improving the existing storm water drains designs, etc. This can give additional recharge of about 25–30 mcm annually.

Roof Top Rainwater Harvesting: Keeping in view the depleting water resources there is an urgent need for harvesting rooftop rain water for groundwater recharge so as to minimize run-off water and evaporation losses. There is as much as 263.17 sq km settlement area available for collecting water as roof top rain water. Hence, the government should seriously think of making a plan to conserve this water. Recently, the Central Ground Water Board has initiated artificial recharge by roof top rainwater harvesting from the major buildings in the urban agglomerates. On experimental basis, rain water harvesting project has been taken up at CGWB, WR, office building. The rain water from building roof top is connected through pipe line and stored in a pit. The water in the pit will be allowed to percolate downward through a recharge tube well. The rain water harvesting by this method is cheaper as well as effective so as to store and recharge groundwater.

Groundwater Regulatory Measures

Groundwater exploitation needs to be regulated. In the peripheral areas of the urban agglomerate, utilization of groundwater for agricultural irrigation purposes should be practiced by employing sprinklers/drip methods only. Registration of drilling agencies, existing groundwater abstraction structures must be made mandatory. Seeking of permission for further construction of groundwater abstraction structures should be made mandatory so as to control exploitation and protection of groundwater from overdraft and quality degradation.

Industrial Sector: Treatment of industrial effluents so as to check pollution of fresh groundwater resources, recycling of industrial wastewater and use of treated industrial waste water for irrigation and groundwater recharge purpose.

Domestic Sector: There are few ways water can be efficiently used, viz. (i) reuse of domestic waste water for gardening; (ii) bathing just with a bucket of water instead of using fountain/bath tub, that can save water to the tube of 100 litres per day per person; (iii) using value system in toilets rather than flushing tanks that can save about 10 litres of water per person per trip; (iv) making use of just ½ a litre container for saving instead of flowing water from taps thus conserving water to the time of about 4–5 litres per shaving; (v) small container may be used for brushing teeth. Stop using taps for this purpose; (vi) don't waste water from taps for washing clothes. A bucket of water may be sufficient for such washing; (vii) leakages from pipelines for water supply to urban/rural areas be checked properly by the organizations/societies concerned; (viii) construction of hand pumps may be further encouraged, groundwater exploitation by hand pump saves water; (ix) try to restore the traditional groundwater harvesting structures; and (x) promote rainwater storage tanks.

Development of Water Resource Monitoring System

The continuous change in the urban land use of a city is the utmost concern of urban planners and decision-makers. The rapid increase of urban population and the urbanization leads to an ever-increasing demand on the urban environment. The unplanned expansion of cities and encroachments by people for various purposes pose serious problems to the environment and the people living in the area. Therefore, it is very much necessary to monitor the land use and its changes in periodical frame. Remote Sensing is the best technology which provides the periodical data with high resolution that can be used to detect the changes and also evaluate its negative and positive impact. By carrying out this exercise one may remove the negative impact of land use in the process of its change or may suggest some remedial measures.

References

Arora, R.K. et al. (1978). 'Jaipur: Profile of a Changing City', *Prashasnika*, W (1–2).

Deckshatulu, B.L. (1987). 'Remote Sensing for Studies on Land Transformation', proceedings of National Symposium on Remote Sensing in Land Transformation and Management, p. 110.

Directorate of Economics and Statistics (2004). *Statistical Abstract, Rajasthan*, Jaipur.

Government of India (1908). *Imperial Gazetteer of India*, Provincial Series, Rajasthan.

Government of Rajasthan (Undated). *Report on Watershed Development Programme in Rajasthan*, Directorate of Watershed and Soil Conservation, Jaipur.

Groundwater Board, Groundwater Resources and Development Potential of Rajasthan (1984). Central Ground Water Board, Government of India, Western Region, Jaipur.

Hanumappa, H.G. (1981). *Urbanization Trend in India: A Case Study of Medium Towns*, Ashish Publishing House, New Delhi.

Imperial Gazetteer of India (1976). Vol. XIII, Government of India Press, Calcutta, p. 214.

——. (1908). Vol. VIII, Provincial Series Rajputana, Books Treasure, Jodhpur, p. 260.

Joshi, K.N. (1993). 'Drought in Semi-Arid', in *Land Studies in Arid Land Management*, Scientific Publishers, Jodhpur.

——. (2002). 'Changing Urban Land Use and its Impact on the Environment', Proc. Con. of 23rd Asian Conference on Remote Sensing, Kathmandu, Nepal November 26–29.

——. (2003). 'Changing Urban Sprawl and its Impact on Hydrological Regime in Nagarlok', XXXV (4).

Master Plan of Jaipur 1971–91. Jaipur: The Chief Town Planner & Architectural Adviser, Government of Rajasthan, May 1976.

Mathur, H.S. (1983). 'Environmental Crisis in Jaipur City: Retrospects and Prospects', in L.R. Singh et al. (eds), *Environment Management*, University of Allahabad, Allahabad.

Mathur, Indu (1985). 'Jaipur: A Social Profile', in G.S. Nathawat et al. (eds), *Human Ecology: An Indian Perspective*, Indian Human Ecology Council, Jaipur, India, pp. 134–35

Nathawat, G.S. (1979). 'The Jaipur City its Growth and Natural Resources, Jaipur and Its Environs', Strategies for Integrated Development in Human Ecology, University of Rajasthan, Jaipur.

Rajasthan Patrika (1989). 'Nagar Parikrama', Jaipur, December 27.

Sharma, H.S. (1984). 'Impact of Unprecedented Rainfall on the City and Its Environs', *Annals of the Association of Geographers, India*, IV (1): 5–9.

Town Planning Report (1981). Jaipur Zone – 1, Department of Town Planning, Jaipur.

Unnithan, T.K.N. and Singh, Y. (1969). *Jaipur City*, University of Rajasthan, Jaipur, p. 21.

12

Delhi's Post Colonial Development Machine

How Can Science and Technology Studies (STS) Help Rethink the Urban?

LEON A. MORENAS

British social and political theorist Isaiah Berlin once said that to compare Dante to a fox and Shakespeare to a hedgehog might seem 'artificial, scholastic and ultimately absurd,' but these metaphors should not 'be rejected as being merely superficial or frivolous.' A metaphor, he argued, 'offers a point of view from which to look and compare, a starting-point for genuine investigation' (Berlin, 1953: 25– 26). More recent studies have demonstrated that metaphors are essential to our understanding of the world; they give form to our concepts and these concepts structure how we perceive and more importantly how we act in our world (Lakoff and Johnson, 1981; Lakoff, 1987, 2004).[1] So how does the conceptual metaphor of the machine help in understanding the urban?

Consider these opening paragraphs of the UN DESA's report *World Urbanization Prospects* (2014: 13):

> Megacities are notable for their size and concentration of economic activity, but are home to only about one in eight of the world's urban dwellers. In 1990 there were 10 cities with more than 10 million inhabitants, and these so-called 'megacities' were home to 153 million people, representing less than 7 per cent of the global urban population. Today, the number of megacities has nearly tripled to 28, the population they contain has grown to 453 million, and these agglomerations now account for 12 per cent of the world's urban

> dwellers. Tokyo is the world's largest city with an agglomeration of 38 million inhabitants, followed by Delhi with 25 million, Shanghai with 23 million, and Mexico City, Mumbai and São Paulo, each with around 21 million inhabitants. By 2020, Tokyo's population is projected to begin to decline, although it will remain the world's largest agglomeration in 2030 with 37 million inhabitants, followed closely by Delhi, whose population is projected to rise swiftly to 36 million.

Using this drizzle of arithmetic, the UN makes a clear prediction: the future of the world is urban. This portrayal of the urban is archetypal of the way the urban is discussed, or at least introduced these days.

I wish to draw attention not to the numbers themselves, but what in my view is the hegemonic portrayal of the inevitable urban condition. My paper counters this representation of the urban and employs qualitative, imprecise and unscientific attributes of the urban-as-machine conceptual metaphor. Through its sensitivity to the machine and its critics, my analysis also aims to guide an alternative appreciation of the city and of its citizens.

India's tryst with urbanization indicates that despite the fact that the majority of the country – around two-thirds – still lives in villages, most national policy decisions envision what our then Home Minister P. Chidambaram has called 'a poverty-free India ... where a vast majority, something like 85 per cent, will eventually live in cities.' He goes on: 'In an urban environment, it is easier and more efficient to provide water, electricity, education, roads, entertainment and security rather than in 6,00,000 villages' (Guha Ray and Chaudhury, 2008: 26). Who could fault Chidambaram for his reasons? The urban is after all the beacon of concentrated, easy efficiency. It must be noted that the present Minister for Urban Development Venkaiah Naidu also concurs with his predecessor. He believes, 'Urbanization is a worldwide phenomenon and you cannot prevent it; you cannot treat it as a problem. You should treat it as a challenge and convert it into an opportunity' (Sethi, 2014). The present government's 'efficient' solution is 100 smart cities. While I discuss this elsewhere (Morenas, 2014), suffice it to say that the urbanization project in India (and globally) is rationalized using efficiency. The urban is global, the arc of history tautly bent in its favour.

But what does this term efficiency mean? After all, this is not just a term bandied about by policymakers alone. It appears in our everyday vocabulary to describe our thoughts and the way we act upon these ideas. American Science and Technology Studies (STS) philosopher Langdon Winner (1977: 12) has argued that efficiency is a form of technique or a mode of human action that is purposive and rational. French STS philosopher Jacques Ellul argues, in turn, that technique is 'any complex of standardized means for attaining a predetermined result ... committed to the quest for continually improved means to carelessly examined ends ... technique transforms means to ends' (1964: 14). This appears to undergird Chidambaram's vision for India and the UN's logic in World Urbanization Prospects; 85 per cent of Indians will live in cities, and ... the megacities are in waiting. These are the ends assured by efficiency, assured by technique.

While both Winner and Ellul focus on the positive dimensions of efficiency and technique, Canadian philosopher of technology Ursula Franklin (1999) draws our attention to its negative side. While on the one hand, efficiency and technique strive *for* greater predictability and profit, on the other, they also embody a set of structures and practices to *prevent* undesirable or unpredictable interventions (1999: 57). These negative attributes are usually subsumed under the larger discourse of efficiency and technique. This is what Ellul (1964) means when he argues that in the quest for continually improved means, larger political ends are either not examined or examined carelessly. Rather than passively accepting the inevitability of India's urban future, this paper focuses on the technological undergirding of urbanization and brings to light some of its negative consequences.

Technique, Ellul further argues, 'transforms everything it touches into a machine' (1964: 3). According to him, the application of technique and efficiency ultimately culminates in what can be termed a machine or apparatus. This is how I am using the conceptual metaphor of the machine. The techniques employed in the production of the urban – through urban and regional planning – transforms the urban into a machine. I present this case through my analysis of the writings of Le Corbusier, the mis-credited 'planner of Chandigarh,' and the writings of the pioneers of the regional planning movement. While the intention of subjecting Le Corbusier's work to close scrutiny is instantly clear, given his involvement with Indian city-building, my reasons for examining the early writings on regional planning require some explanation. Chandigarh was India's first post-colonial city-building enterprise undertaken around 1950, while Delhi was planned soon after, in 1957. Delhi's Master Plan was conceived as a regional plan under the leadership of American regionalist Albert Mayer, who also founded the well-known Regional Planning Association of America along with Henry Wright and Lewis Mumford.

Let's start with the French.

II

> If we eliminate from our hearts and minds all dead concepts in regard to the houses and look at the question from a critical and objective point of view, we shall arrive at the 'House-Machine,' ... healthy (and morally so too) and beautiful in the same way that the working tools and instruments which accompany our existence are beautiful. (Le Corbusier, 1986 [1931]: 227)

With this spirited metaphor in his book, *Towards a New Architecture*, Le Corbusier outlines the prevailing ideology of his time: that the future of housing was the machine-house. According to him, 'the machinery of Society (was) profoundly out of gear,' (1986 [1931]: 269) and his rallying cry 'architecture or revolution' draws inspiration from 'the steamship, the airplane, and the automobile,' and using 'logic, daring, harmony, (and) perfection' produce a new urbanism comprising 'beautiful' and 'healthy' 'house-machines' (Le Corbusier, 1986 [1931]). The time had come, Le Corbusier argued, to create an apparatus[2] – 'both for the house and for the city' – for modern (technological) society to live in; a 'machine for living in,' that was an 'organized, serene, forceful, airy, ordered entity' (1986 [1931]). Anthropologist James Holston calls this vision a 'blueprint utopia' (1989) – through Taylorism, standardization, rationalism, the house and the city would be assembled as a totality, as machines are never designed or constructed partially. This is not unexpected, given that most of the early urban planners, like Le Corbusier, were either architects or engineers. Detailed plans and blueprints were made in order to build either machines or houses. The city too was conceived similarly, as a complete entity guaranteed for efficient functioning.

In order to do this, new conceptual apparatuses were required. The plan for this modern city, therefore, became a conceptual apparatus with a new meaning – for Le Corbusier, the plan was a 'generator' (1986 [1931]: 2). He said: 'The Plan holds in itself the essence of sensation. The great problems of to-morrow, dictated by collective necessities, put the question of 'plan' in a new form. Modern life demands, and is in waiting for, a new kind of plan both for the house and for the city' (1986 [1931]: 3). The term 'Master Plan' is, therefore, a rather apt term, revealing the dictatorial and masculine nature of both the master planner and his purposive creations.

Intriguingly, there is a banality of violence in Le Corbusier's vision. I use banality in homage to Hannah Arendt's phrase 'the banality of evil,' in which she argues that ordinary people, members of 'respectable society,' are capable of terrible acts. Adolf Eichmann and his 'accomplices ... were doctors and lawyers, scholars, bankers and economists' whose 'lack of imagination' and abstraction from reality had caused more destruction than if they were conscious of their evil designs (1994 (1963): 295).

I find many similarities between how Le Corbusier rationalized his role in modern city planning and Arendt's theory about the 'banality of evil'. By emphasizing his non-role in the production of the modernist city, he reduces his agency to a tiny cog in the city machine. Consider the following passage:

> The despot is not a man. It is the Plan. The correct, realistic, exact plan, the one that will provide your solution once the problem has been posited clearly, in its entirety, in its indispensable harmony. This plan has been drawn up well away from the frenzy in the mayor's office or the town hall, from the cries of the electorate or the laments of society's victims. It has been drawn up by serene and lucid minds. It has taken account of nothing but human truths. It has ignored all current regulations, all existing usages, and channels. It has not considered whether or not it could be carried out with the constitution now in force. It is a biological creation destined for human beings and capable of realization by modern techniques. (Le Corbusier (1964 [1933]: 154)

So the Plan is a biological creation that takes account of nothing but human truths and yet it has ignored regulations, history, and context. It is separate from the messy processes of politics, crafted by serene, apolitical minds. It is made by men, but is not a man. And it is the despot. It is in this sense suprahuman – powerful, impressive, desirable.

This is congruous with Arendt's theory that the State and its apparatuses, although responsible for the quality of life of its citizens and their everyday liberties, are not subject to the same rules. Arendt argues 'a government might find itself compelled to commit actions that are generally regarded as crimes in order to assure its own survival and the survival of lawfulness' (1994: 295). In the case of city plans and their apparatuses, they are indeed despotic in that their crimes are considered extraordinary measures used to avert crises like unhygienic sanitary conditions, dangerous building conditions etc. Later in this paper, I discuss Jagmohan Malhotra, the vice-chairman of the DDA and his role during Emergency. First, however, I wish to draw attention to the banality of violence in how the city apparatus was conceived by Le Corbusier and the role that these Plans played in the centralization of power and later in the preservation of these powers.

In *Seeing Like a State*, anthropologist James Scott examines various modernist projects, including those of Le Corbusier, and identifies the prevailing ideology of 'high modernism' (1998). According to him, this ideology is exemplified by 'an uncritical, unskeptical and thus unscientifically optimistic (view) about the possibilities for the comprehensive planning of human settlement'(1998: 4). The writings of Le Corbusier portray an unqualified faith in the city as machine. He suggests that the Plan for the modern apparatus of the city is autonomous, it generates the city-as-machine through its totalizing vision, dictating and demanding that its citizens worship – like the planner – at its altar of modern life.

Scott also identifies three other characteristics of high-modernism; they include (a) an administrative ordering of nature and society where social welfare is often provided by 'a muscle bound, version of self-confidence about scientific and technical progress ... (and) the rational design of social order,' (b) the presence of an authoritarian coercive state and (c) a 'prostrate civil society' incapable of resisting the planner and the State from realizing their modernist idea[l]s (Scott, 1998: 4–5). At the time of Indian Independence, civil society did not view itself as a field of power, so any high-modernist decisions of the State usually passed unopposed. It is particularly striking that this complex of ideology, administration, state, and civil society – these thoughts and the people thinking them – finds no articulation in Le Corbusier's descriptions of the machine as inspiration and the morphology of his modernist city. For him, the Plan is desirable precisely because it is divorced from these things.

While Indian political scientists have voraciously debated the moniker 'civil society,' (Chatterjee, 2004: 173; Chatterjee, 2011; Kaviraj and Khilnani, 2001) suggesting the Gramscian alternative 'political society' to describe Indian citizens in the early years after Independence, there is little argument that modern-city plans like that for Chandigarh and Delhi rendered citizens into invisible 'populations.' In presenting modernist city planning as a neutral technical mission, the expanding bureaucratic power of the State and its coercive powers are rendered apolitical and invisible or in many cases visible but apolitical.

Anthropologist James Ferguson actually terms these high-modernist projects, 'anti-politics machines' (Ferguson, 1994, 1990). These machines are characterized by their highly visible instrumental aims and plans but 'the actual process proceeds silently and often invisibly, masked or rendered even less visible by its contrast with the intentional plans, which appear bathed in the shining light of day'

(Ferguson, 1994, 1990: 276). These plans are the most visible part of a larger mechanism – they cannot, therefore, be dismissed. Ferguson suggests that they should not simply be thought of as blueprints for the machine but should be considered its parts. Perhaps, Le Corbusier said it best: a plan is in fact the 'generator' of his city-machine.

So how is the city-machine generated in the production of its plan? Given the architectural training of most urban planners, it is not surprising that their city designs were rationalized in romanticized aesthetic terms. Once again, the machine provided inspiration for the modernist city form and, therefore, presumed universal. 'Reason ... is an unbroken straight line, 'wrote Le Corbusier, and thus, 'in order to provide himself with a bearable, acceptable framework for his existence, one productive of human well-being and control, man has projected the laws of nature into a system that is a manifestation of the human spirit itself: geometry' (1964 [1933]: 82–83). This obsession with geometry reinforced the notion that a city-machine that looked orderly was also an efficient and rationally organized city.[3] This is the underlying rationale used to describe the Master Plan of Delhi which urban planner Gita Dewan Verma has described as an 'awfully ugly Technicolour map that is such a beautiful work of art' (2006: 14).

These Master Plans simplified city making of human activity and proposed sharply defined mono-functional 'zones.' Urban planning became the functional segregation of everyday activities into over-simplified geometries of work, domicile, commerce and play (Holston, 1989; Scott, 1998). Shopping, for example, was stripped of its experience and became an exercise of 'scientifically' providing access to quantity of goods through calculated floor space. Housing was computed as a variable of employment where the provision of employment dictated the size of the city. Scientific formulas were then applied to determine things like the number of parks, labelled 'green spaces,' the amount of light, or the number of schools measured in terms of square metres. Zoning heightened the emphasis upon transportation in this city, an enterprise of moving people between geometries of land use efficiently and economically across additional categories of automobile, pedestrian, and mass transit.

These plans were particularly destructive when applied to existing settlements especially when their scientific rationality was transcribed and codified into law. On the one hand, scientific formulae justified the creation of shopping and residential areas, to which all city administration resources were allocated. On the other, existing shopping and residential areas were labelled 'non-conforming,' i.e. in contravention to these plans, and the full force of the law was brought to bear upon their removal. Examples abound in Delhi – Commonwealth Games Village[4] housing colony: welcome, Yamuna Pushta[5] slum: non-conforming. Plans in this sense became self-fulfilling prognostications generating the city-as-machine.

III

While urban planning wholeheartedly embraced the city-as-machine model to efficiently organize land and services, regional planning attempted to conceive of urbanism with a more humanistic view. Urban planning placed an overt emphasis on technology as mankind's salvation, regional planning was an attempt to master technology to more humane ends. This provided the basic rationale for the use of a larger scale than that of the city.

In a clarion call to regional planning, its most vociferous progenitor Lewis Mumford wrote:

> Regional Planning asks not how wide an area can be brought under the aegis of the metropolis, but how the population and civic facilities can be distributed so as to promote and stimulate a vivid, creative life throughout a whole region – a region being any geographic area that possesses a certain unity of climate, soil vegetation, industry and culture. The regionalist attempts to plan such an area so that all its sites and resources, from forest to city, from highland to water level, may be soundly developed, and so that the population will be distributed so as to utilize, rather than to nullify or destroy, its natural advantages. It sees people, industry and the land as a single unit. (1925: 151–152)

Regional planning was conceived as a way of unifying people, industry and land at larger scale, a scale large enough to putatively deliver national benefits. In earlier work, I discuss at length how the Tennessee Valley Authority's regional planning model influenced Indian policy makers like Nehru and Mahalanobis precisely by promising to deliver national prosperity (Morenas, 2010). The movement was originally conceived by Scottish biologist and town planner Patrick Geddes, but the champions of regional planning were predominantly in the United States. These American planners viewed cities like Boston, New York and Chicago as 'dinosaur cities,' (Stein, 1925: 134–138) and saw their practice of 'regional planning ... wipe out uneconomic national marketing ... city congestion and terminal wastes ... balance the power load,' and do away with 'the necessity for the skyscraper (and) the subway' (Stein, 1925: 134–138) – defining components of the city-as-machine.

This vision of the region owes much of its legacy to Charles Darwin's concept of evolution. In his seminal 1915 book, *Cities in Evolution*, Patrick Geddes noted that the same technologies that fascinated Le Corbusier were causing cities to disperse rather than conglomerate and coined the term 'conurbation' (1949) to describe the phenomenon. Geddes, a biologist trained by 'Darwin's Bulldog' Thomas Henry Huxley, built his alternative argument by applying an evolutionary logic to regional planning, as the following quotation made by him illustrates:

> The natural eugenic centre is in every home ... Unite these grouped homes into renewed and socialized quarters – parishes, as they should be – and in time you have a better nation, a better world .... Each region and city can learn to manage its own affairs – build its own houses, provide its own scientists, artists and teachers. These developing regions are already in business together; can't they make friends and organize a federation as far as need be? (Geddes in Defries, 1928: 268).

As an applied science, eugenics embraced views on evolution proposed by Darwin to intervene in the human condition through science. Although the movement is infamous for its misuse by the Nazis, at its peak, some of its advocates included politicians Winston Churchill and Theodore Roosevelt and writers George Bernard Shaw and H.G. Wells (Blom, 2008). It even became an academic discipline in many universities until Adolf Hitler, who had earlier praised and incorporated eugenic ideas in his book, *Mein Kampf*, decided to implement them.[6] Nevertheless, the eugenic ideas to which Geddes is referring are of a more liberal stripe; in his application of social Darwinism to human settlements, he sees the region as an evolution of the city.

Fundamental to this vision is the role of technology in the creation of the region. Once again, employing the trope of evolution to the role of technology in determining human settlements, Geddes formulates the region as a product of the 'neotechnic era' (1912: 176–187). He wrote, 'we distinguish the earlier and ruder elements of the Industrial Age as Palaeotechnic,' while 'the newer and still often incipient elements disengaging themselves from these as Neotechnic' (1912: 176–187). These terms are borrowed from the work of Sir John Lubbock, who drew from evolutionary theory to study archaeology and is credited to making the discipline 'scientific' (1865). Just as the Paleolithic age reflected the prehistoric period of human history where humans used primitive stone tools, the Palaeotechnic period referred to that period between 1700 and 1900 that coincided with the rise of the Industrial Revolution. The technology used in the Palaeotechnic period too was crude and comprised coal-fired steam powered factories and the capital-intensive machinery that led to the exploitation of its unskilled machine workers (Lubbock, 1865). The Neotechnic period was conceived as being similar to the Neolithic age, where the relatively sophisticated use of polished tools was eclipsed by larger behavioural and cultural changes in human societies (Lubbock, 1865).

In a similar vein, both Geddes and Mumford argued that the Neotechnic period, through the invention of electricity and the internal combustion machine, freed workers from the tyrannical 'rule of machine and mammon' (Geddes, 1949: 86). Regional conurbations had evolved out of the industrial city and the regional planner/eugenist could intervene. For example in the city, its women, children and workers had little opportunity to visit the salubrious countryside and the regional planner could now, through neotechnic technology ' bring the country to them' (Geddes, 1949: 96). This organic vision of the region is best exemplified by Geddes's poetic statement that 'Towns must now cease to spread like expanding ink-stains and grease-spots: once in true development, they will repeat the star-like opening of the flower, with green leaves set in alternation with its golden rays' (1949: 97). This statement exposes the naivety of Geddes in particular and the regional planning profession in general. Paleotechnic technologies lead to towns becoming 'ink-stains' and 'grease-spots,' products that occur from the use of technologies such as the pen and the automobile; however, despite evidence to suggest technological outcomes, organic and cosmologic metaphors of blossoming flowers stars and rays are used to describe the products of neotechnic technologies.

The fundamental difference between urban planning of Corbusier and regional planning was that while the former called for the assimilation of human societies to the logic of the machine, the latter called for the assimilation of the machine to human ends. Regionalism would find an 'organic ideology,' 'a dynamic equilibrium' (Hall, 2002: 152, 146) by controlling neotechnic technologies not just for its inhabitants, but also for the larger cause of the nation. Whatever their different approaches, the centrality of technology in both city and region is evident.

This brings us back to our STS analysis and to one of its key philosophers, Langdon Winner. Winner defines autonomous technology 'as the rule of a self-generating, self-perpetuating, self-programming mechanism' (1977: 16). We have seen that in their dependence on technology, both city and regional planners organized various technological systems that became totalities. Winner submits that planning, and I would add – both at the city and regional scale – 'is a formalized technique designed to make new connections with a high degree of certainty and manipulability' (1977: 239). Jaques Ellul's views on planning are even more extreme than Winner's. In his view, 'Planning in modern society is *the* technical method,' (1964: 184), per Ellul (1964: 177), a 'trenchant weapon that simplifies and resolves all contradictions, (and) orders incoherencies.'

An important caveat is needed here: the trenchant weapon of planning of the region notwithstanding, it is not as though the region is like a car with no one at its wheel, driving itself. Both Winner and Ellul point out that human beings – planners, administrators, citizens – are ever present in these apparatuses. There are always 'desiring, thinking, deciding, acting' individuals in these systems (Winner, 1977: 227). And yet their desires, thoughts, decisions and actions are stifled, corrupted, invisibilized and even co-opted by technology's larger rationality to guarantee its perpetuation.

This is because a larger process is at play here: regional technological systems become behemoths whose success is in their own perpetuation, in a process called 'reverse adaptation' (Winner, 1977: 226–236, 238–250). Ends are then adapted to suit technological means, and technological systems reprogramme themselves and their environments to ensure their continuation. This is especially true in the case of regional planning, which, by virtue of its scale, has greater size, more interdependencies and interconnectivities than city planning. Even more the case when a city is planned as a region, as we shall see in the case of the Delhi Master Plan.

The phenomenon of 'reverse adaptation' might help explain the remarkable passivity of people most affected by the machinations of planning. While close to 10 million of Delhi's population lives in slums, their disappointment with the planning apparatus does not result in appreciable changes to the system or the planning process. Despite the 74th Constitutional Amendment that mandates the participation of people in the making and execution of plans, the techniques of the expert and the efficient function of the urban machine are still the imperatives of urban planning. These marginalized masses are reduced to individual somnolent users. And as Lefebvre rightly questions, just how is the user of the city perceived?

> As a fairly repulsive character, who causes wear, who fortunately fulfils the function of making the replacement of a thing inevitable, who successfully carries out the process of (technological) obsolescence. (Lefebvre, 2003: 188)

The Delhi Master Plan, a regional plan, was conceived as an instrument to ensure, an 'economically sound, socially balanced and functionally related land use pattern' (DDA, 1962: 1). However, today, over 50 years after its introduction, rather than fulfilling this purpose, the plan has become, to quote Gita Dewan Verma 'a penal code to punish citizens rather than a document of citizens' entitlements and city solutions' (in Bhan, 2006: 13). It is my argument that this is due to the success, not failure, of the Delhi Master Plan, as I explain in the following section on its genesis, closely linked to nationalist discourses on planning.

IV

> I am myself a devotee of science and believe that the world will ultimately be saved, if it is to be saved, by the method and approach of science. (Nehru, 13 December 1947: 2)

This thesis of Nehru's is revealing as it demonstrates his immense faith and devotion to the sciences. If science was the world's saviour, why not leverage the same scientific means to shape India's future? In addition to this almost religious conviction in science, Nehru was equally disdainful of India's villages. Contrary to Gandhi's belief that the 'soul of India' lived in its villages, Nehru was convinced that the village was 'backward intellectually and culturally and no progress can be made,' there (Sisson and Wolpert, 1988: 125). The scientific models of the city and region were, therefore, doubly appealing to the first Prime Minister given that they reinforced his devout faith in science and proffered to be progressive spaces of India's future. The decision to build Chandigarh as a modernist city, and to plan and develop Delhi through the regional planning model bears testament to Nehru's penchant for scientific rationality.

Delhi, India's capital city, saw an explosive population increase – a factor of close to 90 per cent in population between 1941 and 51– and a startling outbreak of jaundice in 1952 (Sundaram, 2010: 28–68). These factors prompted the then Central Minister of Public Health and State Minister for Local Self-Government, Rajkumari Amrit Kaur, to request Douglas Ensminger, representative of the Ford Foundation, that a team of 'US Experts ... advise and guide Delhi in its city planning and development work' (Kaur, 14 January 1956). She specifically requested the involvement of American regional planner Albert Mayer, who was already well on his way to becoming perhaps the single most influential urban, rural and regional planner in India's history. His previous accomplishments included the rural development programme for Etawah district in Uttar Pradesh and the initial design of Chandigarh – that Le Corbusier subsequently claimed as his own achievement.

Mayer happily accepted, and, upon performing a 'reconnaissance survey' for the Ford Foundation, submitted a report with an enclosed Letter Inviting Proposals (from Indian planner counterparts) for the 'Planning of the Delhi Region ... to evolve a long-range plan which will set conscious goals and functions and thus limits to the New Delhi (and Delhi) Regional area, and work out a physical layout and appropriate administrative-governmental set-up to effectuate these' (Mayer, 12 July 1956).

This quote demonstrates Mayer's sensitivity to the growth of the functions of Delhi, over which he wanted to set limits using a regional frame. It also indicates that within this regional confine, a physical city planning enterprise would be undertaken, once again demonstrating the Geddesian ideology that the city and region were simply variations in scale. My own thinking on the subject contradicts this view.

In order to demonstrate the dissimilarity between the region and the city, let us compare their etymologies. The city, according to the *Oxford English Dictionary*, is derived from the Latin word *civitas*, which means 'the body of citizens, the community.' Definitions of the word 'city' keep with the spirit of the root *civitas*: 'a native or other inhabited space,' and 'a self-governing city or state with its dependencies' (OED, 1989a). The city itself was derived from the Greek work *polis* – plural *poleis* – most commonly translated as 'city-state.' The word *polis* originates from the Greek Archaic period (800 BC – 480 BC), which meant city-state, or ancestors of a particular city or state, or simply meant 'citizenship' and is said to have influenced the Latin word *civitas* that means 'citizenhood'. A similar conjoining of the city and the state linked to notions of citizenship is seen in old German and Roman nomenclature.

The word 'region', in contrast, derives from the Latin word *regere*, meaning, 'to direct, rule.' It is defined as 'a kingdom; a realm: a clearly bounded and defined administrative territory' (OED, 1989b). The administrative head of the region was usually the regent, also derived from the same Latin root. Importantly, the forms of governance of the city and region are not the same: the city is administered by its citizens while a region is ruled by a regent or administrator. However, with the change in scale of thinking about urban processes and through the advent of colonialism and then modernity – with the concomitant proliferation of technology into the everyday life of the city, and the iterative interweaving of the processes of industrialization with urbanization – regional administrative measures have gained currency. Yet, as American Marxist geographer David Harvey points out, 'the term 'city' has an iconic and symbolic history that is deeply embedded in the pursuit of political meaning. The city of God, the city on a hill, the relationship between city and citizenship – the city as an object of utopian desire, as a distinctive place of belonging within a perpetually shifting spatio-temporal order – all give it a political meaning that mobilizes a crucial political imaginary' (Harvey, 2012: xvi–vii).

Delhi, like the cities of New York and London, was designed in 1962 under the principles of regional planning. It is interesting to note that self-governing municipalities were set up to administer to the needs of the city. Yet, the regional imperative additionally rationalized the creation of institutions like development authorities,[7] with power to over-rule self-governing mechanisms. The Delhi Development Authority (DDA) is a quintessential example of this power. Legitimized by the First Delhi Master Plan, the DDA represents the banality of violence in its ability to use and manipulate the land-use stratification of the plan to consolidate its power. This power continues to be wielded even to this day. Following are two brief examples, explained at length elsewhere (Morenas, 2010).

Example 1: The Delhi Development Authority and the Making of Jagmohan Malhotra

The OED meaning of the word authority is the 'power to *enforce* obedience' and the 'right to *command* or give *ultimate* decisions (emphases mine)' (OED, 1989c). In other words, authorities in common parlance are not democratic institutions, rather they are authoritarian in that they 'enforce' and 'command' obedience to their decisions.

An acute case of enforcing obedience is the DDA during the Emergency, the period between 1975 and 1977, at which point Indira Gandhi suspended elections, banned all public meetings, processions and agitations, held detainees without trial, and gagged the press (Tarlo, 2003). Much of this was only possible because of the collaboration and enforcement mechanisms of the DDA, perhaps the biggest cog in Delhi's post-colonial development machine.

During this 21-month period, the then vice-chairman of the DDA, Jagmohan Malhotra, colluded with Indira Gandhi's younger son Sanjay Gandhi – who, significantly, held no public office at this time-to forcibly evict and displace 700,000 of Delhi's poorer citizens to the peripheries of Delhi, without any security, services, or entitlements (Tarlo, 2003). What was the official rationale for this? The Delhi Master Plan had deemed Old Delhi a 'slum,' suitable for demolition, the DDA adopted a policy to 'motivate' forced sterilizations of slum-dwellers as a precondition to receive plot allotments at resettlement colonies. This is a clear case of reverse adaptation, where the ends of the plan justified these means of forcing sterilization and relocation. Later, chastised by the Shah Commission, Jagmohan defended his actions under the DDA as 'development not demolition, dawn, not doom' (Tarlo, 2003). Again, this was only possible given the jurisdiction already afforded to the DDA under the regional plan for Delhi and the penchant for technological fixes in the development of the city.

Example 2: Neoliberalism and Delhi Master Plan Revisions

With the precedent set by Jagmohan during the Emergency, the Indian political leadership, the DDA, and its planners decided to retain the faulty instrument of the plan. This is likely because of the authoritarian power that could be wielded through it by selectively regularizing settlements – based on note or vote banks; another case of ends justifying authoritarian means. This process of regularization, laments Gita Dewan Verma, is a form of planning not for the future, but for the past. She says:

> Planning for the past was hot, hip and happening, leaving those in charge free to have their cake and eat it too. They could become humane and pragmatic and 'regularize' those who missed the bus to planned development and add vote banks. Or they could become all disciplined and throw them out if they bothered someone who mattered or if the land they occupied began to look like worthwhile real estate, and thereby add to 'note' banks. Those in charge were already doing this to some measure – in respect of unauthorized colonies, slums, farmhouses, banquet halls, shops and showrooms, petrol pumps, etc. Now they could do it with gay abandon simply by rolling their eyes heavenwards and saying the words 'Master Plan' in an exasperated sort of way ... . This reduced the forthcoming exercise of revising Delhi's Master Plan, which was due for revision in 2001, to a redundant farce. But no one was asking to scrap it, only to amend it. (2003: 61)

By the time of the first revision of the DMP, the DDA, like other Indian state enterprises, had become a bloated white elephant. The Master Plan amendments turned into a mechanism to solicit additional funding without much effort on the part of the planners and an instrument with which to play the real estate market. It was simple: if slums and squatters were bringing down the property values in a particular neighbourhood, the Master Plan could be used to declare them 'unauthorized.' But if these slums were strategically placed and could serve as potential vote banks, then the Master Plan could just be amended to 'regularize' these settlements. Without a larger vision of the city, all that was needed for the postcolonial development machine was to simply re-colour itself and 'amend' the plan!

I go into these two examples in greater detail elsewhere (Morenas, 2010); my purpose in presenting them here was to instantiate Ellul's notion, mentioned at the beginning of this paper, that the development machine of Delhi is 'committed to the quest for continually improved means to carelessly examined ends' (1964).

V

I began this paper with the intention of problematizing the hegemonic representation of the urban, and in doing so I have inherently questioned the techno-scientific logic embedded within urban planning. Does the urban machine ultimately improve or worsen the human condition? Through an STS analysis of both the city and the region, my arguments support the latter. However, as James Scott reminds us, this condemnation needs to be tempered by the historical origins of the urban apparatus (1998: 352–335). The social conditions of colonialism and caste injustice that these urban apparatuses were intended to supplant were so patently unjust and repressive, that the production of a new urban condition (however rationalized) was embraced. Initially, urban machines were exhorted since it was believed that their benefits – including the equitable distribution of space, citizenship for all within the city, rights to subsistence, health, education and shelter, etc. – could be delivered through the efficient deployment of technology. This equitable distribution could in turn lead to systemic equality and emancipation of its urban citizens.

This belief in the urban apparatus, that despite evidence to the contrary, will still deliver these same ideals is as dominant as ever, is evidenced by the former Home Minister's remarks at the beginning of this paper. There is still an underlying belief that even if technology has worsened the human condition in the past, it can still rectify the damage that it has perpetrated, if applied rationally and sensibly.

Delhi's contemporary urbanism is in permanent crisis – the trifurcation of the MCD, the Common Wealth Games Scandal, the numerous deaths of the homeless every winter, the continual encroachment of the Ridge and the River are but a few examples. Torn between its city and regional ideologies, yet united by its technologically driven urbanization, the city is in flux. In the blur and chaos of these scandals, Delhi's machine like tendencies remain imperceptible. This is, perhaps, because, as Heidegger argued, 'technology itself prevents any experience of its own essence' (1977). The belief in a self-correcting technological future may well be naïve, for if technology cannot be experienced, how can we expect it to correct itself?

Technology has, in fact, hastened the decline of the spontaneous, self-organized city and older modes of urbanization present in its historical urban core (Morenas, 2010). STS philosophers contend that technology is intertwined with our very beings. Our usage of technology refashions our humanity and alters our lives through what is offered as a superior rationality. Our obliviousness to this, in Winner's words, is 'technological somnambulism' where we 'willingly sleepwalk' into our technological futures (1986: 10). Berlin, in turn, has warned 'those who rest on such comfortable beds of dogma are victims of forms of self-induced myopia, blinkers that may make for contentment, but not for understanding of what it is to be human '(1998: 11). The hegemonic representation of the urban at the beginning of the paper is precisely this form of somnambulism, myopia, or absence of vision. Despite the compelling evidence of increasing uneven development in Delhi over the past half century, there is a kind of religious and quite profoundly blind faith – characterized as 'somnambulism' by Winner and 'self-induced myopia' by Berlin – in the rhetoric of city and regional machines.

Traditional critiques of spatial inequalities, formulated by Marxist geographers such as Lefebvre (2003) and Harvey (2012), have been insightful about the production of spatial uneven development. Yet, these efforts fall short of critically understanding the means by which a technological rationality inscribes this pattern (Morenas, 2010). Treating technology as neutral like Marx, Marxist geographers believe that the use of the same technology with just political sensibilities, can even uneven development. By applying theories from a Science and

Technology Studies epistemology to the study of the Delhi's urban history and the dominant urban apparatuses of the city and the region, I argue that these urban machines are in fact autonomous. Rather than being employed to pattern space as per the needs of civic life and society, these machines pattern space and society to meet their own technologically determined criteria. Thus, Science and Technology Studies, a discipline that relate means and ends, vitiates the hegemonic rhetoric of technological neutrality allowing debate on (re)focus on relationships between people, technology and our urban future.

Notes

1. American cognitive linguists George Lakoff and Mark Johnson in their exhaustive study of 'conceptual metaphors' argue that these types of metaphors link ideas about things in one domain in terms of another. This cross domain mapping then allows forms of reasoning in that domain to be applied to the other. In their book *Philosophy in the Flesh* (1999), they argue that the metaphor 'Love is a journey' allows a conceptual mapping of a journey to be used to understand love. They demonstrate how when couples use the term, 'We're going in different directions', to describe their problems they are drawing from the conceptual metaphor of 'Love is a journey', to reason about love as well.

   In this paper, I am working backwards. Drawing from mechanistic descriptions of the city, I first establish the conceptual metaphor of 'city is a machine'. Although these extended conceptual descriptions and reasoning are undertaken automatically and without conscious reflection, they form part of the everyday conventionalized descriptions of the city. In tracing their linguistic and historical conceptual metaphors, I describe and discuss the entrenched problems associated with this mapping and reasoning.
2. Italian political philosopher, Giorgio Agamben in his book *What is an Apparatus?* (2009), defines the word apparatus (a) in legal terms, as the judicial decision apart from the opinion; (b) in technical parlance, the assemblage of various parts of a machine or mechanism; and (c) in military usage, a set of means arranged according to a plan. I am using the word 'apparatus' in a similar manner to Agamben especially in the technical and military use of the term.
3. While the Indian ancient cities of Mohenjo-Daro and Harappa were laid out in a gridiron pattern, the ideology informing Le Corbusier can be traced to the writings of Austrian architect Adolf Loos. Loos in his book *Ornament and Crime* asserts, 'The evolution of culture is synonymous with the removal of ornament from utilitarian objects.' Therefore for Le Corbusier, the city as a 'machine for living in' can be seen as a utilitarian

object and the simple geometry and straight lines are the result of a higher evolutionary culture, namely, modernism.

4. In 2010, Delhi hosted the XIX Commonwealth Games. The allocation of land, the execution of construction works and the sale of the apartments of the Commonwealth Games Village designated to house the athletes, has been mired in controversy. I argue elsewhere that this project exemplifies the working of the Delhi Master Plan under a neoliberal ideology (Morenas, 2010).
5. Pushta literally means 'embankment' and Yamuna Pushta refers to the slum on the banks of the river Yamuna in Delhi. The slum settlement began from the Income Tax Office area and stretched up to the Salimgarh Fort near old Delhi. The slum was over 40 years old and housed close to 100,000 inhabitants. In 2004, the slum was demolished by a highly debated Supreme Court judgement that equated slums to garbage. Since then the demolished site has been 'beautified' for the XIX Commonwealth Games. The residents meanwhile have been relocated to the outskirts of Delhi without basic infrastructure, social services and medical facilities.
6. M.S. Golwalkar, the second 'sarsanghchalak' (supreme leader) of the Right wing Rashtriya Swayamsevak Sangh (RSS) was an advocate of eugenics along the lines of Adolf Hilter. In the 1939 book, *We, Our Nationhood Defined*, Golwalkar wrote, 'To keep up the purity of the Race and its culture, Germany shocked the world by her purging the country of the semitic Races – the Jews. Race pride at its highest has been manifested here. Germany has also shown how well nigh impossible it is for Races and cultures, having differences going to the root, to be assimilated into one united whole, a good lesson for us in Hindusthan to learn and profit by' (in Rao, 2003: 698).
7. Just like the Delhi Development Authority was set up in 1957 to administer the region of Delhi, the Greater London Council that later became the Greater London Authority was created to administer the Greater Region of London.

References

'*Authority*' (1989c). *The Oxford English Dictionary*, Second edition, Oxford University Press, Oxford.

Agamben, Giorgio (2009). *What is an Apparatus? and Other Essays*, Trans. David Kishik and Stefan Pedatella, Stanford University Press, Palo Alto.

Arendt, Hannah (1994). *Eichmann in Jerusalem: A Report on the Banality of Evil*, Penguin Twentieth-century Classics, Rev. and Enl. edition, Penguin Books, New York.

Berlin, Isaiah (1953). *The Hedgehog and the Fox: An Essay on Tolstoy's View of History*, Simon & Schuster, New York.

Berlin, Isaiah, Hardy, Henry and Kelly, Aileen (2008). *Russian Thinkers*, Second edition, Penguin Books, London and New York.

Bhan, Gautam (7 Oct 2006). 'Capital's Sealing Drive: Whose Delhi Is It Anyway?' *Tehelka* <http://archive.tehelka.com/story_main20.asp? filename=Ne 100706Whose_Delhi.asp> Last viewed on 23/Jan/2015.

Blom, Philipp (2008). *The Vertigo Years: Change and Culture in the West, 1900–1914*, Weidenfeld & Nicolson, London.

Chatterjee, Partha (2011). *Lineages of Political Society: Studies in Postcolonial Democracy*, Columbia University Press, New York.

——. (2004). *The Politics of the Governed: Reflections on Popular Politics in Most of the World*, Columbia University Press, New York.

'*City*' (1989a). *The Oxford English Dictionary*, Second edition, Oxford University Press, Oxford.

Defries, Amelia (1928). *The Interpreter Geddes: The Man and His Gospel*, Boni & Liveright, New York.

Delhi Development Authority (1962). *Master Plan of Delhi– 1962*, Government Printing Office for Delhi Development Authority, Delhi.

——. (1990). *Master Plan of Delhi– 2001*, Government Printing Office for Delhi Development Authority, Delhi.

——. (2014). *Master Plan of Delhi– 2021*, Government Printing Office for Delhi Development Authority, Delhi.

Ellul, Jacques (1964). *The Technological Society*, Trans. John Wilkinson, Alfred Knopf, New York.

Ferguson, James (1994, 1990). *The Anti-Politics Machine: Development, Depoliticization, and Bureaucratic Power in Lesotho*, University of Minnesota Press, Minneapolis.

Franklin, Ursula (1999, 1990). *The Real World of Technology*, Anansi Press Ltd., Toronto.

Geddes, Patrick (1912). 'The Twofold Aspect of the Industrial Age: Palaeotechnic and Neotechnic', *Town Planning Review*, 31: 176–87.

——. (1905). 'Civics: As Applied Sociology', *Sociological Papers*, 1: 101–44.

——. (1949). *Cities in Evolution*, New and Rev. edition, Williams & Norgate, London.

Guha Ray, Shantanu and Chaudhury, Shoma (2008). 'My Vision is to Get 85 Per cent of India into Cities', *Tehelka*, Sec 5: 21.

Hall, Peter (2002). *Cities of Tomorrow: An Intellectual History of Urban Planning and Design in the Twentieth Century*, Third edition, Blackwell Publishers, Oxford.

Harvey, David (2012). *Rebel Cities: From the Right to the City to the Urban Revolution*, Verso, London.

Holston, James (1989). *The Modernist City: An Anthropological Critique of Brasilia*, University of Chicago Press, Chicago.

Kaur, Amrit (14 Jan 1956). 'Letter to Douglas Ensminger Requesting Ford Foundation Assistance for Planning Delhi (Obtained by Permission from the Ford Foundation Archives),' Ford Foundation: New York.

Kaviraj, Sudipta (1996). 'India: Dilemmas of Democratic Development', in Adrian Leftwich (ed.), *Democracy and Development: Theory and Practice*, Polity Press, Cambridge, UK in association with Blackwell Publishers, pp. 115–38.

Kaviraj, Sudipta and Khilnani, Sunil (2001). *Civil Society: History and Possibilities*, Cambridge University Press, New York.

Khilnani, Sunil (1998). *The Idea of India*, Farrar, Straus and Giroux, New York.

Lakoff, George (2004). *Don't Think of an Elephant!: Know Your Values and Frame the Debate: The Essential Guide for Progressives*, Chelsea Green Publishers, White River Junction, VT.

——. (1987). *Women, Fire, and Dangerous Things: What Categories Reveal about the Mind*, University of Chicago Press, Chicago.

Lakoff, George and Johnson, Mark (1999). *Philosophy in the Flesh: The Embodied Mind and its Challenge to Western Thought*, Basic Books, New York.

——. (1981). *Metaphors We Live By*, University of Chicago Press, Chicago.

Le Corbusier (1986, 1931). *Towards a New Architecture* (Vers Une Architecture), Trans. Frederick Etchells, Dover, New York.

——. (1964, 1933). *The Radiant City: Elements of a Doctrine of Urbanism to be Used as the Basis of Our Machine-Age Civilization* [La Ville Radieuse: Elements d'une Doctrine d'Urbanisme pour L'Équipement de la Civilisation Méchaniste (Boulogne: Éditions de l'Architecture d'Aujourd'hui)], Trans. Charles-Edouard Jeannerret, Orion Press, New York.

Lefebvre, Henri (2003). *The Urban Revolution*, Trans. Robert Bononno, University of Minnesota Press, Minneapolis.

Lubbock, John (1865). *Pre-Historic Times, as Illustrated by Ancient Remains, and the Manners and Customs of Modern Savages*, Williams and Norgate, London.

Mayer, Albert (12 July 1956). 'Letter to Bernard Loshbaugh (Obtained with Permission from the Ford Foundation Archives),' Ford Foundation: New York.

Mayer, Albert (1956). 'Enclosure, Letter to Bernard Loshbaugh', Letters Obtained by Permission from the Ford Foundation Archives, 31 October 2009, Ford Foundation Archives, New York, July 12.

Morenas, Leon (2010). *Planning the City of Djinns: Exorcizing the Ghosts in Delhi's Post-Colonial Development Machine*, Dissertation, Rensselaer Polytechnic Institute, Troy, New York.

Morenas, Leon (2014) 'Dissimulating the Smart City,' Presentation at the *National Seminar on Disciplines, Movements, Policies: The Changing Relationship between Science, State and Society*, Indian Institute of Advanced Study: Shimla.

Mumford, Lewis (1925). 'The Fourth Migration', *Survey*, 54: 130–33.

——. (1925). 'Regions – To Live In', *Survey*, 54: 151–52.

Nehru, Jawaharlal (13 Dec 1947). 'The Function of Universities,' *Selected Speeches and Writings of Nehru*. < http://www.nehruinternationalconference2014.com/nehru_speech24.aspx> Last viewed on 23/Jan/2015.

Rao, Mohan (2003). "'Scientific' Racism: A Tangled Skein," *Economic and Political Weekly*, Vol - XXXVIII No. 08: 697–699.

'Region' (1989 b). *The Oxford English Dictionary*, Second Edition, Oxford University Press, Oxford.

Scott, James (1998). *Seeing Like a State: How Certain Schemes to Improve the Human Condition Have Failed*, Yale University Press, New Haven.

Sethi, Neha (9 July 2014). 'Make urbanization an opportunity: Venkaiah Naidu,' Live Mint. <> Last viewed on 23/ Jan/2015.

Sisson, Richard and Stanley Wolpert (1988). *Congress and Indian Nationalism: The Pre-Independence Phase*, University of California Press, Oakland.

Stein, Clarence (1925). 'Dinosaur Cities', *Survey*, 54: 134–38.

Sundaram, Ravi (2010). 'A City of Order: The Masterplan', in *Pirate Modernity: Delhi's Media Urbanism*, Routledge, New Delhi.

Tarlo, Emma (2003). *Unsettling Memories: Narratives of the Emergency in India*, University of California Press, Berkeley.

The Constitution (Seventy-Fourth Amendment) Act (1992).

United Nations (2014). *World Urbanization Prospects – The 2014 Revision: Highlights*, United Nations Department of Economic and Social Affairs, New York.

Verma, Gita Dewan (2003). *Slumming India: A Chronicle of Slums and their Saviours*, Penguin Books, New Delhi.

Winner, Langdon (1986). *The Whale and the Reactor: A Search for Limits in an Age of High Technology*, University of Chicago Press, Chicago.

——. (1977). *Autonomous Technology: Technics-out-of-Control as a Theme in Political Thought*, MIT Press, Cambridge, Mass.

13

Empowering the Women in Indian Agriculture

Entrepreneurship As a Way

NILABJA GHOSH

In a country aspiring for high economic growth rates, it is important to ensure that women who constitute about half of the nation's population, finds adequate opportunity to participate in the growth process and reap its benefits. Inclusiveness of development and broader concepts of 'well-being' and 'human development' (Sen, 2005, 2006, Nussbaum, 1993, Dasgupta, 2001) are increasingly overriding the conventional focus on economic growth in development policies world over. At the same time, agricultural development began receiving renewed focus when empirical evidences indicated disillusionment in the farming occupation at least partly owing to the poor income potential in the modernizing economy leading to migration and feminization within the sector. In India, it is now widely recognized that policies which leave out a sector that engages more than half of the population and a large majority of the poor cannot generate growth that is sustainable (Sengupta, 2009). The urgency of the time is for developing the human

Acknowledgement: The author thanks Agro-economic Research Center's (AERC), AERC, Punjab Agricultural University, Ludhiana; AERC for North-East India Assam Agricultural University, Jorhat; AERC, Sardar Patel University, Gujartat; AERC, Himachal Pradesh University, Shimla; AERC for Haryana and Uttarakhand; AERC, University of Delhi; AERC for Bihar and Jharkhand; Tilka Manjhi Bhagalpur, Bihar; AERC, University of Allahabad, Uttar Pradesh, AERC, Andhra University Visakhapatnam for collection of information and M. Rajeshwor of IEG-FASAL who processed it in the entire team work.

resources that is contained in Indian agriculture. Training and encouraging farm women for enterprises that present economic potential for both, taking advantage of the rural milieu and integrating agriculture with the larger markets prevalent in industry and urban India can be a potent instrument.

Since economic liberalization started taking shape, the perceived ambit of agriculture broadened towards diversification beyond cereals and value addition to agricultural products as agriculture began to be viewed more comprehensively as a source of income and not merely as a direct source of food security (Gulati, 2011). Agro-processing, food processing in particular, is gaining recognition as a sunrise sector which will link agriculture with industry. There is a serious case for looking at alternative ways to realize the potentials of agriculture and the human resources contained in the agricultural sector as women workforce by integrating at least part of the agro-processing activities with agriculture by broadening the domain of agriculture.

In this paper, we address the issue of promoting entrepreneurship among women in farm households by opening up opportunities of processing agro-products and agro-inputs. 'Oxford American dictionary defines an entrepreneur as a person who organizes or operates a business or businesses taking on greater than normal financial risks to do so. The task is also described as "difficult" and the person seen to undertake it for "commercial risk for profit".' Enterprise, in this sense is oriented to facing market competition and in the present context of farm women, it deviates from conventional practices of 'self-employment' in agriculture which remains unpaid and thereby largely unrecognized as an economic contribution. We cover activities of agricultural (primary) character so far as they connect with newer products as well as others bordering on manufacturing or services provided that the occupation will lead to active risk taking, decision-making and negotiation all of which constitute competitive market behaviour and can be perceived to be 'difficult' or 'challenging'. The merit of this approach to development would lie in the easier availability of certain inputs within the sector and in the traditional skills that the women already possess in such arts as can be further sharpened with training for commercial gain. The activities involved in the choice of enterprise also need to either draw from locally available inputs or cater to the surrounding farm economy. We start with assessing the socio-economic situation of the Indian farm women using secondary data from National Sample Survey Organization (NSSO) and review India's policy directions towards the economic empowerment of women in farm households. Using primary data, we then attempt to evaluate the acceptability of this policy route for the purpose of empowering farm women.

Rural Women in India: Social and Economic limitations

Gender disparity is manifest in the educational attainments of men and women in India suggestive of low human resource development. Property right norms show a bias against females (Agarwal, 1994) reducing their access to land, forcing them to be dependent on the support of men. Even recognition of their role in household welfare and care giving is scarce (Boserup, 1975). In addition there are social evil practices of dowry, son preference and other discriminations, India being one of the few countries with a 'missing' women' syndrome (Klasen, 2006, Sen, 2005). A declining trend of the sex ratio is another concern. Off-farm opportunities are increasingly drawing rural men out of the villages, leaving women to undertake the burden of cultivation which is low-paying.

Work participation of women in India, as recorded both by the NSSO and Census, despite mutual discrepancies, is decidedly lower than that for men (Table 1). It remains confined to a few specific occupations some of which are extension of their domestic work. The extent and nature of the women's economic participation has remained elusive to data protocols (Krishnaraj, 2005).

Table 1

Worker Population Ratio (WPR %) of Rural Male and Female from Census and NSSO Data

	Census (Total)		*Census (Main)*			*NSSO (PS+SS)*		*NSSO(PS)*	
Year	*Male*	*Female*	*Male*	*Female*	*Year*	*Male*	*Female*	*Male*	*Female*
1981	53.8	23.2	52.6	16.0	1987–88	53.9	32.3	51.7	24.5
1991	52.5	26.7	51.8	18.6	1993–94	55.3	32.8	53.8	23.4
2001	52.1	30.8	44.3	16.6	1999–00	53.1	29.9	52.2	23.1
					2004–05	54.6	32.7	53.5	24.2
					2009–10	54.7	26.1	53.7	20.2
2011	—	—	—	—	2011–12*	54.3	24.8	53.5	17.6

Source: Computed from Census 1981, 1991, 2001, 2011, Primary Census Abstract and NSSO, 2009–10, NSSO, 1999–2000, NSSO 2001, 2011, 2013 *Employment and Unemployment Situation in India.* Note: Census categorizes employment as 'Main' and 'Subsidiary' status and NSSO by 'Usual Principal Status' and 'Usual Subsidiary Status'.

* Thin sample.

Table 2, however, suggests that rural women are far more participative in economic life than urban women. In 1999–00 female worker population ratio (WPR) was nearly 30 per cent in rural India compared to 14 per cent in urban areas. A significant part of the participation was in the subsidiary status and a large majority of about 84 per cent of the women workers were occupied in agriculture. Over time, the WPR as well as the women's engagement in agriculture declined, but higher WPR of rural women over urban women is evident even in the 2009–10 survey.

Table 2

Employment (%) in Usual Status of Women in the Two Sectors in India

Workers	*Rural*	*Urban*	*Rural*	*Urban*	*Rural*	*Urban*	*Rural*	*Urban*	*Rural*	*Urban*
Time	*1987–88*		*1993–94*		*1999–00*		*2004–05*		*2009–10*	
Workers (PS+SS)	32.3	15.2	32.8	15.5	29.9	13.9	32.7	16.6	26.1	13.8
Workers (PS)	24.5	11.8	23.4	12.1	23.1	11.7	24.2	13.5	20.2	11.9
In Agriculture (PS)	82.5	21.8	84.7	19.3	84.1	14.6	81.4	14.7	78.9	11.8
Self-employed(PS)	54.9	39.3	51.3	37.2	50.0	38.4	56.4	40.4	50.3	35.4
Casual labour(PS)	40.2	26.5	45.3	27.3	46.1	23.1	38.9	17.4	44.2	20.2

Note: PS=Usual Principal Status, SS=Usual Subsidiary Status.

Source: NSSO 2001 (*Employment and Unemployment Situation in India 1999–00, 2004–05, 2009–10*).

Quality of Employment

Women in farm households mostly work in agriculture rather than non-farm activities and even within agriculture limited specific operations only draw women's participation. The lack of diversity and challenge makes the occupation tedious and not conducive to human resource development. Scientific skills and decision-making hardly have any role in such jobs. Farm women have little association with negotiations in market and communication in public life (except in selling vegetables as vendors in local markets mostly found among the poorest). There is little incentive for even education and skill for conventional farming operations. Mechanization, though shown to be gender neutral made farm jobs easier only for men (Agarwal, 1984), owing to biased societal attitudes, their misplaced beliefs (Wasnik, 2006) and the failure of the government's extension mechanism.

Numerous studies suggested that the operations in which farm women engaged are perceived to be difficult, monotonous and repetitive, described comprehensively as 'drudgery'. The All India Coordinated

Research Project (AICRP) 1999 of the Ministry of Agriculture identified transplanting, weeding, cutting and uprooting, sowing and storage as common female activities of farm job that are ranked high when rated by 'difficulty scores'. The activities are generally manual and many of them require awkward postures that produce body pain and injury that are sometimes known to cause reproductive problems.

The shift of the structure of employment from a self-employment base, (mostly family helpers) towards wage labour and its increased 'casualization' created pressure on wages earned by workers to be the crucial determinant of rural well-being (Hirway and Roy, 1999). Even when considering farm wages women's earnings have been consistently lower than men's even for similar jobs. Data reported by Labour Bureau clearly show that women's wage rates were relatively low for all farm operations, was less than 70 per cent of men's wage in casual labour and not more than 90 per cent even for public works in 2004–05 and 2007–08. Similar disparity in wage rate is also revealed by micro studies (Kaur and Goyal, 1996, Sudha Rani et al, 1990). The gap has narrowed since then especially with the launch of the much debated MGNREGA which has a special place for women workers in villages.

India's Policy on Women's Development

Articles 14, 15, 16 and 39 of the Indian Constitution made provision for gender equality in all spheres of life and Article 15 even empowers the state to make official discrimination in favour of women. Although India's Five Year Plans had a place for the special needs of women, the initial approach was highly discriminatory and rather unfavourable towards human development of Indian women. There was no vision of women forming an enlightened workforce in the First Five Year Plan (1951–56), while the Second Plan (1956–61) actually strengthened the male bias with its lopsided Intensive Area Development Programme (IADP) to bring about the Green Revolution. The only positive impact on women's development indirectly flowed from the welfare efforts.

The International Women's Decade organized under the UN's behest[1] was a turning point starting with the submission of the Report of the *Committee on the Status of Women in India* (CSWI), a National Plan of Action being prepared in 1976. The Sixth Plan (1980–85), devoting a whole chapter on women for the first time shifted the approach towards women from welfare to development. Beneficiary oriented skill development programmes IRDP, TRYSEM, DWCRA were initiated during the Sixth and Seventh Plan periods and domestic violence received attention for the first time.

The Eighth Plan (1992–97) focusing on human resources saw women for the first time as equal partners in development. Training of women in different vocations, formation of the Self-help Groups of women and modification of agricultural extension to cover women beneficiaries were milestone of this period. The Ninth and Tenth Plans (1997–2007) placed women's empowerment and employment among their primary objectives adopting a National Policy for Empowerment of Women (NPEW) in 2001. The Eleventh Plan too has a special focus on 'inclusion', targeting the marginalized and minority communities among women as beneficiaries. Gender budgeting, Gender mainstreaming and Gender outcome assessments became part of the development planning process setting mandated quota of allocation for women in beneficiary oriented projects along with monitoring and evaluation of the impact.

Gender has been gaining space in agricultural extension with the decline of the Training and Visit or TAV system which was criticized for its male bias among other things. Over the last decades a number of programmes mostly funded by external agencies such as the UNDP, the World banks and foreign governments such as the Danish and the Dutch governments have addressed 'women in agriculture' (Ghosh, 2013). In the emerging and more holistic form of extension (ATMA), technology and training with a focus on skill transfer are key methods in extension and gender budgeting is explicit in the mandate of a quota of the developmental resources for women farmers. The National Gender Resources Centre in Agriculture (NGRCA) in Delhi is responsible for the gender mainstreaming. Information on gender friendly tools and technologies in crop production, processing, post harvest management and other allied sector activities is a step towards correction of the past bias and flaws in the erstwhile extension system.

NATP

The National Agriculture Technology Project (NATP), a World Bank-aided project, implemented by the ICAR and the Department of Agriculture and Co-operation (DAC) between November 1998 and 2005 took a group approach towards farmers sensitive to location specific requirements. The institutional mechanism of NATP was the historic creation of autonomous, multi-partite and participatory bodies known as Agricultural Technology Management Agency (ATMA). A major thrust was the technological empowerment of rural women for skill development and income generation, the maximum number of trainings being planned on post-harvest activities, and value-addition mainly on fruits and vegetables, animal husbandry and fishery under the NATP.

Entrepreneurship

Promoting enterprises is not new as a tool for development in India. Several public programmes for self-employment have been implemented in India for decades with disadvantaged sections, including women intended as priority beneficiaries. The Integrated Rural Development Programme (IRDP), later known as Swarnjayanti Gram Swarozgar Yojana (SGSY), was possibly the most outstanding among them. Associated with it were programmes like the Training of Rural Youth for Self-employment (TRYSEM) for creating entrepreneurial competence and technical skills among the youth and the Development of Women and Children in Rural Areas (DWCRA). The success of many of these programmes has been far from satisfactory because viability eluded the enterprises, investment remained at sub-critical levels and best training services were not forthcoming. More noteworthy than the government initiatives were achievements of Self-Employed Women's Association or SEWA (a non-government initiative), acknowledged widely (Nussbaum 1999, Chen 2006), and the Khadi and Village Industries Commission (KVIC), associated with India's freedom movement which have greater commercial orientation with the economic objective of 'producing saleable articles'.

Table 3

Participation in Work of (Adult) Farm Women in India

Principal status workforce (% Population)	40.3
Usual (including Subsidiary) status workforce (% Population)	52.5
Employed in agriculture and forestry (% Principal status workforce)	95.5
Casual labour and public works (% Principal status workforce)	51.1
Unpaid family worker (% Principal status workforce)	37.3

Source: Computed (see Ghosh, 2013).

Economic Activities of Farm Women

At the turn of the century, farm women constituted about 47.9 per cent of Indian women and 48.9 per cent of farm population.[2] Table 3 presenting some summary indicators on the livelihood of farm women computed by analysing unit level data collected by NSSO suggests that the work participation of farm household women is considerably more than for women from other rural households[3] but a very large 95.5 per cent of the workforce is employed in agriculture and forestry related activities. Over 51 per cent of the workers are casual labour with poor quality employment as discussed and 37 per cent of workers are unpaid family workers indicating the potential for unleashing and developing the human resources in farm households. Entrepreneurship as self-employment in non-conventional activities is low in extent among the women and the profile of the enterprises in terms of accountancy and other managerial practices, hired labour and electricity use paints a poor picture (Ghosh, 2013).

Analysis Based on Primary Data: A Team Effort

The evaluation is conducted by analysing primary field level data collected in a country wide survey (AERC, 2009–10) of programmes for promoting women's entrepreneurship. In a coordinated way the sample surveys were conducted by a number of Agro-Economic Research Centres (AERC)[4] or Centres henceforth located in different universities in the country under the overall guidance and coordination of the present author. The states covered under the study were Andhra Pradesh, Punjab, Himachal Pradesh, Haryana, Uttaranchal (now Uttarakhand), Rajasthan, Bihar, Assam and Uttar Pradesh. Nearly all the ventures studied were a result of the NATP programme though not all of them were financially supported and not all the women availed training from the NATP project.

A pilot survey conveyed a sense of regional diversity and complexity making it difficult to apply a perfectly uniform framework for all. It was found that while some areas had witnessed an active programme for promoting entrepreneurship aided by support in various forms such as training, free supply of raw materials, equipment and finance, some had an occasional training programme only while successful entrepreneurship without any training programme was also not uncommon in others. In contrast, some centres found it hard to locate any entrepreneur who was not trained as training was the main instrument that motivated the specific entrepreneurship. In Rajasthan, entrepreneurs benefited from an intensive NATP programme that aimed for all round empowerment of women with multiple support measures but in Punjab entrepreneurs successfully pursued their vocation and did not feel any need for training. Technological modernization, innovative experimentation and improved Extension were at the heart of the programme in Himachal. Questions also surrounded the source of training and it was decided that while ICAR organized training could be a preferred reference point, training received from other creditable government or non-government sources should also be admissible. Entrepreneurs were found to work as individual members or in social groups or as members of Self-help Groups. In some regions an entrepreneur among farm women could be located only with difficulty.

Taking account of the heterogeneities and the knowledge that the centres had on the ground level realities, some degree of flexibility was incorporated in the methodology. While the coordinator framed a detailed questionnaire and a sample framework the centres would use their discretion and judgement in drawing their samples and making their queries to capture the best picture of the reality but under the broad guidelines set by the coordinator for the sake of consistency. While a uniform framework set the procedures, flexibility was permitted at the region level.

Based on information from local authorities like the State Agricultural Universities (SAUs), Non-Governmental Organizations (NGOs), local youth clubs, and Self-Help Groups (SHGs), Commodity Boards and private business entities lists of entrepreneurs were drawn out by the centres who selected random samples of women entrepreneurs. The women belonged to typical farm households though land ownership was not a binding condition. In most cases, the women were beneficiaries in some form from ICAR programmes and received training also. In consultation with knowledgeable authorities of the regions they drew samples of trained and untrained entrepreneurs as appropriate for the region. At least 3 most common enterprises of the areas preferably of agriculture linked character and a sample size of at least 100 were recommended. The indicators were measured either as average (arithmetic mean or mode) used or as percentage shares held by different categories and percentage of respondents. The survey was conducted between 2004 and 2005 but the sample enterprises were initiated and operating between 2001 and 2004. Table 4 lists the districts surveyed in the select states, the sample sizes and the activities described by categories namely (1) Food Processing (FP), (2) Primary Processing (PP), (3) Ecological Processing (EP) and (4) Crafts (CRF).

Table 4

Details of Samples in Various Regions

State (MPCE in ₹)	*Districts*	*Trained No.*	*Untrained No.*	*Activities*
Punjab (847)	Gurdaspur, Amritsar	20	80	Dairy (PP), Bee-keeping (PP), Papad-Badi (FP), Pickles (FP)
Assam (543)	Jorhat, Golaghat	100	50	Live-stock (PP), Bee-keeping (PP), Fruit and Vegetable processing (FP)

Cont'd...

...Cont'd

Rajasthan (591)	Udaipur, Chittorgarh	110	25	Vermi-composting (EP), Improved animal feed (EP), Fruit-vegetable, Preservation (FP), Nursery raising (PP), Papad making (FP), Patta-dona making(CRF), Spice processing (FP),Papad making (FP) Dalia(FP).
Haryana (863)	Hissar	9	30	Dairy (PP), Vermin-composting (EP), Pickle making (FP)
Himachal (798)	Kangra, Bilaspur	180	180	Dairy (PP), Bee-keeping (PP), Vermi-culture (EP), Potato production using Bio-pesticide (EP), Diversified Farming (PP), Fisheries (PP).
Uttarakhand (647)	Udham Singh Nagar	16	66	Beekeeping (PP), Dairy (PP), Poultry (PP), Papad making (FP), Mushroom (PP), Quilt making (CRF)
Uttar Pradesh (533)	Sultanpur	50	50	Agarbatti (CRF), Blanket making (CRF), Spice processing (FP), Dalia making (FP), Milk processing (FP), Basket making (CRF)
Andhra Pradesh (586)	East Godavari, Srikakulam, Vishakhapatnam	75	45	Coir products (CRF), Jute handicrafts (CRF), Leaf plates (CRF)
Bihar (417)	Banka, Bhagalpur, Munger	67	33	Preservation of Fruits vegetables (FP), Preparation of Jamjelly (FP), Preparation of Potato chips, Badi and Papad (FP), Preparation of pickles, and *Murabba* (FP)

Note: Figures of rural monthly per capita consumption expenditures (MPCE) in ₹ for 2004–05 (61st NSSO Round) are given in parentheses below the state names. All India MPCE is ₹ 559.

Type of Enterprises

The enterprises covered drew raw materials from agriculture and the rural commons. The enterprises identified to be more popularly adopted in the study regions were (i) Primary: dairy was more common while others noted were nursery raising, growing fruits, vegetable and pharmaceutical products using organic methods, mushroom culture, poultry, bee-keeping, and fishery, (ii) Food processing: Fruit and vegetable preservation including production of pickles, jam, jelly, *murabba* and potato chips as an important activity, making of *papad* and *badi* from pulses, spice and milk processing and making of health products like *dalia.* (iii) Craft and utilitarian processing: Quilt or blanket making, coir products, jute handicrafts, plate making and weaving of baskets and making *agarbatti* out of leaves, twigs and other forest products. (iv) Newer and eco-friendly product making: Inputs for agriculture with environmental value such as vermi-composting based on locally collected worms, preparation of nutritious animal feed, and crop production using bio-pesticides. Although the study covered only products related with agriculture, in practice NATP had a broader coverage of enterprises like doll making, candle making and shampoo making.

The sample enterprises are found to reasonably diverse falling into the varied categories mentioned above. Some were traditional and others new. Yet others were not new to the area or elsewhere but for the women entrepreneurs in context were new. Fishery in Himachal Pradesh, innovated dairy and diversified farming of vegetables are examples. Most of the inputs used in the enterprises are natural or agricultural in origin and often are freely procurable. Equipment requirement and resource use also vary from moderate to low. Dairy has the least demand for equipment and resources such as land, water and electricity and is said to be 'simple' enough for women of less education to pursue. In Himachal, even this enterprise is enthusiastically modernized by modern techniques and preparation of improved feed. Dairy entrepreneurs found advantage is central crops farming in Punjab and Haryana and in pastures that still abound in Assam, Himachal Pradesh and Uttarakhand. In Rajasthan, improved feed is reported as an enterprise by itself. Bees are migrated in Himachal but not in the other two cases and the pristine environments helps. Food processing is mechanized in different degrees but implements used are simple like mixers, refrigerators and cutter. *Papad, Badi* making in Punjab regions required more mechanization for expansion than the entrepreneurs can afford limiting the scale of enterprise. In Rajasthan and Andhra Pradesh entrepreneurs working as groups are provided with common machines by the promoters. Much richer account is only available in the separate reports submitted by the Centres to the Ministry of Agriculture.

Table 5

Different Aspects of Agro Enterprises Reported by Farm Women

Enterprise	*Product*	*Nature of product*	*Raw Material*	*Equipment*	*Water/Electricity*	*Land(L)/Commons (C)/Workspace(W)*
Dairy	Milk Meat Egg, Dung	Perishable	Fodder Feed straw	Utensils Shed	Low	L, C-Moderate
Bee-keeping	Honey Wax Colony	Fragile (Stored)	Sugar Medicines Sheets	Hive, Extractor	No use	C-Low
Fishery	Fish	Perishable	Seeds, Dung, Chemicals	Low	Wa-high	C-high
Food Products	Papad, Badi, Pickles, Jams, Squash etc.	Fragile Can be Preserved	Salt Spices Oil Pulses Fruits Vegetables Preservatives	Machine for papad Refrigerator Utensils, Knives Mixer	Wa-Low El-High	W-moderate
Agro-Inputs	Animal feed, Vermi-compost Bio-pesticide	Perishable	Vermin Dung Flour	Flour mill	Wa-High	L-High C-High W-Moderate
Crop Diversification	Fruits & Veg. Nursery	—	Seedlings, Fertilizers, Farmyard manure	Farm equipments	Wa-High	L-High
Mushroom Cultivation	Mushroom	Perishable	Spawn	Material as growing medium	Wa-mod	W-Moderate
Leaf plates, patta dona, quilt making, *agarbatti*, coir and jute products	Craft items	Fragile	Leaf, sticks, jute, coir, forest waste	Motorized only in coir craft	El-low	C-High W-Moderate

Note: Land-farmland. Commons-forests, water bodies and open land, Workspace-space within and without premises dedicated for enterprise related activities.

Empowerment of Women

Economic empowerment depends on the commercial viability of the enterprise. For this reason the income from enterprise is calculated as the excess of the revenue from sales over the cost. Only the actual incurred cost is considered though the cost of materials provided by the supporting agencies is imputed. The enterprises in the samples are all found to be financially viable generating moderate amount of profits even when the raw materials provided freely by the promoter is included in the cost. The annual income exceeds a threshold level of ₹ 10,000[5] in all cases except the enterprises producing goods with social and ecological value for which market valuation of the product may be gross underestimates. Enterprises like making of *papad and badi* in Punjab were found extremely lucrative so much so that the diseconomy of scale became a serious limitation. The profitability of the enterprise is a sign of viability. In Rajasthan and certain other cases the scale of operation is low due to various constraints and seasonality. For women who spare limited time to the income earning enterprises bee-keeping, mushroom making and vermin-composting are suitable as subsidiary activities although the total profit and scale may be relatively low. Profit maximization in practice may not be the yardstick nor the objective in short run. Earning from low scales of operation, compatibility with the relevant environment reaching out to distant markets and exposure to larger markets are other important returns to the exercise.

A key strength of the enterprises studied was the cheap and easy availability of inputs that brings down cost considerably. Collection from local commons such as vermins, dung, sticks, leaves and twigs, use of fruits reaped from forests, pastures for grazing, natural, topological waterbodies for fishing and allocation of agricultural land for farming vegetables provided access to free inputs although land would be a constraint for further expansion. In Andhra Pradesh the local coconut crops served as a source of coir used as raw material. For producing leaf plates 'adda' leaves are collected from forests by tribal people and sold to the entrepreneurs. Jute and mesta grown locally help support the handicraft enterprises in Andhra Pradesh.

Other inputs could be procured from neighbouring areas commercially but at low cost. In a few cases inputs were supplied by the promoting agency. Nevertheless, finance was reported to be a constraint. Family funds had to be invested and only in few cases

Figure 1 *Average Profit of Women Entrepreneurs Stateswise*

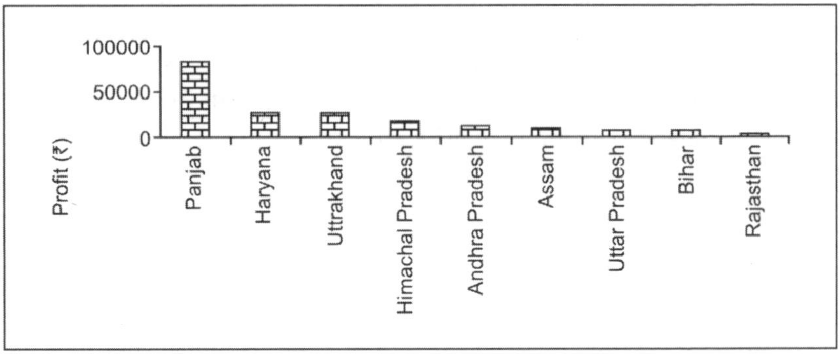

institutional credit was available. In Rajasthan all entrepreneurs received some financial and raw material support for nursery raising and vermin-composting and equipment for *papad* making. In Himachal, technology transmission was the major assistance to which the ATMA, the KVK and the Bee Research Centre contributed. In Andhra Pradesh the coir board and local NGOs helped in providing equipment and in marketing products. In Bihar the women were members of SHGs and got loans through at high interest rates.

Organization

Cooperative activity in dairy was impressive in Punjab where the product was sold with a brand name. Cooperatives did not exist in the study region in Assam. In Haryana the dairy entrepreneurs were served by an SHG in marketing functions. More remarkable was the plan of working in groups in Rajasthan. Without being partners a group-organization served to reduce fixed and overhead costs and enhance bargaining power for procuring inputs. Trainings, mostly arranged by State Agricultural Universities (SAU) and Krishi Vigyan Kendras (KVK), were useful especially in the new and eco-friendly ventures (EP) but were deemed redundant in other activities of traditional practice like dairy and food processing. Besides the Coir Board, NGOs, Khadi Gram Udyog were the agencies that trained the women. Finance was sometimes availed from the NATP itself but otherwise from private sources only and the role of institutional credit was meagre. Access to land was an important factor in adoption of many enterprises. A serious limitation to the ventures was in the inadequacy of marketing channels. However some entrepreneurs were privileged with cooperative support. In a few cases contracts with marketing agencies for nationwide branded sales such as for milk in Punjab, honey in Himachal Pradesh and in craft in Andhra Pradesh was reported. Enterprise was found not only to generate 'visible' monetary earnings of women (Figure 1), but also to help women acquire greater confidence, recognition and awareness in society.

Contribution and Social Empowerment

Time is valuable for the rural woman who has other household chores. In Andhra Pradesh the entrepreneurs were seen to contribute the highest share over 30 per cent of time to the enterprise followed by Haryana while the share in Bihar, Assam, Himachal Pradesh and Rajasthan were low. In return the women could make substantial contribution to their household earnings in Andhra Pradesh, Punjab and Haryana but the sample women in Uttar Pradesh contributed to over half the family income.

Table 6

Results of Entrepreneurship in the Regions Surveyed

State	*Haryana*	*Punjab*	*Himachal*	*Rajasthan*	*Assam*	*Uttara-khand*	*Uttar Pradesh*	*Andhra Pradesh*	*Bihar*
				State APHCE (₹ in thousand)					
Rural Income** (NSSO)	57.3	52.6	48.8	40.5	34.7	39.4	37.8	28.9	27.6
Enterprise Income (Our Survey)	78	100	129	65%<50*	18	31	30	22	23
				Entrepreneur					
Time Share (%)	18.3	13.7	5.8	9.0	7.2	—	14.8	31.4	6.9
Income Share in household (%)	25.0	27.9	3.5	2.0	19	47.0	52.0	31.0	24.0

Note: Figures are weighted averages across enterprises. APHCE is annual per household consumption expenditure. Income and APHCE are given as annual average. * 65 per cent of households earn less than ₹ 50,000 per year. ** APHCE is calculated using monthly per capita consumption expenses (MPCE) and average household size from NSSO report 2004–05.

While contribution to household income is a way to recognition and empowerment, perception based qualitative indicators in Table 7 also suggests positive results, showing that large sections of the respondents found improvement in their family status and role, in their ability to contribute, make decisions, communicate and escape drudgery. Training and occasional participation in marketing (fairs and exhibitions in distant places) imparted confidence, communication skills and exposure to markets and wider society to the rural women. The sample women in Andhra Pradesh were all members of Development of Women and Children in Rural Areas (DWACRA). The men in the household were uniformly reported to be cooperative but the roles remained stereotyped. Men supported in outdoor activities of the enterprise especially where negotiation was needed. Although women were more independent of male support in enterprises working as cooperatives, development potential of individual skills was limited. Some of the beneficiaries gained leadership skills and became resource persons in training programmes.

Table 7

Summary Indicators: Gender Empowerment with Subjective Measures by States

Women (%) reporting improvement State	*Family status*	*Children's education/ health*	*Decision making*	*Freedom to spend*	*Community status/ participation*	*Communication*	*Drudgery*
		Household				*Society*	
Andhra	94	60	68	—	76	56	6
Assam	41	—	48	—	49	51	—
Bihar	46	37	22	22	11	19	22
Himachal	82	84	—	83	51	—	—
Haryana	81	86	—	—	98	—	22
Punjab	27	—	22	—	79	—	—
Rajasthan	72	26	21	42	67	94	33
Uttar Pradesh	89	86	62	69	71	51	—
Uttarakhand	62	71	—	—	62	—	—
Total	68	61	38	55	60	59	22

Note: Blanks indicate 'not reported'.

Inclusiveness

The women who participated seemed to have certain features in common. Majority of them were in the age group 40–50 years and nearly all were above 30. This reflects both the societal attitudes to women of younger age and the responsibility of bringing up young children. Except in Assam education level was low generally not beyond primary level. Only some of the women are widowed, so the entrepreneurship was neither out of distress nor attracted male opprobrium. In

Rajasthan none of the women reported the enterprise as their whole time occupation and in Bihar only 12 per cent did.

In Punjab the farm size of the household is large but the share of small farms in the sample is large in Andhra Pradesh where entrepreneurs from labour households were also in enterprise. Rajasthan and the hill states also find higher coverage of small farmers but on the whole the holding sizes and household incomes as compared to state average from secondary data suggest that the space taken by women from less privileged households remains to be widened. A strong regional dimension is sensed in the findings. Women from the northern states tend to be more privileged belonging to relatively affluent households and earn more but in the eastern and southern states their economic conditions are poorer (Table 8).

Table 8

Socio-economic Status of Women Entrepreneurs

State	*Head or Spouse of head (%)*	*Widow/ Separated (%)*	*Less educated (%)*	*Whole time entre-preneur (%)*	*Average age (years)*	*Holding size (Hectare)*
Punjab	76	10	41	90	44	2.6
Assam	72	2	2	13	46	2–10
Rajasthan	96	2	47	0	45	96* SM
Haryana	95	5	72@	100	43	1.1
Himachal	98	2	24	98	30	88* SM
Uttarakhand	—	—	54@	—	36	0.65
Uttar Pradesh	87	2	100	86	42	93* SM
Andhra	80	20	73	100	35	25* SM & 70* FL
Bihar	50	7	70	12	36	66* SM

Note: SM: Share of small and marginal holders with <2hectares, FL: Farm labour for wage. Less educated: Education not beyond primary schooling (including non-formal education). * denotes % of total. @ Non-schooled (as reported), Blanks indicate 'not reported'.

A Possible Road Ahead

Agriculture, viewed merely as growing of conventional food crops is becoming un-remunerative but considered holistically to encompass diversification, processing, preservation and other agro-services, it may hold a potential for not only empowering women in farm households and communities but also in giving a significant place to women in development and growth. While organized retail and organized food processing involves powerful companies and creates apprehensions of inequality, a more balanced approach for policy makers could be to promote policies for transferring part of the agro-processing activities to farm women linking them with industries or customers. The evaluation exercise indicated signs of potential for empowering farm women and increasing farm income by this route though there are constraints. Support to women entrepreneurs such as in financing, marketing, training, certification and incentive for consumers keeping with regional reality may be helpful.

Notes

1. The UN's first World Conference on Women in Mexico in 1975, subsequent conferences in Copenhagen, Nairobi and Beijing and the UN decade for women (1976–85) mandated self-exploration among the nations on their internal policies further reinforced in 1990 by the millennium development goals (MDG).
2. This is an approximate figure only based on NSSO data.
3. It is also seen that even among non-workers 41 per cent perform jobs that could be potentially priced if market is created.
4. Agro Economic Research Centre of Punjab Agricultural Economics, Ludhiana-Punjab; Agro-economic Research Centre for North-East India in Jorhat-Assam; The Agro-Economic Research Centre of Sardar Patel University Gujarat-Rajasthan; The Agro-economic Research Center of Himachal Pradesh University, Shimla; Agricultural Economics Research Center, University of Delhi-Haryana and Uttaranchal.
5. The threshold for consideration at ₹ 10,000 is purely notional and not based on any cost of living benchmark. It may be compared with the household income that may be expected from participation in the NREGA (now MGNREGA) public work programme that promises to provide employment to at least one member for at least 100 days in a year at a wage rate of ₹ 100 per day. This leads to an income of ₹ 10,000.

References

Agarwal, Bina (1994). *A Field of One's Own*, Cambridge University Press, Cambridge.

Boserup, Ester (1975). *Women's Role in Economic Development*, George Allen and Unwin Ltd., London.

Dasgupta, Partha (2001). *Human Well-Being and the Natural Environment*, Oxford University Press, Oxford.

Ghosh, Nilabja (2010a). *Economic Empowerment of Rural Farm Women through Agro-based Entrepreneurial Ventures*, Report submitted to the Ministry of Agriculture, Government of India from Institute of Economic Growth, Delhi.

——. (2010b). 'Organisational Forms and Market Intermediations: A Study on Rural Women Entrepreneurs in India', *Indian Journal of Labour Economics*, 53 (2): 381–95.

——. (2013). 'Promoting Entrepreneurship among Women in Agriculture', in Sharmila Banerjee and Anjan Chakraborti (eds), *Development and Sustainability: India in a Global Perspective*, Springer, India.

Government of India (1981, 1991 and 2001). Census of India, http://censusindia.gov.in/

——. (2005, 2008). 'Employment and Unemployment Situation in India', National Sample Survey Organization.

——. (2008). Labour Bureau, http://labourbureau.nic.in/WR%20Rural%20India%202k7-8%20Contents.htm

——. (2009–10). *Viable Entrepreneurial Trades of Women in Agriculture (Andhra Pradesh, Bihar, Haryana, Rajasthan, Punjab, Assam, Himachal Pradesh)*, Report submitted by Agro-Economic Research Centres (AERCs) to Ministry of Agriculture.

Gulati, Ashok, Ganguly, Kaveri and Shreedhar, Ganga (2011). *Food and Nutritional Security in India*, International Food Policy Research Institute, New Delhi.

Hirway, Indira and Roy, Anil Kumar (1999). 'Women in Rural Economy: The Case of India', *Indian Journal of Agricultural Economics*, 54 (3).

Kaur, Satnam and Goyal, S.K. (1996). 'A Study of Wage Discrimination against Women Agricultural Labourers', *Agricultural Situation in India*, 53 (4), July.

Klasen, Stephan and Wink, Claudia (2006). 'Missing Women': Revisiting the Debate', in Bina Agarwal, Jane Humphries and Ingrid Robeyns (eds), *Capabilities, Freedom and Equality*, Oxford University Press, Delhi.

Krishnaraj, Maithreyi (2005). 'Food Security: How and for Whom?', *Economic and Political Weekly*, 40 (25), June 18–24: 2508–12.

Nussbaum, Martha and Sen, Amartya (1993). *The Quality of Life*, Clarendon Press, Oxford.

Rani, Sudha, Raju, V.T., Raghuram, P. and Naidu, G. Munaswami (1990). 'Wage Differentials and Factors Governing Employment of Women in Agriculture', *Agricultural Situation in India*, 45 (4), July.

Sen, Amartya (2005). 'Development as Capability Expansion', in Bina Agarwal, Jane Humphries and Ingrid Robeyns (eds), *Capabilities, Freedom and Equality*, Oxford University Press, Oxford.

——. (2006). 'Gender and Cooperative Conflicts', in Bina Agarwal, Jane Humphries and Ingrid Robeyns (eds), *Capabilities, Freedom and Equality*, Oxford University Press, Oxford.

Sengupta, Arjun (2009). 'Mainstreaming Small Farms: A New Approach Needed', Inaugural address delivered at the Conference on the Future of Indian Agriculture: Technology and Institutions, Institute of Economic Growth, Delhi and also forthcoming in a book by the same name edited by Nilabja Ghosh and C.S.C. Sekhar.

14

Rural Non-Agricultural Enterprises in Uttar Pradesh

Continuity and Change

NRIPENDRA KISHORE MISHRA AND UDAI BHAN SINGH

This is a contemporary fact that Rural Non-Farm Sector (RNFS) is expanding throughout India and especially so in Uttar Pradesh. This growth has been witnessed right from the decade of 1980s. But it accelerated in 1990s and has received further boost in the first decade of the 21st century. This has been shown by the rising share of non-farm workers amongst total workers (Ranjan, 2009). Researchers have tried to estimate size and structure of RNFS by looking at employment in RNFS (Sen and Jha, 2005; Alagh, 2005; Mitra and Mitra, 2005; Kundu, Sarangi and Das, 2005; Chadha, 2002; Srivastav and Dubey, 2005; Saith, 1992). However, employment is only a part of this story. Ideally, one would have liked to have some idea of output diversification also. But estimation of RNFS output and its structure is not possible in available data sets. One can have this picture by estimating Gross Value Added (GVA) generated by non-agricultural enterprises in Uttar Pradesh and deducting this from State Domestic Product (SDP). But this method can provide us information only at the state level and it is impossible to know the regional pattern. Estimates of output of RNFS can be also derived from value added per worker as obtained from Employment-Unemployment Survey (EUS) of National Sample Survey (NSS). Most studies on RNFS have been done by following this route. This route assumes that employment and output are either synonymous or coterminous. This is too simplistic and is oblivious of many layers and sub layers of rural economy. It looks at

RNFS as constituted of workers and employers. The fact of the day is that RNFS is principally driven by family labour and self-employment is defining characteristics of RNFS (Shariff and Lanjouw, 2004). Therefore, employment can never capture the complete dynamics of rural non-farm sector. A better picture can be had by looking at rural non-agricultural enterprises. Moreover, whatever has been done is at state level only. The problem with UP is, that this is one state with a very high degree of regional variations. Any aggregated analysis of the state as such is likely to be meaningless. Therefore, it is important to have a disaggregated analysis of UP. Fortunately, now we have two rounds of NSS where this exercise can be done at an enterprise level. These Rounds are 55th Round, 1999–2000 (Non-Agricultural Enterprises in Informal Sector in India) and 67th Round, 2010–11 (Unincorporated Non-Agricultural Enterprises in India). Here the problem is that administrative division of UP does not match with NSS regions. Since NSS regions are based on a much more scientific basis, we are sticking to NSS regions rather than on administrative division. But this procedure too has its problem when we have to compare the different rounds of NSS. This problem occurs because of division of UP and creation of new districts. Earlier, there were five regions in UP and the fifth region, namely, the Himalayan region, has been carved out as Uttarakhand. So Uttar Pradesh was left with four regions only in NSS. Once again, this is not the case that the complete Himalayan region has been cut out. There are districts for which one need to adjust. In the latest 67th Round, NSS has again made five regions in UP. The following section presents results from unit level data set of these two rounds for four zones of Uttar Pradesh and examines changes in some basic characteristics of these enterprises during 1999–2000 to 2010–11.

Regional Spread of Enterprises

The state of Uttar Pradesh is divided into four well defined economic regions: western, eastern, central, and southern. All these regions have different climatic conditions, soil types and infra-structural development. The western region is still the more prosperous region than other regions. Thus, given the wide variations in the level of development, the factors driving non-farm sector would also vary. It is likely that in the more developed western region, diversification of employment away from agriculture would reflect the role of demand pull factors generated by agricultural dynamism, while in the eastern, central and southern regions, distress push can play a role in increasing the volume of non-farm employment. Rural non-agricultural enterprises have a regional pattern in its distribution. Ideally one would have expected a higher percentage of enterprises in western UP. This expectation rested on the assumption that growth of non-agricultural enterprises is intricately linked with growth of surplus in agriculture. This supposition assumes that rural non-agricultural enterprises are either financed by surplus from agriculture or are stimulated by expanding rural markets as a consequence of growth in rural incomes. Given the fact that rural incomes and surplus from agriculture is higher in western UP as compared to eastern UP, the percentage of these enterprises should have been higher there. But 67th Round of NSS presents a different picture. Almost half of enterprises of Uttar Pradesh are located in eastern UP and only one-third are located in western UP. There has been growth in number of enterprises in all regions of the state except central region, where there is a decline in absolute number. That is why share of central regions has declined between 1999–2000 and 2010–11. There has been marginal change in share of other regions. Interestingly, share of western regions, though lower than eastern region, has increased during this period. The most significant change in estimated number of enterprises during 1999–2000 and 2010–11 is in southern region, followed by western region and there is a decline in estimated number of enterprises in central region. However, this is something which goes against common sense. One needs to investigate this and this shall be done later on.

Table 1

Estimated Number and Percentage of Enterprises

Region	*1999–2000*		*2010–11*		
	No.	*%*	*No.*	*%*	*% Change*
Western	1,383,944	31.52	1,593,827	33.73	15.17
Central	7,82,319	17.82	7,46,488	15.8	-4.58
Eastern	2,076,559	47.3	2,208,013	46.73	6.33
Southern	1,47,342	3.36	1,76,896	3.74	20.06
UP	4,390,164	100	4,725,224	100	7.63

Source: Extracted by author from unit data of 55th and 67th Round of NSS.

NSS 67th Round focuses only on three sectors, namely, manufacturing, trade and services. These three groups are further divided into sub groups. These are as follows:

Manufacturing (M)–M1: Food products, beverages and tobacco products, M2: Cotton ginning, cleaning and bailing, textiles, wearing apparel, leather and leather products, M3: Wood and wood products, paper and paper products, printing, etc. M4: Petroleum products, chemicals, pharmaceuticals, rubber, plastics, metals, metal products, machinery and equipment, etc. M5: Remaining manufacturing activities

Trade (T) – T 1: Commission agents for wholesale trade, T 2: Trade and repair of motor vehicles and motor cycles, T 3: Other wholesale trade, T 4: Other retail trade

Other Services (S) – S 1: Accommodation and food service activities, S 2: Transport, storage, information and communication, S 3: Financial and insurance activities, S 4: Real estate, professional, scientific and technical, rental and leasing activities, S 5: Education, S 6: Human health and social work, S 7: Other personal services. In a sense, this round looks at rural non-agricultural enterprises only in above mentioned industry groups. It explicitly excludes construction industry, which it had included in 55th Round (1999–2000) of survey. We have dropped construction from the 55th Round to arrive at a meaningful comparison. Similarly, necessary adjustments have been made in the 55th Round, as it was based on NIC 1998.

Enterprises are of two types, namely Own Account Enterprises (OAE) and establishments. OAEs are enterprises which do not use hired labour regularly and establishments are those which use at least one labour fairly regularly. Obviously, OAEs are family labour intensive and, therefore, operate at low scale of production. This is automatically followed up by low capital intensity and low returns. Establishments are expected to be better off type of enterprises. Hiring of labour is possible only at higher scale of production and with higher level of returns. It may be hypothesised that OAEs are primarily a supplementary source of income used as strategy of coping up either with falling income or providing employment to family labour. It is clear from Table 2 that rural non-agricultural enterprises in Uttar Pradesh are largely OAEs and only a very small percentage (6%) of enterprises are establishments. Incidentally, there are no regional variations. The same pattern holds across all regions of the state. It is also clear from Table 2 that there has been marginal decline in the share of OAEs in all regions and marginal rise in the share of establishments in all regions.

Table 2

OAEs and Establishments by Regions for 1999–2000 and 2010–11

Region	*Year*	*OAEs*	*Establishments*
Western	1999–2000	95.13	4.87
	2010–11	93.88	6.12
Central	1999–2000	97.0	3.0
	2010–11	94.06	5.94
Eastern	1999–2000	94.79	5.21
	2010–11	94.37	5.63
Southern	1999–2000	98.63	1.37
	2010–11	94.02	5.98
UP	1999–2000	95.42	4.58
	2010–11	94.15	5.85

Source: Extracted by author from unit data of 55th and 67th Round of NSS.

In year 2010–11, more than one – third rural non-agricultural enterprises are in category 'other retail trade', followed by 'cotton ginning, cleaning and bailing, textiles, wearing apparel, leather and leather products' (12%) and 'other personal services' (11%) in Uttar Pradesh. That means that these three groups account for half of rural non-agricultural enterprises in Uttar Pradesh. However, there is a regional variation in this story. Other retails trade maintains its predominance in all four regions, but this is followed by cotton ginning, cleaning and bailing, textiles, wearing apparel, leather and leather products in western and central UP, by other personal service in eastern UP and by wood and wood products, paper and paper products, printing, etc. in southern UP. Thus, what we observe is that rural non-agricultural enterprises from industry group wood and wood products, paper and paper products, printing, etc. are not important in western and central UP, but they become significant in percentage in eastern and southern UP.

Since southern UP relatively reports higher percentage (8%) of enterprises in industrial group 'petroleum products, chemicals, pharmaceuticals, rubber, plastics, metals, metal products, machinery and equipment, etc.' one might have expected higher incidence of establishments in this region, as this group is more capital intensive and is difficult to carry out production without hired labour. But this is not the case and at least this is not reflected in Table 3. It needs to be investigated why is it so. During period 1999–2000 and 2010–11, manufacturing has declined in UP. This decline is there in all regions except western. In fact, in western region, share of manufacturing has gone up. Within manufacturing, this decline is there in all sub groups at state level. However, M1 and M2 categories have witnessed rise in western region, M2 in central region, M3 in eastern region and M4 in southern region. Trading has gained substantially in all regions. But within trading it is T4 (other retail trade) which is the main category. Other trading enterprises are almost insignificant. Bulk of these trading enterprises is mainly in other retail trade category and this gain in trading enterprises has come from growth of this category only. It is interesting to note that despite of all hues and cries about growth of service sector, the share of service sector enterprises has come down in rural Uttar Pradesh in all regions except eastern region. The two most important categories in service, namely, S2 (transport, storage, communication and information) and S7 (other personal services) have witnessed decline during 1999–2000 and 2010–11 in all regions of state.

Table 3

Distribution of Enterprises by Industry Group

	Western		*Central*		*Eastern*		*Southern*		*UP*	
Industry/ Year	*1999–2000*	*2010–11*	*1999–2000*	*2010–11*	*1999–2000*	*2010–11*	*1999–2000*	*2010–11*	*1999–00*	*2010–11*
Manufacturing	29.78	34.23	31.81	29.52	35.58	28.48	39.29	30.67	33.21	30.67
M1	8.7	11.91	9.26	4.83	10.46	7.48	9.66	4.57	9.66	8.44
M2	12.3	14.68	12.56	18.46	12.7	8.39	8.33	6.83	12.4	12.04
M3	5.35	3.98	5.28	3.95	7.22	10.05	14.26	10.92	6.52	7.07
M4	3.44	3.66	4.72	2.28	5.2	2.56	7.05	8.35	4.62	3.11
Trading	36.32	38.51	34.8	44.78	31.75	39.08	41.86	45.18	34.07	40.02
T1	0.19	0.15	0.06	0.22	0.07	0.07	0	0.28	0.1	0.13
T2	0.37	0.84	0.17	1.29	0.31	0.45	0.27	1.29	0.3	0.75
T3	4.52	2.75	0.72	1.83	1.27	0.67	0	1.56	2.15	1.59
T4	31.24	34.77	33.86	41.44	30.1	37.89	41.59	42.05	31.52	37.55
Services	33.89	27.26	33.38	25.7	32.67	32.44	18.84	24.15	32.72	29.32
S1	1.39	1.43	0.86	2.36	3.85	5.33	0.82	3.22	2.44	3.47
S2	13.77	10.41	10.77	4.96	7.55	7.03	3.27	4.0	9.94	7.73
S3	0.02	0.17	0	0.58	0.12	0.89	0	0.37	0.06	0.58
S4	0.46	2.21	0.45	1.8	0.87	2.96	0.7	2.12	0.66	2.49
S5	0.83	1.4	0.84	1.35	0.57	1.54	0.36	1.84	0.69	1.47
S6	4.06	3.14	3.52	2.98	2.68	2.87	1.27	3.19	3.21	2.99
S7	13.36	8.5	16.95	11.67	17.04	11.82	12.43	9.41	15.71	10.59
Total	100	100	100	100	100	100	100	100	100	100

Source: Extracted by author from unit data of 55th and 67th Round of NSS.

However, one needs to know how OAEs and establishments are located within different industrial groups. Can it be postulated that there is a definite pattern in type of enterprises and their incidence in different industry groups? It can be seen from Table 4 that earlier, OAEs and establishment were almost uniformly (almost one third each) distributed among manufacturing, trade and services. But in later year, there has been a shift. OAEs have moved out from manufacturing and services to trade. This is so in all regions of state. But, establishment present a discordant note. Establishment are moving out of trade and into manufacturing and services. Once again, the same pattern follows across all regions of state. Thus, there are two quite opposite trends in rural non-agricultural enterprises in Uttar Pradesh.

Table 4

Industry-wise Distribution of OAEs and Establishments

Region	*Year*	*Manufacturing*	*Trade*	*Services*	*Total*
			OAEs		
Western	1999–2000	28.66	37.31	34.03	100
	2010–11	33.63	39.94	26.43	100
Central	1999–2000	31.47	35.52	33.01	100
	2010–11	28.77	46.55	24.68	100
Eastern	1999–2000	34.98	32.72	32.3	100
	2010–11	27.88	40.73	31.39	100
Southern	1999–2000	39.32	42.14	18.54	100
	2010–11	30.1	46.72	23.19	100
UP	1999–2000	32.51	35	32.49	100
	2010–11	30.04	41.61	28.36	100
			Establishments		
Western	1999–2000	51.66	17.05	31.3	100
	2010–11	43.49	16.54	39.97	100
Central	1999–2000	42.81	11.65	45.55	100
	2010–11	41.44	16.67	41.89	100
Eastern	1999–2000	46.49	14.05	39.46	100
	2010–11	38.55	11.39	50.06	100
Southern	1999–2000	37.64	21.75	40.62	100
	2010–11	39.64	21.0	39.36	100
UP	1999–2000	47.7	14.85	37.45	100
	2010–11	40.8	14.42	44.79	100

Source: Extracted by author from unit data of 55th and 67th Round of NSS.

Caste

Caste is an important determinant of growth and viability of enterprise. Of late, Uttar Pradesh has witnessed a lot of social churning out and middle caste group (OBCs) has moved very fast up the economic, social and political ladders. Many studies have pointed this out. NSS 67th round reports that almost three-fourth of enterprises in Uttar Pradesh are owned by OBCs, followed by others, which by default is composed of upper caste groups. SCs still own less than 20 per cent of enterprises in Uttar Pradesh. The predominance of OBCs is maintained in all four regions. The variation comes in the relative importance in category of others and SCs. For example, in western UP, the other category is higher than SC and in eastern and southern UP, it is lower than SCs. The ownership of these enterprises across regions and types shows that share of SCs and OBCs in OAEs are higher than their respective share in establishments. This means that lesser percentage of enterprises is owned by these caste groups in comparison to OAEs. The decline in share of these caste groups in establishments means that 'others' category (which invariably includes upper castes) share a larger percentage. This is quite interesting to note as establishments are run by hired labour and denote higher capital intensity and higher gross value added (GVA). Then it may well be inferred that these upper caste groups are in a better category of enterprises. Interestingly, this pattern follows exactly like this in all four regions of the state. It is only in eastern UP. that the decline in share of OBCs is only marginal. It may be indicative of the fact that OBCs have consolidated their position much more strongly in eastern part of the state. Probably, larger clout of OBCs in politics of eastern UP. is also reflective of this fact.

Table 5

Percentage Distribution of Enterprise Type by Region and Caste, 2010–11

Enterprise type/Caste	*ST*	*SC*	*OBC*	*Others*	*Not Known*	*Total*
				Western		
OAE	0.33	17.71	61.27	20.32	0.37	100
Establishment	0.03	12.4	53.69	32.02	1.86	100
Total	0.31	17.39	60.82	21.02	0.46	100
				Central		
OAE	0.32	17.24	65.49	16.72	0.22	100
Establishment	0.52	6.21	57.31	35.84	0.13	100
Total	0.33	16.6	65.02	17.83	0.22	100

Cont'd...

...Cont'd

				Eastern		
OAE	1.78	19.45	65.16	13.16	0.44	100
Establishment	0.7	7.12	63.32	28.11	0.75	100
Total	1.72	18.78	65.06	13.98	0.46	100
				Southern		
OAE	0.89	24.39	58.92	15.68	0.12	100
Establishment	0	6.36	42.82	50.48	0.34	100
Total	0.84	23.37	58.01	17.64	0.14	100
				UP		
OAE	1.03	18.7	63.67	16.23	0.37	100
Establishment	0.41	8.83	58.16	31.57	1.03	100
Total	0.99	18.14	63.35	17.1	0.41	100

Source: Extracted by author from unit data of 67th Round of NSS.

Different caste groups are distributed across four regions in varying proportions. An examination of Table 6 shows that close to half of SCs in western and southern UP are into trade and only one-third of SCs are into trade in eastern UP. Around 40 per cent OBCs are into trade in all four regions. In central and southern UP, more than half of 'other' caste groups are into trade. In all four regions, the percentage of OBCs in manufacturing is the highest.

Table 6

Distribution of Enterprises by Broad NIC and Caste, 2010–11

Broad NIC/Caste	*ST*	*SC*	*OBC*	*Others*	*Not Known*	*Total*
				Western		
Manufacturing	0.01	16.07	63.74	19.79	0.38	100
Trade	0.72	19.25	58.23	21.58	0.23	100
Services	0.12	16.4	60.8	21.78	0.9	100
Total	0.31	17.39	60.82	21.02	0.46	100
				Central		
Manufacturing	0.66	10	80.86	8.39	0.1	100
Trade	0.22	18.18	57.16	24.11	0.34	100
Services	0.17	21.46	60.5	17.72	0.14	100
Total	0.33	16.6	65.02	17.83	0.22	100
				Eastern		
Manufacturing	3.22	17.48	70.18	9.01	0.11	100
Trade	0.63	17.06	66.41	15.64	0.27	100

Cont'd...

...Cont'd

Services	1.72	22.04	58.84	16.38	1.01	100
Total	1.72	18.78	65.06	13.98	0.46	100
			Southern			
Manufacturing	1.23	22.23	65.17	11.31	0.06	100
Trade	0.86	24.51	53.99	20.56	0.09	100
Services	0.31	22.68	56.41	20.27	0.32	100
Total	0.84	23.37	58.01	17.64	0.14	100
			UP			
Manufacturing	1.55	15.99	69.19	13.06	0.21	100
Trade	0.59	18.29	61.59	19.27	0.26	100
Services	0.96	20.2	59.62	18.39	0.83	100
Total	0.99	18.14	63.35	17.1	0.41	100

Source: Extracted by author from unit data of 67th Round of NSS.

Nature of Operations

Enterprises are of three kinds. Enterprises that are run more or less regularly throughout the year are called perennial enterprises. Seasonal enterprises are those, which are usually run in a particular season or fixed months of a year. Enterprises that are run occasionally, for a total of at least 30 days in the last 365 days, are called 'casual enterprises'. Enterprises are predominantly (more than 94%) perennial in nature. It is only in manufacturing in central UP that percentage of enterprises is lower (85%). Out of these three activities, trade appears to be much more perennial than other activities.

Table 7

Nature of Operation of Enterprise by Industry

Region/Industry Group	*Perennial*		*Seasonal*		*Casual*	
	1999–2000	*2010–11*	*1999–2000*	*2010–11*	*1999–2000*	*2010–11*
			Western			
Manufacturing	89.18	98.51	9.4	1.28	1.42	0.21
Trade	95.86	98.75	3.9	0.63	0.24	0.62
Services	96.89	97.47	2.19	1.9	0.92	0.63
Total	94.22	98.32	4.96	1.2	0.82	0.48
			Central			
Manufacturing	92.87	84.78	6.53	3.21	0.6	12.01
Trade	96.96	100	2.97	0	0.06	0

Cont'd...

...Cont'd

Services	94.72	96.54	2.05	3.15	3.23	0.31
Total	94.91	94.62	3.8	1.76	1.29	3.63
			Eastern			
Manufacturing	92.31	96.61	7.05	3.24	0.64	0.16
Trade	97.78	98.84	1.94	1.04	0.28	0.12
Services	96.34	98.73	1.79	0.66	1.87	0.61
Total	95.36	98.17	3.71	1.54	0.93	0.29
			Southern			
Manufacturing	95.77	97.31	3.81	2.69	0.42	0
Trade	96.83	99.73	3.17	0.16	0	0.11
Services	98.51	94.68	0.74	5.32	0.74	0
Total	96.73	97.77	2.96	2.19	0.3	0.05
			UP			
Manufacturing	91.66	95.55	7.49	2.47	0.84	1.98
Trade	96.95	99.05	2.84	0.69	0.22	0.26
Services	96.27	97.9	1.95	1.54	1.78	0.56
Total	94.97	97.64	4.09	1.48	0.94	0.87

Source: Extracted by author from unit data of 67th Round of NSS.

Moreover, there is no variation across OAEs and establishments in any region. However, it is also clear that establishments show a higher percentage in seasonal enterprises than OAEs. But the most striking inference from Table 8 is that in general rural non-agricultural enterprises in Uttar Pradesh are getting perennial in nature during 1999–2000 and 2010–11. There is rise in percentage of perennial enterprises (OAEs and establishments both) and consequent decline in share of seasonal and casual enterprises. It is only in central region where percentage of OAEs and in eastern region percentage of establishments in casual category has marginally risen during this period.

Table 8

Nature of Operation by Enterprise Type and Region

Region/Type	*Perennial*		*Seasonal*		*Casual*		*Total*
	1999–2000	*2010–11*	*1999–2000*	*2010–11*	*1999–2000*	*2010–11*	
				Western			
OAE	94.59	98.57	4.55	1	0.86	0.43	100

Cont'd...

...Cont'd

Establishment	87	94.48	12.9	4.24	0.1	1.28	100
Total	94.22	98.32	4.96	1.2	0.82	0.48	100
				Central			
OAE	95.26	94.51	3.57	1.63	1.17	3.86	100
Establishment	83.67	96.21	11.03	3.79	5.3	0	100
Total	94.91	94.62	3.8	1.76	1.29	3.63	100
				Eastern			
OAE	95.38	98.37	3.68	1.46	0.93	0.17	100
Establishment	94.97	94.74	4.21	2.98	0.82	2.28	100
Total	95.36	98.17	3.71	1.54	0.93	0.29	100
				Southern			
OAE	96.83	97.85	2.86	2.1	0.31	0.05	100
Establishment	89.8	96.43	10.2	3.57	0	0	100
Total	96.73	97.77	2.96	2.19	0.3	0.05	100
				UP			
OAE	95.16	97.81	3.91	1.35	0.93	0.84	100
Establishment	90.93	94.95	7.98	3.58	1.09	1.48	100
Total	94.97	97.64	4.09	1.48	0.94	0.87	100

Source: Extracted by author from unit data of 67th Round of NSS.

Location of Enterprises

Almost half of enterprises in Uttar Pradesh are located within household premises. This is so in all four regions of the state. However, this high incidence of within household enterprises masks the fact that it is OAEs which are located mainly within households. While almost half of OAEs are located within households in western UP., the corresponding figure is higher in central and southern UP. and lower in eastern UP. Establishments are primarily outside with fixed premises and permanent structure in all four regions of the state. This only verifies our earlier contention that establishments are much more capital intensive than OAEs. During the period 1999–2000 and 2010–11, OAEs and establishments of rural non-agricultural enterprises in western and central region of Uttar Pradesh are coming into household and in eastern and southern region, establishments are going outside the household in this period.

Table 9

Percentage Distribution of Enterprises by Location

Type/Region	Within Household		Outside Household		Total
	1999–2000	2010–11	1999–2000	2010–11	
			Western		
OAE	35.03	50.36	64.97	49.63	100
Establishment	12.66	27.92	87.34	72.09	100
Total	33.94	48.99	66.06	51.01	100
			Central		
OAE	39.7	56.85	60.3	43.15	100
Establishment	16.95	23.14	83.05	76.86	100
Total	39.02	54.85	60.98	45.16	100
			Eastern		
OAE	42.84	43.22	57.16	56.78	100
Establishment	37.13	20.62	62.87	79.38	100
Total	42.55	41.95	57.45	58.05	100
			Southern		
OAE	66.35	65.36	33.65	34.65	100
Establishment	30.5	16.16	69.5	83.84	100
Total	65.86	62.42	34.14	37.58	100
			UP		
OAE	40.63	48.6	59.37	51.39	100
Establishment	26.5	23.43	73.5	76.57	100
Total	39.99	47.13	60.01	52.87	100

Source: Extracted by author from unit data of 55th and 67th Round of NSS.

Secondly, manufacturing is primarily located within households and services are primarily located outside households in all four regions of the state. Close to 60 per cent manufacturing enterprises were within household in western, central and eastern region and this was around 85 per cent in southern region in the year 1999–2000. This percentage rose in the first three regions and declined in the last region. It means that during the period of 1999–2000 and 2010–11 in western, central and eastern region, manufacturing has gone to household and in southern region it has moved away from household. Trading enterprises have also moved into household in all four regions. Similarly, service enterprises have also moved into households except for eastern region.

Table 10

Location of Enterprise by Broad NIC

Type/Region	Within Household		Outside Household		
	1999–2000	2010–11	1999–2000	2010–11	Total
			Western		
Manufacturing	60.01	76.5	39.99	23.5	100
Trade	27.63	41.4	72.37	58.62	100
Services	17.78	25.16	82.22	74.85	100
			Central		
Manufacturing	62.36	82.78	37.64	17.22	100
Trade	32.43	47.72	67.57	52.28	100
Services	23.64	35.16	76.36	64.83	100
			Eastern		
Manufacturing	62.91	66.68	37.09	33.32	100
Trade	29.86	34.96	70.14	65.04	100
Services	32.69	28.64	67.31	71.35	100
			Southern		
Manufacturing	86.56	79.73	13.44	20.27	100
Trade	60.4	64.7	39.6	35.3	100
Services	34.82	36.19	65.18	63.82	100
			UP		
Manufacturing	62.94	73.32	37.06	26.69	100
Trade	30.84	40.56	69.16	59.44	100
Services	26.22	28.68	73.78	71.31	100

Source: Extracted by author from unit data of 55th and 67th Round of NSS.

Status of Enterprises in Last Three Years

NSS 55th and 67th Rounds record the status of rural non-agricultural enterprises in the last three years as whether expanding, stagnant or contracting. Table 11 shows that one-fourth to one-third enterprises are reported to be expanding in all four regions of the state. During periods 1999–2000 and 2010–11, there has been phenomenal growth in enterprises reporting to be expanding. Naturally, the percentage of enterprises reporting contraction has declined during this period. Interestingly, larger percentage of enterprises is reporting expansion during last three years in western region and this expansion is observed in all categories of broad NIC. Thus, it means that this period is characterized by expansion of rural non-agricultural enterprises in all regions of UP and in all sectors.

Table 11

Status of Enterprise by Broad NIC and Region

Broad NIC/Region	Expanding		Stagnant		Contracting		Total
	1999–2000	2010–11	1999–2000	2010–11	1999–2000	2010–11	
				Western			
Manufacturing	12.63	38.82	67.37	51.35	20.0	9.83	100
Trading	17.98	40.85	67.34	43.97	14.68	15.17	100
Services	17.53	40.26	64.01	50.85	18.46	8.89	100
Total	16.2	39.99	66.21	48.46	17.59	11.56	100
				Central			
Manufacturing	13.3	14.61	65.13	72.57	21.56	12.81	100
Trading	15.04	25.6	68.35	68.4	16.61	6	100
Services	10.26	32.81	64.67	55.49	25.07	11.7	100
Total	12.82	23.99	66.03	66.29	21.14	9.73	100
				Eastern			
Manufacturing	17.53	23.93	72.1	55.84	10.37	20.23	100
Trading	22.47	35.24	63.64	48.12	13.89	16.64	100
Services	23.08	31.16	68.79	54.87	8.12	13.97	100
Total	20.88	30.41	68.39	52.82	10.73	16.77	100
				Southern			
Manufacturing	10.2	18.72	66.91	60.78	22.89	20.51	100
Trading	13.93	31.8	66.08	64.01	20	4.19	100
Services	3.62	26.79	80.28	64.24	16.1	8.97	100
Total	10.21	26.12	69.36	62.96	20.43	10.92	100
				UP			
Manufacturing	15.24	27.55	69.49	57.26	15.26	15.19	100
Trading	19.45	35.21	65.72	51.23	14.83	13.56	100
Services	18.68	34.08	66.81	54.02	14.51	11.91	100
Total	17.76	32.4	67.37	54.03	14.87	13.57	100

Source: Extracted by author from unit data of 55th and 67th Round of NSS.

Sub-contracting

Global production networks and rising competition in domestic market accompanied by failure of formal sector to absorb additional labour force or loss of formal sector job has created a situation in many countries, including India, where a substantial section of work force is not working in a central work site. Flexible work contract or sub-contracting and 'putting-out' system of production is becoming a general practice. Businesses are finding it much easier and profitable to procure production from a network of workers/suppliers through intermediaries and middle man (Uchikawa, 2011). The general mode of payment is piece rate. In a way, production process is being decentralized. This decentralization is of a different kind where production is not carried out by the business itself but is out sourced. This phenomenon has expanded in recent times and thus a set of workers have emerged which is known as 'home based workers (HBW)' or 'home workers' or 'outworkers'. These workers are working in enterprises which are essentially in some sort of sub-contracting arrangement with bigger enterprises. Of course, this putting out system of production is not new. But it has expanded tremendously in recent years in all parts of country. We attempt to look at incidence of sub-contracting in different regions of Uttar Pradesh. This is done by looking at industry sub group and type of enterprises.

It is instantly clear from Table 12 that there has been phenomenal expansion in sub-contracting in rural non-agricultural enterprises in Uttar Pradesh. Almost 40 per cent enterprises in western region and 20 per cent in eastern region are in sub-contracting arrangement in the year 2010–11. This expansion in incidence of sub-contracting is pronounced in all regions and in almost all sub-groups of manufacturing. Sub-group M4 (petroleum products, chemicals, pharmaceuticals, rubber, plastics, metals, metal products, machinery and equipment, etc.) is one category where there is either only marginal rise or marginal decline in incidence of sub-contracting. Another exception is sub-group M2 (cotton ginning, cleaning and bailing, textiles, wearing apparel, leather and leather products) in eastern region which has recorded decline in incidence of sub-contracting.

Table 12

Incidence of Sub-Contracting by Sub-Groups of Manufacturing

Region/ Sub-group	*M1*		*M2*		*M3*		*M4*		*Total*	
	1999–2000	*2010–11*	*1999–2000*	*2010–11*	*1999–2000*	*2010–11*	*1999–2000*	*2010–11*	*1999–2000*	*2010–11*
Western	18.84	39.49	27.06	48.63	7.19	14.37	17.33	19.32	19.97	38.32
Central	1.92	1.93	31.20	44.80	1.15	8.79	1.22	0.64	13.25	29.56
Eastern	10.98	11.20	42.25	18.97	1.43	35.12	2.69	0.48	18.99	20.96
UP	11.29	23.59	34.56	37.01	2.78	26.82	5.72	7.94	17.53	28.02

Source: Extracted by author from unit data of 55th and 67th Round of NSS

Note: No enterprise is reported to be in sub-contracting in southern region. Subcontracting is mainly present in manufacturing, therefore, trade and services have been dropped.

The result as shown in Table 12 leads us to a question: Is there any variation in type of enterprises? Table 13 shows that this expansion in sub-contracting has been witnessed by OAEs only. Across all regions, incidence of sub-contracting is many times higher in OAEs than in establishments. Moreover, the observed expansion in sub-contracting during 1999–2000 and 2010–11 is only in OAEs. Rather, the incidence of sub-contracting in establishments has reduced in all regions and in all sub-groups of manufacturing. It is only in M2 that we notice rise in incidence of sub-contracting in establishment in western region and decline in sub-contracting in OAEs in eastern region.

Table 13

Incidence of Sub-Contracting by Type of Enterprise and Manufacturing Sub-Group

Type/Subgroup	M1		M2		M3		M4		Total	
	1999–2000	2010–11	1999–2000	2010–11	1999–2000	2010–11	1999–2000	2010–11	1999–2000	2010–11
					Western					
OAE	19.45	41.79	27.86	50.76	5.88	14.91	18.64	22.09	20.42	40.49
Establishment	12.83	0.55	17.00	24.90	22.10	7.30	6.77	1.83	15.01	12.58
					Central					
OAE	2.02	1.80	30.56	45.94	1.17	10.61	1.27	0.00	12.96	31.49
Establishment	0.00	3.05	44.65	20.57	0.00	0.75	0.00	3.84	19.99	8.35
					Eastern					
OAE	11.40	11.81	42.05	18.49	0.59	36.39	2.84	0.57	18.30	21.84
Establishment	1.81	0.89	43.94	22.66	21.47	0.07	0.00	0.00	28.46	10.28
					UP					
OAE	11.60	25.09	34.37	38.28	1.95	28.42	5.90	9.03	17.18	29.50
Establishment	6.37	1.05	36.65	23.03	20.98	1.88	2.92	1.24	22.46	10.45

Source: Extracted by author from unit data of 55th and 67th Round of NSS.

Note: No enterprise is reported to be in sub-contracting in southern region. Subcontracting is mainly present in manufacturing, therefore, trade and services have been dropped.

Summing up

The above discussion on rural non-agricultural enterprises in Uttar Pradesh clearly brings out the fact that these enterprises are characterized by all sort of conflicting forces. A disaggregated analysis of Uttar Pradesh shows that there are differing and common trends across regions. While central region experienced absolute decline in number of enterprises, there was significant rise in number of enterprises in southern region. Almost half of enterprises of Uttar Pradesh are located in eastern UP and only one-third are located in western UP. Rural non-agricultural enterprises in Uttar Pradesh are largely OAEs and only a very small percentage (6%) of enterprises are establishments. Incidentally, there are no regional variations. The same pattern holds across all regions of the state. It is also clear that there has been marginal decline in the share of OAEs in all regions and marginal rise in share of establishments in all regions. During the period 1999–2000 and 2010–11, manufacturing has declined in UP. This decline is there in all regions except western. In fact, in western region share of manufacturing has gone up. Trading has gained substantially in all regions. But within trading, it is T4 (other retail trade) which is the main category. Other trading enterprises are almost insignificant. The share of service sector enterprises has come down in rural Uttar Pradesh in all regions except eastern region. OAEs have moved out from manufacturing and services to trade. Establishment are moving out of trade and into manufacturing and services. NSS 67th Round reports that almost three-fourth of enterprises in Uttar Pradesh are owned by OBCs, followed by others, which by default is composed of upper caste groups. SCs still own less than 20 per cent of enterprises in Uttar Pradesh. The predominance of OBCs is maintained in all four regions. Almost half of enterprises in Uttar Pradesh are located within household premises. This is so in all four regions of the state. However, this high incidence of within household enterprises masks the fact that it is OAEs, which are located mainly within households. Secondly, manufacturing is primarily located within households and services are primarily located outside households in all four regions of the state. One-fourth to one-third enterprises are reported to be expanding in all four regions of the state. During the period 1999–2000 and 2010–11 there has been phenomenal growth in enterprises reporting to be expanding. There has been phenomenal expansion in sub-contracting in rural non-agricultural enterprises in Uttar Pradesh. Almost 40 per cent enterprises in western region and 20 per cent in eastern region are in sub-contracting arrangement in year 2010–11. This expansion in incidence of sub-contracting is pronounced in all regions and in almost all sub-groups of manufacturing. Across all regions, incidence of sub-contracting is many times higher in OAEs than in establishments. Moreover, the observed expansion in sub-contracting during

1999–2000 and 2010–11 is only in OAEs. In summary, any analysis of rural non-agricultural enterprises in Uttar Pradesh must take into account these varying trends across regions and that is why any generalization about Uttar Pradesh is always fraught with the risk of being too simplistic.

References

Chadha, G.K. (1994). *Employment Earnings and Poverty: A Study of Rural India and Indonesia*, Sage Publications, New Delhi.

——. (2002). 'Rural Non-Farm Employment in India: What Does Recent Experience Teach Us', *Indian Journal of Labour Economics*, 45 (4), October–December.

Kundu, A., Sarangi, N. and Das, B.P. (2005). 'Economic Growth, Poverty and Non-farm Employment: An Analysis of Rural-urban Inter-linkages', in R. Nayyar and A.N. Sharma (eds), *Rural Transformation in India: The Role of Non-farm Sector*, Institute for Human Development, New Delhi.

Papola, T.S. (1987). 'Rural Industrialization and Agriculture Growth: A Case Study of India', in R. Islam (ed.), *Rural Industrialization and Employment in Asia*, ILO (ARETP), New Delhi.

Ranjan, Sharad (2009). 'Growth of Rural Non-farm Employment in Uttar Pradesh: Reflections from Recent Data', *Economic and Political Weekly*, 44 (4): 63–73.

Saith, A. (1992). *The Rural Non-farm Economy: Processes and Policies*, ILO, Geneva.

Sen, Abhijit and Jha, Praveen (2005). 'Rural Employment: Patterns and Trends from National Sample Survey', in R. Nayyar and A.N. Sharma (eds), *Rural Transformation in India: The Role of Non-farm Sector*, Institute for Human Development, New Delhi.

Shariff, A.S. and Lanjouw, P. (2004). 'Rural Non-farm Employment in India', *Economic and Political Weekly*, 39 (40): 4429–46.

Singh, A.K. (2005). 'Role of Rural Non-farm Sector in Rural Transformation: Evidences from Uttar Pradesh', in R. Nayyar and A.N. Sharma (eds), *Rural Transformation in India: The Role of Non-farm Sector*, Institute for Human Development, New Delhi.

Singh, S.P. (2006). 'Rural Non-Farm Employment in Uttar Pradesh: Determinants, Dimensions and Regional Pattern', *Indian Journal of Labour Economics*, 49 (4): 868–82.

Srivastav, N. and Dubey, A. (2005). 'Rural Non-farm Employment in India: Spatial Variation and Temporal Change', *Indian Journal of Labour Economics*, 45 (4).

Uchikawa, Shuji (2011). 'Linkages between Organised and Unorganised Sectors in Indian Machinery Industry', *Economic and Political Weekly*, 46 (1): 45–54.

15

Women as Protectors of Craft

A Case of Ajarak of Barmer

VARSHA JOSHI AND BHUWNESH JAIN

Women are central to the upholding and vivacity of culture in societies worldwide. Their roles in relation to intangible heritage are of great importance, and encompass what may be described as fundamental realms of culture, which are often indispensable in maintaining and transmitting traditional knowledge, cultural identity and familial and cohesive social relations. In most cultures, women play the principle role in raising children, through which the intergenerational transmission and renewal of many forms of intangible heritage occurs. In maintaining and passing on intangible culture to future generations, women often integrate new forms and techniques, thereby recreating and transforming culture (Chaudhuri and Chandra, 2001).

Women's occupational involvement in rural manufacture is not a recent development. Historically, they have participated in production for domestic consumption. Within the caste-based specialization of functions they have evolved gender specific occupations. Even though they mostly remain invisible to the market, they form a significant element in the production process. In recent years, the development of a national and export market has highlighted their role in commodity production. This is a direct consequence of the indispensability of women to the family for survival as well as to the market for low-cost production. Home-based workers, 80 per cent of whom are women, are the most 'invisible' of all unorganized sector workers. Home-based work is found in many different forms in both rural and urban areas. But there has been a lack of recognition and misunderstanding of the principal role of women in the creation, preservation and transmission of traditions and know-how. The role of women as custodians, protectors, transmitters and creators of intangible heritage is very much existent in the state both at the feudalistic set-up as patrons or at the rural grass-root level i.e. the artisans themselves.

The Context

This paper deals with a particular printing tradition of Rajasthan state. Ajarak has existed in Barmer/Kutch/Sindh since the Mohenjo-Daro civilization, or even before that. The true origin of the word 'Ajarak' is unknown. In Arabic, it means blue or indigo. The authentic Ajarak is printed on both sides by method known as resist printing. Sindh was traditionally a large producer of indigo and cotton and exported both to the Middle East (Bilgrami, 2002). The colour blue is also used extensively in Ajarak. It is not known whether the word came from Arabic and was incorporated into Sindhi or vice versa. Men use it as a turban, a *cummerbund* (cloth tied around waist and also wind it around their shoulders. Women use it as a *duppatta*, a *chaddar* or as a *shawl*. The cloth used for these purposes is usually about 2.5–3 metres long.

It is patterned with intense jewel-like colours. The dominant colours are rich crimson and a deep indigo. A little bit of white and black is also used to give definition to the geometric patterns. The geometrical designs in the fabric seem to echo the principles of Sufism (Islamic spiritualism) which was widely followed in the Barmer Sindh region. The geometric patterns which use the concept of symmetry are symbolic of Cosmic process that extends in all directions.

After the Partition of India, the production of Ajarak was carried out in Kutch (Gujarat) and Barmer (Rajasthan) which was once the easternmost part of Sindh. The name and patterns of Ajarak are to a large extent similar to those found in Sindh. The designs are basically geometrical based on the universe and the names of the designs are on stars, moon, etc. Here, the craftsmen who make Ajarak are Khatris. Khatris are both Hindus and Muslims. Hindu Khatris clientele is largely from the Muslim community.

The Khatri families were found in many areas of Pakistan, notably Khairpur, Khairpur Derki, Dabaavada, Khanpur, Hala, Meethiyari, Pithora, Amarkot, Dhoranara, Dund-Aaliyar, Dand-Adam, Saidpur, Said ka Gaon, Sangad Malir, Meethi, Kandiyaari, Pholaria and Nabi-Sar. Most of the Khatri families moved to India after Partition. Ajarak is now made by the Khatris settled in Barmer, Kutch-Bhuj, Ujjain, Bag, and Deesa. Khatri Muslims are present in areas of Balotara and Peepad in Barmer district also carry out Ajarak work.

Role of Women in Protecting this Art

The paper focuses on the role of two women who have played a major role in keeping the tradition of Ajarak alive in two different time periods. One being the *Kuldevi* (clan goddess), Hinglaj Mata and the other is Sukhidevi, a woman from the Khatri community.

Kuldevi Hinglaj

In Rajasthan and part of Sindh now in Pakistan the tradition of Kuldevi has been very strong.

Hinglaj is a Kuldevi of Rajputs, Charans and other Hindu communities like the Khatris. Muslims called her Nani Bai or Lal Chogavali Mai. It is believed that even Juman Muslim unmarried girls called Chagali Mai are the priest at the Hinglaj temple. The Juman Muslims are Brohi Muslims of Baloch clan. Hinglaj is also linked as a Sumerian goddess. The temple is situated in the current Hinglaj, a town on the Makran coast in the Lasbela district of Balochistan, Pakistan, and is the middle of the Hingol National Park. It is said that the Khatri were granted a boon by Hinglaj Mata. Lindsey Harlan says that 'every Kul explicitly associates the appearance of its Kuldevi with a critical act of Divine guardianship; and secondly Kuldevi has the power of protection' (Harlan, 1992: 63). Interestingly, we find that in Greek mythology also there are goddesses like Hera and Athena who are considered as protectors of handicrafts (Hard, 2003: 180). In the case of Ajarak also we find that Hinglaj Mata has a major role to play in creation and protection of printing tradition. As the tradition goes, the Khatris of Sindh would role plain white cloth and keep in front of Hinglaj Devi and would forget about it for six months. The cloth would on its own get the colour and print on it within this period of six months. It is further said that one day a woman needed an Ajarak immediately and could not wait for six months. She requested Hinglaj Mata if it could be prepared in a short period. That was the day, when the goddess told the Khatris that now onwards you will have do the dyeing and printing on your own. Thus, we find that even though she is the protector but at the same time decided to teach the devotees a lesson and thereby handing over the tradition of printing directly into their hands. The Khatris still worship Hinglaj Mata even though the main shrine is situated in Pakistan.

If we look at the process time of making an Ajarak, it actually takes six months if all the steps of washing, colouring, and printing are followed. The procedure of preparation of Ajarak is a long and difficult one involving 23 steps. The intensity and frequency of these can be changed according to the quality of the product to be delivered. In making of original Ajarak, the work is undertaken from November to February each year for a period of three years. This means that the cloth was folded or rolled (*beetana*) and kept under Hinglaj Mata's protection. Interestingly during this rest period the colours mature and the print takes a shape. Thus, the final product is considered to be completed with the blessing of Hinglaj Mata. Therefore, Khatris feel that it is with blessing of the Kuldevi that they were able to learn this tradition and are able to still continue.

Unfortunately, survival of this traditional art is becoming more and more difficult. The procedure of preparation of Ajarak is a long and difficult one involving 23 steps.

Steps of Making Ajarak

Step 1

100 pieces of cloth of 5.5 sq. m. are cut from a big cloth of grey colour. Then, 2 kg soda bicarbonate and 1 kg castor oil are mixed till they mix well with each other. The mixture is added to 300 litre water. The 100 pieces are soaked in the mix for 24 hours.

After 24 hours, the cloth pieces are taken out and washed thoroughly by hitting them on a big stone. This process is continued for 3 days. Then the cloth becomes very soft and is ready to absorb colour.

Step 2

Now, 100 small balls are made by mixing myrrh powder, arandi oil, sesame oil and sakud powder in about 20 litre of water. Then, each piece of cloth is soaked again in water with a small ball added to it.

When the cloth absorbs the mixture, the cloth is squeezed and washed on big stone in such a way that all the creases of the cloth go off and cloth becomes creaseless. Two people hold the cloth from both the corner and let it dry by holding tight.

Step 3

	Ingredients	
1.	Babul gum	10 gms
2.	Limestone powder	10 gms
3.	Mustard oil	250 gms
4.	Water	approximately
5.	*Multani mitti*	5 gms
6.	Cow dung (fresh, wet)	5 gms

These six things are mixed well. The mixture is sieved with a thin cloth after 7 days. This is how Kirana is prepared. Then, required design is drawn in an outline on the cloth.

Step 4 (Printing with Khat)

	Ingredients	
1.	Iron	20 gms
2.	Jaggery (gud)	2 kgs
3.	*Bajra flour*	1 kg
4.	Water	approximately

All these ingredients are mixed in water for 15 to 20 days and left to rot. It turns into black colour which is then used for printing.

Step 5

Kaat is used to develop an outline of the drawing on the cloth. Then, the Kaat Stamp is used to print finer designs inside the outlines.

Step 6 (Kaat Stamp)

Now, the whole cloth is printed with help of Kaat Stamp.

Step 7

Printing is also done with a mix of tamarind seed flour and ferric alum (*fatakadi*).

Step 8 (Printing with Khar)

Ingredients

1. Ghavdi gum
2. *Samuda gum of Kumbhat*
3. *Fitrakis*
4. Water (60 litres)
5. *Multani mitti*
6. *Lal kashish*

All these ingredients are mixed with help of feet. The resulting pulp is used for printing. The wet printing is dried by spraying cow dung powder on it.

Step 9 (Nil Ki Dip)

Ingredients

Local indigo
Soda bicarbonate
Sajji khar
Mustard seeds
Limestone powder
Jaggery

All these ingredients are mixed in about 500 litre of water. After several days, the indigo gets ready for printing. Each cloth piece is soaked in the indigo for 2–3 minutes and spread up-side-down to dry.

Step 10 Bichalana (Washing)

The dyed cloth is thoroughly washed. Now it looks light green. The cloth is boiled in a mix of *dhawdi* flower and sakud oil. Then they are left to dry.

Step 11 Ghana (Colouring)

Each cloth piece is boiled like tea in a copper vessel, in a mix of *sakud, alijer, ghawdi* flower in hot water. Each piece is taken up and down with a wooden stick throughout the boiling. After the cloth is coloured properly, it is washed again with clear water.

Step 12 Tapai (Heating)

1. Camel dung 5 kgs
2. Soda bicarbonate 1 kg

Each cloth piece is soaked in these two ingredients and then it is kept in a folded form overnight.

Step 13 Washing

The cloth pieces are washed next early morning. Now, the single coloured simple Ajarakh is ready for sale.

Step 14 Meena Chapai

Printing with Hansa and Alijer is known as Meena Printing.

Step 15

Indigo dye is for dark blue colour.

Step 16

To get darker colour, indigo deep has to be repeated.

Step 17

If indigo Ajarakh is to be sold, it can be sold after indigo dipping and washing after two days.

Step 18 and 19

If green colour is required, then pomegranate skin, turmeric and kesu flower are mixed to develop yellow colour. It is applied on the indigo cloth to get green colour.

Step 20

The *fitrakis* is applied on the cloth, and then the cloth is left for drying.

Step 21

For 20 pieces of cloth, 1 kg *fitrakis,* 100 gm soda bicarbonate/250 gm turmeric are mixed in water. The half-soaked cloth pieces are left to dry overnight.

Step 22

The cloth pieces are washed for the last time with pomegranate water/*fitrakis*, turmeric, etc. and then left for drying.

Step 23

To get a shining effect on the cloth, water is sprinkled on them. This process is repeated 4–5 times. This results into a fine piece of Ajarak.

The number of people carrying out this work is rapidly diminishing. While in 1950–70, 28 families worked on Ajarak, now only 7 of them do so. There are only 2 families working solely on traditional method of printing Ajarak. The low earning from this craft is the main deterrent in attracting more people to get involved. According to the Khatri families in Barmer region, the income is not even enough to sustain a family.

Besides this, the demand of Ajarak is also decreasing. The traditional demand that arose from certain communities for whom it was customary to wear Ajarak is no longer prominent due to the cultural changes that are taking place. Further, the designs of Ajarak have undergone overwhelming changes. Though traditional designs and modern day designs are co-existing, yet traditional patterns are not that much in demand. Moreover, the use of synthetic colours is detrimental to the health of the workers. Thus, the art of Ajarak has undergone substantial change in terms of production, consumer demand, market and raw material. The traditional Ajarak has been replaced by Screen Ajarak due to its less elaborate production procedure and consequently, reduced labour and costs of production.

The cloth and colours used in the making of Ajarak have also metamorphed over the years. Earlier, cloth of 20 count was used while now a 40 count cloth is used. Instead of organic colours, synthetically produced 'chemical colours' are being used. The benefit of using chemical colours is that a far lesser amount of water is used in the process. While 4,000 litres of water are required when using traditional colours, 100 litres of water shall be used for the same quantity of cloth. A significant change has also come in the demand of the consumers. Since, the customer is mostly from the cities, the demand for traditional items of clothing, like *lungis, odhnis,* etc. has deteriorated considerably and demand for bed sheets, saris, cushions and pillow covers and dress material has begun dominating the market.

Sukhi Devi

In this scenario Sukhi Devi[1] decided to keep the tradition of Ajarak alive. Sukhi Devi got married to Jethanand of Barmer at the age of 16 and was quickly assimilated in his family business of Ajarak printing. Jethanand and his family were refugees from Pakistan who came to Barmer from their native place of *Khairpur Derki* at the time of Partition. They were among the many Khatri families that resided in Khairpur, Khairpur Derki, Dabavada, Khaanpur, Meethi, Haala, Mittiyaari, Kheerpara, Hathunga, Pithora, Amarkot, Dhoranara, Saidpur and Nabisar areas who came to India after Partition. These Khatris then spread in many parts of India like Kutch in Gujarat, Barmer, Deesa and Ujjain.

Sukhi's parental family was not involved in Ajarak printing but in selling of colours for the block prints. Yet, after her marriage, Sukhi started working full-time for Ajarak printing as she found the work interesting though tedious. She did all the manual work from breaking, pulverizing and straining of materials for making colours to dying and printing of cloth. First her mother-in-law and later her daughter-in-law

took care of the household while she was fully involved in managing the family's business.

In the last 20 years of his life, Sukhi's husband Jethamal lost his eyesight. But Sukhi pursued the family business whole-heartedly working full days and was able to earn a decent living.

Later, her work was carried on by her son Ranamal Khatri[2], 43, who had taken to the family business at a very young age. He even tried to expand the business and made some innovative changes in the traditional processes. In fact, Ranamal has also been awarded a national award for his excellent workmanship and is a master craftsman. His products are now being sent to many big cities of the country.

The third generation of this family is also involved in the same business and is dedicated to expanding it. Sukhi Devi's grandson, Manoj Khatri, is a 22-year-old man who has just completed his B.Com. After his initial reluctance to join the family business, Manoj got inspired by his family's commitment to the art and decided to get on board.

Manoj recalls that as a child, he had once made a mistake while tearing off the cloth for printing. 'There is a particular procedure involved in tearing of the cloth. Instead of scolding, his grandmother, Sukhi Devi, taught him the correct technique of tearing off the cloth by hand'. In a similar manner, as a child Manoj got tutored in the various techniques and processes of Ajarak printing by his grand-mother Sukhi Devi. So, he considers his grandmother his real teacher, his *Guru*. Moreover, when any of the workers did not turn up, he got a chance to carry out *bhantana* and printing as well. This clearly underlines the fact that children of such families garner the necessary skills and the required practice while growing up and hence, are seamlessly incorporated into the family business in adulthood. It is not only a trade or occupation to them but a way of life in its own.

Manoj[3] is confident of the fact that he not only has the skills required to run the business successfully but also the practical knowledge of production which he has acquired from his grand mother. An award by the government has motivated him further and he is happy to be able to contribute to preserving the dying art of Ajarak. As a member of the new generation, he has been adopting many novel and innovative means to expand his business. Manoj Hand Prints now has an impressive and vibrant website that gives a detailed overview of their products, and also of the processes and artisans involved in their making. Computers have made inroads into the sphere of designing that until now had been guided by tradition. Manoj's efforts have further led to improved market linkages and greater expansion of export.

Sukhi Devi and her family have played a significant role in preserving and protecting the art of Ajarak over the years. Despite many problems and setbacks, Sukhi continued to practice the art and protect her family tradition. She has not only made efforts to expand her sale of Ajarak, but also trained women from other communities – *Swami, Ravana Rajput, Naai* – in the art. Sukhi believed that if other communities got involved, it would not only lead to increase in production but also help in generating money for sustenance of their families. Sukhi Devi herself trains women and claims that she has trained 30 men and women in this art. Some have even opened their small units of printing and some work from home. In fact, Sukhi Devi and her husband were instrumental in getting removed the restriction that had been imposed by the Khatris on washing by the non-khatri communities.

Ranamal Khatri and his son Manoj further carried on the family's tradition. They both are responsible for expanding the reach and influence of Ajarak to other places. He prepares almost 3 lakh metres of cloth of which 20 per cent is Ajarak. He even tried to open a showroom to showcase his products twice, but was unsuccessful. Ranamal has carved his own separate identity in the world of printing and dying.

Sukhi Devi's grandson Manoj Khatri too is dedicated to expanding his business and hopes to restore Ajarak to its former glory. Currently, he is trying to find more buyers. He believes that Ajarak can only be saved from becoming extinct if more and more art lovers start recognizing it. So, he is also trying to take the art to experts to make it popular among them.

Thus, these two women from different groups have been involved in continuing of traditions in their respective manners. In some ways Hinglaj Mata can be seen as giver and protector of the art to the community and Sukhi Devi as protector and transmitter of a tradition which was and to an extent dying a slow death due to various reasons. Both these women are revered in the Barmer region for their contribution to the art.

Notes

1. Interview with Sukhidevi, Barmer, May 2012.
2. Interview with Ranmal, May 2012.
3. Interview with Manoj Khatri, Barmer, May 2012.

References

Bilgrami, Noorjehan (2002). *Ajrak: Cloth from the Soil of Sindh*, White Orchid Press, Bangkok.

Chaudhuri, Maitrayee and Chandra, Urvashi (2001). *Women, Intangible Heritage and Development: A Feasibility Study*, Report submitted to UNESCO, New Delhi.

Hard, Robin (2003). *The Routledge Handbook of Greek Mythology*, Based on H.J. Rose's *Handbook of Greek Mythology*, Psychology Press, New York.

Harlan, Lindsey (1992). *Religion and Rajput Women: The Ethic of Protection in Contemporary Narratives*, University of California, Berkeley.

16

Democratic Governance at Grassroots Level and Functioning of Local Political Institutions

Evidences from Villages of Madhya Pradesh

YATINDRA SINGH SISODIA

Decentralized governance with the motive of good governance put forward many achievements and dilemmas. The state of Madhya Pradesh assured the peoples' participation in the local governance institutions with adequate gender, class and caste representation as per the need of the constitutional amendment. The performance and efficacy of panchayat members are strongly influenced by the social stratification and class distinctions. The political dynamics at grassroot level is different and has many players and they have their weightage in different context. Against this backdrop, the paper is an attempt to understand the ground realities of the new system. This paper will provide an insight into along with problems and prospects of the new system. The process of implementation of the Panchayat Raj has raised several vital questions linked to the institutional and structural mechanism of governance. The Panchayat Raj Institutions (PRIs) also have far reaching implications for the political and social processes. This paper on the dynamics of local governance in Madhya Pradesh will comprehend and analyse these implications and processes. The paper is an attempt to identify, document and comprehend the broad trends emanating from the field, based on the experience of functioning of Panchayat Raj from the point of view of Panchayat Raj members.

The whole idea of good and responsive governance is that of giving, of serving and of doing good to the people, or solving their problems and making their lives more liveable, satisfying and enjoyable. It comes close to Gandhiji's concept of politics for service of the people and not for becoming masters of the people. The essential pre-requisite for quality governance is that the system should be good and suited to the needs, aspirations, background and ethos of the people concerned and that those selected for operating the system should be endowed with character and competence and remain motivated by the spirit of public service. Governance must be democratic, participatory, transparent and accountable. The issue of governance is more crucial and important from the point of view of grassroot democracy since at local level, the decisions taken by the elected bodies have direct implications for the life of the major chunk of population of the country.

The concept of governance is not new and is as old as human civilization. Governance means the process of decision-making and the process by which decisions are implemented, and not enforced. An analysis of governance focuses on the formal and informal actors involved in decision-making and implementing the decisions made and the formal and informal structures that have been set in place to arrive at and implement the decision. From the Indian point of view, after Independence, efforts have been made to meet the needs and expectations of the people. Special efforts have been taken up to address the rural multifaceted issues with massive investment but the results were not up to the expectations. The idea that produced the 73rd Amendment Act was not a response to pressure from the grassroots but to an increasing recognition that the institutional initiatives of the preceding decades had not delivered expected results, as the extent of rural poverty was still much too large and thus the existing structure of government needed to be reformed. It was a political drive to see Panchayat Raj Institutions (PRIs) as a solution to the governmental crises that India was experiencing.

Decentralization brings government closer to the people. The existence of local political arenas makes it easier for ordinary citizens to participate and exert influence. When power is brought closer to the citizens, the political process becomes more tangible and transparent and more people can become involved. Decentralization may also create a more open political system in that it implies a division of powers in society; many channels of representation and power sharing become available. This counteracts the monopolization of power by certain elite groups, often the consequence of centralized political and administrative structures. A decentralized system is also more accessible to new political movements and minority groups in their attempts to influence politics. This is particularly important in ethnically divided societies, where political exclusion can have seriously polarizing effects (Lijphart, 1977; World Bank, 1997; Grindle, 2000; Hadenius, 2001).

Decentralization has been suggested as an alternative model of government that builds trust, transparency and accountability. Decentralized governance defines the systematic and harmonious interrelationship resulting from the balancing of power and responsibilities between central governments, other levels of government, and non-government actors, and the capacity of local bodies to carry out their responsibilities using participatory mechanisms. United Nations Development Programme's experience with decentralization has demonstrated its significant contributions to improving the population's access to health, education, employment and sustainable livelihoods' opportunities, and various social services (UNDP, 2000).

Fieldwork: Methodology and Context

From the point of view of democratic governance, there are two basic propositions. First, the society with its structural rigidities would get a legal and institutional space through Panchayat Raj in order to operate in an accountable as well as meaningful manner. This means, the introduction of Panchayat Raj should be able to homogenise the difference existing in the society owing to its stratification on caste, class and gender lines. This homogenization will result in an informed decision-making at the grassroot level. Secondly, the policymakers at the macro level have faith in the new system's capability to deliver and the development process, thus, will be more responsible as well as dependable than any of the earlier tested systems of governance. Even if these hitherto untested propositions are true, the fluidity in acceptance of a macro decision to reform the governance will depend on how the micro functionaries at the grassroots are interpreting and adapting the macro process. It is quite likely that traditional power centres still have overbearing influence on the new system of governance for it to operate democratically. More anxious, however, there will be situations where decisions in the newly created institutions succumb to pressures of traditional power centres.

This paper is based on an empirical study which made an attempt to document the processes of change in Madhya Pradesh, which led to the establishment of Panchayat Raj, and also to fully comprehend and analyse the implications of the making as the pivot of grassroot democracy. The data were generated from five regions of Madhya Pradesh viz. Bundelkhand and Baghelkhand, Chambal, Mahakaushal, Bhopal, and Malwa and Nimar. The study was carried out in 25 gram panchayats of five districts representing one district from each socio-cultural region. The forgoing interpretation is based on the indicators of governance which have been analysed on the basis of primary data generated from the field.

Participation

Governmental policies stimulate human development only if they bring the masses into the mainstream of society. That involves participation in decision-making at the regional and local levels. Legitimacy goes hand in hand with participation. The planning process is severely disrupted because: the gram sabha meetings are not regularly held and participation is negligible. The panchayat planners do not enjoy autonomy with regard to plan formulation. There is absence of coordination between governance and planning at different levels. There is very little people's participation in the planning process (Aziz, 1998). While state legislatures provided for the establishment of gram sabha, the statutes remained vague about procedures and power, resulting in dysfunctional instructions (Mander, 1999).

The level of participation of people at grassroot level has been low despite knowing the procedural aspect and gram sabhas are almost a formal institution. The state government transferred nearly all of the powers previously exercised by gram panchayats to gram sabha. It has, thus, gone from representative democracy at the grassroots to direct democracy but the fact remains that despite this endeavour there is a clear cut gap between macro level decisions and grassroots reality (Sisodia, 2005).

Field experiences suggest that a considerably higher number gets the information of gram sabha on regular basis. At the same time, a sizeable number is not receiving the information of gram sabha. Moreover, meetings are not convened regularly. In the gram sabha, the issues discussed mainly revolve around the welfare schemes whereas the mandate given to gram sabha is much wider and comprehensive. The exact frequency of gram panchayat meetings is known to roughly half of the respondents. To come out from the stigma of womanhood and assert the role in panchayat with full vigour and conviction is still a big issue in rural areas. There is overwhelming majority which is of the opinion that all Panchayat Raj representatives are invited in meetings. This is, indeed, a very positive indication and this is testimony of the direct democracy at the grassroots level and participation of the people. The level of participation is by and large medium or higher on the basis of five different major issues. Level of participation is higher among general and SC categories, medium is almost similar in all the categories with slightly higher in OBC and comparatively lower among ST.

Transparency

The efficiency of a government can be seriously reduced, if its regulatory policies are not considered legitimate by the public at large. Regulations and policies can be accepted as legitimate only if they are fundamentally transparent and based on objective criteria. In order to legitimize their policies, governments must provide transparency about state actions, as well as about the procedures that underpin the carrying out of state actions. Transparency requires that governments not only do not impede the flow of information to the public, but also involve actively to make the necessary provisions to ensure that public information can have a feedback effect on governmental performance, since it empowers the public to put pressure on government to deliver services and to do so properly. It can, thus, strengthen the legitimacy of government. In order to instill a stable and predictable policy environment, governments must therefore subject themselves to the scrutiny of the public. This involves subjecting their operations to regular and independent financial audits.

Transparency in terms of Panchayat Raj can be seen in the performance of local political institutions. The gram sabha is based on several extremely important but largely untested assumptions. It is assumed, first, that even in a village society with deep schisms of caste, class and gender, an organic community still exists and that given appropriate legal and institutional spaces, it can act cogently and responsibly as a community. Second, the underlying assumption of the system is that the collectiveness of the gram sabha would be a more reliable vehicle of good governance than a relatively unencumbered bureaucracy or local elected representatives (Sisodia, 2002, 2005).

Grassroot situation brings forward the fact that majority of respondents agree on this point that the information pertaining to schemes is provided and a sizeable majority of respondents give the credit to gram sabha which has been assigned the work of information dissemination. MGNREGA is a flagship scheme and is known to the highest number of respondents. Various pension schemes are also known to a sizeable number. Major issues related to villages are discussed in committee meetings. Gram sabha is the basis of selection of beneficiaries which is the platform designated with this task. Overwhelming majority of respondents refers the right person with regard to maintaining the records of meetings. Sizeable number of respondents feels that finances of panchayat are discussed in meetings. Considerable number of respondents is aware about the financing pattern and again majority of them are also aware that money is utilized for the purpose it is sanctioned for. Usually at village level, taxes are imposed on the services and in majority cases there are no services rendered by the majority of gram panchayats and, therefore, no tax imposition. However, there are many ways wherein the local taxation can be done and funds can be generated but a kind of reluctance is discernible among panchayat representatives in this matter. Considerable number has cited the name of sarpanch/secretary in the selection process of beneficiaries which is not transparent and decisions are confined to sarpanch/secretary. A big number, which has claimed transparency, is unaware of the technicalities of tendering process and, therefore, they seem to be making just passing statement about the transparency in the process. RTI is a new and vibrant law and if it is used at the village level, it can bring transparency and accountability in the system and, therefore, it is a very positive indication. The basis of determination of payment for works is not homogenous whereas in panchayat functioning, there are set rules and procedures laid down for this kind of processes. Almost three-fourth of the respondents agree that the information is provided by an official, which is indeed a big number and a positive sign for panchayats. The level of transparency is medium or higher on the basis of four different major issues. The transparency is by and large of medium level.

Equity and Inclusiveness

Equity means all men and women have equal opportunities to improve or maintain their well-being. And inclusiveness basically means accommodating all sections of society. Despite knowing the importance of tribal regions, the level of participation in the meetings is found to be low for the marginalized sections of the society in general and the tribals in particular. Sarpanch and other influential people dominate in decision-making process. It has been argued that the vibrancy and efficacy of gram sabha will remain dismal if it does not possess the capacity to perform roles and responsibility assigned to it. This question becomes more pertinent in a tribal society where human resource development is low and society is deeply introvert. The experience suggests that the gram sabha and its ever-increasing powers and authority have generated a lot of interest among tribal people. It is expected that this interest is likely to be translated into a more broad based and participative leadership at grassroots level (Sisodia: 2008).

Field experiences unfold that roughly two-third of the respondents feel that the decisions are taken by all which is indeed a positive sign in the rural context. Three-fourth respondents are contacted by the villagers who redress their personal and public problems. Two-third of respondents endorse women participation which is, indeed, very encouraging to notice. There is a mixed viewpoint with regard to the role of SC, ST and women, and a sizeable number believes that these sections have a role to play up to some extent which can be termed as positive. In majority cases, respondents feel that the eligible individuals get benefit of schemes which is a positive sign. Sizeable number of respondents find a kind of togetherness; however, the process of social assimilation in villages is very slow and, therefore, can look forward to changes in future. There is an increase in the attendance rate in meetings and participation in the panchayat decisions and there is an increase in awareness in routine life towards politics which makes a sense in the changing paradigm. In village society, education and age are considered as the main basis of prestige whereas political status is also considered as one of the bases in this category by a considerable number. Overwhelming majority of the respondents endorse this fact that the level of participation of poor people increased in poverty alleviation programmes in villages, which is very positive and significant. Level of equity is medium or higher on the basis of three different major issues.

Effectiveness and Efficiency

Effectiveness can be measured in a narrow, as well as in a broad sense. A broader approach to the concept of effectiveness, however, looks at the extent to which government is fostering an economically efficient system of production and distribution, and to reduce uncertainty. Effectiveness improvements, in a narrow sense, may be achieved either by increasing outputs while employing the same inputs, or by maintaining the same output while employing reduced inputs. Excessive government regulation not only increases the level of economic activity of the informal sector, but it also enables regulators to collect bribes from potential entrants, thus linking efficiency with the issue of transparency.

Overwhelming majority of the respondents is satisfied with works of gram panchayat which signifies a lot in the context of Panchayat Raj functioning. Overwhelming majority of the respondents does not find groupism in village which can be seen in a very positive way. There are many noticeable changes occurring among people due to Panchayat Raj. Sizeable number of respondents finds that there is a decrease in poverty and also village development through various schemes. A considerable number believes that plantation has been carried out which is indeed significant from the point of view of environment conservation. Although a lesser number is giving suggestion nevertheless the suggestions are, indeed, of critical importance for the socio-political development and regeneration of village through Panchayat Raj System. Majority of the respondents believe in panchayats' capability to meet the needs and expectations of the village. Level of effectiveness is medium on the basis of seven different major issues.

Accountability

Accountability means decision-makers in government are answerable to the public, as well as to the institutional stakeholders. This accountability differs depending on the organization and whether the decision is internal or external to an organization. Generally speaking, accountability of public institutions has focused almost wholly on two issues namely: prevention of activities not specifically authorized by law or any subordinate legislation and integrity of the public system or maintenance of financial propriety, which is often equated with adherence to financial rules. While these are important, there are other components also for which the local bodies are expected to be accountable.

Grassroot scenario unravels the fact that there is a significant number which says that there is no benefit in going to gram sabha and this shows that there is no understanding about this important aspect of panchayat functioning. A sizeable majority does inspect the construction work of panchayat which is, indeed, significant. In the opinion of majority, training programmes are conducted. There are different ways whereby efforts are being made to improve presence and participation in gram sabha. Level of accountability is medium or higher on the basis of three different major issues.

Rule of Law

Rule of law means fair and impartial enforcement of legal frameworks, particularly laws on human rights. The prominently prevalent process of decision-making in gram sabha is through unanimity or by majority, which denotes a very positive indication. An overwhelming majority of the respondents points out that education and employment related works are carried out by panchayat for rural development. Roughly half of the respondents find the facilities sufficient totally or up to some extent, which shows the changes occurring in rural areas after arrival of new Panchayat Raj System. Level of rule of law is mostly of medium level on the basis of five different major issues.

Responsiveness

Responsiveness means institutions and processes try to serve all stakeholders. Despite having panchayats at village level, the role of panchayats in settling disputes is negligible. Interestingly, two-third of the respondents find that most of the people are satisfied with the decisions arrived at by different ways of settling the disputes. Respondents engage in one or another activity for the betterment of education in the village. In majority of the cases the respondents feel that the panchayat takes care of the quality of construction of public buildings in the village. Panchayats do make the provision in the budget for the basic services. Overwhelming majority of respondents feels that budget is utilized for eligible persons. Three-fourth of the respondents feels that panchayat representatives are discharging their responsibilities properly. Respondents have come out with a variety of reasons for not attending panchayat meeting, the principle reason being lack of information about the meeting to be held. It is significant to notice that panchayats are engaged in many works at local level. Level of responsiveness is medium or higher on the basis of five different major issues. The responsiveness is by and large of medium level.

Consensus Orientation

Consensus orientation stands for good governance mediating between differing interests to reach at a broad consensus on what is in the best interest of the group and where possible, on policies and procedures. Majority of the respondents are in agreement with this viewpoint and it is, indeed, a positive feedback. Overwhelming majority of respondents feel that there is complete cooperation from government official/departments and remaining have cited the reasons of non-cooperation which are generally prevalent at the local bureaucratic level. Three main areas of interventions for government schemes are endorsed by the overwhelming majority of the respondents. It shows the role and capability of panchayats in rural context. Economic development and development of physical infrastructure are perceived as rural development by the majority of respondents, which is in fact very appropriate in the context of rural scenario as rural people mostly face these deficiencies in routine life. All major problems related to villages have been prioritized for the solution. Level of consensus orientation is mostly of medium level on the basis of three different major issues.

To conclude it can be inferred that participation, transparency, inclusiveness and accountability in gram sabha and gram panchayat meetings have been relatively low. It can be attributed mainly to the strong and invincible caste, class and gender divide in villages. Sarpanch and other influential people dominate in decision-making process. There are two prominent and sharply contrasting groups leading the panchayats – the group of traditionally influential representatives and the other of new entrants. The idea of participation, transparency, inclusiveness accountability as important parts of Panchayat Raj has not been observed fully in practice. In fact, in retrospect, it seems sometimes inevitable that persons of influence would look at larger community engagement with hostility. The vibrancy and efficacy of Panchayat Raj will remain dismal if it does not possess the capacity to perform assigned roles and responsibility. This question becomes more pertinent in a socio-cultural milieu where human resource development is low and society is deeply fragmented and hierarchical. And, therefore, it is urgently needed that marginalized sections of society which have been out from the process of decision-making have to be taken in mainstream through sensitization and capacity building. The experience suggests that the resource flow to gram panchayats and its ever-increasing powers and authority have generated a lot of interest in people. It is expected that this interest is likely to be translated into a more broad based and participative leadership at grassroot level. Transparency and accountability also need to be addressed among panchayat representatives and villagers. Inclusiveness of marginalized sections, and particularly of women, requires urgent attention. The need is to address the issue of awareness generation among masses. Training camps, awareness campaigns and audio-visual mediums can be of critical importance for the sensitisation and capacity building to achieve the goals of governance in true sense.

References

Aziz, Abdul (1998). 'Process of Decentralized Governance and Planning', *Prashasnika*, 25 (2), July–December: 113–19.

Hadenius, A. (2001). *Institutions and Democratic Citizenship*, Oxford University Press, Oxford.

Lijphart, A. (1977). *Democracy in Plural Societies*, Yale University Press, New Haven.

Mander, Harsh (1999). 'Towards Direct Democracy: The Legal Empowerment of Gram Sabha', *Kurukshetra*, New Delhi, 48 (1), October.

Sisodia, Yatindra Singh (2002). 'Decentralised Governance in Madhya Pradesh: Experiences of Gram Sabha in Scheduled Areas', *Economic and Political Weekly*, October 5.

——. (2005). 'A Decade of Panchayat Raj System in Madhya Pradesh', in Yatindra Singh Sisodia (ed.), *Functioning of Panchayat Raj System*, Rawat Publications, Jaipur.

——. (2008). *Implementation of PESA in V Scheduled Areas: An Action Research Study on Working of Panchayat Raj in Tribal Regions of Madhya Pradesh, Rajasthan and Gujarat*, Study Report of Ministry of Panchayati Raj, Government of India, MPISSR, Ujjain.

UNDP (2000). *Decentralised Governance: A Global Matrix of Experiences*, United Nations Development Programme, New York.

World Bank (1997). *World Development Report 1997: The State in a Changing World*, Oxford University Press, Oxford.

17

Occupational Segregation by Gender

Trends and Explanations

RUCHIKA CHAUDHARY

Occupational gender segregation is a strong feature of the Indian labour market. While some occupations have become increasingly integrated over time, others remain highly dominated by either men or women. Occupational segregation is a concern to policy makers for two reasons: Segregation negatively affects the efficiency of the labour market, causes labour market inflexibility because it restrains mobility between male and female occupations. The clustering of women and men in different occupations is a prominent feature of the employment structure and a significant dimension of gender inequality. And high levels of segregation have been considered to be responsible for the discrepancy between men's and women's wages. There are multiple bases of segmentation in the Indian labour market. For example there are large differences in education/skills endowments of workers. There are multiple work arrangements namely, regular (permanent and temporary), casual, self-employed, home-based, contracted, etc. Institutional arrangements are segregated in terms of regulated/unregulated, organized/unorganized sectors and formal/informal. Women are over-represented in mid-skill occupations like crafts, sales and service workers.

Statement of the Problem

Gender segregation of jobs and its perpetuation over time to the disadvantage of women workers has been a widely discussed issue in women's studies. Social, cultural, historical and economic factors all play a role in determining the pattern of occupational segregation.

Marginalization of women can be expressed in various forms. One such form is segregation of women workers in certain specific jobs, which is low in occupational hierarchy, payment and status.

Segregation is the tendency for women and men to be employed in different occupations. Such separation creates gendered occupations which are disproportionately 'female' or 'male', so segregation may be defined as the tendency for women to work in female occupations and male in male occupations. In other words, occupational segregation by gender refers to the inequality in the distribution of men and women across different occupational categories.

Two types of gender segregation have been identified: horizontal and vertical. Horizontal segregation may be defined as concentration of men and women in particular sectors of the labour market or in particular occupations. A labour market showing strong horizontal segregation will have typically male or typically female occupations or sectors.

Vertical segregation is characterized by disproportional participation of women or men at different levels of occupational hierarchy. In other words, it shows the inferior position of women in the labour market in comparison to men.

Objective of the Study

In this paper, the focus is on explaining the differences between the male workers and the female workers i.e. changes in gender segregation of occupations from 1993–94 to 2004–05 (excluding 66th Round), identifying existence of horizontal or vertical segregation and the distribution of women workers across non-agricultural occupations in urban India using the one, two and three digit level national classification of occupations. The latest round (66th Round) used National Classification of Occupations (NCO 2004), which is not comparable to earlier rounds. Hence, the analysis is restricted to three comparable rounds of NSSO i.e. 50th, 55th and 61st.

The analysis here measures the share of women workers within any given occupation as compared to men in order to identify the jobs in which women are engaged in the labour market. Since male employment is much higher (and this is generally so in most occupations), the selected occupations wherein women constitute a significant share have also been identified. Further, the occupational groups which have recorded a relatively higher share of women workers have also been identified.

Database

There are two major sources of data that provide estimates on women's workforce participation in India: the Decennial Censuses and the Quinquennial Employment and Unemployment Surveys (EUS) conducted by the National Sample Survey Organization (NSSO). Unit level data has been used on occupations of men and women workers from different rounds of the NSS i.e. 50th Round (1993–94), 55th Round (1999–00) and 61st Round (2004–05). Data has only been used for urban areas and more specifically for non-agricultural occupations. Further, the information pertaining to the principal usual status workers i.e. the (principal) activity of the person during the reference period of 365 days preceding the date of survey has been used for the purpose of this study.

Research Methodology

The information on occupations is coded according to the National Classification of Occupations (NCO) 1968. The NCO classification has 8 one-digit occupations, 95 two-digit occupations and 462 three-digit occupations. Since agricultural workers have been excluded, the analysis has been done for 7 one-digit, 86 two-digit and 425 three-digit codes.

Two simple indicators that have been used to monitor the share of women in the workforce are: (1) the female work participation rate, and (2) the female share of the total workforce.

The degree of segregation of occupations can be examined in several ways based on the sex ratio or the gender ratio, which is defined as Fi/Mi, where Fi and Mi are the female and male workers, respectively, in i^{th} occupation. Alternatively, female representation or the percentage of women workers in an occupation (PFNA) i.e. Fi/Ti, where Fi and Ti are the female and total workers in the ith occupation, can be used as an indicator of the degree of feminization of an occupation and to examine occupational segregation.

The index of dissimilarity (also known as the displacement index, the segregation index, or the Duncan index) has long been the most widely used segregation index. This index is defined as:

$$ID = \frac{1}{2}\sum_{n=1}^{i}\left|Fi/F - Mi/M\right|$$

Where Fi and Mi are the female and male workers in the ith occupation and F and M are the total female and male workers, respectively.

The Duncan-Duncan index can be interpreted as the proportion of male (female) workers required to be shifted between occupation categories such that the distribution of the proportions of male workers is same as that of the proportions of female workers.

Another index of dissimilarity calculated is DS i.e. size-adjusted index that adjusts for the size of each occupation. It can be defined as:

$$DS = \frac{1}{2}\sum_{i=1}^{n} \left| \{Fi / Ti / (\sum iFi / Ti)\} - \{Mi / Ti / (\sum iMi / Ti\} \right|$$

Descriptive Analysis

Women's participation in labour force is extremely low in urban India. As is visible from the trends in Figure 1; female labour force participation rate has been declining. The Labour Force Participation Rate (LFPR) was 13.2 per cent in 1993–94 according to usual principal status approach and it decreased to 12.8 per cent in 2009–10; whereas the LFPR for urban male was 55.6 per cent in the same year. Similarly Workforce Participation Rate (WPR) for urban male was 53.9 per cent and for urban female it was merely 11.9 per cent in 2000–10 (Figure 1).

Figure 1 *Trends in Labour Force Participation Rates (UPS)*

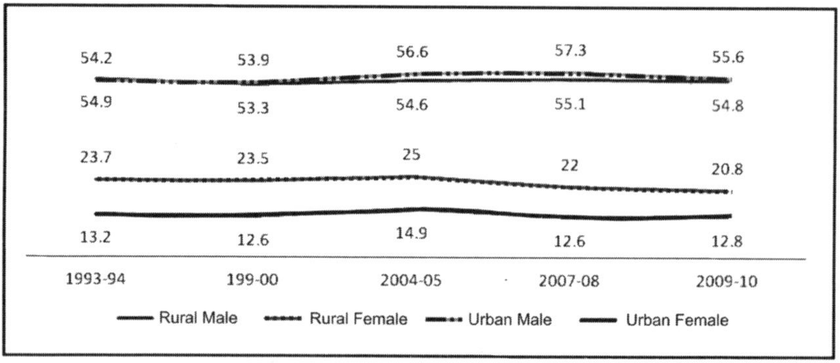

Secondly, corresponding to the low rate of participation in economic activity, female workers accounted for a small share of the total workforce. Women's share of non-agricultural workers, according to the UN statistics is exceptionally low in India (16%) as compared to other countries, e.g. 22 per cent in Bangladesh and 37.6 per cent in Malaysia. It is generally the case that women workers are likely to be undercounted and there also remains a problem with the data collection, but it is also clearly the case that women comprise a significantly lower share of the urban workforce in India than in most other parts of the world. Further, the overall gender discrimination present in the labour market in terms of occupational sex-segregation contributes to the low economic participation of women in the labour market. However, over the years, there has been an increase in the level of employment of women in sectors such as manufacturing, financial services and personal services (see Table A in Appendix), due in part to improved access to education, technological advancement, and increased employment opportunities for women. Women workers are also viewed as less 'troublesome' and cheaper than male labour, thus contributing to their increased presence in certain sectors.

Occupational Structure at the One-digit Level

In terms of numerical importance, for women workers, the three most important occupations at the one-digit level were production and related workers (31.7%), followed by service workers (24%) and professional and technical workers (18.2%) (Figure 2). These three occupations accounted for 74 per cent of female workers in 2004–05. Sales workers and clerical workers were next in importance. Only a small proportion of women workers were in administrative, executive and managerial occupations (6.3%) (Table 1).

Table 1

Distribution of Non-Agricultural Labour Force Across One-digit Occupations

NCO	*Division*	*Share of Female Employment*			*Share of Male Employment*		
		1993–94	*1999–00*	*2004–05*	*1993–94*	*1999–00*	*2004–05*
0–1	Professional, technical and related workers	17.9	18.5	18.2	8.1	8.2	8.1
2	Administrative, executive & managerial workers	4.1	6.4	6.3	7.1	9.6	11.0
3	Clerical and related workers	9.1	8.9	8.1	11.2	10.1	8.7
4	Sales workers	10.9	10.6	11.7	20.6	19.7	21.3
5	Service workers	20.3	20.9	24.0	8.4	8.5	8.3
7–8–9	Production workers, transport equipment operators & lab	37.8	34.7	31.7	44.6	43.9	42.5
	All Non-Agricultural workers	100	100	100	100	100	100

Source: Computed from Unit level data of various rounds of NSSO.

Figure 2 *Share of Female Employment (Fi/F)*

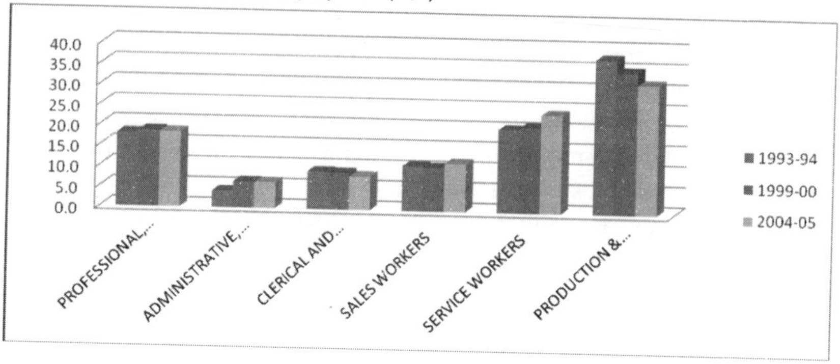

The occupational distribution of male workers was clearly different from that of female workers. 42.5 per cent of male workers were in production related occupations and 21.3 per cent in sales. The remaining male workers were evenly distributed across the other one-digit occupations.

The category of professional, technical and related workers has reported an increase in the share of women as compared to men during the period 1993–94 to 2004–05. This gain is a direct outcome of the increasing educational qualifications among women. This signifies a very positive change in terms of the increase in the number of women UPS workers over time in the 0–1 NCO of professional and technical workers.

Now turn to the female representation across different occupations, measured by the share of the female workforce in each occupation (Table 2).

Table 2

Representation of Women in Different One-digit Occupations

NCO	*Division*	*Percentage Female Workers in Each Occupation (Fi/Ti)*		
		1993–94	*1999–00*	*2004–05*
0–1	Professional, technical and related workers	29.4	30.1	31.8
2	Administrative, executive and managerial workers	9.7	11.3	10.7
3	Clerical and related workers	13.3	14.4	16.2
4	Sales workers	9.0	9.3	10.2
5	Service workers	31.1	31.9	37.4
7–8–9	Production and related workers, transport equipment operators and labourers	13.7	13.1	13.4
	Total Non-Agricultural labour force	15.8	15.9	17.2

Source: Computed from unit level data of various rounds of NSSO.

Figure 3 *Percentage Female Workers in Each Occupation (Fi/Ti)*

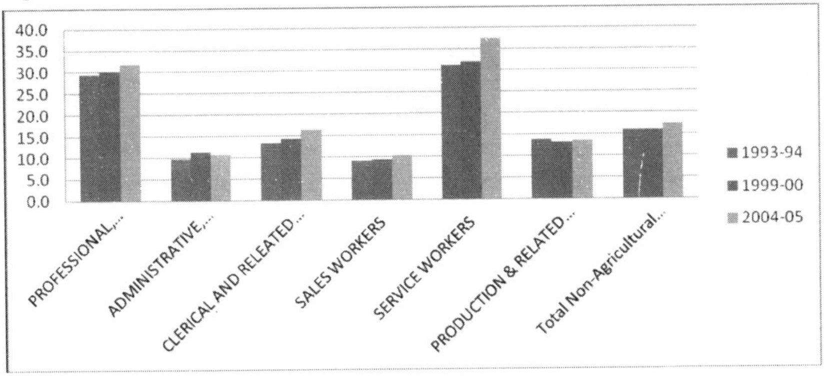

By this measure, female representation was highest among service workers (37.4%) followed by professional, technical and related workers (31.8%). But this shows remarkably low representation of women in different occupations in India as compared to the other countries. For e.g. in Malaysia, women accounted for 45 per cent of workers in clerical occupations. In China, women accounted for more than 40 per cent of the workforce in sales and services (Anker, 1998).

Occupational Structure at the Two-digit Level

The more interesting findings on occupational distribution come from data at the two-digit level of the NCO as shown below (Table 3).

Table 3

Women's Representation in Two-digit Occupations

Category	*% of Women Workers in Each Occupation*	*Number of 2 digit Occupations*			*Share of Female Workforce*		
		1993–94	*1999–00*	*2004–05*	*1993–94*	*1999–00*	*2004–05*
Male dominated	0-PFNA	58	61	62	34.4	37.6	36.8
Female under-represented	>PFNA&< 50	22	18	18	45.2	28.5	30.9
Female over-represented	50–80	2	3	2	8.5	21.7	17.3
Female dominated	80+	1	1	1	11.9	12.2	15.1
All		83	83	83	100	100	100

Note: PFNA stands for the aggregate proportion of females in the non-agricultural workforce in the relevant survey year. PFNA was 15.8 per cent in 1993–94, 15.9 per cent in 1999–00 and 17.2 per cent in 2004–05.

Source: Computed from Unit level data of various rounds of NSSO.

In total there are 83 non-agricultural occupations in all the three survey years. Throughout all the survey years, there was only one occupation which was female dominated (Code 53) namely, 'maids and related housekeeping service workers, n.e.c'. Further, there were two occupations in which women comprised between 50 and 80 per cent of the workforce. These were 'tobacco preparers and tobacco product makers' (Code 78) and 'teachers' (Code 15). In 2004–05, one-third of women workers were concentrated in these three occupations. Not surprisingly, the large majority of the occupations at the two-digit level remained male-dominated and it also increased from 61 in 1999–00 to 62 in 2004–05.

In all the survey years, there were major 15 two-digit occupations, in which each employed at least 2 per cent female labour force (Table 4). Women in these occupations accounted for 80.5 per cent of the total female labour force in 1993–94, 78.2 per cent in 1999–00 and 78.3 per cent in 2004–05. Thus, we observe a small overall decline in the concentration of women in selected major occupations in the last decade.

Table 4

Major Occupations among Female Workers (Two-digit level)

Two-digit occupations	*Distribution of female labour force across the top 15 occupations of NSS 2004–05*		
	1993–94	*1999–00*	*2004–05*
Maids and related housekeeping services workers, n.e.c	11.9	12.2	15.1
	85.7	**86.4**	**92.1**
Teachers	13.2	13.0	13.1
	49.5	**51.0**	**51.0**
Tailors, dress makers, sewers, upholsterers and related workers	5.7	5.7	7.5
	25.5	**26.6**	**29.7**
Merchants and shopkeepers, wholesale and retail trade	7.2	6.2	5.5
	9.7	**9.2**	**9.6**
Salesmen, shop assistants and related workers	3.1	3.3	5.0
	9.0	**9.7**	**11.6**
Spinners, weavers, knitting, dyers and related workers	7.1	4.9	4.5
	24.5	**26.7**	**25.6**
Clerical and related workers, n.e.c	5.4	4.7	4.4
	14.2	**14.7**	**17.4**

Cont'd...

...Cont'd

Tobacco preparers and tobacco product makers	6.0	5.6	4.1
	70.6	**75.0**	**74.3**
Bricklayers and other construction workers	3.7	4.0	3.8
	15.2	**12.8**	**12.4**
Labourers, n.e.c.	5.9	5.7	3.3
	16.5	**16.7**	**17.1**
Building caretakers, sweepers, cleaner and related workers	3.1	3.1	3.3
	31.4	**30.2**	**34.0**
Production and related workers, n.e.c	2.1	2.4	2.6
	44.5	**34.5**	**30.1**
Working proprietors, directors and managers, mining construction, manufacturing and related concerns	1.9	2.4	2.4
	10.4	**11.0**	**11.5**
Nurses and other medical and health technicians	2.5	3.1	2.3
	60.0	**56.9**	**47.4**
Launderers, drycleaners and pressers	1.7	1.9	1.5
	30.3	**35.6**	**28.4**
Combined	80.5	78.2	78.3

Note: Numbers in bold show female share of total workforce. The table can be read as follows: in 2004–05 15.1 per cent of the female workforce belonged to the occupation 'maids and related housekeeping workers' and among maids, 92 per cent of the workforce was female.

Until 1999–00, among these 15 major 'female' occupations, 'Teachers' constituted the largest percentage of the female workforce. But in 2004–05, 'maids and related occupations' took precedence over teachers. 15.1 per cent of the female workforce belonged to the occupation 'maids and related services' and among 'maids and related housekeeping workers', 92 per cent of the workforce was female.

Among these 15 major female occupations, some such as maids, teachers and nurses are well recognized internationally as 'female' occupations. Tobacco related occupations, particularly *bidi*-making is specifically an Indian occupation undertaken predominantly by women and is generally a low-paid and home-based activity. Among tobacco related occupations, 74.3 per cent of the workforce was female in 2004–05 (down from 75 per cent in 1999–00). Clerical occupations such as typists and book-keepers are not as important as elsewhere while production workers such as weavers and spinners, *bidi* makers and labourers including, general labourers, construction workers and sweepers, have a greater weight in the female occupational structure. Thus there is a relative predominance of unskilled work among women workers in India.

Occupational Structure at the Three-digit Level

For three-digit analysis, occupations without proper 3-digit codes are excluded. The number of male dominated occupations increased from 304 in 1993–94 to 309 in 2004–05. The number of female dominated occupations also increased to 11 in 2004–05. And there was a corresponding decline in all other categories, particularly in female under-represented and over-represented occupations.

Table 5

Women's Representation in Three-digit Level Occupations

Category	*Percentage of women workers in each occupation*	*Number of 3-digit occupations*		*Share of Female workforce*	
		1993–94	*2004–05*	*1993–94*	*2004–05*
Male dominated	0 – PFNA	304	309	23	29.1
Female under-represented	>PFNA – < 50	89	83	48.5	39.9
Female over-represented	50–80	17	12	14.9	13.3
Female dominated	80+	8	11	13.5	17.7
All	All	418	415	100	100

Note: PFNA stands for the aggregate proportion of females in the non-agricultural workforce in the relevant survey year. PFNA was 15.8 per cent in 1993–94, 15.9 per cent in 1999–00 and 17.2 per cent in 2004–05.

Source: Computed from Unit level data of various rounds of NSSO.

In 2-digit occupation category, 'maids and related housekeeping service workers, n.e.c.' increased significantly from 69 per cent in 1993–94 to 92 per cent in 2004–05. Similarly, in 3-digit level category, percentage of female workers in domestic servants increased from 87 per cent to 91 per cent in 2004–05. Percentage of female workers as *bidi* makers has also increased from 73 per cent to 76 per cent in 2004–05. There were no female supervisors and foremen in tobacco occupation category in 1993–94 and it increased to 30 per cent in 2004–05. Female representation in teacher's occupation has also increased in all sub-categories, except primary school teachers. The gender composition in the profession of teaching is more equal, where more than 50 per cent of the teachers are women.

So females are mainly concentrated in occupations that require limited skills and education, that pay low wages with less scope for career advancement (Table 6).

Table 6

Representation of Women Workers in Selected Three-digit Level Occupations in 4 Major Two-digit Occupations (Vertical Segregation)

Occupations	*Percentage of Female Workers in Each Occupation*	
	1993–94	*2004–05*
Maids and related housekeeping service workers, n.e.c.	**69.2**	**92.3**
Domestic servants	87.2	91.1
Tobacco preparers and tobacco product makers	**70.6**	**74.3**
Supervisors and foremen, tobacco and tobacco product making	0	30.4
Tobacco preparers	65.8	56.4
Bidi makers	72.7	75.8
Teachers	**49.5**	**51**
Teachers, university and colleges	25.3	37.4
Teachers, higher secondary and high school	39.8	44.6
Teachers, middle school	48.7	50.8
Occupations	*Percentage of Female workers in each occupation*	
	1993–94	*2004–05*
Teachers, primary school	65	58.6
Teachers, pre-primary	90.2	93.8
Nursing and other medical and health technicians	**60**	**47.4**
X-ray technicians	10.3	12.6
Veterinary assistants	1.6	1.7
Nursing, sanitary and other medical health technicians, n.e.c	35.6	26.9
Midwives and health visitors	89.8	88.1
Ayahs, nurse, maids	87.8	96.7
Nurses	91.5	94.6

Note: Below each 2-digit occupation (in bold letters), the component 3-digit occupations are listed.

Source: Computed from unit level data of various rounds of NSSO.

Table 7
Measures of Occupational Segregation

Occupation	*Year*	*Index of Dissimilarity (ID)*	*Size-adjusted ID (DS)*
One-digit	1993–94	0.205	0.287
	1999–00	0.225	0.282
	2004–05	0.300	0.305
Two-digit	1993–94	0.423	0.445
	1999–00	0.417	0.415
	2004–05	0.413	0.411

Source: Computed from unit level data of various rounds of NSSO.

Results of the Segregation Indices

The value of ID ranges from 0 (no segregation) to 1 (total segregation). The index can be interpreted as the minimum proportion of men plus the minimum proportion of women workers who would need to change occupations to ensure that the proportion of women workers in all occupations is identical and equal to the female proportion of the labour force (Anker, 1998). When there is no segregation i.e. when occupations are integrated, the share of women (men) in each occupation will be the same as the share of women (men) in the workforce. The ID measure satisfies certain basic axioms desirable in an aggregate index of segregation, however, that the value of the ID depends on the level of aggregation of occupations. As the level of disaggregation rises, the value of the index also rises. So the DS index is also used that adjusts for the size of each occupation.

The value of these two indices calculated is higher at the two-digit level i.e. when the classification of occupations becomes more detailed, the value of the segregation index rises as expected. The ID and DS measures are showing different trends at the one-digit and two-digit level of occupations. There is a clear decline in segregation between 1993–94 to 2004–05, as measured by the ID and DS index at the two digit level of occupations. Further this decline in the value of ID and DS is more in 1993–94 to 1999–00.

Conclusion

Our analysis of trends shows that despite having high economic growth, women's participation in the labour market has been declining. Gender segregation and segmentation has been a strong characteristic of the

Indian labour markets. Women in India (and globally) are over-represented in certain occupations. The three most important occupations for Indian women (at the one-digit level in 2009–10) were elementary occupations (26%), followed by craft and related trade workers (19%) and service and sales workers and technicians (11%). Only a small proportion of women workers were in administrative, executive and managerial occupations (7%). The tasks and jobs performed by women are generally influenced by the traditional gender division of labour. Thus, domestic responsibilities extending to labour market contexts constitute the most common jobs, including those of maids, cooks, tailors, and nurses, among others.

Higher gender segregation in the labour market reflects concentration of women in a few occupations; while men are differentiated into a wide range of occupations. In this context, the detailed analysis shows that occupational segregation is extensive: both horizontally as well as vertically. Women workers were found to be concentrated in three 1-digit occupations – 'production and related workers', 'service workers' and 'professional and technical workers'. An analysis at the 2-digit level shows that four occupations-maids, teachers, tobacco preparers and nurses accounted for one-third of the total female workforce in 2004–05 (Horizontal segregation). It means that women are dominating those occupations that are internationally recognized as 'female' occupations. And there is relative predominance of unskilled work among women workers in India. Analysis at the 3-digit level shows that females are mainly concentrated in lower range of professional hierarchy, thus establishing prevalence of vertical segregation. There is a clear segregation of women in sectors that are characterized by low pay, long hours and, often, informal working arrangements. Even within the sectors where women dominate, they rarely hold upper managerial jobs. Part-time work continues to be a predominantly female domain.

It is clear that feminization of the workforce has not occurred in India in the same way as in many other countries, developed and less developed. Women's work participation in urban India has remained very low. The stereotyped jobs of teaching, sales and service, and a host of production-related occupations continue to utilize women's labour. And beyond just the policy environment, the segregation of women is the reflection of a complex interaction between economic and social factors such as gender discrimination and biases, which lead young women to focus on a narrow range of occupations.

References

Anker, Richard (1998). *Gender and Jobs: Sex Segregation of Occupations in the World*, International Labour Office, Geneva.

Chakravarty, Satya and Chakravarty, Sumita (1995). 'On Employment Segregation by Sex', *Demography India*, 24 (2): 269–74.

Duncan, Otis Dudley and Duncan, Beverly (1955). 'A Methodological Analysis of Segregation Indices', *American Sociological Review*, 20: 210–17.

Gunderson, Morley and Sebastian, Alice (2008). 'Gender, Education and Employment: An Analysis of Higher Education and Labour Market Outcome in Kerala', *The Indian Journal of Labour Economics*, 51 (4).

Swaminathan, Madhura and Majumdar, Sharmila (2006). 'Workers in Urban India: Changes in Gender Segregation of Occupations, 1983–00', *The Indian Journal of Labour Economics*, 42 (2).

Watts, Martin and Rich, Judith (1993). 'Occupational Sex Segregation in Britain, 1979–1989: The Persistence of Sexual Stereotyping', *Cambridge Journal of Economics*, 17: 159–77.

Appendix

Table A

Distribution of Workers by Industrial Affiliation (UPS) for 15–59 Age Group Workers

Industries/Sectors	*Sectoral Share in Employment*					
	1993–94			*2009–10*		
Sector	*Male*	*Female*	*Total*	*Male*	*Female*	*Total*
Primary Sector	56.4	78.0	63.6	45.0	67.9	51.5
Mining and Quarrying	0.9	0.4	0.8	0.8	0.3	0.7
Manufacturing	11.3	9.2	10.6	11.5	11.0	11.4
Utilities	0.6	0.1	0.4	0.4	0.1	0.3
Construction	4.3	1.3	3.3	11.9	5.4	10.0
Secondary Sector	17.2	11.0	15.1	24.6	16.7	22.4
Trade, hoteling etc.	9.7	3.0	7.5	13.5	4.2	10.9
Transport and communication etc.	4.4	0.2	3.0	6.3	0.4	4.6
Finance, business activities etc.	1.3	0.3	1.0	2.7	1.0	2.2
CSP	11.0	7.4	9.8	7.9	9.7	8.4
Tertiary Sector	26.4	11.0	21.3	30.4	15.3	26.1
Non-Agricultural Sector	43.6	22.0	36.4	55.0	32.1	48.5
Total	100	100	100	100	100	100

18

Gender, Development and Radicalism

Rise of the Naxalite Movement in India

KSHIPRA SHARMA

Radicalism is a reflection of rising discontentment, deviation and demand for change. Over the decades, world has witnessed significant forms and scales of radicalism with varying backgrounds. This paper broadly examines the multidimensional nature of such radical formations in the changing global order, from the point of view of women. The idea is to go beyond the theoretical underpinnings and examine the major consequential gender debates, in context of the Naxalite movement in India.[1]

It is noteworthy that radicalism stirs greater base in developing countries due to the growing gap between the rich and the poor. This paper brings to light the incomplete, distorted growth in selected pockets of developing societies like India, which in its struggle to compete with the international standards continues to push certain urgencies under the carpet. In India, failed land reforms, exploitative developmental projects, draconian laws on wildlife protection, forest reservation policy have added to the hardships of the marginalized sections, particularly women, robbing them of their means of subsistence and even dignity. Today, rights of these sections (mostly tribal) over resources on which they had subsisted for centuries without formal ownership title are destroyed in the name of 'development'. Having lost their control over traditional livelihood resources, they are impoverished, displaced, homeless; their frustration, anger automatically driving them towards radicalism in the form of Naxalite movement. This paper explores the causes and consequences of the rising relationship between women and radicalism in India. Conscious attempt is made to surpass facts and figures, and concentrate more on the changing trends from the point of view of the affected.

For analytical convenience this paper is divided into two sections – the first section deals with relationship between development and radicalism (in developing countries) from gender perspective; and the second section deals with various dimensions of the relationship between women and the Naxalite movement. Special attention is given to India, keeping in mind the overall theme of the paper.

Development and Radicalism: Gender Perspective

Contemporary time witnesses a plethora of development discourses. The concept of development is undoubtedly 'contested ... complex, and ambiguous' (Thomas, 2004: 1 in (Sumner, 2007: 10). Amidst definitional debates, there is a general agreement on the view that 'development' encompasses 'change' – 'change for the better' (Slim, 1995: 143). Dimensions of development touch upon the economical, political, social, legal, institutional, environment, religion, etc. Thomas broadly divides definitions of 'development' into three types. The first is 'historical and long term and arguably relatively value free; second definition is policy related evaluative or indicator led, based on value judgments; the third is post-modernist, drawing attention to ethnocentric and ideologically loaded western conceptions of 'development', raising possibility of alternative conceptions' (Sumner, 2007: 11).

Development is a universal goal for all but multidimensional developmental change is particularly critical for developing nations where conducive socio-economic and political environment is the prime prerequisite for people to utilise their potential for growth. Development is closely bound with ideologies and belief systems. Hugo rightly says that it is about 'continuity' as well. For development to be foundational, one has to connect with the concerned community or society in question. It must represent their values and capacity. Contrast to the west imitation, effective development 'safeguards and thrives on difference and produces diversity' (Slim, 1995: 144). Development must be moulded to suit concerned interests.

Clearly, development means different things to different people. For a successful development scheme, however, two ingredients are the keys, i.e. equality and justice. Development paradigm must ensure people's representation and involvement in decision-making for the holistic improvement. Some scholars define this paradigm as 'democracy' (Slim, 1995, 144). Clearly, there is more to development than economic development. According to Sunanda Sen, development relates to people *per se* and as such covers diverse aspects of the economy and the polity relating to nation state. She elaborates that different dimensions of development definitely cannot be captured by a single statistic (Sen, 2007: 84). John Clark in his 1991 book, *Democratizing Development* rightly says:

> Development is not a commodity to be weighed or measured by GNP statistics. It is a process of change that enables people to take charge of their own destinies and realize their full potential. It requires building up in people the confidence, skills, assets and freedoms necessary to achieve this goal. (Clark as cited in Slim, 1995: 144)

Real human development concerns more intangible factors that relate to the quality of change in people's lives, along with the quantity of change (Slim, 1995: 144). The context for international development has been changing rapidly. While previously reference was made to an apparently 'homogeneous' Third World is now an emphasis on diversity. It is noteworthy that most of the experts on the subject highlight the error of equating development with growth particularly in case of developing countries. They argue that growth parameter in terms of the GDP (Gross Domestic Product) of a country is a poor indicator of the qualitative dimensions of development which reaches out to people within the country. In the last few years, there has been an enormous effort to move beyond the World Bank's economic development indicators, to a new broad range of indicators which include the personal, social, cultural, and environmental dimensions of development. Out of the new range of development indicators, the World Bank's programme of social indicators of development currently has 94 indicators and UNDP'S Human Development Index has 253 human development indicators (UNDP, 1993). These range from infant mortality rates to air quality, through human rights, etc. The HDI also claims to be gender sensitive (Slim, 1995: 176).

Gender balance in the development paradigm is an important concern. This concern is based on the premise that development initiatives cannot succeed or the impact be sustained if the people affected do not consent to and avail them fully. It also identifies how development paradigm may impact differently on women and men. Gender mainstreaming can be called as a promising answer to haunting questions of social inequalities/injustices, particularly in developing countries like India. Without going into myriad of theoretical development debates, here I attempt to give only a brief sketch of the nature and significance of the links between gender and development, mainly in the context of developing countries.

Gender mainstreaming can be one of the first steps towards a holistic developmental framework. The *Human Development Report 1995* (HDR, 1995) of the United Nations Development Program (UNDP) is specifically concerned with gender disparities and ways to address them. The report has simple but far-reaching message: 'Human Development if not engendered is endangered' (UNDP, 1995: 1 as cited in Rao, Rurup, Sudharshan eds., 1996: 29) Feminist notion of gender mainstreaming provided by Emanuela Lombardo and Petra Meier (2006), helps in providing a better perspective into gender and development paradigm. According to them, at least five shifts in the policy-making process must be found to be able to say that gender mainstreaming has been put into practice. These include: 'a shift towards a broader concept of gender equality that necessarily implies ... evidence of incorporation of a gender perspective into the mainstream political agenda; an equal political representation of women as a way to ensure that women will, at least numerically, be part of the mainstream; shift in the institutional and organizational cultures of political decision-making; and a shift that requires both 'displacement' and 'empowerment' for mainstreaming to be a transformative feminist concept' (Swaminathan and Jayarajan, 2008: 77).

Unfortunately, this significant equation between the two falls short in the developmental projects undertaken in developing countries like India. In its race for speedy growth, India appears to subordinate pressing problems concerning half of its population (i.e, women).

Close examination shows that in post-Independence period, the Indian leaders took cautious steps for nation-building. Throughout the decades of the 1950s, 1960s and 1970s, India emphasized on the policy of self-reliance through indigenous efforts in a fully or semi-protected environment (Adhikari, 2010: 3–4). In the mid-1980s, the then prime minister decided to partially open the Indian economy to western capital but markets were still not entirely free in India. Nevertheless, India took the giant step of liberalization in the 1990s which advocated a more open and market oriented economy.

In the era of globalization, process of development becomes much more complex. It's no hidden fact that globalization is a two faced mirror, one reflecting the profit of the few while the other reflecting the plight of the many. According to scholars like Sunanda Sen, '... deprivation and exclusion, operating at multiple layers of their struggle for survival ...' can be observed for large marginalized section (like the tribals), even in the high-growth countries of the developing region like India (Sen, 2007: 83). Paradox truly defines the second nature of globalization. In metropolitan cities of most developing countries, such features are more apparent with common sites of posh sky scrappers clubbed with nearby slums. Conditions are distressing as wages are low, regulation is weak, and production is increasingly oriented towards global market rather than domestic needs. Gender disparity amidst such disorders seem further subordinated. In a feudal-patriarchal society like India there are innumerable challenges for women. Despite being legally and constitutionally at par with men, women are subordinated and mistreated both in and out of home. They get very little of deserved respect and position. Not surprising, according to 2013 UNDP report, India's Gender Inequality Index (GII) is 0.61, ranking it 132 out of the 148 countries for which data exists.[2] India still grapples with the four major gender based discriminations (as listed by HDR, 1995) in the form of: 'denial of human capabilities, denial of economic opportunities, denial of political power and legal inequality combined with inadequate social protection against violence' (Rao, Rurup, Sudharshan eds., 1996: 17)

Government initiatives to address the wide-ranging disadvantages Indian women face have not made much of difference either. Unfortunately, even today, Indian women continue to face wide-ranging disadvantages, whether it is in terms of property rights, workforce participation, educational opportunities, access to health care or political representation. Even the National Rural Employment Guarantee Act (NREGA), which is considered as a premium source of women empowerment, is yet to overcome traditional mechanism of gender disparity. Overall, the economic and social disadvantages of women in Indian society reflect a whole gamut of '... patriarchal norms and practices such as patrilineal inheritance, patrilocal residence, the gender division of labour, and the gender segregation of public spaces'(Report of an Expert Group, 2010: 10–11).

Undoubtedly, the role of women in India has been shifting and women are making their presence felt in many sectors. However, the position of women cannot alone be judged by the increasing number of women coming out of their households. In fact, there is a complex interaction of historical, social, cultural, religious and economic factors that influences the overall status of women. According to some scholars, women are said to suffer twofold. Often they work two full time jobs. One in public spaces, where they are paid minimal, second in the private spaces where they are not paid at all (Anderson and Rajkumar, 2001). With the establishment of international free trade policies, such as North America Free Trade Agreement (NAFTA) and General Agreement on Tariffs and Trades (GATT), transnational corporations establish economic equations with developing nations in search of flexible, cheap female labour (Goldstein, 2004: 310). Even today, statistics on employment, wage (and work condition) showcase the gap between men and women. As far as the question of job opportunities and unemployment status is concerned, the unemployment rate in India in the year 2009–2010 was 20 for males and 23 for females (for rural and urban areas/'usual status' distribution).[3] As far as wages are concerned, statistics received by NSS reveals that disparity exists not only across rural-urban areas but also on the grounds of gender. Looking at all the above statistics and trends, India's development undoubtedly appears lopsided.

Tribals/Adivasis, though an integral part of India's social fabric, are probably the most affected by this kind of lopsided development. Repetitive, the harmony between the tribals and the natural world was ruptured right from the colonial period. The worst consequence was the unlimited power to the state paving way for state control and management of forests (Xaxa, 2008: 107). With the advent of variety of development policies, most of tribals have been displaced from their residing lands without justifiable rehabilitation and resettlement.[4] Despite past initiatives like scheduled tribes (Recognition of Forest Rights) Bill 2005 and the so called reformatory bodies like Joint Forest Management (under the Forest Conservation Act, 2008), the aim of balancing governance with conservation of resources seems distant. According to some scholars, such efforts are actually reversing state policies by their latent support for private use of forest produce.[5] Expert group's report to the Planning Commission in 2008 is one important publication that gives a detailed analysis of the conditions of Dalits, Adivasis, women and their increasing resortment to radicalism in the form of Naxalism.[6]

No doubt, the situation of women among these communities is comparatively more complicated. Tribal women face greater challenges in attaining a sustainable livelihood and a decent life due to environmental degradation and outside interference. Situation worsens because they are equally responsible for their family livelihood. In addition to household chores, they even work as men's partners outside their homes. They are essentially responsible for collecting water, fuel and edibles. By being detached from their traditional resources which they occupied for generations, their very family survival is endangered. Situation becomes acute when male members of the family migrate to cities in search of jobs. They have no choice but to bear the burden of family subsistence and reproduction. Even recent legislations like The Scheduled Tribes and Other Traditional Forest Dwellers (Recognition of Forest Rights) Act, (2006), claiming to recognize and vest forest rights to the dependent communities, have failed to cater to the diverse needs of these women.[7] According to some, the law crafted only provides for the issuance of deeds to single men or married couples. It is silent about the rights of single women, whether widowed, deserted or not yet married.

These trends are a sure indication that much hyped 'development' paradigm is causing deprivations, discontentment and alienation. Noteworthy, such deep discontentments take form of radical collective actions in most of the developing countries. Such voices garner higher support in these countries due to unparallel experiences shared by different sections of the population. Facing innumerable hardships on everyday basis, women are the most vulnerable and automatically drawn towards radicalism in hopes of emancipation, in hopes of change.

Conceptually, radicalism stands vague and ill-defined. However, it can be broadly identified as revolutionary activism advocating 'institutional change' (Snow and Cross, 2011: 116). Noteworthy, some prefer to define forms of radicalism using the social movement theory while others look for novel theoretical groundings. According to certain scholars, radical activism is often the result of 'close bonds amongst activists' (may or may not be following certain ideologies) and development of a 'collective identity' that places them in opposition to the traditional way of achieving social change.[8] Naxalite movement is one such radical movement with multiple contextualization as social or political movement.

In the next section, I look at various aspects of Naxalite movement by placing it within the domain of social movements, knowing its birth at Naxalbari as an agrarian movement. More importantly, causes and consequences of the movement from the point of view of women is the main area of concern.

Women and the Naxalite Movement in India: A Critical Analysis

Twentieth century has borne witness to several radical social movements where participation of women has been phenomenal.

Scholars like U. Vindhya attribute participation of women in such 'collective protest actions' as part of their efforts to come out of their 'own situations', or '... in response to 'abstract' ideas of freedom, justice and equality'(Vindhya, 2003: 148).

In India, relationship between women and radicalism has a vibrant history. Radical movements like Tebhaga (1940s), Telangana (1940s) and Naxalbari (1960s) movement actually paved novel ways for women to assert their rights. First time, women embraced non-conventional ways to fight against social injustice. In the later years of 1970s, activism in the form of Chipko movement and Shramik Sangathan of Dhulia not only challenged the fundamental tenets of the state developmental policy but also brought to forefront, the women-specific perspective into the political arena (Ilina, 2004: 194–95).

Empowerment of women through radical movements (participating or otherwise) can be weighed by the availability of adequate space for women's issues within such platforms. Keeping such factors in mind, it will be interesting to explore not only contributions of women in the Naxalite movement in India but also the contribution of the movement towards women's question, if at all.

The 'Naxalite movement' basically is a product of communist ideology of Marxist-Leninist variety, which emerged in the spring of 1967, at Naxalbari, West Bengal.[9] It emerged as a social/political movement with the aim at establishing an alternative regime. Its increasing area of influence is linked to their fundamental fight against persistent rural poverty, unemployment, ineffective state reforms and most importantly for securing the dignity of the citizens. Ideologically, the movement is anti-imperialist and anti-capitalist. It stands opposed to the whole mechanism of capitalist exploitation. According to their Marxist framework, it was the gradual increase in wealth that gave birth to the concept of patriarchal family and slowly manipulated entry of women into the labour market (capitalism).[10]

Today, even after many ups and down, the movement appears to have a large social base with a considerable presence of women population. Besides the increasing number of women in cadres (in different Naxalite groups), the role and position of their participation has also transformed tremendously (Dasgupta, 2009: 32–35). Heavily armed in uniforms, women cadres are strenuously trained for military operations.[11] The objective of this section is to examine this participation and support of women in the movement and find out if the movement has been truly liberatory and empowering against the alleged negative implications of state controlled 'development'.

I shall briefly discuss three issues central to the relationship between Women, Development and Naxalite movement i.e, land, wages and dignity/identity.[12]

Over the years, despite the movement's repeated claims for revolutionizing the entire system, it seems incapable of putting to rest, some of the major feminist anxieties. Feminists have repeatedly highlighted inadequacies within their revolutionary agendas saying the movement has not made efforts to include and negotiate gender issues into their larger political model. Now, I shall briefly examine the above mentioned three concerns:

(a) *Question of Land:* In an agrarian economy like India, land confers personality to an individual or a group. It imparts social identity and is a means of political empowerment. Apart from direct production from fields, land titles increase access to credit and serve as a saleable asset during crisis. Although access to land remains important for most of rural households, it becomes a lifeline especially for women. As known, lack of legal control over economic assets puts them at mercy of males of the family. Unfortunately, despite several land reforms initiated by Indian government, the situation looks grim. Even though land has been distributed among the poor, landless labourers for agricultural purposes out of ceiling surplus land or *bhoodan* land or *gair majarua khas* land (common land), but new settlers were often dispossessed by the landlords or the latter were in practical possession of these lands, distribution of land is only on paper (Bandhopadhyay, 2007: 13). Women in middle of such a situation are left with nothing much. Joint entitlement for husbands and wives, though often recommended, are useless as land is mostly controlled by the male of the patriarchal Indian family. Having lost their right over forest land and resources, tribal women are suffering great loss. Rising deprivations makes these women highly vulnerable and easy targets of radical groups. Marginalized tribal women search for alternatives that would at least bring their crisis to the forefront, if not fully address it. As mentioned earlier, Naxalite movement is one such movement that recognizes such survival issues and promises to replace this trail of exploitation by a revolutionary new order based on equality and justice.

However, looking at its record, the Naxalite movement itself shows certain loopholes. In its early stage, the male dominated movement failed to recognize women's plight due to non-ownership of land.

On account of the past events like the Telangana struggle in 1940s and Gaya struggle in 1970s, the Communist-led movement (with male majority) appeared uncomfortable with the idea of distribution of land in name of women.[13] Often the argument, 'land to the 'real' tillers' was forwarded to the anticipating women population. Though certain changes were witnessed at later years (1983) in the form of combined efforts of Sangharsh Vahini and Naxalite movement on the issue of women's land rights, nothing concrete came out of such efforts (Omvedt, 1993: 208). Naxalites have often advocated redistribution of seized crops and land among the landless poor, but entitlements in the name of women are hardly ever part of their larger agenda.[14]

(b) *Question of Wages:* It is no hidden fact that women face different form of inequalizing processes in economic realm. The most detrimental is the issue of wages. Over-representation of women in informal sector and economic activities where wages and working conditions are generally inferior to the formal sector is a major concern (Rao, Rurup, Sudarshan, 1996: 18). The Second Labour Commission points out that not only are women hired on a large scale in these sectors, but are '... exploited inhumanly ...' (Report of Expert Group, 2008: 14). As far as the Naxalite movement is concerned, though it has raised issue of minimum wages over the years, on the question of equal wages it seems to lack the required seriousness. Naxalite groups like CPI-ML (Liberation), though has mentioned the need for equal wages in some of its party documents, but no long-term strategy has been forwarded as yet.[15]

(c) *Question of Dignity:* As mentioned earlier, with denial of own resources developmental project have not only produced subsistence problems but has also robbed citizens off their dignity and identity.[16] Deprived of their right to decent life, dignity and identity, women among all deprived sections are becoming increasingly alienated and searching for liberatory outlets. If one closely examines the attitude of the Naxalite movement towards dignity/identity of women in society and within its working groups, one can locate serious shortcomings. According to critics, the phrase 'dignity of women' apparently meant only physical security and honour of women for the movement. Probably this is the reason why all these years they concentrated more on the issue of sexual abuse of labouring class women by the upper caste landlords and chose to subordinate the economic rights of women in terms of land and wages where power play exists in the most strategic forms.[17] Noteworthy, even the issue of patriarchal fencing of female desires and rights within the movement continue to be raised by feminists in the past. Not only were the women revolutionaries denied the right to marriage, motherhood, there were a number of cases of sexual abuses within the party workings. Overall, question of individual identity and dignity seem subsumed under the line of collective identity/ideology.

Interestingly in spite of the movement's changing gears, the Naxalite movement's attention to gender issues remains inadequate. According to critics, it has not really been able to address its own inner-party contradictions. Ironically, on the one hand, the movement appears to raise questions against the institution of private property, marriage, and family as agencies of gender oppression while on the other hand it seems unable to shed their own feudal-patriarchal mindset. Available narratives by female ex-naxalites of the early stages like Ajitha (Kerala) and Krishna Bandhopadhyay (Bengal) bring to light, trail of pervasive violence against women under the facade of revolution. Whether it was the question of division of labour, leadership or sexual freedom within the movement, women were always dominated. At later stages however, after the introduction of overground activities, certain changes have been initiated like the women's front, education department, introduction of magazines, etc. How far these steps have been effective is still a question unanswered.

Conclusion

The development process affects women and men in different ways. The after effects of colonialism and the peripheral position of developing countries in today's globalizing world worsen the effects of discrimination on women (Momsen, 2004: 1). Indeed, gender inequalities have led to not only huge loss of human potential but also costs development. In countries like India, growing gender disparities demand gender-centric responses. To improve the status of women in different regions and locales in India, 'specific interventions varying from state to state based on specific needs and priorities' should be the priority (Rustagi, 2004: 334).[18]

More importantly, in order to realize the dream of 'growth with development', India will have to mainstream women's issues within its strategic developmental paradigm. Policies must focus more on the subjugated sections, weaving diverse interests together. Review and debates on state development policies and actions from gender perspective can provide the much needed momentum. Not surprising, silencing of gender perspective all these years has only deepened the crisis. It is; indeed, time to address the marginalized women's voices, facilitating all-round, meaningful dialogue. Development essentially must be founded on the greater understanding of equality, justice and productivity.

Notes

1. The phrases, 'Naxalite movement' and 'Naxalites' are used to broadly encompass members of different Naxalite groups who have their common history in Naxalbari, a place on the north-eastern tip of India, situated in the state of Bengal (1967). Special attention is given to CPI-ML (Liberation) to understand the different aspects of the movement due to very limited information on the underground Naxal groups. Moreover, the term 'gender' is used in a broad sense in this paper. The Oxford dictionary describes gender as a socially constructed difference between men and women. See *Oxford Dictionary of Sociology* (1998: 250).

   Certain sections of this article have been borrowed from my own contribution in a published anthology of essays. See, Shantanu Chakrabarti and Kingshuk Chatterjee (eds), *Globalisation and Development: Current Trends*, K.W. Publishers, New Delhi, 2012.
2. For details on India's Human Development Index value and ranks, refer to 'India', HDI Value and Rank Changes in 2013 Human Development Report. Noteworthy, Gender Development Index (GDI) and Gender Empowerment Index (GEI) have been replaced by Gender Inequality Index (GII).
3. See Press Note: Key Indicators of Employment and Unemployment in India, 2009–2010, NSSO, Government of India, p. 3. These data are, according to the 'usual status' of persons as defined in terms of their work status, over the last one year. See Sen (2007: 89).
4. In spite of past government initiatives for rehabilitation and resettlement, there is no adequate database of persons displaced and rehabilitated. Moreover, there's not enough involvement of inhabitants for production of 'impact appraisals' before development projects commence. See Government of India, Report of an Expert Group, *Development Challenges in Extremist Affected Areas*, 2010, pp. 15–17.
5. Ibid., p. 11.
6. Ibid., p. 3.
7. For detailed see 'India's Forest Law and Women', *Yojna,* (2008), pp. 44.
8. Ibid., p. 118.
9. For detailed background on the Naxalite movement, see Banerjee (1984) and Ray (2002).

10. For details on Marxist views on women's question see 'Women under Capitalism: Advancement and Retrogression', *Women's Movement and Communist Party: Ideology, Programme, Practice*, 2008, p. 21.
11. Pictures supplemented in the articles of Roy (2010) and Navalakha (2010) clearly show women in uniforms and carrying guns.
12. The term 'dignity' is used in context of respect and recognition. Detailed explanation is given in the coming section 'Question of Dignity'. 'Identity' in general terms signifies unique character of one's own that is linked to its existence; see *Oxford Dictionary of Sociology* (1998: 296). I have used the two terms, dignity and identity interchangeably, in some places (in general sense).
13. In spite of a tremendous support of women in Telangana struggle, communist leaders failed to evolve a long term policy for women's upliftment. In terms of distribution of land, women were not counted as individuals. See Stree Shakti Sangathan (1989: 15–23).

    Bodhgaya movement was a movement led by Chhatra Yuva Sangharsh Vahini (a youth organization) against the feudal order of Bodhgaya Math (Bihar). Women constituted large part of this movement whose main aim was to fight for equal rights of men and women. See Louis (2002: 142–44).
14. Sarbani Bandhyopadhyay, 'The Revolutionary Patriarchs' http://www.pragoti.org/node/2053 (accessed 11 April 2009) and Madhu Kishwar and Ruth Vanita, ed., *In Search of Answers: Indian Women's Voices From Manushi,* (New Delhi: Manohar, 1999: 135–148), and Political Organisational Report adopted at the 5th All India Party Congress, CPI-ML Publication (2007: 46–48).
15. Party Congress Report, CPI-ML Publication.
16. To have a greater understanding of 'dignity' and 'identity', refer to Nancy Fraser's (1997) work on 'justice' as recognition.
17. See the Congress reports of CPI-ML (Liberation) 1988–1990 and *The General Programme, The Party Constitution* adopted at different Party Congress, CPI-ML Publication.
18. Rustagi, Preet (2004), 'Importance of Gender related Development Indicators: An Analysis of Indian States' *Indian Journal of Gender Studies,* 11(3): 293–343. available at http:/dise.in/Downloads/Use%20of%20Dise%20Rustagi.pdf Accessed on 25 March 2013.

References

Anderson-Rajkumar, Evangeline (2001). 'Women Missing the World: Globalisation through a Gender Lens', available at http://www.reformiert-online.net/agora2/docs/113.pdf. Accessed on 29 August 2012.

Apffel-Marglin, Frederique, Kumar, Sanjay and Mishra, Arvind (2010). *Interrogating Development: Insights from the Margins*, Oxford University Press, New Delhi.

Bandhopadhyay, D. (2007). 'Rural Unrest', *Yojna*, A Special Issue on Naxalism, 51: 11–14.

Bandhyopadhyay, Sarbani (2009). *The Revolutionary Patriarchs*, http://www.pragoti.org/node/2053 Accessed 11 April 2009.

Banerjee, Sumanta (1984). *India's Simmering Revolution: The Naxalite Uprising*, Zed Books, London.

Communist Party of India (Marxist-Leninist) (2008). *Women's Movement and Communist Party: Ideology, Programme, Practice*, CPI-ML Publication.

—- (1988–2007). *All India Party Congress Reports*, CPI-ML Publication.

Dasgupta, Abhijit (2009). 'Equally Extreme', *India Today*, November 9, available at http://indiatoday.intoday.in/calendar/130/2009/magazine.html. Accessed on 12 February 2010.

Fraser, Nancy (1997). *Justice Interrupts: Critical Reflections on the Post Socialist Conditions*, Routledge, New York.

Goldstein, Joshua (2004). *International Relations*, Pearson Education, Delhi.

Government of India (2010). Report of an Expert Group, *Development Challenges in Extremist Affected Areas*, pp. 10–11, available at http://planningcommission.nic.in/reports/publications/rep_dce.pdf. Accessed on 18 February 2013.

Guttal, Shalmali (2007). 'Globalisation', *Development in Practice*, 17 (4/5): 523–31.

'India: Country Profile of Human Development Indicators', available at http://hdrstats.undp.org/en/countries/profiles/IND.html. Accessed on 23 June 2013.

'India', HDI Value and Rank Changes in the 2013 Human Development Report, *The Rise of the South: Human Progress in a Diverse World*, available at http://hdrstats.undp.org/images/explanations/IND.pdf. Accessed on 24 March 2013.

Kishwar, Madhu and Vanita, Ruth. eds (1999). *In Search of Answers: Indian Women's Voices From Manushi*, Manohar, New Delhi.

Lawal, Gbenga (2006). 'Globalisation and Development: Implications for the African Economy', *Humanity and Social Sciences Journal*, 1 (1): 65–78.

Lombardo, E. and Meier, P. (2006). 'Gender Mainstreaming in the EU: Incorporating a Feminist Reading?', *European Journal of Women's Studies*, 13 (2): 151–66.

Louis, Prakash (2002). *People Power: The Naxalite Movement in Central Bihar*, Wordsmith, Delhi.

Marshall, Gordon (ed.) (1998). *Oxford Dictionary of Sociology*, Oxford University Press, Oxford.

Momsen, Janet Henshal (2004). *Gender and Development*, Routledge, London/New York.

Navalakha, Gautam (2010). 'Days and Nights in the Heartland of Rebellion: Maoist Land', available at http://indianvanguard.wordpress.com/2010/

04/02/gautam-navlakha-days-and-nights-in-the-heartland-of-rebellion / Accessed on July 2010.

Omvedt, Gail (1993). *Reinventing Revolution: New Social Movements and the Socialist Tradition in India*, M.E. Sharpe, New York.

Petras, James and Veltmeyer, Henry (2001). *Globalization Unmasked: Imperialism in the 21st Century*, Madhyam Books, Delhi.

Press Note: Key Indicators of Employment and Unemployment in India, 2009–2010, NSSO, Government of India, http://indiacurrentaffairs.org/national-sample-survey-key-indicators-of-employment-and-unemploy ment-in-india-2009–10/Accessed on 11 January 2013.

Rao, N., Rurup L., and Sudarshan R. eds (1996). *Sites of Change: The Structural Context for Empowering Women in India*, FES and UNDP, New Delhi.

Ray, Rabindra (2002). *The Naxalites and Their Ideology*, Oxford University Press, New Delhi.

Roy, Arundhati (2010). 'Walking with the Comrades', *Outlook*, available at http://www.outlookindia.com/article.aspx?264738. Accessed on 23 April 2012.

Rustagi, Preet (2004). 'Importance of Gender-related Development Indicators: An Analysis of Indian States', *Indian Journal of Gender Studies*, 11 (3): 293–343, available at http://dise.in/Downloads/Use%20of%20Dise%20Data/Preet%20Rustagi.pdf. Accessed on 25 March 2013.

Sen, Ilina (2004). 'Women's Politics in India', in Maitrayee Choudhari (ed.), *Feminism in India*, Kali for Women, New Delhi, Section 4, pp. 187–210.

Sen, Sunanda (2007). *Globalisation and Development*, National Book Trust, New Delhi.

Slim, Hugo (1995). *What is Development*, National Book Trust, New Delhi.

Snow, David A. and Cross, Remy (2011). 'Radicalism within the Context of Social Movements: Processes and Types', *Journal of Strategic Security*, 4 (4): 115–30, available at scholarcommons.usf.edu/cgi/viewcontent.cgi?article=1143&context... Accessed on 27 April 2013.

Stree Shakti Sangathan (1989). *We Were Making History: Life Stories of Women in the Telangana People's Struggle*, Kali for Women, New Delhi.

Sumner, Andrew (2007). *What is Development*, International Development Studies, http:/www.sagepub.in/upm-data/18296_5070_Sumner_Ch01.pdf, Accessed 4 February 2015.

Swaminathan, Padmini and Jayarajan, J. (2008). 'Mainstreaming Gender, Engendering Development: Reflections on a Case Study', *Economic and Political Weekly*, 43 (17): 77–86.

Thomas, A. (2004). *The Study of Development*, Paper prepared for DSA Annual Conference, 6 November, Church House, London.

Vindhya, U. (2003). 'Question of Revolutionary Identity and Sexuality in the Contemporary Radical Left Movement in Andhra Pradesh', *Psychology and Developing Societies*, 15 (2): 143–64.

Xaxa, Virginia (2008). *State, Society and Tribes: Issues in Post Colonial India*, Pearson Longman, New Delhi.

Index